Outspoken Women

Speeches by American Women Reformers, 1635–1935

Judith Anderson
University of Rhode Island

KENDALL/HUNT PUBLISHING COMPANY
2460 Kerper Boulevard P.O. Box 539 Dubuque, Iowa 52004-0539

Copyright © 1984 by Kendall/Hunt Publishing Company

Library of Congress Catalog Card Number: 84–80377

ISBN 0–8403–3298–X

Printed in the United States of America
10 9 8 7 6 5 4 3 2

This book is dedicated with love to:

my parents, Bernice and George Anderson, who inspired their five daughters to be outspoken women;

and to my sisters, Joan Anderson Davis, Joyce Anderson Brungardt, June Anderson Lafollette and Jill Anderson Winn, who lived up to their inspiration.

Contents

Acknowledgments

I would like to express special appreciation to:

my favorite librarian, Joanne Costanza, for her professional assistance; and my favorite transcriber and typist, Rae Ann Calkins, for her professional assistance;

my professionally dedicated and personally generous colleagues in Women's Studies and friends in the Feminist Community, Winnie Brownell, Marge Caldwell, Lib Clark, Greta Cohen, Adria Evans, Beth Evans, Roseann Evans, Pat Farnes, Sylvia Feldman, Lorry Garvin, Mathilda Hills, Dale Howard, Tally Kampen, Irene Lefebvre, Bernice Lott, Dorrie McCaffrey, Marilyn McCrory, Dawn Paul, Mary Ellen Reilly, Beverly Rochon, Diane Seleen and Karen Stein;

my closest friends who rescheduled and rearranged their lives on numerous occasions to offer love and support, Gunda Georg, Bea Schultz, Karen Schroeder, Steve and Sheila Grubman, Sharon Strom, Yvonne Lutter and, especially, Barbara Margolis.

Introduction

The Times That Try Men's Souls
Confusion has seized us, and all things go wrong,
    The women have leaped from "their spheres,"
And instead of fixed stars, shoot as comets along,
    And are setting the world by the ears!
In courses erratic they're wheeling through space,
In brainless confusion and meaningless chase.

In vain do our knowing ones try to compute
    Their return to the orbit designed;
They're glanced at a moment then onward they shoot,
    And are neither "to hold nor to bind";
So freely they move in their chosen elipse,
The "Lords of Creation" do fear an eclipse.

They've taken a notion to speak for themselves,
    And are wielding the tongue and the pen;
They've mounted the rostrum; the termagant elves,
    And—oh horrid!—are talking to men!
With faces unblanched in our presence they come
To harrangue us, they say, in behalf of the dumb.

A Satire written by Maria Weston Chapman in 1838
The History of Woman Suffrage, Vol. I, pp. 82–83

The "times that try men's souls" which Maria Weston Chapman refers to in the title of her satire are specifically the years of 1837–38 when Angelina and Sarah Grimké toured New England to speak out against slavery. However, any scholar examining the history of American women reformers between the years 1635–1935 would find this satire to be an appropriate epithet for the entire period. For throughout this three hundred years of American history the public repeatedly debated four basic issues concerning women reformers: "*if* women should speak," "*where* women should speak, "*who* women should speak to," and "*what* women should speak about." The arguments over "if women should speak" and "where women should speak" emerged from religious interpretations which contended women should "learn in silence with all subjection" and "keep to their rightful sphere in the home." (I Timothy, 2:11–12) The arguments over "who women should speak to" and "what women should speak about" emanated from social etiquette rules which forbade women to address "promiscuous" audiences (audiences composed of men and women) and to refrain from speaking out on any issue deemed "unseemly" for the "morally superior" sex. Fortunately for American society in general, and American reform movements in particular, American women refused to heed these arguments. First by ones and twos, then by scores, and finally by hundreds and thousands, they defied religious and social dicta alike and mounted the public platform to assume their roles as "outspoken women."

The following brief historical essay provides a glimpse into the lives of the first outspoken women, outspoken women of early reform movements and outspoken women of later reform movements. The names of the women reformers who appear in this essay are limited to the forty outspoken women whose speeches fill the remainder of this book.

The First "Outspoken Women"

The honor of being titled "America's First Outspoken Woman" unquestionably belongs to Anne Hutchinson. Her dedicated belief in John Cotton's "Covenant of Grace" inexorably pitted her against the Puritan Theocracy's belief in the "Covenant of Works"; but this theological conflict would probably have passed unnoticed if she had not dared to invite her neighbors to attend twice-weekly gatherings in her home where she began to progressively espouse her own personal interpretations and conclusions while incautiously criticizing local ministers. This "sin," too, might have been unworthy of serious attention if she had not been so effective in converting a large number of enthusiastic followers to her cause who then proselytized her teachings throughout the colony. Ultimately, it was both her audacity to advance her own thoughts and her success as a persuasive speaker which led to her eventual banishment from Massachusetts in 1637 and her excommunication from the church in 1638. The severity of Anne Hutchinson's punishment is a tribute to her achievements as an "outspoken woman."

Deborah Sampson gallantly followed in Anne Hutchinson's footsteps when she flaunted 18th century societal rules of propriety in more than one unorthodox way. Her first bold step was to enlist in the Continental forces in 1782 under the name of Robert Shurtleff. For almost three years she served as a revolutionary soldier before a stay in a hospital exposed her true sex and resulted in her discharge from the army. Her heroic adventures might have garnered only a small unusual footnote in recorded history if she had not also taken her second courageous step and launched a brief and daring career as a public lecturer. For seven months in 1802 she toured throughout various cities and towns in New England and New York delivering her "address" about life as a female soldier. Both steps brought only a small degree of fame and fortune to Deborah Sampson in her lifetime, but her pioneering efforts as soldier and public lecturer enliven and enrich the early American history of "outspoken women."

Frances Wright stormed on to the public lecture platform not long after Deborah Sampson, but, unlike Deborah, she had more than one "address" to deliver. In her lecture tour in 1828–29 she: condemned organized religion as the chief obstacle to human happiness, barring the way to a free, unbiased pursuit of knowledge; advocated a compensated-emancipation plan for the abolition of slavery while simultaneously attacking racism and segregated schools; attacked capital punishment as an excuse for sanctioned murder; and demanded improvements in the status of women, including equal education, legal rights for married women, liberal divorce laws, and birth control. The pulpit and the press pilloried her unmercifully, labelling her as "The Great Red Harlot of Infidelity" and threatening her life on numerous occasions. In response to her persecutions, Frances replied: "The injury and inconvenience of every kind and every hour to which, in these days, a really consistent reformer stands exposed, none can conceive but those who experience them. Such become, as it were, excommunicated after the fashion of the old Catholic Mother Church, removed even from the protection of law, such as it is, and from the sympathy of society, for whose sake they consent to be crucified."[1] Little did Frances Wright realize at the time that her reputation would become such that later woman's rights advocates would be tagged "Fanny Wrightists" as the worst kind of abuse. But she also could not realize that such a tag would be worn with pride and honor.

Maria Stewart climbed the steps to the public rostrum two years after Frances Wright had stepped down. She delivered only four addresses, all of them in Boston, but her place in the honor roll of early "outspoken women" rests assured. She was the first black woman to speak in public and also the first black woman to speak out against slavery. Unfortunately, public pressure from both the black and white community compelled her to retire after having spoke only four times.

However, she refused to quietly and passively take leave of the public stage and in her Farewell Address, delivered on October 21, 1833, she eloquently defended her right as a woman to speak out: "What if I am a woman; is not the God of ancient times the God of these modern days? Did he not raise up Deborah to be a mother and a judge in Israel? Did not Queen Esther save the lives of the Jews? And Mary Magdalena first declare the resurrection of Christ from the dead? . . . If such women as are here described once existed, be no longer astonished then, my brethern and friends, that God at this eventful period should raise up your own females to strive by their example, both in public and in private, to assist those who are endeavoring to stop the strong current of prejudice that flows so profusely against us at present. . . . What if such women as are here described should rise among our sable race? And it is not impossible; for it is not the color of the skin that makes the man or the woman, but the principle formed in the soul."[2]

Angelina and Sarah Grimké arrived in New England four years after Maria Stewart delivered her farewell address. As southern women raised on a plantation, they knew first-hand the travesties of slavery and they were determined to have a voice in abolishing it. Initially they had been satisfied to write treatises and address audiences of women in New York, but when the American Anti-Slavery Society invited them to tour New England and address audiences of all types they unhesitantly accepted the challenge. In a year-long tour which culminated with a series of lectures in Boston in 1838, the two women addressed "mixed" audiences which numbered from the hundreds to the thousands. This daring venture infuriated the Congregational Ministerial Association who issued a "Pastoral Letter" strongly objecting to their "unwomanly" behavior and warning their flock of "the dangers which at present seem to threaten the female character with widespread and permanent injury."[3] But Angelina and Sarah would not be daunted, nor would they allow this public rebuke to circulate without public confrontation. Angelina argued in 1837: "If we surrender the right to *speak* in public this year, we must surrender the right to *petition* next year, and the right to *write* the year after, and so on. What *then* can *woman* do for the slave, when she herself is under the feet of man and shamed into *silence*?"[4] And Sarah concluded in 1838: "To me it is perfectly clear *that whatsoever it is morally right for man to do, it is morally right for woman to do.*"[5] Thus, with both their courageous actions and their bold words, Angelina and Sarah Grimké won a major battle for women's right to be "outspoken women."

Outspoken Women and Early Reform Movements

Two early reform movements attracted large numbers of females into their folds and served as training schools for "outspoken women": the Abolitionist Movement and the Woman's Suffrage Movement. The Abolitionist Movement emerged in the early 1830's, and from its inception it had to contend with women who insisted on active participation. When the American Anti-Slavery Society formed in Philadelphia in 1833 they allowed a few women to attend and even to speak from the floor, but they wouldn't permit them to join the society or to vote on resolutions. Disgruntled with their second-class status, the twenty or so women who had attended decided to form the Philadelphia Female Anti-Slavery Society. By 1837 a large enough number of similar societies had been formed in the surrounding states to convene the first National Female Anti-Slavery Society convention in New York City. Eighty-one women from twelve states gathered to debate resolutions, argue over strategies and organize lecture campaigns and petition drives. With a new-found confidence in their individual abilities to persuade, these courageous women set out to challenge 19th century notions of a "woman's rightful sphere." For the next twenty-five years they tramped throughout their states addressing all kinds of audiences, despite frequent harassment and threats of mob violence. Mathilda Joslyn Gage, chronicling "Preceding Causes" for her introduction to Volume I of *The History of Woman Suffrage*, provides a poignant glimpse into the activities of one of these brave early abolitionists: "Abby Kelley was the most untiring and the most persecuted of all the women who labored throughout the Anti-Slavery struggle. She travelled up and down, alike in winter's cold and summer's heat, with scorn, ridicule, violence, and mobs accompanying her, suffering all kinds of persecutions, still speaking whenever and wherever she gained an audience; in the open air, in schoolhouse, barn, depot, church, or public hall; on week-day or Sunday, as she found opportunity. For listening to her, on Sunday, many men and women were expelled from their churches. Thus through continued persecution was women's self-assertion and self-respect sufficiently developed. . . ."[6]

In June, 1840 a World's Anti-Slavery Convention convened in London, England. Female abolitionists had achieved sufficient recognition by then to have eight of their number selected as members of the American delegation. However, when the women arrived at the convention hall, "the excitement and vehemence of protest and denunciation could not have been greater, if the news had come that the French were about to invade England," noted a young observer named Elizabeth Cady Stanton, who had accompanied her delegate husband to the convention. "In vain those obdurate women had been conjured to withhold their credentials, and not thrust a question that must produce such discord on the Convention. Lucretia Mott, in her calm, firm manner, insisted that the delegates had no discretionary power in the proposed action, and the responsibility of accepting or rejecting them must rest on the Convention."[7] After hours of much heated debate on the convention floor, the women were denied their seats and instructed to sit in the gallery with other observers. Historians would record this event as yet one more example of the suppression of women. However, feminist historians would also refer to this event as the starting point for the woman's suffrage movement; for, up in the observer's gallery, sitting side by side, were Lucretia Mott and Elizabeth Cady Stanton, and their conversations included plans to hold a woman's rights convention in the near future.

It was highly fitting that the woman's suffrage movement blossomed at an abolitionist convention; for, as abolitionists, many women first gained their place on the public platform and first learned of their own second-class status in American society. And so it was a natural expansion for those women who pleaded to free the slave to plead for the liberation of their own kind. Lucretia Mott, Abby Kelley Foster, Susan B. Anthony, Elizabeth Cady Stanton, Frances Harper, Ernestine Rose, Lucy Stone, Sojourner Truth, and many more would go down in history as civil rights champions for both the slave and the female. Until the post-Civil War years, most women who fought for both causes only encountered individual conflicts; as when Lucy Stone, for example, had to work out an arrangement with the anti-slavery society who hired her as a lecturer to speak for them on the weekends and woman's rights during the week. After the Civil War, when abolitionists fought for Negro suffrage and suffragists insisted on universal suffrage, many women were forced to choose between support for Negro suffrage irregardless of its inclusion of women, or to withdraw support for Negro suffrage if it did not include women as well. This unfortunate conflict resulted in the formation of two woman suffrage associations in 1869, which coexisted until their merger into one association in 1890. Except for this incidence of pitting one group's rights against the other group's rights, the abolitionist movement and the woman's suffrage movement nourished each other for over a quarter of a century.

From a twentieth-century perspective it is difficult to comprehend the magnitude of time and energy dedicated to the woman's suffrage movement. After the vote had finally been won in 1920,

Carrie Chapman Catt attempted an estimate of the amount of effort exerted: "To get the word 'male' in effect out of the Constitution cost the women of the country fifty-two years of pauseless campaign. During that time they were forced to conduct fifty-six campaigns of referenda to male voters; 480 campaigns to get Legislatures to submit suffrage amendments to voters; 47 campaigns to get state constitutional conventions to write woman suffrage into state constitutions; 277 campaigns to get state party conventions to include woman suffrage planks; 30 campaigns to get presidential party conventions to adopt woman suffrage planks in party platforms; and 19 campaigns with 19 successive congresses."[8] As astounding as Carrie's assessment appears, however, it did not cover the twenty years of active work which preceded the first introduction of the woman suffrage amendment before Congress. Hence, most historians consider the Seneca Falls Convention of 1848 as the beginning of the woman suffrage movement; the very convention that Lucretia Mott and Elizabeth Cady Stanton plotted in London in 1840.

The Seneca Falls convention produced a number of "firsts" in the history of American women reform movements: it was the first woman's rights convention, it was the first time the concept of woman suffrage appeared in resolution form, and it was the first occasion for Elizabeth Cady Stanton to deliver a public address. All three of these premiers would prove to be momentous for the advancement of women's rights and would be repeated in various forms over the next half of a century. Three of the resolutions unanimously passed at this convention also revealed the participants' keen awareness of societal obstacles they must overcome if they were to succeed as reformers:

Fifth: Resolved, that inasmuch as man, while claiming intellectual superiority, does accord to woman moral superiority, it is preeminently his duty to encourage her to speak and teach, as she has the opportunity, in all religious assemblies.

Seventh: Resolved, that the objection of indelicacy and impropriety, which is so often brought against woman when she addresses a public audience, comes with very ill-grace from those who encourage, by their attendance, her appearance on the stage, in the concert, or in feats of the circus.

Eleventh: Resolved, therefore, that, being invested by the Creator with the same capabilities, and the same consciousness of responsibility for their exercise, it is demonstrably the right and duty of woman, equally with man, to promote every righteous cause by every righteous means; and especially in regard to the great subjects of morals and religion, it is self-evidently her right to participate with her brother in teaching them, both in private and in public, by writing and by speaking, by any instrumentalities proper to be used, and in any assemblies proper to be held; and this being a self-evident truth growing out of the divinely implanted principles of human nature, any custom or authority adverse to it, whether modern or wearing the hoary sanction of antiquity, is to be regarded as a self-evident falsehood, and at war with mankind.[9]

Of course, recognizing the barriers which lie in their path was but the first step, and countless future conventions would be required to develop the strategies for their removal.

The hundreds of national and state woman's rights conventions held after Seneca Falls cultivated generations of women reformers, the like of which America has never quite experienced again. The hesitant, the unsure and the inexperienced delivered their first public addresses, argued in their first debates, chaired their first assemblies and were transformed into the audacious, the confident and the outspoken. Moreover, conventions continuously brought issues of concern to women before the public eye. The press, regardless of their prejudices in favor or against woman's rights, could not afford to ignore the newsworthiness of these highly publicized events. Hence, proponents and opponents alike were forced to debate women's issues openly and publicly and, consequently, the uninformed and the undecided became informed and involved. Among the women reformers who rose to national stature as a result of this public exposure were such extraordinary orators as: Elizabeth Cady Stanton, Susan B. Anthony, Ernestine Rose, Lucy Stone, Sojourner Truth, Anna Howard Shaw and Carrie Chapman Catt. The history of American "outspoken women" would be immeasurably diminished without their contributions.

Outspoken Women and Later Reform Movements

The rapid rise of industrialization and the subsequent explosion of city populations revolutionized American society in the last decades of the 19th century and the first decades of the 20th century. In the wake of this revolution a host of new reform movements sprang into existence in the hope of finding solutions to a myriad of new problems. With the doors to the public platform flung open by their abolitionist and suffrage sisters in the preceding decades, thousands of American women marched in to assume their roles as reformers for a wide variety of causes. By far the largest proportion devoted their talents to social reforms, but a dedicated number also joined the ranks of labor reformers. Regardless of the focus of their attention, women active in the later reform movements firmly established themselves as "outspoken women."

A brief overview of some of the social reform causes women engaged in provides clear evidence of both the diversity of women's concerns and the tendency of many individual women to be involved in more than one cause at a time. The Temperance Movement is a case in point. Frances Willard and Carry Nation achieved the most notoriety advancing this movement against alcohol abuse, but Susan B. Anthony, Elizabeth Cady Stanton, Ernestine Rose, Sojourner Truth, Abby Kelley Foster, Frances Harper, Anna Howard Shaw and others also lectured far and wide on behalf of this cause. The pre-World War I Peace Movement is a second case in point. Although Jane Addams and Emily Greene Balch were the only pacifists honored for their efforts with the Nobel Peace Prize, the Women's Peace Party and the Women's International League for Peace and Freedom could never have succeeded without the additional efforts of Crystal Eastman, Alice Paul, Florence Kelley, Lillian Wald, Charlotte Perkins Gilman, or Carrie Chapman Catt, among others. Nor can the tireless battles against military conscription and the Espionage Act waged by Emma Goldman, Elizabeth Gurley Flynn and Kate Richards O'Hare be omitted from any assessment of anti-war activities at that time. Similar cases can be made for the causes of prison reform, birth control and social work. Dorothea Dix first espoused prison reform, but Kate Richards O'Hare, Emma Goldman and Elizabeth Gurley Flynn championed its cause as well. Margaret Sanger gained national and international recognition as the founder of the Birth Control Movement, but Emma Goldman, Mary Ellen Lease and Charlotte Perkins Gilman also actively campaigned for this reform. The names of Jane Addams and Lillian Wald became synonymous with social work, but Florence Kelley, Leonora O'Reilly and Rose Schneiderman also served as activists in the social settlement movements of their time.

Other social reform causes attracted fewer women to their ranks, but the women they did attract gained national attention because of their involvement in them. Dorothea Dix led the way in mental health reform and her efforts alone helped to establish 32 mental hospitals throughout the country. Florence Kelley served as the first general secretary of the National Consumer's League and it was largely due to her organizing skill that 60 Consumer Leagues sprang up in cities across the nation. Mary Baker Eddy founded the Christian Science movement and in a period of eight years she cultivated 20 churches, ninety societies and 33 teaching centers. Ida Tarbell indicted the Standard Oil Company through articles and speeches and achieved national fame as a female muckraker. Susette LaFlesche, as an Omaha Indian, overcame her culture's reticence to speak in public and travelled throughout the east winning recognition for Indian rights. Along similar lines, Mary McLeod Bethune, Ida Wells-Barnett and Mary Church Terrell exposed racism against blacks with their valiant campaigns against unequal education, lynching and segregation. Finally, Victoria Woodhull, Charlotte Perkins Gilman, Crystal Eastman, Alice Paul and Emma Goldman broke new ground in the rich field of feminist thought with their daring lectures on free love, liberal divorce laws, jealousy, prostitution and equal economic opportunities for women.

Labor reform causes allured a smaller number of women into their camps, but the women who joined their ranks proved more than equal to the task. Elizabeth Gurley Flynn, Mary Harris "Mother" Jones, Kate Richards O'Hare, Mary Ellen Lease, Leonora O'Reilly and Rose Schneiderman dedicated their lives to organizing working men and women into strong labor armies equipped to fight for fair wages and better working conditions. Each of them allied themselves with a particular labor organization or party which hired them as organizers and trouble shooters: Elizabeth Gurley Flynn campaigned throughout the country for the Industrial Workers of the World; Mary Harris "Mother" Jones fought chiefly for the United Mine Workers and the Western Federation of Miners; Kate Richards O'Hare agitated on behalf of the Socialist Party; Mary Ellen Lease battled for both the Knights of Labor and the Populist Party; and Leonora O'Reilly and Rose Schneiderman became key organizers for the Women's Trade Union League. Between these six women reformers alone, it is impossible to calculate the number of rallies they addressed, strikes they actively participated in, trials and hearings they testified at, or months and years they spent in jail on behalf of their various constituencies. Each in their own right earned widespread recognition and respect from the working people whose causes they championed.

Organizing workers into viable unions was the principle goal of most labor reformers, but a second major aim was to draw public attention to particular labor issues. Through this second activity labor reformers attracted additional advocates into their fold. Numerous suffragists and social reformers joined with labor reformers to fight for improvements in working conditions of women workers, urging such reforms as the elimination of the sweatshop system and the establishment of the eight-hour day. A similar collaboration evolved to expose the travesties of child labor. Thus, any honor roll of women labor reformers would be incomplete without the addition of such reformers as: Florence Kelley, a dedicated investigator of the working conditions of women workers and a vigorous advocate of child labor reform; Jane Addams, who through the auspices of Hull House, sponsored numerous studies of both the work conditions of women and children in Chicago; Lillian Wald, who through the auspices of the Henry Street Settlement, sponsored similar studies in New York City; Crystal Eastman, a pioneer investigator into work related accidents and a leading figure in establishing worker compensation laws; and Charlotte Perkins Gilman and Emma Goldman, both tireless writers and speakers for reform of labor conditions which threatened the lives of women and children.

The remainder of this book is a living monument to forty "outspoken women" whose speeches and lives enriched American reform movements in ways impossible to match in contemporary times. Every effort was made to locate complete extant copies of the speeches, and in most cases this was possible to achieve. However, when only an incomplete or edited speech was all that was available, the text was included with proper notation. Several initial attempts to organize the speeches in chronological order or into categories of reform movements proved unwieldy; hence, the simple solution to let each woman speak for herself in the order by which her last name fell in the alphabet. It is my deepest hope that readers of these biographies and speeches will be as profoundly touched as I have been while compiling this collection of truly extraordinary "outspoken women."

Judith Anderson
Jamestown, Rhode Island

Notes

1. Mathilda Joslyn Gage, "Preceding Causes," *The History of Woman Suffrage,* Vol. I (Rochester, N.Y., 1881), pp. 25–42.
2. Maria W. Stewart, "Farewell Address," *Meditations of Mrs. Maria W. Stewart* (Washington, D.C., 1879), pp. 76–78.
3. Elizabeth Cady Stanton, Susan B. Anthony and Mathilda Joslyn Gage, Editors, *The History of Woman Suffrage,* Vol. I, p. 61.
4. Gilbert Barnes and Dwight L. Dummond, Editors, *The Letters of Theodore Weld, Angelina Grimke Weld and Sarah Grimke, 1822–1844* (New York, N.Y., 1934), I, pp. 429–430, letter of Angelina Grimké to Theodore Weld and John Greenleaf Whittier, August 20, 1837.
5. Sarah Grimké, *The Equality of the Sexes and the Condition of Women* (Boston, Ma., 1838), p. 122.
6. Mathilda Joslyn Gage, "Preceding Causes," pp. 25–42.
7. *The History of Woman Suffrage,* Vol. I, pp. 53–62.
8. Carrie Chapman Catt and Nettie Rogers Shuler, *Woman Suffrage and Politics* (New York, N.Y., 1923), p. 107.
9. *The History of Woman Suffrage,* Vol. I, pp. 67–74.

Jane Addams
(1860–1935)

Jane Addams was born on September 6, 1860 in Cedarville, Illinois. The eighth of nine children, she lost her mother at the age of two and subsequently became closely attached to her father, a noted Illinois politician and abolitionist. After completing public school in 1877, Jane entered the Rockford Female Seminary and graduated first in her class in 1882. For the next eight years Jane confronted numerous challenges in her personal life: her father's sudden death, surgery for a disabling spinal condition followed by six months of convalescence, two years travelling in Europe and encountering severe urban poverty for the first time, two years in Baltimore struggling with her stepmother and her own nervous depression, and a second two-year trip to Europe where she began to envision her future work with the urban poor while continuing to combat her own physical and emotional illnesses. In February, 1889, Jane and a close friend, Ellen Starr, returned to Chicago and began looking for a suitable house in a poor neighborhood where they could translate Jane's vision into reality. In September of 1889 "Hull House" opened its doors to Chicago's urban poor and became Jane's "home" for the remaining forty-six years of her life. By 1893 Hull House was the center of some forty clubs, functions, and activities and 2,000 people crossed its threshold each week. In the mid 1890's Jane and a remarkable group of talented associates she had attracted to her side expanded Hull House influence to include a broad range of social reforms: tenement conditions, sweatshops, child labor, factory work inspections, limited working hours for women, improved welfare procedures, protection of immigrants, to mention a few. By the turn of the century Jane's accomplishments brought her national recognition and she became a sought-after lecturer and writer. In 1902 she published her first book, *Democracy and Social Ethics,* and followed it with ten other books, including her memorable autobiographies *Twenty Years at Hull House* (1910) and *The Second Twenty Years at Hull House* (1930). Considered a pioneer in the American settlement movement, Jane became the first woman president of the National Conference of Charities and Correction (later the National Conference of Social Work) in 1909, and the first head of the National Federation of Settlements in 1911. As an activist and reformer, Jane also participated in other social movements of her time. In 1907 she served on the Chicago municipal suffrage campaign, and as first vice president of the National American Suffrage Association (1911–14) she spoke widely for the cause. Long an outspoken opponent of militarism, Jane was elected as the first chairperson of the Women's Peace Party and president of the International Congress of Women at The Hague (both in 1915), and as the first president of the Women's International League for Peace and Freedom (in 1919). Her many years of pacifist efforts were recognized in 1931 when she shared the Nobel Peace Prize with Nicholas Murray. In 1933 Jane suffered a severe heart attack but remained active until May 21, 1935, when she died of intestinal cancer at the age of seventy-four.

The following lecture was delivered in the summer of 1892 at the Ethical Culture Societies summer school in Plymouth, Massachusetts. The summer school theme focused on the subject of philanthropy and social progress. The lecture was later printed in Jane Addams, *Philanthropy and Social Progress* (New York, N.Y., 1893), pp. 1–26.

"The Subjective Necessity for Social Settlements"

Hull House, which was Chicago's first Settlement, was established in September, 1889. It represented no association, but was opened by two women, backed by many friends, in the belief that the mere foothold of a house, easily accessible, ample in space, hospitable and tolerant in spirit, situated in the midst of the large foreign colonies which so easily isolate themselves in American cities, would be in itself a serviceable thing for Chicago. Hull House endeavors to make social intercourse express the growing sense of the economic unity of society. It is an effort to add the social function to democracy. It was opened on the theory that the dependence of classes on each other is reciprocal; and that as "the social relation is essentially a reciprocal relation, it gave a form of expression that has peculiar value."

This paper is an attempt to treat of the subjective necessity for Social Settlements, to analyze the motives which underlie a movement based not only upon conviction, but genuine emotion. Hull House of Chicago is used as an illustration, but so far as the analysis is faithful, it obtains wherever educated young people are seeking an outlet for that sentiment of universal brotherhood which the best spirit of our times is forcing from an emotion into a motive.

I have divided the motives which constitute the subjective pressure toward Social Settlements into three great lines: the first contains the desire to make the entire social organism democratic, to extend democracy beyond its political expression; the second is the impulse to share the race life, and to bring as much as possible of social energy and the accumulation of civilization to those portions of the race which have little; the third springs from a certain *renaissance* of Christianity, a movement toward its early humanitarian aspects.

It is not difficult to see that although America is pledged to the democratic ideal, the view of democracy has been partial, and that its best achievement thus far has been pushed along the line of the franchise. Democracy has made little attempt to assert itself in social affairs. We have refused to move beyond the position of its eighteenth-century leaders, who believed that political equality alone would secure all good to all men. We conscientiously followed the gift of the ballot hard upon the gift of freedom to the negro, but we are quite unmoved by the fact that he lives among us in a practical social ostracism. We hasten to give the franchise to the immigrant from a sense of justice, from a tradition that he ought to have it, while we dub him with epithets deriding his past life or present occupation, and feel no duty to invite him to our houses. We are forced to acknowledge that it is only in our local and national politics that we try very hard for the ideal so dear to those who were enthusiasts when the century was young. We have almost given it up as our ideal in social intercourse. There are city wards in which many of the votes are sold for drinks and dollars; still there is a remote pretence, at least a fiction current, that a man's vote is his own. The judgment of the voter is consulted and an opportunity for remedy given. There is not even a theory in the social order, not a shadow answering to the polls in politics. The time may come when the politician who sells one by one to the highest bidder all the offices in his grasp, will not be considered more base in his code of morals, more hardened in his practice, than the woman who constantly invites to her receptions those alone who bring her an equal social return, who shares her beautiful surroundings only with those who minister to a liking she has for successful social events. In doing this is she not just as unmindful of the common weal, as unscrupulous in her use of power, as is any city "boss" who consults only the interests of the "ring"?

In politics "bossism" arouses a scandal. It goes on in society constantly and is only beginning to be challenged. Our consciences are becoming tender in regard to the lack of democracy in social affairs. We are perhaps entering upon the second phase of democracy, as the French philosophers entered upon the first, somewhat bewildered by its logical conclusions. The social organism has broken down through large districts of our great cities. Many of the people living there are very poor, the majority of them without leisure or energy for anything but the gain of subsistence. They move often from one wretched lodging to another. They live for the moment side by side, many of them without knowledge of each other, without fellowship, without local tradition or public spirit, without social organization of any kind. Practically nothing is done to remedy this. The people who might do it, who have the social tact and training, the large houses, and the traditions and custom of hospitality, live in other parts of the city. The club-houses, libraries, galleries, and semi-public conveniences for social life are also blocks away. We find working-men organized into armies of producers because men of executive ability and business sagacity have found it to their interests thus to organize them. But these working-men are not organized socially; although living in crowded tenement-houses, they are living without a corresponding social contact. The chaos is as great as it would be were they working in huge factories without foreman or superintendent. Their ideas and resources are cramped. The desire for higher social pleasure is extinct. They have no share in the traditions and social energy which make for progress. Too often their only place of meeting is a saloon, their only host a bartender; a local demagogue forms their public opinion. Men of ability and refinement, of social power and university cultivation, stay away from them. Personally, I believe the men who lose most are those who thus stay away. But the paradox is here: when cultivated people do stay away from a certain portion of the population, when all social advantages are persistently withheld, it may be for years, the result itself is pointed at as a reason, is used as an argument, for the continued withholding.

It is constantly said that because the masses have never had social advantages they do not want them, that they are heavy and dull, and that it will take political or philanthropic machinery to change them. This divides a city into rich and poor; into the favored, who express their sense of the social obligation by gifts of money, and into the unfavored, who express it by clamoring for a "share"—both of them actuated by a vague sense of justice. This division of the city would be more justifiable, however, if the people who thus isolate themselves on certain streets and use their social ability for each other gained enough thereby and added sufficient to the sum total of social progress to justify the withholding of the pleasures and results of that progress from so many people who ought to have them. But they cannot accomplish this. "The social spirit discharges itself in many forms, and no one form is adequate to its total expression." We are all uncomfortable in regard to the sincerity of our best phrases, because we hesitate to translate our philosophy into the deed.

It is inevitable that those who feel most keenly this insincerity and partial living should be our young people, our so-called educated young people who accomplish little toward the solution of this social problem, and who bear the brunt of being cultivated into unnourished, over-sensitive lives. They have been shut off from the common labor by which they live and which is a great source of moral and physical health. They feel a fatal want of harmony between their theory and their lives, a lack of co-ordination between thought and action. I think it is hard for us to realize how seriously many of them are taking to the notion of human brotherhood, how eagerly they long to give tangible expression to the democratic ideal. These young men and women, longing to socialize their democracy, are animated by certain hopes.

These hopes may be loosely formulated thus: that if in a democratic country nothing can be permanently achieved save through the masses of the people, it will be impossible to establish a higher political life than the people themselves crave; that it is difficult to see how the notion of a higher civic life can be fostered save through common intercourse; that the blessings which we associate with a life of refinement and cultivation can be made universal and must be made universal if they are to be permanent; that the good we secure for ourselves is precarious and uncertain, is floating in mid-air, until it is secured for all of us and incorporated into our common life.

These hopes are responsible for results in various directions, pre-eminently in the extension of educational advantages. We find that all educational matters are more democratic in their political than in their social aspects. The public schools in the poorest and most crowded wards of the city are inadequate to the number of children, and many of the teachers are ill-prepared and overworked; but in each ward there is an effort to secure public education. The schoolhouse itself stands as a pledge that the city recognizes and endeavors to fulfil the duty of educating its children. But what becomes of these children when they are no longer in public schools? Many of them never come under the influence of a professional teacher nor a cultivated friend after they are twelve. Society at large does little for their intellectual development. The dream of transcendentalists that each New England village would be a university, that every child taken from the common school would be put into definite lines of study and mental development, had its unfulfilled beginning in the village lyceum and lecture courses, and has its feeble representative now in the multitude of clubs for study which are so sadly restricted to educators, to the leisure class, or only to the advanced and progressive wage-workers.

The University Extension movement—certainly when it is closely identified with Settlements—would not confine learning to those who already want it, or to those who, by making an effort, can gain it, or to those among whom professional educators are already at work, but would take it to the tailors of East London and the dock-laborers of the Thames. It requires tact and training, love of learning, and the conviction of the justice of its diffusion to give it to people whose intellectual faculties are untrained and disused. But men in England are found who do it successfully, and it is believed there are men and women in America who can do it. I also believe that the best work in University Extension can be done in Settlements, where the teaching will be further socialized, where the teacher will grapple his students, not only by formal lectures, but by every hook possible to the fuller intellectual life which he represents. This teaching requires distinct methods, for it is true of people who have been allowed to remain undeveloped and whose faculties are inert and sterile, that they cannot take their learning heavily. It has to be diffused in a social atmosphere. Information held in solution, a medium of fellowship and goodwill can be assimilated by the dullest.

If education is, as Froebel defined it, "deliverance," deliverance of the forces of the body and mind, then the untrained must first be delivered from all constraint and rigidity before their faculties can be used. Possibly one of the most pitiful periods in the drama of the much-praised young American who attempts to rise in life is the time when his educational requirements seem to have locked him up and made him rigid. He fancies himself shut off from his uneducated family and misunderstood by his friends. He is bowed down by his mental accumulations and often gets no farther than to carry them through life as a great burden. Not once has he had a glimpse of the delights of knowledge. Intellectual life requires for its expansion and manifestation the influence and assimilation of the interests and affections of others. Mazzini, that greatest of all democrats, who broke his heart over the condition of the South European peasantry, said: "Education is not merely a necessity of true life by which the individual renews his vital force in the vital force of humanity; it is a Holy Communion with generations dead and living, by which he fecundates all his faculties. When he is withheld from this Communion for generations, as the Italian peasant

4

has been, we point our finger at him and say, 'He is like a beast of the field; he must be controlled by force.' " Even to this it is sometimes added that it is absurd to educate him, immoral to disturb his content. We stupidly use again the effect as an argument for a continuance of the cause. It is needless to say that a Settlement is a protest against a restricted view of education, and makes it possible for every educated man or woman with a teaching faculty to find out those who are ready to be taught. The social and educational activities of a Settlement are but differing manifestations of the attempt to socialize democracy, as is the existence of the settlement itself.

I find it somewhat difficult to formulate the second line of motives which I believe to constitute the trend of the subjective pressure toward the Settlement. There is something primordial about these motives, but I am perhaps over-bold in designating them as a great desire to share the race life. We all bear traces of the starvation struggle which for so long made up the life of the race. Our very organism holds memories and glimpses of that long life of our ancestors which still goes on among so many of our contemporaries. Nothing so deadens the sympathies and shrivels the power of enjoyment as the persistent keeping away from the great opportunities for helpfulness and a continual ignoring of the starvation struggle which makes up the life of at least half the race. To shut one's self away from that half of the race life is to shut one's self away from the most vital part of it; it is to live out but half the humanity which we have been born heir to and to use but half our faculties. We have all had longings for a fuller life which should include the use of these faculties. These longings are the physical complement of the "Intimations of Immortality" on which no ode has yet been written. To portray these would be the work of a poet, and it is hazardous for any but a poet to attempt it.

You may remember the forlorn feeling which occasionally seizes you when you arrive early in the morning a stranger in a great city. The stream of laboring people goes past you as you gaze through the plate-glass window of your hotel. You see hard-working men lifting great burdens; you hear the driving and jostling of huge carts. Your heart sinks with a sudden sense of futility. The door opens behind you and you turn to the man who brings you in your breakfast with a quick sense of human fellowship. You find yourself praying that you may never lose your hold on it at all. A more poetic prayer would be that the great mother breasts of our common humanity, with its labor and suffering and its homely comforts, may never be withheld from you. You turn helplessly to the waiter. You feel that it would be almost grotesque to claim from him the sympathy you crave. Civilization has placed you far apart, but you resent your position with a sudden sense of snobbery. Literature is full of portrayals of these glimpses. They come to shipwrecked men on rafts; they overcome the differences of an incongruous multitude when in the presence of a great danger or when moved by a common enthusiasm. They are not, however, confined to such moments, and if we were in the habit of telling them to each other, the recital would be as long as the tales of children are, when they sit down on the green grass and confide to each other how many times they have remembered that they lived once before. If these tales are the stirring of inherited impressions, just so surely is the other the striving of inherited powers.

"There is nothing after disease, indigence, and a sense of guilt so fatal to health and to life itself as the want of a proper outlet for active faculties." I have seen young girls suffer and grow sensibly lowered in vitality in the first years after they leave school. In our attempt then to give a girl pleasure and freedom from care we succeed, for the most part, in making her pitifully miserable. She finds "life" so different from what she expected it to be. She is besotted with innocent little ambitions, and does not understand this apparent waste of herself, this elaborate preparation, if no work is provided for her. There is a heritage of noble obligation which young people accept

5

and long to perpetuate. The desire for action, the wish to right wrong and alleviate suffering, haunts them daily. Society smiles at it indulgently instead of making it of value to itself. The wrong to them begins even farther back, when we restrain the first childish desires for "doing good" and tell them that they must wait until they are older and better fitted. We intimate that social obligation begins at a fixed date, forgetting that it begins with birth itself. We treat them as children who, with strong-growing limbs, are allowed to use their legs but not their arms, or whose legs are daily carefully exercised that after awhile their arms may be put to high use. We do this in spite of the protest of the best educators, Locke and Pestalozzi. We are fortunate in the mean time if their unused members do not weaken and disappear. They do sometimes. There are a few girls who, by the time they are "educated," forget their old childish desires to help the world and to play with poor little girls "who haven't playthings." Parents are often inconsistent. They deliberately expose their daughters to knowledge of the distress in the world. They send them to hear missionary addresses on famines in India and China; they accompany them to lectures on the suffering in Siberia; they agitate together over the forgotten region of East London. In addition to this, from babyhood the altruistic tendencies of these daughters are persistently cultivated. They are taught to be self-forgetting and self-sacrificing, to consider the good of the Whole before the good of the Ego. But when all this information and culture show results, when the daughter comes back from college and begins to recognize her social claim to the "submerged tenth," and to evince a disposition to fulfil it, the family claim is strenuously asserted; she is told that she is unjustified, ill-advised in her efforts. If she persists the family too often are injured and unhappy, unless the efforts are called missionary, and the religious zeal of the family carry them over their sense of abuse. When this zeal does not exist the result is perplexing. It is a curious violation of what we would fain believe a fundamental law—that the final return of the Deed is upon the head of the Doer. The deed is that of exclusiveness and caution, but the return instead of falling upon the head of the exclusive and cautious, falls upon a young head full of generous and unselfish plans. The girl loses something vital out of her life which she is entitled to. She is restricted and unhappy; her elders, meanwhile, are unconscious of the situation, and we have all the elements of a tragedy.

We have in America a fast-growing number of cultivated young people who have no recognized outlet for their active faculties. They hear constantly of the great social mal-adjustment, but no way is provided for them to change it, and their uselessness hangs about them heavily. Huxley declares that the sense of uselessness is the severest shock which the human system can sustain, and that, if persistently sustained, it results in atrophy of function. These young people have had advantages of college, of European travel and economic study, but they are sustaining this shock of inaction. They have pet phrases, and they tell you that the things that make us all alike are stronger than the things that make us different. They say that all men are united by needs and sympathies far more permanent and radical than anything that temporarily divides them and sets them in opposition to each other. If they affect art, they say that the decay in artistic expression is due to the decay in ethics, that art when shut away from the human interests and from the great mass of humanity is self-destructive. They tell their elders with all the bitterness of youth that if they expect success from them in business, or politics, or in whatever lines their ambition for them has run, they must let them consult all of humanity; that they must let them find out what the people want and how they want it. It is only the stronger young people, however, who formulate this. Many of them dissipate their energies in so-called enjoyment. Others, not content with that, go on studying and go back to college for their second degrees, not that they are especially fond of study, but because they want something definite to do, and their powers have been trained in the direction of mental accumulation. Many are buried beneath mere mental ac-

manitarianism. It is difficult to analyze a living thing; the analysis is at best imperfect. Many more motives may blend with the three trends; possibly the desire for a new form of social success due to the nicety of imagination, which refuses worldly pleasures unmixed with the joys of self-sacrifice; possibly a love of approbation, so vast that it is not content with the treble clapping of delicate hands, but wishes also to hear the bass notes from toughened palms, may mingle with these. . . .

Susan B. Anthony
(1820–1906)

Susan B. Anthony was born on February 15, 1820 on a farm near Adams, Massachusetts. The second of eight children, she moved with her family in 1826 to Battenville, New York, where she attended the district school and learned the tenets of the Quaker religion. At an early age Susan began teaching in local schools to help support her family and in 1839 she left home to teach, first at Eunice Kenyon's Friends' Seminary in New Rochelle, New York, and in 1846 at Canajoharie Academy in Rochester, New York, where she served as headmistress of the Female Department. Dissatisfied with teaching, in 1849 she returned to manage the family farm and began to immerse herself in the reform movements of the day, including temperance, antislavery, and women's rights. In 1850 Susan met Elizabeth Cady Stanton and by 1853 Elizabeth had convinced her to devote her lifetime work to the woman's rights movement. In the years prior to the Civil War she worked behind the scenes to secure speakers, arrange dates, raise money, organize New York state woman's rights conventions and implement county-by-county canvasses to obtain signatures on petitions demanding suffrage and property rights for women. Never abandoning her concern for the abolition of slavery, Susan also served from 1856 until the Civil War as the principal New York agent for William Lloyd Garrison's American Anti-Slavery Society. During the Civil War she and Elizabeth organized the Women's Loyal National League, which secured hundreds of thousands of signatures on petitions calling for Negro emancipation. After the war Susan campaigned to gain women the right to vote along with Negro males, waging her campaign in the East, in a lengthy tour of Kansas, for two years in the new weekly *Revolution* launched by she and Elizabeth in 1868, and through various organizations and conventions. In 1869 she and Elizabeth formed the National Woman Suffrage Association which they used for the rest of their lives as a forum to guide, steady and prod generations of women suffragists. For the next thirty years Susan travelled almost ceaselessly throughout the country working for a federal suffrage amendment and in various state campaigns. In 1872 Susan decided to test the 14th and 15th amendments and voted in New York in the presidential election; whereupon she was arrested and indicted for voting illegally, tried by a district judge, pronounced guilty and fined $100. In 1876, she and two colleagues dramatically presented a "Woman's Declaration of 1876" at the Fourth of July ceremonies at the Centennial Exposition in Philadelphia. In the early 1870's Susan and Elizabeth and Mathilda Joslyn Gage began writing the monumental historical work, *History of Woman Suffrage*, which would eventually fill over 5,000 pages and six volumes. From 1892 to 1900, Susan served as president of the National American Woman Suffrage Association after over twenty years of serving as vice president under Elizabeth. In the late 1890's she travelled to Europe and helped to found the International Council of Women, and at the turn of the century helped to found the International Woman Suffrage Alliance. In February, 1906 Susan attended her last suffrage convention and on March 13, at the age of eighty-six, she died of heart failure at her home in Rochester, New York.

The following speech was delivered on May 4, 1894 in Kansas City, Kansas at the opening of the campaign to pressure inclusion of a woman suffrage plank in both the Republican party platform and the Populist party platform. The speech appears in printed form in Ida Harper (Ed.), *The Life and Work of Susan B. Anthony* (Indianapolis, In. and Kansas City, Mo., 1899), II, pp. 1015–1021.

"Demand for Party Recognition"

I come to you tonight not as a stranger, not as an outsider but, in spirit and in every sense, as one of you. I have been connected with you by the ties of relationship for nearly forty years. Twenty-seven years ago I canvassed this entire State of Kansas in your first woman suffrage campaign. During the last decade I have made a speaking tour of your congressional districts over and over again. Now I come once more to appeal to you for justice to the women of your State.

To preface, I want to say that when the rebellion broke out in this country, we of the woman suffrage movement postponed our meetings, and organized ourselves into a great National Women's Loyal League with headquarters in the city of New York. We sent out thousands of petitions praying Congress to abolish slavery, as a war measure, and to these petitions we obtained 365,000 signatures. They were presented by Charles Sumner, that noblest Republican of them all, and it took two stalwart negroes to carry them into the Senate chamber. We did our work faithfully all those years. Other women scraped lint, made jellies, ministered to sick and suffering soldiers and in every way worked for the help of the government in putting down that rebellion. No man, no Republican leader, worked more faithfully or loyally than did the women of this nation in every city and county of the North to aid the government.

In 1865 I made my first visit to Kansas and, on the 2d of July, went by stage from Leavenworth to Topeka. O, how I remember those first acres and miles of cornfields I ever had seen; how I remember that ride to Topeka and from there in an open mail wagon to Ottumwa, where I was one of the speakers at the Fourth of July celebration. Those were the days, as you recollect, just after the murder of Lincoln and the accession to the presidential chair of Andrew Johnson, who had issued his proclamation for the reconstruction of Mississippi. So the question of the negro's enfranchisement was uppermost in the minds of leading Republicans, though no one save Charles Sumner had dared to speak it aloud. In that speech, I clearly stated that the government never would be reconstructed, that peace never would reign and justice never be uppermost until not only the black men were enfranchised but also the women of the entire nation. The men congratulated me upon my speech, the first part of it, every word I said about negro suffrage, but declared that I should not have mentioned woman suffrage at so critical an hour.

A little later the Associated Press dispatch came that motions had been made on the floor of the House of Representatives at Washington to insert the word "male" in the second clause of the Fourteenth Amendment. You remember the first clause, "All persons born or naturalized in the United States, and subject to the jurisdiction thereof, are citizens of the United States and of the State wherein they reside. No State shall make or enforce any law which shall abridge the privileges and immunities of citizens." That was magnificent. Every woman of us saw that it included the women of the nation as well as black men. The second section, as Thaddeus Stevens drew it, said, "If any State shall disfranchise any of its citizens on account of color, all that class shall be counted out of the basis of representation;" but at once the enemy asked, "Do you mean that if any State shall disfranchise its negro women, you are going to count all the black race out of the basis of representation?" And weak-kneed Republicans, after having fought such a glorious battle, surrendered; they could not stand the taunt. Charles Sumner said he wrote over nineteen pages of foolscap in order to keep the word "male" out of the Constitution; but he could not do it so he with the rest subscribed to the amendment: "If any State shall disfranchise any of its male citizens all of that class shall be counted out of the basis of representation."

There was the first great surrender and, in all those years of reconstruction, Elizabeth Cady Stanton, the great leader of our woman suffrage movement, declared that because the Republicans were willing to sacrifice the enfranchisement of the women of the nation they would lose eventually the power to protect the black man in his right to vote. But the leaders of the Republican party shouted back to us, "Keep silence, this is the negro's hour." Even our glorious Wendell Phillips, who said, "To talk to a black man of freedom without the ballot is mockery," joined in the cry, "This is the negro's hour;" but we never yielded the point that, "To talk to women of freedom without the ballot is mockery also." But timidity, cowardice and want of principle carried forward the reconstruction of the government with the women left out.

Then came in 1867 the submission by your Kansas legislature of three amendments to your constitution: That all men who had served in the rebel army should be disfranchised; that all black men should be enfranchised; and that all women should be enfranchised. The Democrats held their State convention and resolved they would have nothing to do with that "modern fanaticism of woman's rights." The Germans held a meeting in Lawrence, and denounced this "new-fangled idea." The Republicans held their State convention and resolved to be "neutral." And they were neutral precisely as England was neutral in the rebellion. While England declared neutrality, she allowed the *Shenandoah,* the *Alabama* and other pirate ships to be fitted up in her ports to maraud the seas and capture American vessels. The fact was not a single stump speaker appointed by the Republican committee advocated the woman suffrage amendment and, more than this, all spoke against it.

Then, of course, we had to make a woman suffrage campaign through the months of September and October. We did our best. Everywhere we had splendid audiences and I think we had a larger ratio of men in those olden times than we have nowadays. Election day came, that 5th day of November, 1867, when 9,070 men voted yes, and over 18,000 voted no. On the negro suffrage amendment, 10,500 voted yes and the remainder voted no. Both amendments were lost. All the political power of the national and State Republican party was brought to bear to induce every man to vote for negro suffrage; on the other hand, all the enginery and power of the Republican, as well as of the Democratic party, were against us; and many were so ignorant they absolutely believed that to vote for woman suffrage was to vote against the negro. It was exactly like declaring here tonight that if every woman in this house should fill her lungs with oxygen, she would rob all you men of enough to fill yours. Nobody is robbed by letting everybody have equal rights.

Since 1867 seven other States have submitted the question. Let me run them over.

[Miss Anthony then gave a graphic description of the campaigns in Michigan, 1874; Colorado, 1877; Nebraska, 1882; Oregon, 1884; Rhode Island, 1886; Washington, 1889; South Dakota, 1890; all of which failed for lack of support from the political platforms, editors and speakers.]

But at last in Colorado, in the second campaign, we won by the popular vote, *gained through party endorsement,* the enfranchisement of women. During the summer of 1893 nearly every Republican and Populist and not a few Democratic county conventions put approving planks in their platforms. When the fall campaign opened every stump orator was authorized to speak favorably upon the subject; no man could oppose it unless he ran counter to the principles laid down in his party platform. That made it a truly educational campaign to all the voters of the State. A word to the wise is sufficient. Let every man who wants the suffrage amendment carried, demand a full and hearty endorsement of the measure by his political party, be it Democrat, Republican, Populist or Prohibition, so that Kansas shall win as did her neighbor State, Colorado.

12

The Republicans of Kansas made the Prohibition amendment a party measure in 1880. After they secured the law they had planks in their platform for its enforcement from year to year, until they were tired of fighting the liquor dealers, backed by the Democrats in the State and on the borders. They wearied of being taunted with the fact that they had not the power to enforce the law. Then in 1887 they gave municipal suffrage to women as a sheer party necessity. Just as much as it was a necessity of the Republicans in reconstruction days to enfranchise the negroes, so was it a political necessity in the State of Kansas to enfranchise the women, because they needed a new balance of power to help them elect and re-elect officers who would enforce the law. Where else could they go to get that balance? Every man in the State, native and foreign, drunk and sober, outside of the penitentiary, the idiot and lunatic asylums, already had the right to vote. They had nobody left but the women. As a last resort the Republicans, by a straight party vote, extended municipal suffrage to women.

This political power was put into the hands of the women of this State by the old Republican party with its magnificent majorities—82,000, you remember, the last time you bragged. It was before you had the quarrel and division in the family; it was by that grand old party, solid as it was in those bygone days!

Last year, and two years ago, after the Peoples' party was organized, when their State convention was held, and also when the Republican convention was held, each put a plank in its platform declaring that the time had come for the submission of a proposition for full suffrage to women. What then could the women infer but that such action meant political help in carrying this amendment? If I had not believed this I never would have come to the State and given my voice in twenty-five or thirty political meetings, reminding the Republicans what a grand and glorious record they had made, not only in the enfranchisement of the black men but in furnishing all the votes on the floor of Congress ever given for women's enfranchisement there, and in extending municipal suffrage to the women of Kansas. I have vowed, from the time I began to see that woman suffrage could be carried only through party help, that I never would lend my influence to either of the two dominant parties that did not have a woman suffrage plank in its platform.

I consider, by every pledge of the past, by the passage of the resolution through the legislature when the representatives of the two parties, the Peoples' and Republican, vied with each other to see who would give the largest majority, that both promised to make this a party measure and I speak tonight to the two parties as the old Republican party. You are not the same men altogether, but you are the descendants, the children, of that party; and I am here tonight, and have come all the way from my home, to beg you to stand by the principles which have made you great and strong, and to finish the work you have so nobly begun.

The Republicans are to have their State convention the 6th of June. I shall be ashamed if the telegraph wires flash the word over the country, "No pledge for the amendment," as was flashed from the Republican League the other day. Should this happen, as I have heard intimated, and there is a woman in the State of Kansas who has any affiliation with the Republican party, any sympathy with it, who will float its banner after it shall have thus failed to redeem its pledge, I will disown her; she is not one of my sort.

The Populist convention is to be held the 12th of June. If it should shirk its responsibility, and not put a strong suffrage plank in its platform, pledging itself to use all its educational powers and all its party machinery to carry the amendment, then I shall have no respect for any woman who will speak of work for its success.

The Democrats have declared their purpose. They are going to fight us. What does the good Book say? "He that is not for me is against me." We know where the Democratic party is, it is against us. If the Republican and Peoples' parties say nothing for us, they say and do everything against us. No plank will be equivalent to saying to every woman suffrage Republican and Populist speaker, "You must not advocate this amendment, for to do so will lose us the whisky vote, it will lose us the foreign vote." Hence, no plank means no word for us, and no word for us means no vote for us. But while no word can be spoken in favor, every campaign orator, as in 1867, is free to speak in opposition.

Men of the Republican party, it comes your time first to choose whom you will have for your future constituents, to make up the bone and sinew of your party; whether you will have the most ignorant foreigners, just landed on our shores, who have not learned a single principle of free government—or the women of your own households; whether you will lose to-day a few votes of the high license or the low license Republicans, foreign or native, black or white, as the case may be, and gain to yourselves hereafter the votes of the women of the State. These are the alternatives. It has been stated that you can not have a suffrage plank in the Republican platform in Saline county because it would lose the votes of the Scandinavians. Will those 1,000 Scandinavian men be of more value to the Republicans than will be the votes of their own wives, mothers, daughters and sisters in all the years to come?

The crucial moment is upon you now, and I say unto you, men of both parties, you will have driven the last nail in the coffin of this amendment and banished all hope of carrying it at the ballot-box if you do not incorporate woman suffrage in your platforms. I know what the party managers will say, I have talked with and heard from many of them. I read Mr. Morrill's statement that "this question should go to the ballot-box on its merits and should not be spoken of in the political meetings or made a party measure."

The masses are rooted and grounded in the old beliefs in the inferiority and subjection of women, and consider them born merely to help man carry out his plans and not to have any of their own. Now, friends, because this is true, because no man believes in political equality for woman, except he is educated out of every bigotry, every prejudice and every usage that he was born into, in the family, in the church and in the state, so there can be no hope of the rank and file of men voting for this amendment, until they are taught the principles of justice and right; and there is no possibility that these men can be reached, can be educated, through any other instrumentality than that of the campaign meetings and campaign papers of the political parties. Therefore, when you say this is not to be a political question, not to be in your platform, not to be discussed in your meetings, not to be advocated in your papers, you make it impossible for its merits to be brought before the voters.

Who are the men that come to our women's meetings? We have just finished the tour of the sixty counties in the State of New York. We had magnificent gatherings, composed of people from the farthest townships in the county, and in many of them from every township, with the largest opera houses packed, hundreds going away who could not get in. Our audiences have been five-sixths women, and the one man out of the six, who was he? A man who already believed there was but one means of salvation for the race or the country, and that was through the political equality of women, making them the peers of men in every department of life. How are we going to reach the other five-sixths of the men who never come to women's meetings? There is no way except through the political rallies which are attended by all men. Now if you shut out of these the discussion of this question, then I say the fate of this amendment is sealed.

Even if it were possible to reach the men through separate meetings, the women of Kansas can not carry on a fall campaign. They can not get the money to do it unless you men furnish it. Our eastern friends have already contributed to the extent of their ability to hold these spring meetings, and you very well know that after the husbands shall have paid their party assessments there will be nothing left for them to "give to their wives" to defray the expenses of a woman suffrage campaign. Therefore, no discussion in the regular political meetings means no discussion anywhere. But suppose there were plenty of money, and there could be a most thorough fall campaign, what then? Why, the same old story of "women talking to women," not one of whom can vote on the question.

Again, with what decency can either of the parties ask women to come to their political meetings to expound Populist or Republican doctrines after they have set their heels on the amendment? Do you not see that if it will lose votes to the parties to have the plank, it will lose votes to allow women to advocate the amendment on their platforms? And what a spectacle it would be to see women pleading with men to vote for the one or the other party, while their tongues were tied on the question of their own right to vote! Heaven and the Republican and Populist State Conventions spare us such a dire humiliation!

But should the Republicans refuse to insert the plank on June 6 and the Populists put a good solid one in their platform on June 12, what then? Do you suppose all the women in the State would shout for the Republicans and against the Populists? Would they pack the Republican meetings, where no word could be spoken for their liberty, and leave the benches empty in the Populist meetings where at every one hearty appeals were made to vote for woman's enfranchisement? My dear friends, woman surely will be able to see that her highest interest, her liberty, her right to a voice in government, is the great issue of this campaign, and overtops, outweighs, all material questions which are now pending between the parties.

I know you think your Kansas men are going to vote on this amendment independently of party endorsement. You are no more sanguine today than were the men and women, myself included, in 1867, that those Free State men, who had given up every comfort which human beings prize for the sake of liberty, who had fought not only through the border ruffian warfare but through the four years of the rebellion, would vote freedom to the heroic women of Kansas. Where would you ever expect to find a majority more ready to grant to women equal rights than among those old Free State men? You have not as glorious a generation of men in Kansas today as you had in 1867. I do not wish to speak disparagingly, but in the nature of things there can not be another race of men as brave as those. If you had told me then that a majority of those men would have gone to the ballot-box and voted against equal rights for women, I should have defended them with all my power; but they did it, two to one.

Do you mean to repeat the experiment of 1867? If so, do not put a plank in your platform; just have a "still hunt." Think of a "still hunt" when it must be necessarily a work of education! My friends, I know enough of this State, to feel that it is worth saving. I have given more time and money and effort to Kansas than to any other State in the Union, because I wanted it to be the first to make its women free. Women of Kansas, all is lost if you sit down and supinely listen to politicians and candidates. Both reckon what they will lose or what they will gain. They study expediency rather than principle. I appeal to you, men and women, make the demand imperative: "The amendment must be endorsed by the parties and advocated on the platform and in the press." Let me propose a resolution:

WHEREAS, From the standpoint of justice, political expediency and grateful appreciation of their wise and practical use of school suffrage from the organization of the State, and of municipal suffrage for the past eight years, we, Republicans and Populists, descendants of that grand old party of splendid majorities which extended these rights to the women of Kansas, in mass meeting assembled do hereby

Resolve, That we urgently request our delegates in their approaching State conventions to endorse the woman suffrage amendment in their respective platforms.

[The resolution was adopted by a unanimous vote.]

That vote fills my soul with joy and hope. Now I want to say to you, my good friends, I never would have made a 1,500 mile journey hither to appeal to the thinking, justice-loving men of Kansas. They already are converted, but they are a minority. We have to consider those whose votes can be obtained only by that party influence and machinery which politicians alone know how to use. This hearty response is a pledge that you will demand of your State conventions that the full power of this political machinery shall be used to carry the woman suffrage amendment to victory.

Emily Greene Balch
(1867–1961)

Emily Greene Balch was born on January 8, 1867 in Jamaica Plain, Massachusetts. The second of six children, she attended Miss Catherine Ireland's School in Boston before entering Bryn Mawr College in 1886. Upon graduation from Bryn Mawr in 1889, she embarked for Europe to study at the Sorbonne as the first recipient of the Bryn Mawr European Fellowship. Returning to Boston in 1891, Emily apprenticed herself to the Boston Children's Aid Society for two years and resumed her education with stints at the Harvard Annex and the University of Chicago. In 1895 she returned to Europe to study at the University of Berlin for a year. Emily began her academic career at Wellesley in 1896 and maintained a stormy association with the College until 1919 when the trustees voted not to renew her appointment. Her twenty-three years at Wellesley were constantly affected or interrupted by her radical extracurricular activities and, hence, Emily chose not to fight her termination on the grounds she had knowingly risked her position in order to live for her causes. The causes Emily championed were many and varied. She fought for minimum wages for women and served as cofounder and president of the Boston Women's Trade Union League. She declared herself a socialist in 1906 and organized several socialist conferences in Boston and New York. She campaigned vigorously on behalf of immigrants and achieved scholarly recognition for her major work, *Our Slavic Fellow Citizens,* published in 1910. But it was through her dedication to the cause of peace that Emily Balch achieved her greatest fame. In 1915 she joined the American delegation to the International Congress of Women at The Hague, and from that time on she became a tireless political activist for pacifist causes. She staunchly opposed World War I, military conscription and espionage legislation and defended the civil liberties of conscientious objectors and the foreign born. She helped found the Emergency Peace Federation in 1917 and supported its radical successor, the People's Council of America. From 1919 until her death, she held numerous offices in the Women's International League for Peace and Freedom, travelling worldwide to organize congresses and to undertake special missions. In 1946 her years of pacifist efforts brought her the much deserved Nobel Peace Prize. In the last years of her life Emily lived peacefully in Massachusetts until she died of pneumonia on January 9, 1961 at the age of 94.

The following address was delivered at the International Congress of Women at The Hague in 1915. It appeared in printed form in Jane Addams, Emily Greene Balch and Alice Hamilton, *Women at The Hague* (New York, N.Y., 1915), pp. 111-23.

"The Time to Make Peace"

There is a widespread feeling that this is not the moment to talk of a European peace. On the contrary there is reason to believe that the psychological moment may be very close upon us. If, in the wisdom that comes after the event, we see that the United States was dilatory when it might have helped to open a way to end bloodshed and make a fair and lasting settlement, we shall have cause for deep self-reproach.

The question of peace is a question of terms. Every country desires peace at the earliest possible moment at which it can be had on terms satisfactory to itself. Peace is possible the moment that each side would accept what the other would grant, but from the international or human point of view a satisfactory peace is possible only when these claims and concessions are such as to forward and not to hinder human progress. If Germany's terms are the annexation of Belgium and part of France and a military hegemony over the rest of Europe, or if on the other hand the terms of France or of England include "wiping Germany off the map of Europe" there is no possibility of peace at the present time nor at any time that can be foreseen, nor does the world desire peace on these terms.

In one sense the present war is a conflict between the two great sets of belligerent powers, but in a different and very real sense it is a conflict between two conceptions of national policy. The catch words "democracy" and "imperialism" may be used briefly to indicate the opposing ideas. In every country both are represented, though in varying proportions, and in every country there is strife between them.

In each belligerent nation there are those that want to continue the fight till military supremacy is achieved, in each there are powerful forces that seek a settlement of a wiser type which, instead of containing such threats to stability as are involved in annexation, humiliation of the enemy, and in competition in armaments, shall secure rational independence all round, protect the rights of minorities and foster international cooperation.

One of the two little realized effects of the war is the overriding of the regular civil government by the military authorities in all the warring countries. The forms of constitutionalism may be undisturbed but as *inter arma leges silent* so in time of war military power—no less really because unobtrusively—tends to control the representatives of the people. Von Tirpitz, Kitchener, Joffre, have in greater or less degree overshadowed their nominal masters.

Another effect of war is that as between the two contending voices, the one is given a megaphone, the other is muffled if not gagged. Papers and platforms are open to "patriotic" utterances as patriotism is understood by the jingo; the moderate is silenced not alone by the censor, not alone by social pressure, but also by his own sense of the effect abroad of all that gives an impression of internal division and of a readiness to quit the fight. In our own country during the height of tension with Germany, loyal Americans who believed that the case of the United States was not a strong one (and a hundred million people cannot all think alike on such an issue), those who loathe the thought of war over such a quarrel, could not and would not give any commensurate expression to their views for fear that they might make it harder for our government to induce Germany to render her warfare less inhuman.

Everywhere war puts out of sight the moderates and the forces that make for peace and gives an exaggerated influence to militaristic and jingo forces creating a false impression of the pressure for extreme terms.

Of course each country desires as favorable terms as it can get and therefore would prefer to make peace at a moment when the great struggle—which in a rough general sense is a stalemate—is marked by some incident advantageous to itself. Germany would like to make peace from the crest of the wave of her invasion of Russia; Russia and England would like to make terms from a conquered Constantinople. If the disinterested neutrals, who alone are free to act for peace, wait for a moment when neither side has any advantage they will wait long indeed.

But the minor ups and downs of the war, shifting and unpredictable, are relatively much less important than they appear. The grim unchanging fact which affects both sides and which is to the changing fortunes of battle as the miles of immovable oceans depths are to the waves on the surface—this all outweighing fact is the intolerable burden of continued war. This it is which makes momentary advantage comparatively unimportant. All the belligerents want peace, though probably with different intensity; none of them wants it enough to cry "I surrender."

The making of peace involves not only questions of the character of the terms, of demands more or less extreme; it also involves the question of the principle according to which settlements are to be made. There are again two conflicting conceptions.

On the one hand is the assumption that military advantage must be represented *quid pro quo* on the terms—so much victory, so much corresponding advantage in the settlement. There is even the commercial conception of war as an investment and the idea that the fighter has a right to indemnity for what he has spent.

On the other hand it is assumed that the war having thrown certain international adjustments into the melting pot, the problem is to create a new adjustment such as shall on the whole be as generally satisfactory and contain as much promise of stability as practicable.

Even in a settlement based on such considerations the balance of physical force could not be merely ignored. Gains won by force create no claim that anyone is bound to respect yet while the expenditure of blood and treasure gives no right to reimbursement (and it is to the general interest that such expenditure, undertaken more or less on speculation, should never prove a good investment), nevertheless the arbitrament of war, being an arbitrament of violence, relative power is bound to tell in the resulting adjustment.

It is important, therefore, to consider that, with a given balance of relative strength as between the contending sides, an equilibrium may be expressed in more than one way, as there are equations which admit of more than one solution. The equilibrium of opposing claims might be secured by balancing unjust acquisition against unjust acquisition or by balancing magnanimous concession against magnanimous concession. A neutral mediator or mediating group acting in the interest of civilization in general and of the future might, without throwing any weight into the scale of one or the other side, help them to find the equilibrium on the higher rather than on the lower level.

On the basis of military advantage or on the basis of military costs the neutrals have no claim to be heard in the settlement. The soldier is genuinely aggrieved and outraged that they should mix in the matter at all. Yet even on the plane of fighting power the unexhausted neutral may fling a sword into the scale and on the plea of costs suffered the neutral may demand a voice. It is, however, supremely as representatives of humanity and civilization and the true interests of all sides alike that those who are not in the thick of the conflict can and should be of use in the settlement and help to find it on the higher plane.

The settlement of a war by outsiders—not their mere friendly cooperation—is something that has often occurred, exhibiting that curious mixture of the crassest brute force with the most ambitious idealism which often characterizes the conduct of international dealings. The fruits of victory were refused to Russia by the Congress of Berlin in 1878, Europe forbade Japan the spoils of her war with China in 1895, the results of the Balkan wars were largely determined by those who had done none of the fighting. While mere might played a large part in such interferences from the outside there is something beside hypocrisy in the claim of the statesmen of countries which had not taken part in the war to speak on behalf of freedom, progress and peace.

A peace involving annexation of unwilling peoples could never be a lasting one. The widespread sense of irritation at all talk of peace at present seems to be due to a feeling that a settlement now would be a settlement which would leave Belgium if not part of France in German hands. Such a settlement would be as disastrous to Germany as to any other nation. It might put

19

an end to military operations but it certainly would not bring peace if we give any moral content to that much abused word. Europe was not at peace before August, 1914, nor Ireland for long before, nor Poland, nor Alsace, nor Finland. Any community which, if it could, would fight to change its political status, may be quiet under coercion but it is not at peace. Neither would Europe be at peace with Germany in Belgium.

The question then is what sort of peace may we at least hope for now—on what terms, on what principles?

We may be sure that each side is ready to concede more and to demand less than appears on the surface or than it is ready to advertise. The summer campaign, in which marked advantages are most likely, is nearly over and a winter in the trenches will cost on all sides money and suffering out of all proportion to the advances that can be hoped for. It must be remembered too, that the advantages hitherto gained are not all on one side but that each has something to concede. The British annexations of Egypt and Cyprus may be formal rather than substantial changes but the conquest of the German colonies large and small—South West Africa, Togo Land, Samoa, Neu Pommern, Kaiser Wilhelmsland, the Solomon, Caroline and Marshall Islands, to say nothing of Kiao-Chao—and probably Russian gains at the expense of Turkey in the East—give bargaining power to the Allies. So also, even without success in the Dardanelles, does their ability to thwart or forward the Germans in Asia Minor and Mesopotamia.

Friends of Finland and of Poland must see to it that the debatable lands of the eastern as well as of the western frontier are kept in mind. From the point of view of Poland the main thing to be desired is the union of the three dismembered parts—Russian, German and Austrian Poland—and their fusion in some sort of a buffer state, independent or at least essentially autonomous. Something like this appears to be the purpose of both Germany and Russia with the difference that this Polish state would be in the one case under Teutonic, in the other under Russian, auspices. No one knows which would be the choice as between the two of the majority of the Poles concerned. Concessions to Germany in Finland and Poland are at least conceivable and would make the concession of complete withdrawal in the West easier for her to make. Still more important are the concessions in regard to naval control of the seas which Great Britain ought to be willing to make if the safety of her commerce and intercolonial communications can be adequately secured otherwise, and this would seem to be the natural counterpart of substantial steps toward disarmament on land.

But all this is speculation. The fact obvious to those who look below the surface, is that every belligerent power is carrying on a war deadly to itself, that bankruptcy looms ahead, that industrial revolt threatens, not at the moment but in a none too distant future, that racial stocks are being irreparably depleted. The prestige of Europe, of the Christian church, of the white race is lowered inch by inch with the progress of the struggle which is continually closer to the débâcle of a civilization.

Each power would best like peace on its own terms. Our common civilization would suffer by the imposition of extreme terms by any power. Each people would be thankful indeed to secure an early peace without humiliation a long way short of its extreme demands.

There is thus every reason to believe that a vigorous initiative by representatives of the neutral powers of the world could at this moment begin a move toward negotiations and lead the way to a settlement which, please God, shall be a step toward a nobler and more intelligent civilization than we have yet enjoyed.

Mary McLeod Bethune
(1875–1955)

Mary McLeod Bethune was born on July 10, 1875 near Mayesville, South Carolina. The fifteenth of seventeen children, she grew up on a farm purchased by her parents after they were freed as slaves at the conclusion of the Civil War. Mary's lengthy career as an educator began at a small black mission school near Mayesville where she excelled as an elementary student. In 1888 she received a scholarship to attend Scotia Seminary in Concord, North Carolina, a Presbyterian school for black girls that emphasized religion and industrial education. After graduating in 1894, she received another scholarship to attend the Bible Institute for Home and Foreign Missions (later the Moody Bible Institute) in Chicago to prepare for a career as a missionary to Africa. When no assignments for Africa opened up, Mary taught for a year in Augusta, Georgia, before returning to South Carolina to teach at Kindell Institute in Sumter. In 1898 she married a fellow teacher named Albert Bethune and a few months later they moved to Savannah, Georgia. Two years later Mary and her husband and infant daughter moved to Palatka, Florida to open their own mission school. After five years in Palatka Mary divorced her husband and resettled in Daytona Beach to establish a school for girls patterned after her alma mater Scotia Seminary. Beginning in 1904 with $1.50, borrowed essentials, a rented house and six students, Mary's business skills and persuasive oratorical talents converted some meager resources into a major educational institution. In less than twenty years the Daytona Normal and Industrial Institute for girls had acquired twenty acres with an attractive campus and eight buildings and a farm, and employed a faculty and staff of 25 for a student body of 300 girls. During this same time period Mary also led successful black voter registration drives despite threats from the Ku Klux Klan, campaigned for women's suffrage, and helped establish a much-needed regional hospital for blacks. After World War I she devoted much of her energy to transform her Institute into a college, and in 1929 it was officially renamed Bethune-Cookman College. While directing the school Mary rose to national prominence through her work in several organizations for black women. In the 1920's she actively worked for the National Association of Colored Women and assumed its presidency in 1924. In 1935 she created the National Council of Negro Women, formed by uniting the major national black women's associations, and served as its President until 1949. Recognized as a forceful and articulate leader in the field of education, Mary also served as president of the National Association of Teachers in Colored Schools, as vice-president of the Commission on Interracial Cooperation, and as president of the Association for the Study of Negro Life and History. In 1935, through Eleanor Roosevelt's influence, Mary was appointed to the 35-member National Advisory Committee to the National Youth Administration. For the next nine years she assumed the role of advocate to the federal government for all black interests, implementing the Federal Council on Negro Affairs (popularly called the "Black Cabinet") in 1936, organizing National Negro conferences in 1937 and 1939, and continuously promoting policies of nondiscrimination in government facilities. In 1944 Mary left her government post and retired to her home in Daytona Beach, which she soon transformed into an educational foundation. On May 18, 1955 Mary died from a heart attack at the age of 80.

The following speech was delivered before the Chicago Women's Federation on June 30, 1933. The original typescript is located at the Amistad Research Center, Dillard University, New Orleans, Louisiana.

"A Century of Progress of Negro Women"

To Frederick Douglass is credited the plea that, "the Negro be not judged by the heights to which he is risen, but by the depths from which he has climbed." Judged on that basis, the Negro woman embodies one of the modern miracles of the New World.

One hundred years ago she was the most pathetic figure on the American continent. She was not a person, in the opinion of many, but a thing—a thing whose personality had no claim to the respect of mankind. She was a household drudge,—a means for getting distasteful work done; she was an animated agricultural implement to augment the service of mules and plows in cultivating and harvesting the cotton crop. Then she was an automatic incubator, a producer of human live stock, beneath whose heart and lungs more potential laborers could be bred and nurtured and brought to the light of toilsome day.

Today she stands side by side with the finest manhood the race has been able to produce. Whatever the achievements of the Negro man in letters, business, art, pulpit, civic progress and moral reform, he cannot but share them with his sister of darker hue. Whatever glory belongs to the race for a development unprecedented in history for the given length of time, a full share belongs to the womanhood of the race.

By the very force of circumstances, the part she has played in the progress of the race has been of necessity, to a certain extent, subtle and indirect. She has not always been permitted a place in the front ranks where she could show her face and make her voice heard with effect. But she has been quick to seize every opportunity which presented itself to come more and more into the open and strive directly for the uplift of the race and nation. In that direction, her achievements have been amazing.

Negro women have made outstanding contributions in the arts. Meta V. W. Fuller and May Howard Jackson are significant figures in Fine Arts development. Angelina Grimke, Georgia Douglass Johnson and Alice Dunbar Nelson are poets of note. Jessie Fausett has become famous as a novelist. In the field of Music Anita Patti Brown, Lillian Evanti, Elizabeth Greenfield, Florence Cole-Talbert, Marion Anderson and Marie Selika stand out pre-eminently.

Very early in the post-emancipation period women began to show signs of ability to contribute to the business progress of the Race. Maggie L. Walker, who is outstanding as the guiding spirit of the Order of Saint Luke, in 1902 went before her Grand Council with a plan for a Saint Luke Penny Savings Bank. This organization started with a deposit of about eight thousand dollars and twenty-five thousand in paid-up capital, with Maggie L. Walker as the first Woman Bank President in America. For twenty-seven years she has held this place. Her bank has paid dividends to its stockholders; has served as a depository for gas and water accounts of the city of Richmond and has given employment to hundreds of Negro clerks, bookkeepers and office workers.

With America's great emphasis on the physical appearance, a Negro woman left her wash-tub and ventured into the field of facial beautification. From a humble beginning Madame C. J. Walker built a substantial institution that is a credit to American business in every way.

Mrs. Annie M. Malone is another pioneer in this field of successful business. The C. J. Walker Manufacturing Company and the Poro College do not confine their activities in the field of beautification to race. They serve both races and give employment to both.

When the ballot was made available to the Womanhood of America, the sister of darker hue was not slow to seize the advantage. In sections where the Negro could gain access to the voting booth, the intelligent, forward-looking element of the Race's women have taken hold of political issues with an enthusiasm and mental acumen that might well set worthy examples for other groups. Oftimes she has led the struggle toward moral improvement and political record, and has compelled her reluctant brother to follow her determined lead.

In time of war as in time of peace, the Negro woman has ever been ready to serve for her people's and the nation's good. During the recent World War she pleaded to go in the uniform of the Red Cross nurse and was denied the opportunity only on the basis of racial distinction.

Addie W. Hunton and Kathryn M. Johnson gave yeoman service with the American Expeditionary Forces with the Y.M.C.A. group.

Negro women have thrown themselves whole-heartedly into the organization of groups to direct the social uplift of their fellowmen, one of the greatest achievements of the race.

Perhaps the most outstanding individual social worker of our group today is Jane E. Hunter, founder and executive secretary of the Phillis Wheatley Association, Cleveland, Ohio.

In November, 1911, Miss Hunter, who had been a nurse in Cleveland for only a short time, recognizing the need for a Working Girls' Home, organized the Association and prepared to establish the work. Today the Association is housed in a magnificent structure of nine stories, containing one hundred thirty-five rooms, offices, parlours, a cafeteria and beauty parlour. It is not only a home for working girls but a recreational center and ideal hospice for the young Negro woman who is living away from home. It maintains an employment department and a fine, up-to-date camp. Branches of the activities of the main Phillis Wheatley are located in other sections of Cleveland, special emphasis being given to the recreational facilities for children and young women of the vicinities in which the branches are located.

In no field of modern social relationship has the hand of service and the influence of the Negro woman been felt more distinctly than in the Negro orthodox church. It may be safely said that the chief sustaining force in support of the pulpit and the various phases of missionary enterprise has been the feminine element of the membership. The development of the Negro church since the Civil War has been another of the modern miracles. Throughout its growth the untiring effort, the unflagging enthusiasm, the sacrificial contribution of time, effort and cash earnings of the black woman have been the most significant factors, without which the modern Negro church would have no history worth the writing.

Both before and since emancipation, by some rare gift, she has been able to hold onto the fibres of family unity and keep the home one unimpaired whole. In recent years it has become increasingly the case where in many instances, the mother is the sole dependence of the home, and single-handed, fights the wolf from the door, while the father submits unwillingly to enforced idleness and unavoidable unemployment. Yet in myriads of instances she controls home discipline with a tight rein and exerts a unifying influence that is the miracle of the century.

The true worth of a race must be measured by the character of its womanhood.

As the years have gone on the Negro woman has touched the most vital fields in the civilization of today. Wherever she has contributed she has left the mark of a strong character. The educational institutions she has established and directed have met the needs of her young people; her cultural development has concentrated itself into artistic presentation accepted and acclaimed by meritorious critics; she is successful as a poet and a novelist; she is shrewd in business and capable in politics; she recognizes the importance of uplifting her people through social, civic and religious activities; starting at the time when as a "mammy" she nursed the infants of the other race and taught him her meagre store of truth, she has been a contributing factor of note to interracial relations. Finally, through the past century she has made and kept her home intact—humble though it may have been in many instances. She has made and is making history.

Carrie Chapman Catt
(1859–1947)

Carrie Chapman Catt was born on January 9, 1859 in Ripon, Wisconsin. The second of three children, she moved with her family to Charles City, Iowa in 1866 where she attended public schools and graduated from high school in 1875. After a year of teaching, Carrie entered Iowa State College at Ames and graduated with a Bachelor of Science degree in 1880. In 1881 she accepted the position of principal of the Mason City, Iowa high school, and in 1883 she assumed the job of superintendent of schools. After her marriage in 1885 to Leo Chapman, Carrie turned her energies to her husband's newspaper business. However, his untimely death less than two years later abruptly ended this part of her professional life. In 1887 she joined the Iowa Woman Suffrage Association, little knowing that the next thirty-plus years of her life would be devoted to gaining the vote for women. After marrying George Catt in 1890 and moving to New York City in 1892, Carrie immersed herself in the National American Woman Suffrage Association. In 1895 she set up an Organizational Committee which directed the national association's field work, and within the next five years her superb organizational talents had succeeded in creating a highly efficient nationwide structure unmatched in the long history of the association. In 1900 Susan B. Anthony selected Carrie to replace her as president of the association, a position which Carrie held until 1904 when she was forced to resign because of her husband's poor health. After her husband's death in 1905, Carrie worked to set up the Woman Suffrage Party in New York State and chaired the Empire State Campaign Committee to gain a state suffrage referendum. In 1915 Carrie once again assumed the presidency of the National American Woman Suffrage Association and quickly developed the "Catt Winning Plan" to press for suffrage on the Federal and State level simultaneously. Five years later on August 26, 1920, she realized her greatest lifework when the nineteenth amendment finally became official law. In addition to her American suffrage efforts, Carrie was the prime moving force of the International Woman Suffrage Alliance, presiding over its Congresses in 1904, 1906, 1908, 1909, 1911, 1913, 1920, and 1923 in various capitols of Europe. In 1919 Carrie also helped found the League of Women Voters to provide an educational forum for women to discuss the major political issues of the day. In the 1920's and 1930's Carrie devoted much of her remaining reform career to pacifist causes, campaigning for the League of Nations and helping to establish the Committee on the Cause and Cure of War which met annually from 1925 until 1939. On March 9, 1947, Carrie died of a heart attack at the age of eighty-eight.

The following speech was delivered on December 15, 1915 in Washington, D.C. before the United States Senate Hearing on Woman Suffrage. The speech appears in printed form in *The History of Woman Suffrage*, Vol. V, Appendix, pp. 752–754.

"Why Are Only Women Compelled to Prove Themselves?"

Mr. Chairman and Gentlemen of the Committee:

Since our last appeal was made to your committee a vote has been taken in four Eastern States upon the question of amending their constitutions for woman suffrage. The inaction of Congress in not submitting a Federal amendment naturally leads us to infer that members believe the proper method by which women may secure the vote is through the referendum. We found in those four States what has always been true whenever any class of people have asked for any form of liberty and was best described by Macaulay when he said: "If a people are turbulent they are unfit for liberty; if they are quiet, they do not want it." We met a curious dilemma. On the one hand a great many men voted in the negative because women in Great Britain had made too emphatic a demand for the vote. Since they made that demand it is reported that 10,000,000 men have been killed, wounded or are missing through militant action, but all of that is held as naught compared with the burning of a few vacant buildings. Evidently the logic that these American men followed was: Since some turbulent women in another land are unfit to vote, no American woman shall vote. There was no reasoning that could change the attitude of those men. On the other hand the great majority of the men who voted against us, as well as the great majority of the members of Legislatures and Congress who oppose this movement, hold that women have given no signal that they want the vote. Between the horns of this amazing dilemma the Federal amendment and State suffrage seem to be caught fast.

So those of us who want to learn how to obtain the vote have naturally asked ourselves over and over again what kind of a demand can be made. We get nothing by "watchful waiting" and if we are turbulent we are pronounced unfit to vote. We turned to history to learn what kind of a demand the men of our own country made and determined to do what they had done. The census of 1910 reported 27,000,000 males over 21. Of these 9,500,000 are direct descendants of the population of 1800; 2,458,873 are negroes; 15,040,278 are aliens, naturalized or descendants of naturalized citizens since 1800. The last two classes compose two-thirds of the male population over 21. The enfranchisement of negro men is such recent history that it is unnecessary to repeat here that they made no demand for the vote. The naturalization laws give citizenship to any man who chooses to make a residence of this country for five years and automatically every man who is a citizen becomes a voter in the State of his residence. In the 115 years since 1800 not one single foreigner has ever been asked whether he wanted the vote or whether he was fit for it—it has literally been thrust upon him. Two-thirds of our men of voting age today have not only made no demand for the vote but they have never been asked to give any evidence of capacity to use it intelligently.

We turned again to history to see how the men who lived in this country in 1800 got their votes. At that time 8 per cent of the total population were voters in New York as compared with 25 per cent now. There was a struggle in all the colonial States to broaden the suffrage. New York seemed always to have lagged behind the others and therefore it forms a good example. It was next to the last State to remove the land qualification and it was not a leader in the extension of the suffrage to any class.

In 1740 the British Parliament disqualified the Catholics for naturalization in this country. That enactment had been preceded in several of the States by their definite disfranchisement. In 1699 they were disfranchised by an Act of the Assembly of New York. Although the writers on the early franchise say that Jews were not permitted to vote anywhere in this country in 1701, as they certainly were not in England, yet occasionally they apparently did so. In New York that year there was a definite enactment disfranchising them. In 1737 the Assembly passed another disfranchising Act. Catholics and Jews were disfranchised in most States. It is interesting to learn how they became enfranchised. One would naturally suppose that together or separately they would make some great demand for political equality with Protestants but there is no record that they did. I find that the reason why our country became so liberal to them was not because there was any demand on their part and not because there was any special advocacy of their enfranchisement by statesmen. It was due to the fact that in the Revolution, Great Britain, having difficulty with the American colonies on the south side of the St. Lawrence River, did as every belligerent country does and tried to hold Canada by granting her favors. In order to make the Canadian colonies secure against revolution the British Parliament, which had previously disfranchised the Catholics and the Jews, now extended a vote to them. The American Constitution makers could not do less than Great Britain had done, and so in every one of the thirteen States they were guaranteed political equality with Protestants.

The next great movement was the elimination of the land qualification and on this we find that history is practically silent. In Connecticut and Rhode Island a small petition was presented to the Assembly asking for its removal. In New York in the constitutional convention of 1821 when some members advocated its removal others asked, "Where is the demand? Who wants to vote that has no land?" The answer was that there had been some meetings in New York in behalf of removing this qualification. No one of them had seen such a meeting but some members had heard that a few had been held in the central districts of the State. This constitutes the entire demand that has been made by the men of our country for the vote.

In contrast we may ask what have women done? Again I may say that New York is a fair example because it is the largest of the States in population and has the second city in size in the world and occupies perhaps the most important position in any land in which a suffrage referendum has been taken. Women held during the six months prior to the election in 1915, 10,300 meetings. They printed and circulated 7,500,000 leaflets or three-and-a-half for every voter. These leaflets weighed more than twenty tons. They had 770 treasuries in the State among the different groups doing suffrage work and every bookkeeper except two was a volunteer. Women by the thousands contributed to the funds of that campaign, in one group 12,000 public school teachers. On election day 6,330 women watched at the polls from 5:45 in the morning until after the vote was counted. I was on duty myself from 5:30 until midnight. There were 2,500 campaign officers in the State who gave their time without pay. The publicity features were more numerous and unique than any campaign of men or women had ever had. They culminated in a parade in New York City which was organized without any effort to secure women outside the city to participate in it, yet 20,000 marched through Fifth Avenue to give some idea of the size of their demand for the vote.

What was the result? If we take the last announcement from the board of elections the suffrage amendment received 535,000 votes—2,000 more than the total vote of the nine States where women now have suffrage through a referendum. It was not submitted in Wyoming, Utah or Illinois. Yet New York suffragists did not win because the opponents outvoted them. How did this happen? Why did not such evidence of a demand win the vote? Because the unscrupulous men of the State worked and voted against women suffrage, aided and abetted by the weakminded and illiterate, who are permitted a vote in New York. In Rochester the male inmates of the almshouse and rescue home were taken out to vote against the amendment. Men too drunk to sign their own names voted all over the State, for drunkards may vote in New York. In many of the polling places the women watchers reported that throughout the entire day not one came to vote who did not have to be assisted; they did not know enough to cast their own vote.

Those are some of the conditions women must overcome in a referendum. One can eventually be carried even in New York but we believe we have made all the sacrifices which a just Government ought to expect of us. Even the Federal Amendment is difficult enough, with the ratification of 36 Legislatures required, but we may at least appeal to a higher class of men. We were obliged to make our campaign in twenty-four different languages. . . . It is too unfair and humiliating treatment of American women to compel us to appeal to the men of all nations of the earth for the vote which has been so freely and cheaply given to them. We believe we ought to have the benefit of the method provided by the Federal Constitution.

Dorothea Dix
(1802–1887)

Dorothea Dix was born on April 4, 1802 in Hampden, Maine. The oldest of three children, she spent an unhappy childhood marred by her father's frequent absences and her mother's semi-invalidness. At the age of twelve Dorothea moved to Boston to live with her grandmother, and at age fourteen she moved again to live with her great-aunt in Worcester, Massachusetts. After attending school in Worcester, Dorothea opened a school for young girls in Boston in 1821 and published an elementary science textbook (1824) and an anthology of poetry for children (1825). A serious bout with tuberculosis forced Dorothea to spend six years (1825–31) recuperating with various family friends in Rhode Island and the Virgin Islands. In 1831 she opened a new school in Boston, but by 1836 she suffered a nervous and physical collapse and was ordered by her doctor to travel abroad and rest. In late 1837 Dorothea returned to America and spent several more years travelling in the South trying to regain her health. In 1841 she returned to Boston and was asked by a Harvard divinity student to teach a class for women in the East Cambridge jail. Dorothea's discovery of mentally ill women housed in the same jail with drunkards, vagrants and prostitutes affected her so deeply that she was determined to rectify the situation and investigate other such Boston facilities. Little did Dorothea realize that this event would prompt her to dedicate the remainder of her life to crusading for the mentally ill. After a thorough investigation of Massachusetts jails, almshouses and houses of correction, she presented her findings in 1843 to the state legislature and succeeded in convincing them to appropriate funds to expand facilities for the proper care and treatment of the mentally ill. From 1843 to 1854 Dorothea repeated her investigations and presentations of "memorials" to state legislatures across the country, playing a direct role in the founding of thirty-two state mental hospitals and serving as the inspiration for many more. In between state travels, she also lobbied for six years for a Federal bill which would set up a perpetual trust for the mentally ill, but after the bill had finally passed both houses of Congress in 1854, President Pierce vetoed the bill. Exhausted and disappointed, Dorothea went to Europe to recuperate and to visit various mental institutions being developed abroad. With the coming of the Civil War Dorothea returned to the United States in 1860 and agreed to become superintendent of army nurses in 1861. Five tumultuous years later, she resumed her visitations of hospitals and prisons until 1881, when she retired to the New Jersey State Hospital she had helped bring into existence thirty-five years earlier. On July 18, 1887, Dorothea died there at the age of eighty-three.

The following address was presented before the Kentucky State Legislature in Frankfort, Kentucky in February, 1846. The address appeared in printed form in Dorothea Dix, *Memorial Soliciting an Appropriation for the State Hospital for the Insane, at Lexington; and Also Urging the Necessity for Establishing a New Hospital in the Green River Country* (Frankfort, Ky., 1846), pp. 1–16.

"On Behalf of the Insane Poor in Kentucky"

To the General Assembly of the Commonwealth of Kentucky:

GENTLEMEN:—I ask the indulgence of placing before you some remarks suggested by re-peated and careful inspection of the State Hospital for the Insane, at Lexington; and also the results of journeys recently made through forty four counties of your State, in view of ascertaining, as far as possible, the numbers and condition of this class of sufferers who have not been brought under remedial hospital care.

I would respectfully and earnestly urge the duty of providing a remedy for prominent defects and deficiencies in the present establishment, and suggest some reasons which appear absolute and consistent, for early additional provision in a southern district of the State for this numerous and increasing class of sufferers. Justice and humanity unite to present these claims, and it may be added, that both present and future *economy* in the administration of the public funds sustain their plea.

I approach you with confidence as the advocate of those who, alas, cannot plead their own cause—of those in whom the light of the understanding is darkened, and who are crushed under the weight of an overwhelming malady—yes, I approach you with confidence, for I am told that the citizens of Kentucky have heretofore been neither slow nor reluctant in responding to the calls of duty, and acknowledging the claims of those, who through privation and disease are made *wards* of the State—legalized dependents on its beneficent and guardian care.

Legislators of Kentucky, I do not now urge the necessities of these afflicted ones, so much in the *hope* of your effective and generous action, as in the *belief* that you will not hesitate to provide amply for those who, in the providence of God, cannot provide for themselves: yes, I *believe* that with united mind and will, you will act wholly upon that sacred rule of universal obligation, which enjoins upon Legislators no less than upon individuals in their social relations, to do for others what they in similar circumstances would have meted to themselves.

Of all the calamities to which humanity is subject, none is so dreadful as insanity. Pinching want, hideous deformity, acute disease, mutilation, deafness, blindness; all these are distressing in their effects alike upon the sufferer and those with whom he is connected; but sad as are these distresses they leave to the unfortunate, human sympathies and priceless affections. They admit the assuaging influence of consolation and tender care, *recognizing* through these the love that prompts, and the hand that ministers. Not so is it with those who are smitten with the visitation of *insanity*—that disease which produces utter dependence for the supply of all physical wants, and rends away the noblest attributes of humanity.

The heart grows cold, and no gentle or generous affections flourish there. The brain no longer exercising its functions healthfully, reveals only distorted images of the mind. Healthful, intellec-tual vigor is prostrated, and man, from bearing affinity with spiritual natures, becomes in an hour, transformed to a mere brute existence, manifesting little beside low animal instincts.This malady, the offspring of civilization, increases annually in our country, and demands not on the solid ground of *humanity,* and the less stable basis of *expediency,* but through the uncompromising law of *necessity,* that its progress be arrested and its controllable causes subdued. The evil and the remedy are both before us. Experience and observation have dispelled that long received error which as-cribed to the *mind* the production of insanity, and have demonstrated the physiological fact that the proximate cause of this disease is bodily. The *manifestations* of the mind are distorted through physical disease, or disturbance of that organ through which the reasoning faculties find expression. Insanity in strict definition, has ceased to be called *mental disease;* it is rather mental disability. This fact established, we seek for insanity, as for other bodily ailments, those remedies which will *soonest* and *most surely* restore the lost balance of the system. Moral means in various measure, in all diseases, but eminently so in this, comes in aid of medical agents, and it is both conceded and urged by the highest authorities, that *these can be effectually combined only in an establishment specially devoted to the remedial treatment of the various forms of this malady.*

It is a prominent characteristic of insanity, manifested with rare exceptions, in all varieties of this disease, that many of the persons and objects amongst which it is developed, become sources of discomfort, or of serious annoyance and excitement to the patient, thereby nourishing and aggravating irritation and morbid susceptibilities.

Disagreeable thoughts are continually revived by things with which they are associated, as well as by persons whose kindest attentions are construed into proofs of ill-will and ill-design. Thus the mind of the patient is disquieted sufficiently to counteract any curative process the administration of medicine might be preparing. Withdrawal from all outward and familiar disturbing causes counteracts morbid associations, and wholesome influences obtain predominance.

Friends at home rarely possess the means of relief which a violent and sudden exhibition of insanity demands, even if in all cases they can have the advantage of the services of a skillful medical practitioner, familiar with the Protean phases of this disease. The discriminating and watchful *hourly* attention these often, for considerable periods require, can be had only within the walls of a judiciously organized and vigilantly governed Hospital. Here, where mild and gentle, but firm and decided influences are brought to bear, the raving maniac becomes yielding and calm, and the insensible are roused to an interest in the affairs of life, and throw off melancholy and inertia.

Although for a given time a patient may live at greater expense in a hospital than in a poor-house, or in a private family, this is no argument against the former; for granting that expense alone is the consideration, the number of cures wrought through the agency of hospital treatment timely adopted, will in a short period leave the balance-sheet of expense altogether in favor of the latter. But it is not a question of expense which is to be discussed, it is the *rights of suffering humanity;* in Kentucky it is no longer a question whether the poor and friendless maniac, and the helpless subject of dementia shall be provided for; and whether the well-established hospital shall open its doors to but a few favored ones, and reject the many; heretofore it has, I think, been the purpose to provide for *all.* But numbers have now increased vastly beyond the capacity of the present establishment to receive; and it is well known to all who have inquired into the facts, that the lodging apartments are in many cases, crowded to the great disadvantage and discomfort of the occupants. What was once an *ample* provision is no longer *sufficient.* The increased population of the State, and of course the increased number of patients, call for accommodations in measure with this increase.

The first consideration however seems to be attention to the *comfort* and *safety* of the patients resident in the hospital which is already established, by adding such improvements as will place it in rank with the best institutions for the management of the insane in the United States, and put it in the power of the able and devoted Superintendent to do that justice to his patients, and the cause of humanity, which his judgment and skill as a physician, and his kind and humane dispositions suggest.

Within the last three months, I have repeatedly visited the hospital at Lexington, and have been permitted freely to see every department of the entire establishment. With such ample opportunities for observation, I think I am able to do justice to all who share in the administration of the affairs of the institution. The judicious and watchful attention of the resident physician and his assistant, have commanded my confidence and respect. The Commissioners, as official visitors, are as vigilant as they are disinterested. The Steward and Matron are devoted to their very onerous duties, through a hearty interest in the welfare of those whose daily comforts so much depend on their fidelity. One cannot sufficiently commend the neatness and order which are maintained in this large establishment; and that these circumstances are preserved under existing inconveniences, must surprise even the most casual observer. This is done at an expense of manual labor and continual oversight, laborious in the extreme.

A transient visitor, passing through the Institution, giving perhaps but a few hours to an examination of its various departments, unacquainted with the details of its domestic economy, and knowing little or nothing of the peculiar and unremitting care which most of those two hundred and twenty patients require; seeing little of the special labors which the defective construction, and the inconvenient arrangements of the present buildings produce,—such a visitor may come away from the hospital, as many I have known, even within the short period of my acquaintance with the Institution; and believe that all is as it should be, and that nothing is wanting to make this a complete and effective establishment.

The most obvious defects may be briefly enumerated as follows:—The kitchen is much too small for the variety and amount of labor to be performed in it. It is deficient in *all* arrangements which would facilitate the accomplishment of work in that department. For the want of a well constructed *range,* with boilers and bakers, the cooking is done by a large iron stove, not the least objection to which is the greater quantity of fuel which it consumes than would a properly adjusted fire, and cooking-apparatus. It is estimated that the saving in fuel alone for a year or eighteen months would cover the expense of erecting a well-constructed and commodious kitchen.

The establishment affords but *one dining-room,* and in this long and cheerless hall must be congregated nearly all the patients, both from the men and women's departments, to partake their meals at one and the same time. That these should be disposed with less comfort than is requisite for a large part of the patients is, under existing arrangements inevitable. And here we see congregated all classes of patients, the incurable and the convalescent; the mirthful and the sad; the unconscious and those whose keen sensibilities are quickened to acutest suffering; these all must come together, and on these are wrought healthful, or oftener injurious influences, according to the form of the malady under which the patient labors. It is deemed an imperative necessity in all well-organized hospitals that the patients be classified with reference to their mental condition and physical wants. Here your Superintendent has *no choice;* it cannot be done, so remarkably defective is the internal construction of these buildings.

There are in this whole establishment, neither bathing-rooms nor washing-rooms of any description. In ordinary domestic arrangements these are needful for comfort and refreshment, as well as for their essential hygienic influences; how much more at all seasons, must this be the case in establishments which receive several hundred inmates, and most of these variously diseased. In no class of diseases indeed, is either warm or cold bathing considered so essential to the curative process, as in that of insanity; yet we have here a hospital which should be complete in all remedial appliances, wholly destitute of even the most simple accommodations for water-bathing. How the benefits of personal cleanliness are commanded at all here, is the wonder. First, laboriously, the water must be "packed" from the spring to the kitchen; next heated in small quantities at a time, in a receiver upon the cooking-stove; thirdly, it must be conveyed in buckets over two flights of stairs (if for the women's department, if for the men's, across the yards, &c.,) into one of the *day-rooms,* where, after use, it must again and finally, be borne in buckets over one flight of stairs to some waste-drain on the premises. It cannot be necessary to enlarge upon this subject.

The necessity is urgent for the early introduction of water throughout the State hospital; it is requisite in the culinary department, and in all beside. Here again would be a diminution of expense in the item of labor. The quantity of water required for daily consumption in large institutions is not comparable with that demanded in private households. Of thirteen hospitals, with the internal arrangements of which I am acquainted, there is *daily* consumed in each, for all purposes, from *one hundred and twenty,* to *one hundred and sixty barrels,* and this for purposes only of absolute necessity. At Utica, N. York, when the number of patients as yet did not reach two hundred, the daily consumption of water was nearly *four thousand gallons.* Nor did this, in whole, supply the baths, the house-cleansing, washing, and cooking departments. The water at Utica was forced from a well by means of a pump driven by horse-power, to the attic story of the centre building, and thence distributed through pipes over the entire establishment. One horse will force from forty-five to fifty hogsheads in an hour. Every arrangement is made to guard against a conflagration. The roofs are all fireproof. An engine, and large number of buckets are always *in order and in place,* for instant use. There is an engine at the State Hospital here, but the distance from the spring to the rear buildings, would render its use of little avail. In fine, the first and greatest necessity is to secure an ample supply of water *in* the buildings, as well for security, as for health and convenience.

The laundry is very defective. The ground floor, occupied for cleansing the apparel, &c., is so imperfectly constructed that the health of those who labor there is seriously exposed. The ironing-room is but half the size necessary for the ready and convenient performance of that branch of labor. There is no drying nor airing room at all. In damp and wet weather, therefore, several days sometimes intervene before the requisite changes of body or of bed-garments can be had. A properly constructed washing-house appears desirable, not less for health than for the reduction of labor, and the great reduction in the expenditure of fuel. There is no infirmary in the hospital, nor are there apartments either in the men, or the women's ward, where, in the event of special sickness from fevers, or other incidental illnesses, patients might be kept quiet, and receive all the cares their condition would claim.

Dr. Luther V. Bell, whose reputation not only in our own country but in Europe, gives authority to his opinions, remarks as follows, upon the treatment of the insane: "The value of properly adapted architectural arrangements; of a complete classification of patients; of a well educated, morally elevated, and well paid class of attendants; of well directed and perseveringly applied employment; of mechanical and of agricultural labor; of such amusements of mind and body as experience proves to be best adapted to occupy and direct the diseased intellectual functions and moral susceptibilities; and lastly, such an intercommunication with the sane, in social intercourse, public and private devotional exercises, and in the lighter and gayer re-unions of life, as the peculiarities of each case demand, must be felt and acknowledged, wherever the insane are entrusted to the care of the refined, the well-informed, and the conscientious. Beyond the judicious, energetic, and experienced application of such moral agents as these, and an adequate medical treatment, there is, and can be no mystery in the treatment of the insane."

The State Hospital at Lexington is pleasantly situated, and at convenient distance from the city. There is attached to this institution about thirty acres of land, but it is much to be regretted that it has not the advantage of owning a farm of one or two hundred acres, whereon those of the patients who are able to labor, and who would be benefited thereby, might be employed. All recent experience shows that a tract of land for agricultural purposes is almost, if not quite, indispensable to the interest both of the patients, and to the domestic economy of the hospital. Whatever shall seem to aid remedial measures, and advance recovery to health, seems demanded at the hands of those who, possessed of this priceless blessing, owe as a thank-offering to heaven, every care to such as are smitten with disease.

Dr. Earle, of the Bloomingdale Asylum refers repeatedly in his valuable reports, to the advantage of well-directed employment for the insane, and offers examples illustrative of this opinion, from which I select the following, "During the Spring of 1844, two farmers, each of whom possessed a good farm, were admitted to our Asylum within a week of each other. They were laboring under the most abject form of melancholy, and had both attempted suicide. In less than a month, their condition being somewhat improved, they expressed a willingness, and one of them a strong desire to work out of doors. Being furnished with implements, they daily went out together, and worked upon the farm with as much apparent interest as if it belonged to themselves. Under this course they continued rapidly to improve, and both were discharged recovered, one at the end of six weeks, the other at the expiration of three months from the time of their respective admissions."

"Another man was brought to the Asylum, laboring under a high degree of active mania. His appetite was poor, and his frame emaciated. He was careless of his personal appearance, restless, turbulent, and almost incessantly talking, in an incoherent manner, upon the delusions attending upon his disease. When out of doors, he was constantly wandering to and fro, talking to himself, and digging the earth with his hands, without end or object, and generally having his mouth filled with grass. For some months there was but little change in his condition. At length, having become somewhat less bewildered, his attendant succeeded in inducing him to assist in making beds. Shortly afterwards he was employed with the painters and glaziers upon the green-house; after this, he went into the carpenter's shop, where he worked regularly for several weeks. Meanwhile, his bodily health improved, his mind gradually returned to its former integrity, and he was discharged cured of his mental disorder."

"These cases are fair examples of the utility of a combination of medical and moral treatment, for in all of them medicine was regularly administered until within a comparatively short period before their departure from the institution. They are presented also as cogent arguments in favor of giving to manual labor that preeminence which has already been assigned to it."

The following schedule of the productions from fifty acres of the Bloomingdale farm, cultivated by the patients under the direction of the farmer and gardener, may be read with interest.

Hay,	40 tons.	Mangel Wurtzel,	50 bushels.
Oats cut in the milk,	4 "	Turnips,	325 "
Butter,	728 lbs.	Parsnips,	100 "
Milk,	4700 gallons.	Carrots,	30 "
Pork,	2706 lbs.	Onions,	50 "
Potatoes,	500 bushels.	Cabbages,	3000 heads.
Corn,	75 "	Leeks,	4000 "
Sugar Beets,	250 "	Celery,	2600 "
Blood Beets,	125 "	Salsify,	1500 heads.

Beside these there was a full supply, for the *whole* establishment, of peas, beans, squashes, tomatoes, radishes, cucumbers, asparagus, spinach, lettuce, egg-plant, and turkey-plant, beside a good supply of water-melons and musk-mellons. Of *fruits,* we had

Apples	500 bushels.	Cherries,	100 bushels.
Pears,	60 "	Grapes,	800 lbs.
Peaches,	18 "		

Beside currants in abundance, strawberries and raspberries.

By the labor of the patients and gardener three years since, I observe from the annual report of the Connecticut Hospital, that the garden, which contains *an acre and a quarter* of land, surrounded by a carriage-road, and a border planted with evergreens, rose-bushes, and other flowering plants, produced as follows:

Lettuce, 1100 large solid heads.	Cucumbers for pickles, 7 barrels.
Cabbages, 1400 do. do.	Beets, 147 bushels.
Radishes, 700 bunches.	Carrots, 24 "
Asparagus, 2800 do.	Parsnips, 25 "
Rhubarb, 300 lbs.	Onions, 120 "
Marrowfat peas, 14 bushels.	Turnips, 80 "
Sweet Corn, 419 dozen ears.	Tomatoes, 40, "
Summer Squash, 715 dozen.	Early potatoes, 35 bushels.
Squash peppers, 48 dozen.	Winter squashes, 7 wagon loads.
Cucumbers, (table) 756 dozen.	Celery, 500 large heads.

These articles, all of the very best and earliest kinds, and valued at market prices in Hartford, would have amounted to more than 625 dollars. The farm was like the garden, well cultivated." I have quoted these examples, which might be greatly multiplied, to show the excellent economy of a judicious cultivation of the lands pertaining to public institutions, and to enforce the double argument for attaching good farming and gardening land to Hospitals for the treatment of the insane.

I have referred at some length to the special wants and deficiencies of the only establishment for the reception of the insane within the bounds of this wide Commonwealth, and have urged perhaps with importunity, that these wants should be supplied, and that these deficiencies should be remedied. I leave this subject with those whose good sense and convictions of justice will, I trust, conduct to such effectual legislation as shall be in harmony with the humane sentiments of the citizens at large, creditable to the Legislators, and honorable to the Commonwealth.

Many States are active in laying broad and deep foundations of numerous charitable institutions; in enhancing that real greatness which knows no decline or extinction; let not these outstrip Kentucky in moral elevation, and enlightened wisely directed beneficence. Let it not be said here as of old, in Attica: "The Athenians *know* what is right; but the Lacedemonians *practice* it.

I have yet another plea to urge, another boon to crave. It is for *yourselves and your children* that I ask *additional* benefits. More complete and entire provision is needed for the unruly or unconscious idiot, the helpless epileptic, and the raving maniac. Heretofore your appropriations from the State Treasury since the establishment of the Hospital, have appeared to keep pace with the public need, at least it seems to me that this has been the intention. The Report of the Superintendent of the Hospital reveals the facts of an overcrowded institution, and of numerous applications for admission, for which, of course, there is now no provision. Several hundred insane persons according to the most moderate estimate, are now suffering, in various parts of the State, for want of well-directed remedial treatment. As yet, I have visited but forty-four counties; but from the best sources of information I have been able to consult, it is evident that much suffering exists, and many patients are annually becoming *hopelessly* insane through want of seasonable appropriate care. Friends are often indisposed to place the patient away from home, but if the dispositions were usually favorable to hospital treatment, there at present exists no accommodations for receiving them. In Kentucky alone, of all the States I have traversed, it has not been my painful experience to find the insane poor, filling the cells of poorhouses, or the dungeons of the jails. I have not a single example to offer of an insane person found either in a poor-house or jail, except one patient, whose violent paroxysms and homicidal propensities made it necessary to place him for his own safety, and that of his family, in a county jail, till the session of the court, when the legal measures required for his transfer to the hospital could be adopted. The fact that the *State* assumes the expenses of the pauper insane, explains the entire absence of similar cases of culpable neglect, and dreadful suffering and privation, exposure and distress, which are to this hour frequent in almost, if not quite; every State in the Union.

In Kentucky the affluent and self-supporting classes are the severest sufferers. Just views respecting the healing and kindly influence of hospital care are not so widely diffused as could be wished, and except in the event of sudden and very violent attacks of this fearful malady, the patient is detained by mistaken tenderness within the family circle, till the disease is confirmed, and hope of cure is extinct.

All experience shows that insanity *seasonably treated is as certainly curable as a cold or a fever.* Recovery is the rule; permanent disease the exception.

Dr. Bell, in one of his Reports of the McLean Hospital, at Somerville, states that the records of the institution justify the declaration, that *"all cases certainly recent,* that is, whose origin does not directly or obscurely run back more than a year, *recover under a fair trial."* In this opinion Dr. Ray, formerly of the Main State Hospital, now physician elect to the Butler Asylum, R. Island, fully concurs.

The Directors of the Ohio Hospital, at Columbus, observe in their third annual report, "that the importance of remedial means in the *first* stages of insanity, cannot be too strongly impressed upon the public mind."

Dr. Woodward, of the Massachusetts State Hospital, repeats in nearly every report, and renews arguments, for the *seasonable* treatment of the insane.

Dr. Chandler, late of the New Hampshire Hospital, says, in the report of 1843, that "it *is well established,* that the *earlier* patients are placed under curative treatment in hospitals, the *more sure and speedy* is the recovery."

Dr. Brigham, Superintendent of the State Asylum at N. York, states that, "few things relating to the management of the insane are so *well established,* as the necessity of their *early* treatment, and their removal from home in order to effect recovery. By examining the records of well constructed lunatic asylums, it appears that *more than eight in ten recent cases recover,* while *not more than one in six* of the old cases are cured."

Dr. Awl, of Ohio, remarks in his fifth report, "that fearful as is the disease of insanity, the experience of this and other institutions of the United States, have clearly shown, that *with seasonable* aid, it is by no means an incurable disease; that under *proper medical* and *moral treatment,* a large proportion do perfectly recover. And of those who are absolutely incurable, a vast number can always be greatly improved, and made comfortable and useful. We unhesitatingly conclude, that the *only safe* and correct course, either for the insane themselves, or for their friends and society, is to provide ample accommodations for them, where there will be opportunity for every one to experience comfort and relief."

Dr. Earle, of the Bloomingdale Hospital, in the report for 1844, states that "it appears to be very satisfactorily proved, that of cases where there is no eccentricity or constitutional weakness of intellect, and where the proper remedial measures are adopted in the *early* stages of the disorder, no less than eighty of every one hundred are cured. *There are few acute diseases from which so large a per centage* of the persons attacked are restored."

"*One of the chief obstacles* to a more general recovery of the patients admitted into public institutions, and one of the principal causes of the great accumulation of deranged people in the community, *is the neglect* of removing them to an Asylum, as soon *as possible after* the commencement of the disease. The mistaken kindness of friends in detaining the patient at home until the period most favorable to recovery is past, has undoubtedly been the cause of rendering the disease of hundreds of maniacs permanent." "After the first three months of the existence of derangement, the probabilities of cure rapidly diminish, and at the expiration of a year, it is believed that they are not half so great as at first. If continued beyond that time, the diminution progresses, so that of such as have been deranged more than two years, the number that recover is comparatively very small; supposed by some physicians to be about one in thirty; yet hope is left, and cures are sometimes effected of those whose disorder has existed five, ten, and even fifteen years. *It would seem that every consideration of humanity and duty requires a greater practical attention to these important truths.*"

An experienced writer on insanity, says, "It appears to me, that no idea relating to this unfortunate portion of our fellow-beings is more essential to keep before the community, than *the importance of attending to the first indications of insanity, and the immediate adoption of judicious medical and moral treatment.* The records of hospitals establish the fact that insanity is a disease that can be generally cured, if early and properly treated, while it is equally well established, that if the disease is neglected, or suffered to continue for two or three years it is difficult of remedy. That such should be the result is evident from the nature of the disease. Insanity is a disease of the physical system—a disease of the brain, and the *mental disorder is but one of its symptoms.* Insanity never arises till the *brain,* the *organ* of the mind, becomes affected."

Dr. Rockwell, of the Vermont Asylum says, "It is *very important that the insane should be placed under treatment in the early stages of the disease.*"

Dr. Kirkbride expressly urges in his reports of the Pennsylvania Hospital for the Insane, "the exceeding importance under every aspect of the case, of *early, prompt removal* to suitable hospitals; by which large numbers would be restored to health and to society, who now are a burthen to themselves and their friends."

Drs. Allen, Stribbling, Fisher, Butler, Stedman, Galt, and others who conduct the hospitals in the United States, concur in these views, and urge them in all or nearly all the reports which are annually issued from their respective institutions.

In the Ohio State Asylum, 1842, *twenty-five* old cases, suffered to become incurable, had cost to the State and counties $50,600, while *twenty-five recent* cases, brought under seasonable treatment, had cost but $1,130, that is, forty-five dollars twenty cents for each individual.

In the Massachusetts State Hospital, *twenty-five* old cases had cost the State $54,157, while the whole average number of recent cases recovered, cost but *fifty-eight* dollars, *forty-five* cents. Similar facts are exhibited upon the records of other institutions, and we have thus positive demonstration of the usefulness of hospital treatment in the two-fold, but not comparable results of health-restoring, and property-saving advantages.

Surely, if partial deafness, or failing sight, or inflammation upon the lungs assail our friend, we do not rashly defer calling on the physician to aid, by his superior knowledge our own cares, nor do we fail to surround the invalid with all those circumstances which shall seem most likely to control and cure the disease. On the access of fever or pneumonia, we lose no time in applying the most approved remedies, together with the most skillful nursing, yet we venture, with a strange hardihood, to tamper with that delicate organ, the brain, and delay the remedial measures till the case becomes, if not quite hopeless, nearly so. I have paused longer on this topic than I was aware, but its exceeding importance, the influence the decisions of friends and relatives exert on *life and health, and all life's dearest interests,* urge all who have knowledge on this subject, to enforce earnestly and firmly the duty of seasonable attention to appropriate care, and medical treatment for the insane. Numerous and deeply affecting examples of domestic trial, and individual suffering, through ill-judging and ill-judged management of the insane, exist in many private families in Kentucky. These cases not being a *public* charge, and not under official control, I do not feel at liberty to record; but sure I am, that there will be few readers of these pages who will not be able to furnish, through their own recollection, examples which will sustain my position,—examples powerfully appealing to every just and humane sentiment in the community.

Are there not many who will read this page, who, like myself, can recall the lone husband and father wearing out a woeful life in the dreary blockhouse, almost within the shadow of his own roof; 'without clothes, for if he was furnished, he would rend them in pieces; without bed, for if that was supplied, it would be destroyed; without bathing or shaving, till he resembles the beasts of the forest; without fire, for with it he would burn the building; in a cheerless block-house, for if a less solid structure, he would break through it!'

Are there none who remember the dull victim of melancholy delusions, harrassed by unreflecting neighbors, hurrying away to find refuge from their thoughtless persecutions, beneath the waters of the nigh flowing river? Are there none who recollect the son and brother, swinging his clanking chain within a slight and comfortless cabin, clamoring and hooting at the passers by, vociferous, dangerous, and destitute of all appropriate care; dangerous when at large, and wretched under the weary bondage of his chains? Will none have heard of the delirious epileptic girl, whose troublesome habits and mischievous propensities bring upon her the cutting lash, and who, driven by this merciless discipline, to wilder freaks, and more frequent paroxysms, is an object of deepest pity. These scenes, these hapless conditions of the insane are terrible, but these, and others not dissimilar, are not unusually the result, so much of barbarious dispositions on the part of kindred, (the last case excepted,) as the consequence of ignorance upon the right treatment demanded for the insane, and a failure to *realize* the great sufferings which ill-directed management create and aggravate. Let all, and each, throughout our country, learn the benefits of hospital treatment, and unite to secure these benefits to all the insane, of whatever rank or condition.

The dread of severe measures, in the treatment of the insane in hospitals is passing away from the minds of all who seek information concerning them. In these *the rule of right, and the law of kindness* are known to prevail. Severity and harsh measures of coercion are long since abandoned. Gentleness and persuasion unite with a mild decision, to control the wayward and the perverse, and to quiet the raving maniac.

The good and truly noble St. Vincent de Paul, was the first apostle in this holy work to turn men's thoughts in Europe, to more humane and more rational modes of treatment. With a devotion which no hardships could subdue, he traversed vast regions, and taught men the sublime lesson, that to be humane, was to be allied to Deity. Pinel, in France, carried to this blessed reform the manly tenderness and clear reasonings of his noble heart and intellect; thousands owe to his determined exertions their salvation from a bondage more terrible than death; their recovery of the lapsed powers of the mind; their restoration to reason, to usefulness, and to happiness. England and the United States are far advanced in this humane work; but, all is not done; too much remains to be done; let none supinely rest while such loud calls are raised through the land for the succour of these afflicted beings.

Gentlemen of the Legislature, I ask of you such an appropriation from the State Treasury for the hospital at Lexington, as shall place that, your first and most liberally established institution for the insane, upon a suitable foundation. As this, when completed, will be altogether inadequate to the necessities of your citizens, I ask for the establishment of a new hospital in the Southern, or Green River Country; and to this end, solicit the early adoption of such preliminary measures as shall enable you the next year, rapidly to carry forward and complete that work. The evils of delay are incalculable; they must be obvious; they should not be allowed to increase. I ask, that in the choice of a site for a new hospital, the very important appropriation of a tract of land of sufficient extent to furnish labor for the patients, and supplies for the institution, may be a first consideration. This should be chosen in a healthful district, command cheerful views, be accessible to and from a shire-town, be of convenient access by good stage-routes and water conveyances from different portions of the State; it should have an ample and unfailing supply of pure water; be so situated as to command fuel at moderate rates; and abundant stores of provisions at reasonable cost. It is worthy of consideration to embrace in this view the advantage of vicinity to a stone-quarry, or to clay strata suitable for the manufacture of brick. I respectfully suggest the appointment of an efficient Board of Commissioners to carry these objects into effect.

Legislators of Kentucky, from the discussions arising out of conflicting interests, and diverse opinions, questions of various weight, and some, possibly, of doubtful advantage; before you shall dissolve this session, consecrate one hour, uninfluenced by selfish aims, local prejudices, or political differences, to the solemn and sacred interests of suffering humanity. United by an exalted motive, be the instruments of a wide spreading happiness, and the creators of enduring benefits. The heart of many a child of misfortune, released from pangs of deep distress, through your just legislation, shall upbear you daily to the gates of heaven in prayers of gratitude. To use the language of one of our high-souled citizens, "the truest tokens of grandeur in a State are, the diffusion of the greatest happiness among the greatest number; and that God-like JUSTICE which controls the relations of the State to all the people who are committed to its charge." Let your hospitals and your asylums rival your schools and your colleges; so multiply the "links in that golden chain by which Humanity shall connect itself with the throne of God!"

The clarion note of "Kentucky, old Kentucky"!—rings through the land. She claims eminence in her political station amidst the Star-crowned Sisters; she exults in the far told history of her military renown; but there is a moral eminence far transcending political distinctions; and a more glorious renown than is sounded from the trumpet of victorious battles:—bid her to a place in the firmament of heaven; there enthroned by her holy deeds of charity and love, inscribe her name on that scroll of history borne by angels—and sealed by arch-angels for the archives of eternity!

Crystal Eastman
(1881–1928)

Crystal Eastman was born on June 25, 1881 in Marlborough, Massachusetts. The third of four children, she became closely attached to her mother, Annis, who achieved fame as an ordained Congregational Minister and advocate of woman's rights, and to her brother, Max, who later became a prominent writer, editor and socialist. The family moved to Elmira, New York, when Crystal was still a child and she attended local schools until she entered Vassar College, graduating in 1903. The next year she received a master's degree in sociology from Columbia University, and in 1907 she earned her LL.B degree from New York University Law School. After passing the bar examination Crystal joined Paul Kellogg in the monumental "Pittsburgh Survey", which was the first attempt to study the effects of industrialization on urban workers. Her findings were published in *Work Accidents and the Law* in 1910 and helped to advance the movement for workmen's compensation laws. In 1911 Crystal married Wallace Benedict and moved with him to Milwaukee, Wisconsin. For the next four years she worked actively for the Wisconsin Political Equality League and served as its campaign manager during the unsuccessful drive for woman suffrage in 1912. In 1913 Crystal joined with Alice Paul and Lucey Burns in founding the Congressional Union for Woman Suffrage, which became the National Woman's Party, and served as its delegate to the International Woman Suffrage Alliance in Budapest. In 1915 Crystal returned to New York, divorced her first husband, married Walter Fuller, and became increasingly active in the peace movement. As chairperson of the New York state branch of the Woman's Peace Party and a member of the executive committee of the American Union Against Militarism, she campaigned tirelessly against the National Defense Bill. When America entered the war she helped organize the Civil Liberties Bureau (forerunner of the American Civil Liberties Union) to aid conscientious objectors. In 1917 she and her brother Max launched the radical journal *Liberator* and she assumed the position of managing editor as well as contributing author of numerous articles on war, women and labor. In 1919 Crystal helped organize a Feminist Congress in New York where many women gathered to demand their rights. From 1921 to 1927 she lived mostly in England with her husband and children continuing her active work on behalf of feminist and labor movements. In 1927, Crystal returned to New York to resume activist reform work, but on July 8, 1928 she died of nephritis after a lengthy illness.

The following speech was delivered several times as a lecture in New York City in September and October, 1920. It later appeared in article form in the *Liberator* (December, 1920).

"We Have the Vote, Now We Can Begin"

Most women will agree that August 23, the day when the Tennessee legislature finally enacted the Federal suffrage amendment, is a day to begin with, not a day to end with. Men are saying perhaps "Thank God, this everlasting woman's fight is over!" But women, if I know them, are saying, "Now at last we can begin." In fighting for the right to vote most women have tried to be either non-committal or thoroughly respectable on every other subject. Now they can say what they are really after; and what they are after, in common with all the rest of the struggling world, is *freedom*.

Freedom is a large word.

Many feminists are socialists, many are communists, not a few are active leaders in these movements. But the true feminist, no matter how far to the left she may be in the revolutionary movement, sees the woman's battle as distinct in its objects and different in its methods from the workers' battle for industrial freedom. She knows, of course, that the vast majority of women as well as men are without property, and are of necessity bread and butter slaves under a system of society which allows the very sources of life to be privately owned by a few, and she counts herself a loyal soldier in the working-class army that is marching to overthrow that system. But as a feminist she also knows that the whole of woman's slavery is not summed up in the profit system, nor her complete emancipation assured by the downfall of capitalism.

Woman's freedom, in the feminist sense, can be fought for and conceivably won before the gates open into industrial democracy. On the other hand, woman's freedom, in the feminist sense, is not inherent in the communist ideal. All feminists are familiar with the revolutionary leader who "can't see" the woman's movement. "What's the matter with the women? My wife's all right," he says. And his wife, one usually finds, is raising his children in a Bronx flat or a dreary suburb, to which he returns occasionally for food and sleep when all possible excitement and stimulus have been wrung from the fight. If we should graduate into communism tomorrow this man's attitude to his wife would not be changed. The proletarian dictatorship may or may not free women. We must begin now to enlighten the future dictators.

What, then, is "the matter with women"? What is the problem of women's freedom? It seems to me to be this: how to arrange the world so that women can be human beings, with a chance to exercise their infinitely varied gifts in infinitely varied ways, instead of being destined by the accident of their sex to one field of activity—housework and child-raising. And second, if and when they choose housework and child-raising to have that occupation recognized by the world as work, requiring a definite economic reward and not merely entitling the performer to be dependent on some man.

This is not the whole of feminism, of course, but it is enough to begin with. "Oh! don't begin with economics," my friends often protest, "Woman does not live by bread alone. What she needs first of all is a free soul." And I can agree that women will never be great until they achieve a certain emotional freedom, a strong healthy egotism, and some un-personal sources of joy—that in this inner sense we cannot make woman free by changing her economic status. What we can do, however, is to create conditions of outward freedom in which a free woman's soul can be born and grow. It is these outward conditions with which an organized feminist movement must concern itself.

Freedom of choice in occupation and individual economic independence for women: How shall we approach this next feminist objective? First, by breaking down all remaining barriers, actual as well as legal, which make it difficult for women to enter or succeed in the various professions, to go into and get on in business, to learn trades and practice them, to join trades unions. Chief among these remaining barriers is inequality in pay. Here the ground is already broken. This is the easiest part of our program.

Second, we must institute a revolution in the early training and education of both boys and girls. It must be womanly as well as manly to earn your own living, to stand on your own feet. And it must be manly as well as womanly to know how to cook and sew and clean and take care of yourself in the ordinary exigencies of life. I need not add that the second part of this revolution will be more passionately resisted than the first. Men will not give up their privilege of helplessness without a struggle. The average man has a carefully cultivated ignorance about household matters—from what to do with the crumbs to the grocer's telephone number—a sort of cheerful inefficiency which protects him better than the reputation for having a violent temper. It was his mother's fault in the beginning, but even as a boy he was quick to see how a general reputation for being "no good around the house" would serve him throughout life, and half-consciously he began to cultivate that helplessness until to-day it is the despair of feminist wives.

A growing number of men admire the woman who has a job, and, especially since the cost of living doubled, rather like the idea of their own wives contributing to the family income by outside work. And of course for generations there have been whole towns full of wives who are forced by the bitterest necessity to spend the same hours at the factory that their husbands spend. But these bread-winning wives have not yet developed home-making husbands. When the two come home from the factory the man sits down while his wife gets supper, and he does so with exactly the same sense of fore-ordained right as if he were "supporting her." Higher up in the economic scale the same thing is true. The business or professional woman who is married, perhaps engages a cook, but the responsibility is not shifted, it is still hers. She "hires and fires," she orders meals, she does the buying, she meets and resolves all domestic crises, she takes charge of moving, furnishing, settling. She may be, like her husband, a busy executive at her office all day, but unlike him, she is also an executive in a small way every night and morning at home. Her noon hour is spent in planning, and too often her Sundays and holidays are spent in "catching up."

Two business women can "make a home" together without either one being over-burdened or over-bored. It is because they both know how and both feel responsible. But it is a rare man who can marry one of them and continue the home-making partnership. Yet if there are no children, there is nothing essentially different in the combination. Two self-supporting adults decide to make a home together: if both are women it is a pleasant partnership, more fun than work; if one is a man, it is almost never a partnership—the woman simply adds running the home to her regular outside job. Unless she is very strong, it is too much for her, she gets tired and bitter over it, and finally perhaps gives up her outside work and condemns herself to the tiresome half-job of housekeeping for two.

Cooperative schemes and electrical devices will simplify the business of home-making, but they will not get rid of it entirely. As far as we can see ahead people will always want homes, and a happy home cannot be had without a certain amount of rather monotonous work and responsibility. How can we change the nature of man so that he will honorably share that work and responsibility and thus make the home-making enterprise a song instead of a burden? Most assuredly not by laws or revolutionary decrees. Perhaps we must cultivate or simulate a little of that highly prized helplessness ourselves. But fundamentally it is a problem of education, of early training—we must bring up feminist sons.

Sons? Daughters? They are born of women—how can women be free to choose their occupation, at all times cherishing their economic independence, unless they stop having children? This is a further question for feminism. If the feminist program goes to pieces on the arrival of the first baby, it is false and useless. For ninety-nine out of every hundred women want children, and seventy-five out of every hundred want to take care of their own children, or at any rate so closely superintend their care as to make any other full-time occupation impossible for at least ten or fifteen years. Is there any such thing then as freedom of choice in occupation for women? And is not the family the inevitable economic unit and woman's individual economic independence, at least during that period, out of the question?

The feminist must have an answer to these questions, and she has. The immediate feminist program must include voluntary motherhood. Freedom of any kind for women is hardly worth considering unless it is assumed that they will know how to control the size of their families. "Birth control" is just as elementary an essential in our propaganda as "equal pay." Women are to have children when they want them, that's the first thing. That ensures some freedom of occupational choice; those who do not wish to be mothers will not have an undesired occupation thrust upon them by accident, and those who do wish to be mothers may choose in a general way how many years of their lives they will devote to the occupation of child-raising.

But is there any way of insuring a woman's economic independence while child-raising is her chosen occupation? Or must she sink into the dependent state from which, as we all know, it is so hard to rise again? That brings us to the fourth feature of our program—motherhood endowment. It seems that the only way we can keep mothers free, at least in a capitalist society, is by the establishment of a principle that the occupation of raising children is peculiarly and directly a service to society, and that the mother upon whom the necessity and privilege of performing this service naturally falls is entitled to an adequate economic reward from the political government. It is idle to talk of real economic independence for women unless this principle is accepted. But with a generous endowment of motherhood provided by legislation, with all laws against voluntary motherhood and education in its methods repealed, with the feminist ideal of education accepted in home and school, and with all special barriers removed in every field of human activity, there is no reason why woman should not become almost a human thing.

It will be time enough then to consider whether she has a soul.

Mary Baker Eddy
(1821–1910)

Mary Baker Eddy was born on July 16, 1821 in Bow, New Hampshire. The last of six children, she attended school irregularly due both to physical and emotional frailties, and between her ninth and thirteenth years was largely tutored at home by her older brother Albert. In 1843 Mary married George Glover and travelled through the South with him before his sudden death in 1844. She returned to New England and settled in Sanborton Bridge, New Hampshire, where she gave birth to a son and soon became too ill to take care of herself or her son. For the next nine years Mary suffered recurrent bouts of nervous and emotional exhaustion and could only intermittently teach or write to supplement her income. In 1853 she married again, this time to a dentist named Daniel Patterson. For the next several years Mary moved with her itinerant husband around the New England area, frequently suffering from the same kinds of illness which had previously plagued her. In 1862 she travelled to Portland, Maine, to see if Dr. Phineas Quimby, a believer in the "science of mental and spiritual healing", might be able to help her. This encounter both improved Mary's health and converted her to the theory of mental and spiritual healing. After Dr. Quimby died in 1866, Mary decided to assume his role as teacher and healer, little realizing at the time that she would devote the rest of her life to this vocation. For the next nine years Mary travelled around New England visiting various spiritualists and healers and formulating her own "science" of healing. In 1875 she ended her nomadic existence and bought a house in Lynn, Massachusetts, which she used both as a residence and as a "Christian Scientists' Home" where classes and meetings could be held. In the same year some of her students who had formed a publishing house issued her book *Science and Health.* Having divorced her second husband in 1873, Mary married her third husband, Dan Eddy, in 1877. In that same year a Christian Science Association was formed, two years later the Church of Christ (Scientist) was formally chartered, and in 1881 a charter was obtained for the Massachusetts Metaphysical College as a degree-granting institution. In 1882 the Christian Science movement consisted of one fractious fifty-member congregation, but by 1890 it had twenty churches, ninety societies, at least 250 practitioners, and 33 teaching centers scattered across the country. Mary, herself, had almost single-handedly instructed at least six hundred students in the lower and higher elements of her science by 1890, and her gifts and talents as a teacher were touted far and wide, even by those who later became estranged or dissident. In 1883 Mary founded the monthly *Christian Scientist Journal* and published her *Key to the Scriptures,* both of which were highly popular and highly profitable. In 1892 Mary went into semi-retirement and only emerged to confront political conflicts within the association, several of which gained national attention due to their often bizarre circumstances. Partly to counter some of the adverse publicity generated by these conflicts, she founded the *Christian Science Monitor* in 1908, which soon became a widely known and highly respected newspaper. Mary's last years were once again marred by emotional and physical ill health and on December 3, 1910 she found relief through death at the age of eighty-nine.

The following sermon was delivered in Boston in 1886 at the First Church of Christ, Scientist. It was later published by the Trustees under the Will of Mary Baker G. Eddy in 1908 through the auspices of the Christian Science Foundation.

"Christian Healing"

TEXT: *And these signs shall follow them that believe; In my name shall they cast out devils; they shall speak with new tongues; they shall take up serpents; and if they drink any deadly thing, it shall not hurt them; they shall lay hands on the sick, and they shall recover.*
—MARK XVI. 17,18.

History repeats itself; to-morrow grows out of today. But Heaven's favors are formidable: they are calls to higher duties, not discharge from care; and whoso builds on less than an immortal basis, hath built on sand.

We have asked, in our selfishness, to wait until the age advanced to a more practical and spiritual religion before arguing with the world the great subject of Christian healing; but our answer was, "Then there were no cross to take up, and less need of publishing the good news." A classic writes,—

> "At thirty, man suspects himself a fool;
> Knows it at forty, and reforms his plan;
> At fifty, chides his infamous delay,
> Pushes his prudent purpose to resolve."

The difference between religions is, that one religion has a more spiritual basis and tendency than the other; and the religion nearest right is that one. The genius of Christianity is works more than words; a calm and steadfast communion with God; a tumult on earth,—religious factions and prejudices arrayed against it, the synagogues as of old closed upon it, while it reasons with the storm, hurls the thunderbolt of truth, and stills the tempest of error; scourged and condemned at every advancing footstep, afterwards pardoned and adopted, but never seen amid the smoke of battle. Said the intrepid reformer, Martin Luther: "I am weary of the world, and the world is weary of me; the parting will be easy." Said the more gentle Melanchthon: "Old Adam is too strong for young Melanchthon."

And still another Christian hero, ere he passed from his execution to a crown, added his testimony: "I have fought a good fight, . . . I have kept the faith." But Jesus, the model of infinite patience, said: "Come unto me, all ye that labor and are heavy laden, and I will give you rest." And he said this when bending beneath the malice of the world. But why should the world hate Jesus, the loved of the Father, the loved of Love? It was that his spirituality rebuked their carnality, and gave this proof of Christianity that religions had not given. Again, they knew it was not in the power of eloquence or a dead rite to cast out error and heal the sick. Past, present, future magnifies his name who built, on Truth, eternity's foundation stone, and sprinkled the altar of Love with perpetual incense.

Such Christianity requires neither hygiene nor drugs wherewith to heal both mind and body; or, lacking these, to show its helplessness. The primitive privilege of Christianity was to make men better, to cast out error, and heal the sick. It was a proof, more than a profession thereof; a demonstration, more than a doctrine. It was the foundation of right thinking and right acting, and must be reestablished on its former basis. The stone which the builders rejected must again become the head of the corner. In proportion as the personal and material element stole into religion, it lost Christianity and the power to heal; and the qualities of God as a person, instead of the divine Principle that begets the quality, engrossed the attention of the ages. In the original text the term

God was derived from the word *good*. Christ is the idea of Truth; Jesus is the name of a man born in a remote province of Judea,—Josephus alludes to several individuals by the name of Jesus. Therefore Christ Jesus was an honorary title; it signified a "good man," which epithet the great goodness and wonderful works of our Master more than merited. Because God is the Principle of Christian healing, we must understand in part this divine Principle, or we cannot demonstrate it in part.

The Scriptures declare that "God is Love, Truth, and Life,"—a trinity in unity; not three persons in one, but three statements of one Principle. We cannot tell what is the person of Truth, the body of the infinite, but we know that the Principle is not the person, that the finite cannot contain the infinite, that unlimited Mind cannot start from a limited body. The infinite can neither go forth from, return to, nor remain for a moment within limits. We must give freer breath to thought before calculating the results of an infinite Principle,—the effects of infinite Love, the compass of infinite Life, the power of infinite Truth. Clothing Deity with personality, we limit the action of God to the finite senses. We pray for God to remember us, even as we ask a person with softening of the brain not to forget his daily cares. We ask infinite wisdom to possess our finite sense, and forgive what He knows deserves to be punished, and to bless what is unfit to be blessed. We expect infinite Love to drop divinity long enough to hate. We expect infinite Truth to mix with error, and become finite for a season; and, after infinite Spirit is forced in and out of matter for an indefinite period, to show itself infinite again. We expect infinite Life to become finite, and have an end; but, after a temporary lapse, to begin anew as infinite Life, without beginning and without end.

Friends, can we ever arrive at a proper conception of the divine character, and gain a right idea of the Principle of all that is right, with such self-evident contradictions? God must be our model, or we have none; and if this model is one thing at one time, and the opposite of it at another, can we rely on our model? Or, having faith in it, how can we demonstrate a changing Principle? We cannot: we shall be consistent with our inconsistent statement of Deity, and so bring out our own erring finite sense of God, and of good and evil blending. While admitting that God is omnipotent, we shall be limiting His power at every point,—shall be saying He is beaten by certain kinds of food, by changes of temperature, the neglect of a bath, and so on. Phrenology will be saying the developments of the brain bias a man's character. Physiology will be saying, if a man has taken cold by doing good to his neighbor, God will punish him now for the cold, but he must wait for the reward of his good deed hereafter. One of our leading clergymen startles us by saying that "between Christianity and spiritualism, the question chiefly is concerning the trustworthiness of the communications, and not the doubt of their reality." Does any one think the departed are not departed, but are with us, although we have no evidence of the fact except sleight-of-hand and hallucination?

Such hypotheses ignore Biblical authority, obscure the one grand truth which is constantly covered, in one way or another, from our sight. This truth is, that we are to work out our own salvation, and to meet the responsibility of our own thoughts and acts; relying not on the person of God or the person of man to do our work for us, but on the apostle's rule, "I will show thee my faith by my works." This spiritualism would lead our lives to higher issues; it would purify, elevate, and consecrate man; it would teach him that "whatsoever a man soweth, that shall he also reap." The more spiritual we become here, the more are we separated from the world; and should this rule fail hereafter, and we grow more material, and so come back to the world? When I was told the other day, "People say you are a medium," pardon me if I smiled. The pioneer of something new under the sun is never hit: he cannot be; the opinions of people fly too high or too low. From my earliest investigations of the mental phenomenon named mediumship, I knew it was misinterpreted, and I said it. The spiritualists abused me for it then, and have ever since; but they take pleasure in calling me a medium. I saw the impossibility, in Science, of intercommunion between the so-called dead and the living. When I learned how mind produces disease on the body, I learned how it produces the manifestations ignorantly imputed to spirits. I saw how the mind's ideals were evolved and made tangible; and it matters not whether that ideal is a flower or a cancer, if the belief is strong enough to manifest it. Man thinks he is a medium of disease; that when he is sick, disease controls his body to whatever manifestation we see. But the fact remains, in metaphysics, that the mind of the individual only can produce a result upon his body. The belief that produces this result may be wholly unknown to the individual, because it is lying back in the unconscious thought, a latent cause producing the effect we see.

"And these signs shall follow them that believe; In my name shall they cast out devils." The word *devil* comes from the Greek *diabolos;* in Hebrew it is *belial,* and signifies "that which is good for nothing, lust," etc. The signs referred to are the manifestations of the power of Truth to cast out error; and, correcting error in thought, it produces the harmonious effect on the body. "Them that believe" signifies those who understand God's supremacy,—the power of Mind over matter. "The new tongue" is the spiritual meaning as opposed to the material. It is the language of Soul instead of the senses; it translates matter into its original language, which is Mind, and gives the spiritual instead of the material signification. It begins with motive, instead of act, where Jesus formed his estimate; and there correcting the motive, it corrects the act that results from the motive. The Science of Christianity makes pure the fountain, in order to purify the stream. It begins in mind to heal the body, the same as it begins in motive to correct the act, and through which to judge of it. The Master of metaphysics, reading the mind of the poor woman who dropped her mite into the treasury, said, "She hath cast in more than they all." Again, he charged home a crime to mind, regardless of any outward act, and sentenced it as our judges would not have done to-day. Jesus knew that adultery is a crime, and *mind* is the criminal. I wish the age was up to his understanding of these two facts, so important to progress and Christianity.

"They shall take up serpents; and if they drink any deadly thing, it shall not hurt them." This is an unqualified statement of the duty and ability of Christians to heal the sick; and it contains no argument for a creed or doctrine, it implies no necessity beyond the understanding of God, and obedience to His government, that heals both mind and body; God,—not a person to whom we should pray to heal the sick, but the Life, Love, and Truth that destroy error and death. Understanding the truth regarding mind and body, knowing that Mind can master sickness as well as sin, and carrying out this government over both and bringing out the results of this higher Christianity, we shall perceive the meaning of the context,—"They shall lay hands on the sick, and they shall recover."

The world is slow to perceive individual advancement; but when it reaches the thought that has produced this, then it is willing to be made whole, and no longer quarrels with the individual. Plato did better; he said, "What thou seest, that thou beest."

The mistaken views entertained of Deity becloud the light of revelation, and suffocate reason by materialism. When we understand that God is what the Scriptures have declared,—namely, Life, Truth, and Love,—we shall learn to reach heaven through Principle instead of a pardon; and this will make us honest and laborious, knowing that we shall receive only what we have earned. Jesus illustrated this by the parable of the husbandman. If we work to become Christians as honestly and as directly upon a divine Principle, and adhere to the rule of this Principle as directly as we do to the rule of mathematics, we shall be Christian Scientists, and do more than we are now doing, and progress faster than we are now progressing. We should have no anxiety about what is or what is not the person of God, if we understood the Principle better and employed our thoughts more in demonstrating it. We are constantly thinking and talking on the wrong side of the question. The less said or thought of sin, sickness, or death, the better for mankind, morally and physically. The greatest sinner and the most hopeless invalid think most of sickness and of sin; but, having learned that this method has not saved them from either, why do they go on thus, and their moral advisers talk for them on the very subjects they would gladly discontinue to bring out in their lives? Contending for the reality of what should disappear is like furnishing fuel for the flames. Is it a duty for any one to believe that "the curse causeless cannot come"? Then it is a higher duty to know that God never cursed man, His own image and likeness. God never made a wicked man; and man made by God had not a faculty or power underived from his Maker wherewith to make himself wicked.

The only correct answer to the question, "Who is the author of evil?" is the scientific statement that evil is unreal; that God made all that was made, but He never made sin or sickness, either an error of mind or of body. Life in matter is a dream: sin, sickness, and death are this dream. Life is Spirit; and when we waken from the dream of life in matter, we shall learn this grand truth of being. St. John saw the vision of life in matter; and he saw it pass away,—an illusion. The dragon that was wroth with the woman, and stood ready "to devour the child as soon as it was born," was the vision of envy, sensuality, and malice, ready to devour the idea of Truth. But the beast bowed before the Lamb: it was supposed to have fought the manhood of God, that Jesus represented; but it fell before the womanhood of God, that presented the highest ideal of Love. Let us remember that God—good—is omnipotent; therefore evil is impotent. There is but one side to good,—it has no evil side; there is but one side to reality, and that is the good side.

God is All, and in all: that finishes the question of a good and a bad side to existence. Truth is the real; error is the unreal. You will gather the importance of this saying, when sorrow seems to come, if you will look on the bright side; for sorrow endureth but for the night, and joy cometh with the light. Then will your sorrow be a dream, and your waking the reality, even the triumph of Soul over sense. If you wish to be happy, argue with yourself on the side of happiness; take the side you wish to carry, and be careful not to talk on both sides, or to argue stronger for sorrow than for joy. You are the attorney for the case, and will win or lose according to your plea.

As the mountain hart panteth for the water brooks, so panteth my heart for the true fount and Soul's baptism. Earth's fading dreams are empty streams, her fountains play in borrowed sunbeams, her plumes are plucked from the wings of vanity. Did we survey the cost of sublunary joy, we then should gladly waken to see it was unreal. A dream calleth itself a dreamer, but when the dream has passed, man is seen wholly apart from the dream.

We are in the midst of a revolution; physics are yielding slowly to metaphysics; mortal mind rebels at its own boundaries; weary of matter, it would catch the meaning of Spirit. The only immortal superstructure is built on Truth; her modest tower rises slowly, but it stands and is the miracle of the hour, though it may seem to the age like the great pyramid of Egypt,—a miracle in stone. The fires of ancient proscription burn upon the altars of to-day; he who has suffered from intolerance is the first to be intolerant. Homœopathy may not recover from the heel of allopathy before lifting its foot against its neighbor, metaphysics, although homœopathy has laid the foundation stone of mental healing; it has established this axiom, "The less medicine the better," and metaphysics adds, "until you arrive at no medicine." When you have reached this high goal you have learned that proportionately as matter went out and Mind came in as the remedy, was its potency. Metaphysics places all cause and cure as mind; differing in this from homœopathy, where cause and cure are supposed to be both mind and matter. Metaphysics requires mind imbued with Truth to heal the sick; hence the Christianity of metaphysical healing, and this excellence above other systems. The higher attenuations of homœopathy contain no medicinal properties, and thus it is found out that Mind instead of matter heals the sick.

While the matter-physician feels the pulse, examines the tongue, etc., to learn what matter is doing independent of mind, when it is self-evident it can do nothing, the metaphysician goes to the fount to govern the streams; he diagnoses disease as mind, the basis of all action, and cures it thus when matter cannot cure it, showing he was right. Thus it was we discovered that all physical effects originate in mind before they can become manifest as matter; we learned from the Scripture and Christ's healing that God, directly or indirectly, through His providence or His laws, never made a man sick. When studying the two hundred and sixty remedies of the Jahr, the characteristic peculiarities and the general and moral symptoms requiring the remedy, we saw at once the concentrated power of thought brought to bear on the pharmacy of homœopathy, which made the infinitesimal dose effectual. To prepare the medicine requires time and thought; you cannot shake the poor drug without the involuntary thought, "I am making you more powerful," and the sequel proves it; the higher attenuations prove that the power was the thought, for when the drug disappears by your process the power remains, and homœopathists admit the higher attenuations are the most powerful. The only objection to giving the unmedicated sugar is, it would be dishonest and divide one's faith apparently between matter and mind, and so weaken both points of action; taking hold of both horns of the dilemma, we should work at opposites and accomplish less on either side.

The pharmacy of homœopathy is reducing the one hundredth part of a grain of medicine two thousand times, shaking the preparation thirty times at every attenuation. There is a moral to this medicine; the higher natures are reached soonest by the higher attenuations, until the fact is found out they have taken no medicine, and then the so-called drug loses its power. We have attenuated a grain of aconite until it was no longer aconite, then dropped into a tumblerful of water a single drop of this harmless solution, and administering one teaspoonful of this water at intervals of half an hour have cured the incipient stage of fever. The highest attenuation we ever attained was to leave the drug out of the question, using only the sugar of milk; and with this original dose we cured an inveterate case of dropsy. After these experiments you cannot be surprised that we resigned the imaginary medicine altogether, and honestly employed Mind as the only curative Principle.

What are the foundations of metaphysical healing? *Mind,* divine Science, the truth of being that casts out error and thus heals the sick. You can readily perceive this mental system of healing is the antipode of mesmerism, Beelzebub. Mesmerism makes one disease while it is supposed to cure another, and that one is worse than the first; mesmerism is one lie getting the better of another, and the bigger lie occupying the field for a period; it is the fight of beasts, in which the bigger animal beats the lesser; in fine, much ado about nothing. Medicine will not arrive at the science of treating disease until disease is treated mentally and man is healed morally and physically. What has physiology, hygiene, or physics done for Christianity but to obscure the divine Principle of healing and encourage faith in an opposite direction?

Great caution should be exercised in the choice of physicians. If you employ a medical practitioner, be sure he is a learned man and skillful; never trust yourself in the hands of a quack. In proportion as a physician is enlightened and liberal is he equipped with Truth, and his efforts are salutary; ignorance and charlatanism are miserable medical aids. Metaphysical healing includes infinitely more than merely to know that mind governs the body and the method of a mental practice. The preparation for a metaphysical practitioner is the most arduous task I ever performed. You must first mentally educate and develop the spiritual sense or perceptive faculty by which one learns the metaphysical treatment of disease; you must teach them how to learn, together with what they learn. I waited many years for a student to reach the ability to teach; it included more than they understood.

Metaphysical or divine Science reveals the Principle and method of perfection,—how to attain a mind in harmony with God, in sympathy with all that is right and opposed to all that is wrong, and a body governed by this mind.

Christian Science repudiates the evidences of the senses and rests upon the supremacy of God. Christian healing, established upon this Principle, vindicates the omnipotence of the Supreme Being by employing no other remedy than Truth, Life, and Love, understood, to heal all ills that flesh is heir to. It places no faith in hygiene or drugs; it reposes all faith in mind, in spiritual power divinely directed. By rightly understanding the power of mind over matter, it enables mind to govern matter, as it rises to that supreme sense that shall "take up serpents" unharmed, and "if they drink any deadly thing, it shall not hurt them." Christian Science explains to any one's perfect satisfaction the so-called miracles recorded in the Bible. Ah! why should man deny all might to the divine Mind, and claim another mind perpetually at war with this Mind, when at the same time he calls God almighty and admits in statement what he denies in proof? You pray for God to heal you, but should you expect this when you are acting oppositely to your prayer, trying everything else besides God, and believe that sickness is something He cannot reach, but medicine can? as if drugs were superior to Deity.

The Scripture says, "Ye ask, and receive not, because ye ask amiss;" and is it not asking amiss to pray for a proof of divine power, that you have little or no faith in because you do not understand God, the Principle of this proof? Prayer will be inaudible, and works more than words, as we understand God better. The Lord's Prayer, understood in its spiritual sense, and given its spiritual version, can never be repeated too often for the benefit of all who, having ears, hear and understand. Metaphysical Science teaches us there is no other Life, substance, and intelligence but God. How much are you demonstrating of this statement? which to you hath the most actual substance,—wealth and fame, or Truth and Love? See to it, O Christian Scientists, ye who have named the name of Christ with a higher meaning, that you abide by your statements, and abound in Love and Truth, for unless you do this you are not demonstrating the Science of metaphysical healing. The immeasurable Life and Love will occupy your affections, come nearer your hearts and into your homes when you touch but the hem of Truth's garment.

A word about the five personal senses, and we will leave our abstract subjects for this time. The only evidence we have of sin, sickness, or death is furnished by these senses; but how can we rely on their testimony when the senses afford no evidence of Truth? They can neither see, hear, feel, taste, nor smell God; and shall we call that reliable evidence through which we can gain no understanding of Truth, Life, and Love? Again, shall we say that God hath created those senses through which it is impossible to approach Him? Friends, it is of the utmost importance that we look into these subjects, and gain our evidences of Life from the correct source. Jesus said, "I am the way, the truth, and the life. No man cometh unto the Father, but by me,"—through the footsteps of Truth. Not by the senses—the lusts of the flesh, the pride of life, envy, hypocrisy, or malice, the pleasures or the pains of the personal senses—does man get nearer his divine nature and present the image and likeness of God. How, then, can it be that material man and the personal senses were created by God? Love makes the spiritual man, lust makes the material so-called man, and God made all that was made; therefore the so-called material man and these personal senses, with all their evidences of sin, sickness, and death, are but a dream,—they are not the realities of life; and we shall all learn this as we awake to behold His likeness.

The allegory of Adam, when spiritually understood, explains this dream of material life, even the dream of the "deep sleep" that fell upon Adam when the spiritual senses were hushed by material sense that before had claimed audience with a serpent. Sin, sickness,and death never proceeded from Truth, Life, and Love. Sin, sickness, and death are error; they are not Truth, and therefore are not TRUE. Sin is a supposed mental condition; sickness and death are supposed physical ones, but all appeared through the false supposition of life and intelligence in matter. Sin was first in the allegory, and sickness and death were produced by sin. Then was not sin of mental origin, and did not mind originate the delusion? If sickness and death came through mind, so must they go; and are we not right in ruling them out of mind to destroy their effects upon the body, that both mortal mind and mortal body shall yield to the government of God, immortal Mind? In the words of Paul, that "the old man" shall be "put off," mortality shall disappear and immortality be brought to light. People are willing to put new wine into old bottles; but if this be done, the bottle will break and the wine be spilled.

There is no connection between Spirit and matter. Spirit never entered and it never escaped from matter; good and evil never dwelt together. There is in reality but the good: Truth is the real; error, the unreal. We cannot put the new wine into old bottles. If that could be done, the world would accept our sentiments; it would willingly adopt the new idea, if that idea could be reconciled with the old belief; it would put the new wine into the old bottle if it could prevent its effervescing and keep it from popping out until it became popular.

The doctrine of atonement never did anything for sickness or claimed to reach that woe; but Jesus' mission extended to the sick as much as to the sinner: he established his Messiahship on the basis that Christ, Truth, heals the sick. Pride, appetites, passions, envy, and malice will cease to assert their Cæsar sway when metaphysics is understood; and religion at the sick-bed will be no blind Samson shorn of his locks. You must admit that what is termed death has been produced by a belief alone. The Oxford students proved this: they killed a man by no other means than making him believe he was bleeding to death. A felon was delivered to them for experiment to test the power of mind over body; and they did test it, and proved it. They proved it not in part, but as a whole; they proved that every organ of the system, every function of the body, is governed directly and entirely by mind, else those functions could not have been stopped by mind independently of material conditions. Had they changed the felon's belief that he was bleeding to death, removed the bandage from his eyes, and he had seen that a vein had not been opened, he would have resuscitated. The illusive origin of disease is not an exception to the origin of all mortal things. Spirit is causation, and the ancient question, Which is first, the egg or the bird? is answered by the Scripture, He made "every plant of the field before it was in the earth."

Heaven's signet is Love. We need it to stamp our religions and to spiritualize thought, motive, and endeavor. Tireless Being, patient of man's procrastination, affords him fresh opportunities every hour; but if Science makes a more spiritual demand, bidding man go up higher, he is impatient perhaps, or doubts the feasibility of the demand. But let us work more earnestly in His vineyard, and according to the model on the mount, bearing the cross meekly along the rugged way, into the wilderness, up the steep ascent, on to heaven, making our words golden rays in the sunlight of our deeds; and "these signs shall follow them that believe; . . . they shall lay hands on the sick, and they shall recover."

Elizabeth Gurley Flynn
(1890–1964)

Elizabeth Gurley Flynn was born on August 7, 1890 in Concord, New Hampshire. The eldest of four children, she attended school sporadically until her family finally settled permanently in a working-class district of the South Bronx in New York City in 1900. In the Bronx she attended Public School 9 and Morris High School while learning much about Marxism at home from her actively socialist parents. Elizabeth's career as a radical agitator began in 1906, when she was sixteen, with a speech to the Harlem Socialist Club on the subject of women under socialism. By the following year she had achieved such success as a soapbox speaker that she often spoke for the Socialist party, the Socialist Labor party and the Industrial Workers of the World (IWW). Invited by John Archibald Jones, and IWW organizer, to join a Minnesota speaking tour, she dropped out of high school in late 1907 and began her national career. In 1908 she married Jones and in 1910 gave birth to a son. However, her love for her organizing work kept her often on the road and she soon separated from her husband and often left her son to be cared for by her mother. Elizabeth quickly acquired a national reputation as an organizer, leading successful free speech fights in Missoula, Montana and Spokane, Washington in 1909 and attracting widespread press coverage. In 1910 she returned to New York City and participated in all of the IWW's major activities in the Northeast, the most spectacular of these being the textile strikes at Lawrence, Massachusetts in 1912 and at Paterson, New Jersey in 1913. In Lawrence, Elizabeth met Carlo Tresca, a leader of the Italian anarchists in the United States, and the two of them lived together for more than twelve years while each was still legally married. In the years before World War I, Elizabeth continued her work with the IWW, although by 1916 she had less to do with the organization because of feuds between her and Big Bill Haywood, its chief officer. The pre-war "red scare" which contributed to the demise of the IWW turned Elizabeth from organizing workers to defending them and upholding their rights. In 1918 she established the Worker's Defense Union (WDU) which affiliated itself with the National Civil Liberties Bureau, the forerunner of the American Civil Liberties Union which she helped to found in 1920. By 1925 the WDU merged with the International Labor Defense which was affiliated with the Communist party, and in 1926 Elizabeth became its chairman. In the same year she fell ill while on a speaking tour in the West and doctors diagnosed her problem as heart disease and recommended complete rest. For the next ten years Elizabeth retired from active organizing work and recuperated in the home of a close activist friend, Dr. Marie Equi of Portland, Oregon. In 1936, having recovered her health, Elizabeth returned to New York City and joined the Communist party, which eagerly welcomed her. She soon became a national organizer and a member of the party's women's commission and began writing a column for the *Daily Worker*. In 1938 Elizabeth was elected to the party's national committee and in 1941 was elected to the party's political bureau, elevating her to the inner circles of leadership. In 1942 she ran for congressman-at-large in New York state and after her defeat spent the duration of the war publicizing women's contributions to the war effort. After the war Elizabeth travelled to Paris as part of the American delegation to the socialist-dominated Women's Congress. In the late 1940's she headed the defense committee for the party, formed to aid the top party leaders arrested under the Smith Act. In 1951 Elizabeth was indicted under the same Act and served two years in the federal penitentiary for women in Alderson, West Virginia. In the 1950's she continued to work for the party and in 1961 she became the first woman selected as national chairman. On a third trip to the Soviet Union in 1964, Elizabeth died of gastroenterocolitis on September 5 and was given a state funeral in Red Square.

The folowing speech was delivered before the New York Civic Club Forum in New York City on January 31, 1914. The typescript is located in the Labadie Collection, the University of Michigan Library, Ann Arbor, Michigan.

"The Truth About the Paterson Strike"

Comrades and Friends:

The reason why I undertake to give this talk at this moment, one year after the Paterson strike was called, is that the flood of criticism about the strike is unabated, becoming more vicious all the time, drifting continually from the actual facts, and involving as a matter of course the policies and strike tactics of the I.W.W. To insure future success in the city of Paterson it is necessary for the past failure to be understood, and not to be clouded over by a mass of outside criticism. It is rather difficult for me to separate myself from my feelings about the Paterson strike, to speak dispassionately. I feel that many of our critics are people who stayed at home in bed while we were doing the hard work of the strike. Many of our critics are people who never went to Paterson, or who went on a holiday; who did not study the strike as a day-by-day process. Therefore it's rather hard for me to overcome my impatience with them and speak purely theoretically.

What is a labor victory? I maintain that it is a twofold thing. Workers must gain economic advantage, but they must also gain revolutionary spirit, in order to achieve a complete victory. For workers to gain a few cents more a day, a few minutes less a day, and go back to work with the same psychology, the same attitude toward society is to have achieved a temporary gain and not a lasting victory. For workers to go back with a class-conscious spirit, with an organized and a determined attitude toward society means that even if they have made no economic gain they have the possibility of gaining in the future. In other words, a labor victory must be economic and it must be revolutionizing. Otherwise it is not complete. The difference between a strike like Lawrence and a garment workers' strike in New York is that both of them gained certain material advantages, but in Lawrence there has been born such a spirit that even when 10,000 workers were out of employment, the employers did not dare reduce the wages of a single man still in the mills. When the hours were reduced by law in New Hampshire and Connecticut in the midst of the industrial panic prevailing throughout the textile industry it was impossible for those manufacturers to reduce the wages at the same time, knowing full well that to do so would create a spontaneous war. Among the garment workers in New York there has unfortunately been developed an instrument known as the protocol, whereby this spirit is completely crushed, is completely diverted from its main object against the employers. This spirit has now to assert itself against the protocol.

So a labor victory must be twofold, but if it can only be one it is better to gain in spirit than to gain economic advantage. The I.W.W. attitude in conducting a strike, one might say, is pragmatic. We have certain general principles; their application differs as the people, the industry, the time and the place indicate. It is impossible to conduct a strike among English-speaking people in the same way that you conduct a strike among foreigners, it is impossible to conduct a strike in the steel industry in the same manner you conduct a strike among the textile workers where women and children are involved in large numbers. So we have no ironclad rules. We realize that we are dealing with human beings and not with chemicals. And we realize that our fundamental principles of solidarity and class revolt must be applied in as flexible a manner as the science of pedagogy. The teacher may have as her ultimate ideal to make the child a proficient master of English, but he begins with the alphabet. So in an I.W.W. strike many times we have to begin with the alphabet, where our own ideal would be the mastery of the whole.

The Paterson strike divides itself into two periods. From the 25th of February, when the strike started, to the 7th of June, the date of the pageant in New York City, marks the first period. The second period is from the pageant to the 29th of July, when every man and woman was back at work. But the preparation for the strike had its roots in the past, the development of a four-loom system in a union mill organized by the American Federation of Labor. This four-loom irritated the workers and precipitated many small outbreaks. At any rate they sent to Mr. John Golden, the president of the United Textile Workers of America, for relief, and his reply was substantially, "The four-loom system is in progress. You have no right to rebel against it." They sought some other channel of expressing their revolt, and a year before the historic strike the Lawrence strike occurred. It stimulated their spirit and it focused their attention on the I.W.W. But unfortunately there came into the city a little group of Socialist Labor Party people who conducted a strike ending in disaster under what they were pleased to call the auspices of the "Detroit I.W.W." That put back the entire movement for a year.

But in the beginning of last year, 1913, there was a strike in the Doherty mill against the four-loom system. There had been agitation for three months by the Eight-Hour League of the I.W.W. for the eight-hour day, and it had stimulated a general response from the disheartened workers. So we held a series of mass meetings calling for a general strike, and that strike broke on the 25th of February, 1913. It was responded to mostly by the unorganized workers. We had three elements to deal with in the Paterson strike; the broad silk weavers and the dyers, who were unorganized and who were as you might say, almost virgin material, easily brought forth and easily stimulated to aggressive activity. But on the other hand we had the ribbon weavers, the English-speaking conservative people, who had behind them craft antecedents, individual crafts unions that they had worked through for thirty years. These people responded only after three weeks, and then they formed the complicating element in the strike, continually pulling back on the mass through their influence as the English-speaking and their attitude as conservatives. The police action precipitated the strike of many workers. They came out because of the brutal persecution of the strike leaders and not because they themselves were so full of the strike feeling that they could not stay in any longer. This was the calling of the strike.

The administering of the strike was in the hands of a strike committee formed of two delegates from each shop. If the strike committee had been full-force there would have been 600 members. The majority of them were not I.W.W.; were nonunion strikers. The I.W.W. arranged the meetings, conducted the agitation work. But the policies of the strike were determined by that strike committee of the strikers themselves. And with the strike committee dictating all the policies of the strike, placing the speakers in a purely advisory capacity, there was a continual danger of a break between the conservative element who were in the strike committee and the mass who were being stimulated by the speakers. The socialist element in the strike committee largely represented the ribbon weavers, this conservative element making another complication in the strike. I want if possible to make that clear before leaving it, that the preparation and declaration as well as the stimulation of the strike was all done by the I.W.W., by the militant minority among the silk workers; the administering of the strike was done democratically by the silk workers themselves. We were in the position of generals on a battlefield who had to organize their forces, who had to organize their commissary department while they were in battle but who were being financed and directed by people in the capital. Our plan of battle was very often nullified by the democratic administration of the strike committee.

The industrial outlook in Paterson presented its difficulties and its advantages. No one realized them quicker than we did. There was the difficulty of 300 mills, no trustification, no company that had the balance of power upon whom we could concentrate our attack. In Lawrence we had the American Woolen Company. Once having forced the American Woolen Company to settle, it was an easy matter to gather in the threads of the other mills. No such situation existed in Paterson. Three hundred manufacturers, but many of them having annexes in Pennsylvania, meant that they had a means whereby they could fill a large percentage of their orders unless we were able to strike Pennsylvania simultaneously. And those mills employed women and children, wives and children of union weavers, who didn't need actually to work for a living wage, but worked simply to add to the family income. We had the difficulty that silk is not an actual necessity. In the strike among coal miners you reached the point eventually where you had the public by the throat, and through the public you were able to bring pressure on the employers. Not so in the silk industry. Silk is a luxury. We had the condition in Paterson, however, that this was the first silk year in about thirty years. In 1913 fortunately silk was stylish. Every woman wanted a silk gown, and the more flimsy it was the more she wanted it. Silk being stylish meant that the employers were mighty anxious to take advantage of this exceptional opportunity. And the fact that there were over 300 of them gave us on the other hand the advantage that some of them were very small, they had great liabilities and not very much reserve capital. Therefore we were sort of playing a game between how much they could get done in Pennsylvania balanced off with how great the demand for silk was and how close they were to bankruptcy. We had no means of telling that, except by guesswork. *They* could always tell when our side was weakening.

The first period of the strike meant for us persecution and propaganda, those two things. Our work was to educate and stimulate. Education is not a conversion, it is a process. One speech to a body of workers does not overcome their prejudices of a lifetime. We had prejudices on the national issues, prejudices between crafts, prejudices between competing men and women,—all these to overcome. We had the influence of the minister on the one side, and the respect that they had for government on the other side. We had to stimulate them. Stimulation, in a strike, means to make that strike and through it the class struggle their religion; to make them forget all about the fact that it's for a few cents or a few hours, but to make them feel it is a "religious duty" for them to win that strike. Those two things constituted our work, to create in them a feeling of solidarity and a feeling of class-consciousness,—a rather old term, very threadbare among certain elements in the city of New York, but meaning a great deal in a strike. It means, to illustrate, this: the first day of the strike a photographer came on the stage to take a picture, and all over the hall there was a quiver of excitement: "No, no, no. Don't let him take a picture." "Why not?" "Why, our faces might show in the picture. The boss might see it." "Well," I said, "doesn't he know you are here? If he doesn't know now, he will know tomorrow."

From that day, when the strikers were afraid to have their pictures taken for fear they might be spotted, to the day when a thousand of them came to New York to take part in a pageant, with a friendly rivalry among themselves as to which one would get their picture in the paper, was a long process of stimulation, a long process of creating in them class spirit, class respect, class consciousness. That was the work of the agitator. Around this propaganda our critics center their volleys: the kind of propaganda we gave the strikers, the kind of stimulation and education we gave them. Many of our critics presume that the strikers were perfect and the leaders only were human; that we didn't have to deal with their imperfections as well as with our own. And the first big criticism that has been made—(of course they all criticize: for the socialists we were too radical, for the anarchists we were too conservative, for everybody else we were impossible) is that we didn't advocate violence. Strange as it may seem, this is the criticism that has come from more sources than any other.

I contend that there was no use for violence in the Paterson strike; that only where violence is necessary should violence be used. This is not a moral or legal objection but a utilitarian one. I don't say that violence should *not* be used, but where there is no call for it, there is no reason why we should resort to it. In the Paterson strike, for the first four months there wasn't a single scab in the mills. The mills were shut down as tight as a vacuum. They were like empty junk boats along the banks of the river. Now, where any violence could be used against non-existent scabs, passes my understanding. Mass action is far more up-to-date than personal or physical violence. Mass action means that the workers withdraw their labor power, and paralyze the wealth production of the city, cut off the means of life, the breath of life of the employers. Violence may mean just weakness on the part of those workers. Violence occurs in almost every American Federation of Labor strike, because the workers are desperate, because they are losing their strike. In the street car strikes, for instance, every one of them is marked with violence, because the men in the power-house are at work, the power is going through the rails and the scabs are able to run the cars. The men and women in desperation, seeing that the work is being done, turn the cars off the track, cut the wires, throw stones, and so on. But the I.W.W. believes that it is far more up to date to call the men in the power house out on strike. Then there won't be any cars running, any scabs to throw stones at or any wires that are worth cutting. Physical violence is dramatic. It's especially dramatic when you talk about it and don't resort to it. But actual violence is an old-fashioned method of conducting a strike. And mass action, paralyzing all industry, is a new-fashioned and a much more feared method of conducting a strike. That does not mean that violence shouldn't be used in self-defense. Everybody believes in violence for self-defense. Strikers don't need to be told that. But the actual fact is that in spite of our theory that the way to win a strike is to put your hands in your pocket and refuse to work, it was only in the Paterson strike of all the strikes in 1913 that a strike leader said what Haywood said: "If the police do not let up in the use of violence against the strikers the strikers are going to arm themselves and fight back." That has, however, not been advertised as extensively as was the "hands in your pockets" theory. Nor has it been advertised by either our enemies or our friends: that in the Paterson strike police persecution did drop off considerably after the open declaration of self-defense was made by the strikers. In that contingency violence is of course a necessity and one would be stupid to say that in either Michigan or West Virginia or Colorado the miners have not a right to take their guns and defend their wives and their babies and themselves.

The statement has been made by Mrs. Sanger in the "Revolutionary Almanac" that we should have stimulated the strikers to do something that would bring the militia in, and the presence of the militia would have forced a settlement of the strike. That is not necessarily true. It was not the presence of the militia that forced a settlement of the Lawrence strike. And today there is militia in Colorado, they have been there for months. There is the militia in Michigan, they have been there for a long period. There was the militia in West Virginia, but *that* did not bring a successful termination of the strike, because coal was being produced,—and copper was being produced,—in other parts of the world, and the market was not completely cut off from its product. The presence of the militia may play a part in stimulating the strikers or in discouraging the strikers, but it does not affect the industrial outcome of the strike, and I believe to say so is to give entirely too much significance to political or military power. I don't believe that the presence of the militia is going to affect an industrial struggle to any appreciable extent, providing the workers are economically in an advantageous position.

Before I finish with this question of violence I want to ask you men and women here if you realize that there is a certain responsibility about advocating violence. It's very easy to say, "We will give up our own lives in behalf of the workers," but it's another question to ask them to give up their lives; and men and women who go out as strike agitators should only advocate violence when they are absolutely certain that it is going to do some good other than to spill the blood of the innocent workers on the streets of the cities. I know of one man in particular who wrote an article in the "Social War" about how "the blood of the workers should dye the streets in the city of Paterson in protest" but he didn't come to Paterson to let his blood dye the streets, as the baptism of violence. In fact we never saw him in the city of Paterson from the first day of the strike to the last. This responsibility rests heavily upon every man and woman who lives with and works with and loves the people for whom the strike is being conducted.

The second criticism is "Why did we go to Haledon? Why didn't we fight out the free speech fight in Paterson?" One of the humorous features of it is that if Haledon had been a Democratic city instead of a Socialist city, that criticism would probably not have been made at all. It was not that we went to Haledon, it was that we went to a Socialist city, that irritates our critics. I want to point out to you something that you possibly never realized before, and that is that we had the "right" to speak in Paterson. There was no conventional free speech fight in Paterson. A conventional free speech fight is where you are not permitted to speak at all, where you are immediately arrested and thrown into jail and not given the right to open your mouth. That is not the kind of free speech fight that existed in Paterson. We had the right to speak in the halls of Paterson, and we would have had the right to the last day of the strike if it had not been for the position of the hallkeepers. It was not the police that closed the halls, it was the hallkeepers, and for the reason that they could not afford to lose their licenses. And a hallkeeper is usually a saloon-keeper first and a renter of halls afterwards. If there had been any hall in Paterson where a saloon was not attached we would probably have been able to secure that hall with but very little trouble. Some of the hallkeepers in fact, if I may speak from personal experience, were very glad to get rid of us, because we were not paying any rent and we were making a lot of work around their places. We had the right to speak on Lafayette Oval. We hired a piece of land on Water Street and used it during the entire time of the strike. The only time meetings were interfered with was on Sunday, and that involved not a free speech issue but a Sunday issue, the blue law of the State of New Jersey. When you are fighting a strike with 25,000 people and you are focussing your attention on trying to keep those people lined up to win that strike, it is a mighty dangerous procedure to go off at a tangent and dissipate your energies on something that is not important, even though you may have a right to do it. We had a right to speak on Sundays, but it meant to divide our energies and possibly to spend our money in ways that did not seem absolutely advisable at the time. The free speech fight that we have in Paterson is something far more intricate than just having a policeman put his hand over your mouth and tell you you can't speak. They let you talk. Oh yes. If I had invited all of you to come to Paterson and speak they would have let you talk, and the police and the detectives would have stood off at one side and listened to you. Then you have been indicted by the grand jury for what you said, arrested and put under bonds and a long legal process started to convict you for what you said.

Therefore to call in the free speech fighters of the country would have been an absurdity, since every one of them would have been permitted to say their say and afterward would have been indicted for the language they used. There was quite a different situation from Lawrence. In Lawrence the halls were never interfered with. In Paterson we had this peculiar technicality, that while you had the right to speak they said, "We hold you responsible for what you say, we arrest you for what you say, what you meant, what you didn't say, what we thought you ought to have said, and all the rest of it." Our original reason for going to Haledon, however, was not on account of the Sunday law only, but goes deep into the psychology of a strike. Because Sunday is the day before Monday! Monday is the day that a break comes in every strike, if it is to come at all during the week. If you can bring the people safely over Monday they usually go along for the rest of the week. If on Sunday, however, you let those people stay at home, sit around the stove without any fire in it, sit down at the table where there isn't very much food, see the feet of the children with shoes getting thin, and the bodies of the children where the clothes are getting ragged, they begin to think in terms of "myself" and lose that spirit of the mass and the realization that all are suffering as they are suffering. You have got to keep them busy every day in the week, and particularly on Sunday, in order to keep that spirit from going down to zero. I believe that's one reason why ministers have sermons on Sunday, so that people don't get a chance to think how bad their conditions are the rest of the week. Anyhow, it's a very necessary thing in a strike. And so our original reason for going to Haledon—I remember we discussed it very thoroughly—was to give them novelty, to give them variety, to take them en masse out of the city of Paterson some place else, to a sort of picnic over Sunday that would stimulate them for the rest of the week. In fact that is a necessary process in every strike, to keep the people busy all the time, to keep them active, working, fighting soldiers in the ranks. And this is the agitator's work,—to plan and suggest activity, diverse, but concentrated on the strike. That's the reason why the I.W.W. has these great mass meetings, women's meetings, children's meetings; why we have mass picketing and mass funerals. And out of all this continuous mass activity we are able to create that feeling on the part of the workers, "One for all and all for one." We are able to make them realize that an injury to one is an injury to all, we are able to bring them to the point where they will have relief and not strike benefits, to the point where they will go to jail and refuse fines, and go hundreds of them together.

This method of conducting strikes has proved so successful and so remarkable with the I.W.W. that the United Mine Workers have taken it up, and in Michigan they are holding women's meetings, children's meetings, mass picketings and mass parades, such as never characterized an American Federation of Labor strike before.

This is the agitator's work, this continual activity. And we lay awake many nights trying to think of something more we could give them to do. I remember one night in Lawrence none of us slept. The strike spirit was in danger of waning for lack of action. And I remember Bill Haywood said finally, "Let's get a picket line out in Essex street. Get every striker to put a little red ribbon on and walk up and down and show that the strike is not broken." A few days later the suggestion was carried out, and when they got out of their homes and saw this great body that they were, they had renewed strength and renewed energy which carried them along for many weeks more in the strike. That was the original object in going to Haledon.

It has been asked "Why didn't we advocate short strikes, intermittent strikes? Why didn't we practice sabotage? Why didn't we do everything we didn't do? It reminds me of the story Tom Mann told. A very pretty young lady, you know how many of them there are around New York of this type, fluttering sentimentalists, came up to him with a sweet smile and said, "Can you tell me, Mr. Mann, why the women and the miners and the railroad people and all these people don't get together in England," and he said, "Can you tell me why you didn't cut your dress on the other side instead of this side?" People are not material, you can't lay them down on the table and cut them according to a pattern. You may have the best principles, but you can't always fit the people to the best principles. And for us to have gone into Paterson for the first three months of the strike and to have advocated a short strike would have said "Aha, they got theirs, didn't they? That's what happens in every strike. They are very revolutionary until the boss gives them theirs, and then they say 'Boys, go back to work.' " In other words, we would simply have duplicated what every grafting, corrupt labor leader has done in Paterson and the United States: to tell them "Go back to work, your strike is lost." And so it was necessary for us first to gain the confidence of the people and to make them feel that we were willing to fight just as long as they were; that we were not the first ones to call quits. And why should we? We were not the ones that were making the sacrifices, we were not the ones that were paying the price. It was the strikers that were doing that. But for us to advocate a short strike, on the other hand, would have been directly contrary to our own feelings. We felt that the strike was going to be won. And it may seem to you a very foolish piece of optimism when I say that I believed the Paterson strike was going to be won up to the Sunday before the Paterson strike was lost. We didn't tell the people to stay out on a long strike knowing in our hearts that they were losing. We couldn't have talked to them if we had felt that way. But every one of us was confident they were going to win that strike. And you all were. Throughout the United States the people were. To successfully advocate an intermittent strike or to go back to work and use sabotage was impossible for the simple reason that the people wanted a long strike, and until they themselves found out by experience that a long strike was a waste of energy it was no use for us to try to dictate to them.

People learn to do by doing. We haven't a military body in a strike, a body to which you can say "Do this" and "Do that" and "Do the other thing" and they obey unfailingly. Democracy means mistakes, lots of them, mistake after mistake. But it also means experience and that there will be no repetition of those mistakes.

Now, we can talk short strike in Paterson, we can talk intermittent strike, we can talk sabotage, because the people know we are not afraid of a long strike, that we are not cowards, that we haven't sold them out, that we went through the long strike with them and that we all learned together that the long strike was not a success. In other words, by that six months they have gained the experience that will mean it never needs to be repeated.

Sabotage was objected to by the Socialists. In fact they pursued a rather intolerant attitude. It was the Socialist organizer and the Socialist secretary who called the attention of the public to the fact that Frederic Sumner Boyd made a sabotage speech. Why "intolerant"? Because nobody ever objected to anything that the Socialists said. We tried to produce among those strikers this feeling: "Listen to anything, listen to everybody. Ministers come, priests come, lawyers, doctors, politicians, Socialists, anarchists, A. F. of L., I.W.W.,—listen to them all and then take what you think is good for yourselves and reject what is bad. If you are not able to do that then no censorship over your meetings is going to do you any good." And so the strikers had a far more tolerant attitude than had the Socialists. The strikers had the attitude: "Listen to everything." The Socialists had the attitude: "You must listen to us but you must not listen to the things we don't agree with, you must not listen to sabotage because we don't agree with sabotage." We had a discussion in the executive committee about it, and one after the other of the members of the executive committee admitted that they used sabotage, why shouldn't they talk about it? It existed in the mills, they said. Therefore there was no reason why it should not be recognized on the platform. It was not the advocacy of sabotage that hurt some of our comrades but denial of their right to dictate the policy of the Paterson strike.

What the workers had to contend with in the first period of this strike was this police persecution that arrested hundreds of strikers, fined hundreds, sentenced men to three years in state's prison for talking; persecutions that meant beating and clubbing and continual opposition every minute they were on the picket line, speakers arrested, Quinlan arrested, Scott convicted and sentenced to 15 years and $1500 fine. On the other side, what? No money. If all these critics all over the United States had only put their interest in the form of finances the Paterson strike might have been another story. We were out on strike five months. We had $60,000 and 25,000 strikers. That meant $60,000 for five months, $12,000 a month for 25,000 strikers; it meant an average of less than 50 cents a month. And yet they stayed out on strike for six months. In Ireland today there is a wonderful strike going on and they are standing it beautifully. Why? Because they have had half a million dollars since the thirty-first of August (five months) given into the relief fund, and every man that goes on the picket line has food in his stomach and some kind of decent clothes on his back.

I saw men go out in Paterson without shoes, in the middle of winter and with bags on their feet. I went into a family to have a picture taken of a mother with eight children who didn't have a crust of bread, didn't have a bowl of milk for the baby in the house,—but the father was out on the picket line. Others were just as bad off. Thousands of them that we never heard of at all. This was the difficulty that the workers had to contend with in Paterson: hunger; hunger gnawing at their vitals; hunger tearing them down; and still they had the courage to fight it out for six months.

Then came the pageant. What I say about the pageant tonight may strike you as rather strange, but I consider that the pageant marked the climax in the Paterson strike and started the decline in the Paterson strike, just for the reason that the pageant promised money for the Paterson strikers and it didn't give them a cent. Yes, it was a beautiful example of realistic art, I admit that. It was splendid propaganda for the workers in New York. I don't minimize its value but am dealing with it here solely as a factor in the strike, with what happened in Paterson before, during and after the pageant. In preparation for the pageant the workers were distracted for weeks, turning to the stage of the hall, away from the field of life. They were playing pickets on the stage. They were neglecting the picketing around the mill. And the first scabs got into the Paterson mills while the workers were training for the pageant, because the best ones, the most active, the most energetic, the best, the strongest ones of them went into the pageant and they were the ones that were the best pickets around the mills. Distraction from their real work was the first danger in Paterson. And how many times we had to counteract that and work against it!

And then came jealousy. There were only a thousand that came to New York. I wonder if you ever realized that you left 24,000 disappointed people behind? The women cried and said "Why did *she* go? Why couldn't I go?" The men told about how many times they had been in jail, and asked why couldn't they go as well as somebody else. Between jealousy, unnecessary but very human, and their desire to do something, much discord was created in the ranks.

But whatever credit is due for such a gigantic undertaking comes to the New York silk workers, not the dilettante element who figure so prominently, but who would have abandoned it at the last moment had not the silk workers advanced $600 to pull it through.

And then comes the grand finale—no money. Nothing. This thing that had been heralded as the salvation of the strike, this thing that was going to bring thousands of dollars to the strike,— $150 came to Paterson, and all kinds of explanations. I don't mean to say that I blame the people who ran the pageant. I know they were amateurs and they gave their time and their energy and their money. They did the best they could and I appreciate their effort. But that doesn't minimize the result that came in Paterson. It did not in any way placate the workers of Paterson, to tell them that people in New York had made sacrifices, in view of the long time that *they* had been making sacrifices. And so with the pageant as a climax, with the papers clamoring that tens of thousands of dollars had been made, and with the committee explaining what was very simple, that nothing *could* have been made with one performance on such a gigantic scale, there came trouble, dissatisfaction, in the Paterson strike.

Bread was the need of the hour, and bread was not forthcoming even from the most beautiful and realistic example of art that has been put on the stage in the last half century.

What was the employers' status during all this time? We saw signs of weakness every day. There was a minister's committee appointed to settle the strike. There was a businessmen's committee appointed to settle the strike. The governor's intervention, the President's intervention was sought by the manufacturers. Every element was brought to bear to settle the strike. Even the American Federation of Labor; nobody believes that they came in there uninvited and no one can believe that the armory was given to them for a meeting place unless for a purpose. What was this purpose but to settle the strike? The newspapers were clamoring that the strike could and must be settled. And we looked upon all this,—the newspapers that were owned by the mill owners, the ministers and the business men who were stimulated by the mill owners,—we looked upon all this as a sign that the manufacturers were weakening. Even the socialists admitted it. In the New York *Call* of July 9 we read this: "The workers of Paterson *should* stay with them another round or two after a confession of this kind. What the press had to say about the strike looks very much like a confession of defeat." This was on the 9th of July. Every sign of weakness on the part of the manufacturers was evident.

But there came one of the most peculiar phenomena that I have ever seen in a strike; that the bosses weakened simultaneously with the workers. Both elements weakened together. The workers did not have a chance to see the weaknesses of the employers as clearly, possibly, as we who had witnessed it before, did, which gave us our abiding faith in the workers' chances of success, but the employers had every chance to see the workers weaken. The employers have a full view of your army. You have no view of their army and can only guess at their condition. So a tentative proposition came from the employers of a shop-by-shop settlement. This was the trying-out of the bait, the bait that should have been refused by the strikers without qualification. Absolute surrender, all or nothing, was the necessary slogan. By this we did not mean that 100 per cent of the manufacturers must settle, or that 99 per cent of the workers must stay out till 1 per cent won everything. The I.W.W. advice to the strikers was—an overwhelming majority of the strikers must receive the concession before a strike is won. This was clearly understood in Paterson, though misrepresented there and elsewhere. Instead, the committee swallowed the bait and said, "We will take a vote on the shop-by-shop proposition, a vote of the committee." The minute they did that, they admitted their own weakness. And the employers immediately reacted to a position of strength. There was no referendum vote proposed by this committee, they were willing to take their own vote to see what they themselves thought of it, and to settle the strike on their own decision alone.

Then it was that the I.W.W. speakers and Executive Committee had to inject themselves in contradistinction to the strike committee. And the odd part of it was that the conservatives on the committee utilized our own position against us. We had always said, "The silk workers must gain their own strike." And so they said, "We are the silk workers. You are simply outside agitators. You can't talk to this strike committee even." I remember one day the door was virtually slammed in my face, until the Italian and Jewish workers made such an uproar, threatening to throw the others out of a three-story building window, that the floor was granted. It was only when we threatened to go to the masses and to get this referendum vote in spite of them that they took the referendum vote. But all this came out in the local press and it all showed that the committee was conservative and the I.W.W. was radical, more correctly the I.W.W. and the masses were radical. And so this vote was taken by the strikers. It resulted in a defeat of the entire proposition. Five thousand dyers in one meeting voted it down unanimously. They said, "We never said we would settle shop by shop. We are going to stick it out together until we win together or until we lose together." But the very fact that they had been willing to discuss it made the manufacturers assume an aggressive position. And then they said, "We never said we would settle shop-by-shop. We never offered you any such proposition. We won't take you back now unless you come under the old conditions."

One of the peculiar things about this whole situation was the attitude of the socialists on that committee. I want to make myself clearly understood. I don't hold the socialist party officially responsible, only insofar as they have not repudiated these particular individuals. The socialist element in the committee represented the ribbon weavers, the most conservative, the ones who were in favor of the shop-by-shop settlement. They were led by a man named Magnet, conservative, Irish, Catholic, Socialist. His desire was to wipe the strike off the slate in order to leave the stage free for a political campaign. He had aspirations to be the mayoralty candidate, which did not however come to fruition. This man and the element that were behind him, the socialist element, were willing to sacrifice, to betray a strike in order to make an argument, the argument given out in the "Weekly Issue" a few days before election: "Industrial action has failed. Now try political action." It was very much like the man who made a prophecy that he was going to die on a certain date, and then he committed suicide. He died, all right. Industrial action failed, all right. But they forgot to say that they contributed more than any other element in the strike committee to the failure of the strike. They were the conservatives, they were the ones who wanted to get rid of the strike as quickly as possible. And through these ribbon weavers the break came.

On the 18th of July the ribbon weavers notified the strike committee, "We have drawn out of your committee. We are going to settle our strike to suit ourselves. We are going to settle it shop by shop. That's the way they have settled it in New York at Smith and Kauffmann." But a visit had been made by interested parties to the Smith and Kauffmann boys prior to their settlement, at which they were informed that the Paterson strike was practically lost: "These outside agitators don't know anything about it, because they are fooled in this matter. You had better go back to work." When they went back to work on the nine-hour day and the shop-by-shop settlement, then it was used by the same people who had told them that, as an argument to settle in the same way in Paterson. And the ribbon weavers stayed out till the very last. Oh yes. They have all the glory throughout the United States of being the last ones to return to work, but the fact is that they were the first ones that broke the strike, because they broke the solidarity, they precipitated a position that was virtually a stampede. The strike committee decided, "Well, with the ribbon weavers drawing out, what are we going to do? We might as well accept;" and the shop-by-shop proposition was put through by the strike committee without a referendum vote, stampeded by the action of the English-speaking, conservative ribbon weavers.

So that was the tragedy of the Paterson strike, the tragedy of a stampede, the tragedy of an army, a solid phalanx being cut up into 300 pieces, each shop-piece trying to settle as best for themselves. It was absolutely in violation of the I.W.W. principles and the I.W.W. advice to the strikers. No strike should ever be settled without a referendum vote, and no shop settlement should ever have been suggested in the city of Paterson, because that was the very thing that had broken the strike the year before. So this stampede came, and the weaker ones went back to work and the stronger ones were left outside, to be made the target of the enemy, blacklisted for weeks and weeks after the strike was over, many of them on the blacklist yet. It produced discord among the officers in the strike. I remember one day at Haledon, the chairman said to Tresca and myself, "If you are going to talk about the eight-hour day and about a general strike, then you had better not talk at all." And we had to go out and ask the people, "Are we expected here today and can we say what we think, or have we got to say what the strike committee has decided?" We were unanimously welcomed. But it was too late. Just as soon as the people saw that there was a break between the agitators and the strike committee, that the ribbon weavers wanted this and others wanted that, the stampede had started and no human being could have held it back.

It was the stampede of hungry people, people who could no longer think clearly. The bosses made beautiful promises to the ribbon weavers and to everybody else, but practically every promise made before the settlement of the Paterson strike was violated, and the better conditions have only been won through the organized strikes since the big strike. Not one promise that was made by the employers previous to breakup on account of the shop-by-shop settlement was ever lived up to. Other places were stranded. New York, Hoboken, College Point were left stranded by this action. And on the 28th of July everybody was back at work, back to work in spite of the fact that the general conviction had been that we were on the eve of victory. I believe that if the strikers had been able to hold out a little longer by any means, by money if possible, which was refused to us, we could have won the Paterson strike. We could have won it because the bosses had lost their spring orders, they had lost their summer orders, they had lost their fall orders and they were in danger of losing their winter orders, one year's work; and the mills in Pennsylvania, while they could give the bosses endurance for a period, could not fill all the orders and could not keep up their business for the year round.

I say we were refused money. I wish to tell you that is the absolute truth. The New York *Call* was approached by fellow-worker Haywood, when we were desperate for money, when the kitchens were closed and the people were going out on the picket line on bread and water, and asked to publish a full page advertisement begging for money, pleading for money. They refused to accept the advertisement. They said, "We can't take your money." "Well, can you *give* us the space?" "Oh, no, we can't afford to give you the space. We couldn't take money from strikers, but we couldn't give space either." And so in the end there was no appeal, either paid for or not, but a little bit of a piece that did not amount to a candle of light, lost in the space of the newspaper. However, on the 26th of July, while the ribbon weavers and some of the broad silk weavers were still out, the *Call* had published a criticism by Mr. Jacob Panken of the Paterson strike. Lots of space for criticism, but no space to ask bread for hungry men and women. And this was true not only of the *Call*, but of the other socialist papers. So, between these two forces, we were helpless. And then we had to meet our critics. First came the socialist critic who said, "But the I.W.W. didn't do enough for the socialist party. Look at all the money we gave you. And you don't say anything about it." Dr. Korshet had a long article in the New York *Call*. Anyone may read it who likes to refresh his memory. Just this: "We gave you money and you didn't thank us." Well, I would like to know why we *should* thank them. Aren't the socialists supposed to be workingmen, members of the working class, just the same as we are? And if they do something for their own class we have got to thank them the next ten years for it. They are like the charity organization that gives the poor working woman a little charity and then expects her to write recommendations to the end of the end of the earth. We felt that there was no need to thank the socialist party for what they had done, because they had only done their duty and they had done very little in comparison with what they have done in A. F. of L. strikes, in the McNamara cases.

They make the criticism that we didn't give them any credit. How about the 5,000 votes that the I.W.W. membership gave the party in Paterson for a candidate who was a member of the A. F. of L. and who did not get a single vote from his own union? All his votes came from the I.W.W. If they wanted to invest money, the money that they invested for each vote in Paterson was well spent, on a purely business basis.

Abigail Kelley Foster
(1810–1887)

Abigail Kelley Foster was born on January 15, 1810 in Pelham, Massachusetts. The fifth of seven children, she grew up in a modest Quaker household in a rural district near Worcester, Massachusetts. After attending school in Worcester and at the Friends' school in Providence, Rhode Island, she became a teacher in the Friends' school in Lynn, Massachusetts. While in Lynn Abigail became a dedicated abolitionist and served as secretary of the Lynn Female Anti-Slavery Society from 1835-37. After a successful first speech at the second woman's anti-slavery convention held in Philadelphia in 1838, she began her long and tempestuous career as a lecturer and agitator. During the next fifteen years she travelled throughout New England, New York, Pennsylvania, Ohio, Indiana and Michigan espousing Garrison's doctrine of "No Union with Slaveholders" and helping to advance the feminist cause by opening public platforms to women. In 1845 she helped establish the *Anti-Slavery Bugle* in Salem, Ohio, and worked for years to raise money to ensure its survival. In the same year she married a fellow abolitionist, Stephen Foster, and they often travelled together as a lecture team. During the 1850's Abigail also found time to address feminist and temperance meetings, attending numerous national and state conventions. With the exception of a final fundraising tour of New England for the American AntiSlavery Society in 1870, Abigail's poor health kept her from being nationally active during the post Civil War years. On January 14, 1887, several months after attending an abolitionists' reunion, Abigail died quietly in Worcester at the age of seventy-seven.

The following speech was delivered at the 4th Ohio Woman's Rights Conference in Cleveland, Ohio on October 6, 1853. The speech was in response to the clergy's argument that *women* cast out "licentious" women from the church and community, *not* the clergy. It appeared in printed form in *The History of Woman Suffrage*, Vol. I (Rochester, N.Y., 1881) pp. 134-136.

"It Is the Pulpit Who Casts Out 'Impure' Women"

I want to say here that I believe the law is but the writing out of public sentiment, and back of that public sentiment, I contend lies the responsibility. Where shall we find it? " 'Tis education forms the common mind." It is allowed that we are what we are educated to be. Now if we can ascertain who has had the education of us, we can ascertain who is responsible for the law, and for public sentiment. Who takes the infant from its cradle and baptizes it "in the name of the Father, Son, and Holy Ghost;" and when that infant comes to childhood, who takes it into Sabbath-schools; who on every Sabbath day, while its mind is "like clay in the hands of the potter," moulds and fashions it as he will; and when that child comes to be a youth, where is he found, one-seventh part of the time; and when he comes to maturer age, does he not leave his plow in the furrow, and his tools in the shop, and one-seventh part of the time go to the place where prayer is wont to be made? On that day no sound is heard but the roll of the carriage wheels to church; all are gathered there, everything worldly is laid aside, all thoughts are given entirely to the Creator; for we are taught that we must not think our own thoughts, but must lay our own wills aside, and come to be moulded and fashioned by the priest. It is "holy time," and we are to give ourselves to be wholly and entirely fashioned and formed by another. That place is a holy place, and when we enter, our eye rests on the "holy of holies;" he within it is a "divine." The "divines" of the thirteenth century, the "divines" of the fifteenth century, and the "divines" of the nineteenth century, are no less "divines." What I say to-day is taken for what it is worth, or perhaps for less than it is worth, because of the prejudice against me; but when he who educates the people speaks, "he speaks as one having authority," and is not to be questioned. He claims, and has his claim allowed, to be specially ordained and specially anointed from God. He stands mid-way between Deity and man, and therefore his word has power.

Aye, not only in middle age does the man come, leaving everything behind him; but, in old age, "leaning on the top of his staff," he finds himself gathered in the place of worship, and though his ear may be dull and heavy, he leans far forward to catch the last words of duty—of duty to God and duty to man. Duty is the professed object of the pulpit, and if it does not teach that, what in Heaven's name does it teach? This anointed man of God speaks of moral duty to God and man. He teaches man from the cradle to the coffin; and when that aged form is gathered within its winding-sheet, it is the pulpit that says, "Dust to dust and ashes to ashes."

It is the pulpit, then, which has the entire ear of the community, one-seventh part of the time. If you say there are exceptions, very well, that proves the rule. If there is one family who do not go to church, it is no matter, its teachings are engendered by those who do go; hence I would say, not only does the pulpit have the ear of the community one-seventh part of the time of childhood, but it has it under circumstances for forming and moulding and fashioning the young mind, as no other educating influence can have it. The pulpit has it, not only under these circumstances; it has it on occasions of marriage, when two hearts are welded into one; on occasions of sickness and death, when all the world beside is shut out, when the mind is most susceptible of impressions from the pulpit, or any other source.

I say, then, that woman is not the author of this sentiment against her fallen sister, and I roll back the assertion on its source. Having the public ear one-seventh part of the time, if the men of the pulpit do not educate the public mind, who does educate it? Millions of dollars are paid for this education, and if they do not educate the public mind in its morals, what, I ask, are we paying our money for? If woman is cast out of society, and man is placed in a position where he is respected, then I charge upon the pulpit that it has been recreant to its duty. If the pulpit should speak out fully and everywhere, upon this subject, would not woman obey it? Are not women under the special leading and direction of their clergymen? You may tell me, that it is woman who forms the mind of the child; but I charge it back again, that it is the minister who forms the mind of the woman. It is he who makes the mother what she is; therefore her teaching of the child is only conveying the instructions of the pulpit at second hand. If public sentiment is wrong on this (and I have the testimony of those who have spoken this morning, that it is), the pulpit is responsible for it, and has the power of changing it. The clergy claim the credit of establishing public schools. Granted. Listen to the pulpit in any matter of humanity, and they will claim the originating of it, because they are the teachers of the people. Now, if we give credit to the pulpit for establishing public schools, then I charge them with having a bad influence over those schools; and if the charge can be rolled off, I want it to be rolled off; but until it can be done, I hope it will remain there.

Charlotte Perkins Gilman
(1860–1935)

Charlotte Perkins Gilman was born on July 3, 1860 in Hartford, Connecticut. One of four children, she grew up in dire poverty, moving nineteen times in eighteen years with her mother and siblings trying to economically survive with little financial support from her estranged father. Charlotte's schooling was thus limited, although she did attend the Rhode Island School of Design for awhile and became a voracious reader. In her teens, she helped support herself and her family by working as a commercial artist, art teacher and governess. In May 1884, Charlotte married Charles Stetson and gave birth to a daughter less than a year later. Feeling increasingly despondent, in 1885 Charlotte traveled alone to California in hopes of regaining her health. Discovering her illness improved with her separation from her husband, she remained in California and finally divorced her husband in 1894. In order to support herself, Charlotte began writing short stories and poetry and published *In This Our World* in 1893, which was well received and earned her a small reputation. She also begain lecturing to earn fees and toured widely from the early 1890's to 1900. During this time period she also helped plan the California Woman's Congresses of 1894 and 1895, lived for a brief while at "Hull House" in Chicago, and in 1896 served as a delegate to the International Socialist and Labor Congress. In 1898 Charlotte Published *Women and Economics,* a persuasive feminist manifesto upon which her reputation primarily rests. But other major works were also published: *Concerning Children* (1900), *The Home* (1903), *Human Work* (1904), *Man-Made World* (1911), and *His Religion and Hers* (1923). In 1900 Charlotte married George Gilman and the two lived in New York City until 1922, when they moved to Norwich, Connecticut. In 1909 she wrote, edited, and published her own monthly magazine, the *Forerunner,* which contained works of fiction, editorials, news and poems, all focusing on the position of women and the need for social reorganization. In 1913 Charlotte addressed the International Suffrage Convention in Budapest, and in 1915 she helped to found the Women's Peace Party. In the 1920's she continued lecturing and writing on women, although the fervor for feminism had paled and her audiences were often small. In 1932 Charlotte discovered she had breast cancer and on August 17, 1935 she carried out her plan to commit suicide in the event her disease could not be arrested.

The following speech was delivered several times in New York City and nearby cities in New Jersey and Connecticut during the years 1909-1910. It was later printed in article form in *The Forerunner,* vol. No. 3 (January, 1910), pp. 12-14.

"The Humanness of Women"

A woman by the river's brim,
A wife and servant is to him-
And she is nothing more.

WE HAVE made mistakes, as old as humanity, about the world, and about women.
First, as to the world:

This we have assumed to be a general battlefield for men to struggle in; a place for free competition; full of innumerable persons whose natural mode of life was to struggle for existence with one another.

This is the individualist view, and is distinctly masculine.

Males are essentially individualistic—born to vary and compete; and an exclusively masculine world must be individualistic and competitive.

We have been wrong. The new Social Philosophy recognizes Society as an orderly life-form, having its own laws of growth; and that we, as individuals, live only as active parts of Society. Instead of accepting this world of warfare, disease, and crime, of shameful, unnecessary poverty and pain, as natural and right, we now see that all these evils may be removed, and we propose to remove them. Humanity is waking up, is beginning to understand its own nature, is beginning to face a new and a possible problem, instead of the dark enigma of the past.

Second, as to the women.

Our mistake about her was a very strange one. No one knows yet how or why it was made; yet there it stands; one of the most colossal blunders ever made by mankind. In the face of all creation, where the female is sometimes found quite self-sufficient, often superior, and always equal to the male, our human race set up the "andro-centric theory," holding that man alone was the race type; and that woman was "his female." In what "Mr. Venus" described as "the vicious pride of his youth," our budding humanity distinguished itself by discrediting its mother. "You are a female," said Ancient Man, "and that's all. We are the People!"

This is the alpha and omega of the old idea about woman. It saw in her only sex—not Humanity.

The New Woman is Human first, last and always. Incidentally she is female; as man is male. As a male he has done his small share in the old physical process of reproduction; but as a Human Creature he has done practically all in the new Social processes which make civilization.

He has been Male—and Human:—She has been Female—and nothing else;—that is, in our old idea.

Holding this idea; absurd, erroneous, and mischievous to a terrible degree; we strove to carry it out in our behavior; and human history so far is the history of a wholly masculine world, competing and fighting as males must, forever seeking and serving the female as males must; yet building this our world as best they could alone.

Theirs is the credit—and the shame—of the world behind us, the world around us; but the world before us was a new element—the Humanness of Woman.

For a little over a century we have become increasingly conscious of a stir, an uprising, and protest among women. The long-suppressed "better half" of humanity has begun to move and push and lift herself. This Woman's movement is as natural, as beneficial, as irresistible as the coming of spring; but it has been misunderstood and opposed from the first by the glacial moraine of old ideas, the inert force of sheer blank ignorance, and prejudice as old as Adam.

At first the women strove for a little liberty, for education; then for some equality before the law, for common justice; then, with larger insight, for full equal rights with men in every human field; and as essential base of these, for the right of suffrage.

Woman suffrage is but one feature of the movement, but it is a most important one. The opposition to it is wholly one of sex-prejudice, of feeling, not of reason; the opposition of a masculine world; and of an individualism also masculine. The male is physiologically an individualist. It is his place in nature to vary, to introduce new characteristics, and to strive mightily with his rivals for the favor of the females. A world of males must fight.

With the whole of history of this combative sort; with masculinity and humanity identical in the average mind; there is something alien, unnatural, even revolting, in the claim of woman to her share in the work and management of the world. Against it he brings up one constant cry—that woman's progress will injure womanhood. All that he sees in woman is her sex; and he opposes her advance on the ground that "as a woman" she is unfit to take part in "a man's world"—and that if she did, it would mysteriously but inevitably injure her "as a woman."

Suggest that she might be able to take part in "a woman's world,"—and has as much right to a world made her way as he has to his man-made world! Suggest that without any such extreme reversal, she has a right to half the world; half the work, half pay, half the care, half the glory!

To all this replies the Male-Individualist:

"The World has to be as it is. It is a place to fight in; fight for life, fight for money. Work is for slaves and poor people generally. Nobody would work unless they had to. You are females and no part of the world at all. Your place is at home; to bear and rear children—and to cook."

Now what is the position toward women of this new philosophy that sees Society as one thing, and the main thing to be considered; that sees the world as a place open to ceaseless change and improvement; that sees the way so to change and improve it that the major part of our poor silly sins and sorrows will disappear utterly for lack of cause?

From this viewpoint male and female fall into two lower positions, both right and proper; useful, beautiful, essential for the replenishment of the race on earth. From this viewpoint men and women rise, together, from that lower relation, to the far higher one of Humanness, that common Humanness which is hers as much as his. Seeing Society as the real life-form; and our individual lives as growing in glory and power as we serve and develop Society; the movement of women becomes of majestic importance. It is the advance of an entire half the race, from a position of arrested development, into full humanness.

The world is no longer seen as a battlefield, where it is true, women do not belong; but as a garden—a school—a church—a home, where they visibly do belong. In the great task of cultivating the earth they have an equal interest and an equal power. Equality is not identity. There is work of all kinds and sizes—and half of it is woman's.

In that vast labor of educating humanity, till all of us understand one another; till the thoughts and feelings necessary to our progress can flow smooth and clear through the world-mind, women have pre-eminent part. They are the born teachers, by virtue of their motherhood, as well as in the human joy of it.

In the power of organization which is essential to our progress we have special need of women, and their rapid and universal movement in this direction is one of the most satisfactory proofs of our advance. In every art, craft and profession they have the same interests, the same power. We rob the world of half its service when we deny women their share in it.

In direct political action there is every reason for women's voting that there is for men's; and every reason for a spreading universal suffrage that there is for democracy. As far as any special power in government is called for, the mother is the natural ruler, the natural administrator and executive. The functions of democratic government may be wisely and safely shared between men and women.

Here we have our great position fairly before us:—the improvement of the world is ours to make; women are coming forward to help make it; women are human with every human power; democracy is the highest form of government—so far; and the use of the ballot is essential to democracy; therefore women should vote!

Against this rises the tottering fortress of the ultra-masculine abetted by a petty handful of witless traitors—those petticoated creatures who also see in women nothing but their sex. They may be, in some cases, honest in their belief; but their honesty does no credit to their intelligence. They are obsessed by this dominant idea of sex; due clearly enough to the long period of male dominance—to our androcentric culture. The male naturally sees in the female, sex; first, last and always. For all these centuries she has been restricted to the exercise of feminine duties only, with the one addition of house-service.

The wife-and-mother sex, the servant sex, she is to him; and nothing more. The woman does not look at men in this light. She has to consider them as human creatures, because they monopolize the human functions. She does not consider the motorman and conductor as males, but as promotors of travel; she does not chuck the bellboy under the chin and kiss the waiter!

Inextricably mingled with the masculine view is the individualist view, seeing the world forever and ever as a place of struggle.

Then comes this great change of our time, the dawning of the Social consciousness. Here is a world of combination, of ordered grouping and interservice. Here is a world now wasting its wealth like water—all this waste may be saved. Here is a world of worse than unnecessary war. We will stop this warfare. Here is a world of hideous diseases. We will exterminate them. Here is a world of what we call "Sin"—almost all of which is due to Ignorance, Ill-health, Unhappiness, Injustice.

When the world learns how to take care of itself decently; when there are no dirty evil places upon it, with innocent children born daily and hourly into conditions which inevitably produce a certain percentage of criminality; when the intelligence and good breeding which now distinguish some of us are common to all of us—we shan't hear so much about sin!

A socially conscious world, intelligent, courageous, earnest to improve itself, seeking to establish a custom of peaceful, helpful interservice—such a world has no fear of woman, and no feeling that she is unfit to participate in its happy labors. The new social philosophy welcomes woman suffrage.

But suppose you are not in any sense Socialistically inclined. Suppose you are still an Individualist, albeit a believer in votes for women. Even so, merely from the woman's point of view, enough can be said to justify the promise of a New World.

What makes the peace and beauty of the Home—its order—comfort—happiness?—the Woman.

Her service is given, not hired. Her attitude is of one seeking to administer a common fund for the common good. She does not set her children to compete for their dinner—does not give most to the strongest and leave the weakest to go to the wall. It is only in her lowest helplessness; under the degrading influence of utter poverty, that she is willing to exploit her children and let them work before their time.

If she, merely as Woman, merely as wife and mother, comes forward to give the world the same service she has given the home, it will be wholly to its advantage.

Go and look at the legislation initiated or supported by women in every country where women vote—and you will see one unbroken line of social service. Not self-interest—not mercenary profit—not competition; but one steady upward pressure; the visible purpose to uplift and help the world.

This world is ours as much as man's. We have not only a right to half its management but a duty to half its service. It is our duty as human beings to help make the world better—quickly! It is our duty as Women to bring our Motherhood to comfort and help humanity—our children every one!

Emma Goldman
(1869–1940)

Emma Goldman was born on June 27, 1869 in Kovno, Russia (Kaunus in modern Lithuania). As the only child of her parent's union, but as the third child of her mother, Emma grew up in an unpleasant environment in which her father resented the fact she was a girl and her halfsisters and mother resented his resentment on her account. Thus, Emma's first sixteen years were clouded by family disapproval and constant moving from one Russian village to the next. In 1885, Emma escaped an arranged marriage by emigrating to America with one of her half sisters and settling in Rochester, New York. After several years work in a clothing factory and a brief marriage to Jacob Kersner, Emma's "real life" began (as she claims) when she moved to New York City in 1889. Already a critic of capitalism and a budding socialist, her contacts with anarchists in New York completed her radical education and she devoted the rest of her life to the anarchist movement and socialist reform causes. Emma's most serious setbacks surrounded her early acceptance of individual acts of violence. Her support of Alexander Berkman's attempt to kill Henry Clay Fisk during the Homestead conflict resulted in his imprisonment for fourteen years and the government's notice of her. In 1893 Emma, herself, began a one-year term in prison for advising unemployed workers of their sacred right to take bread if they were starving, and in 1901 the government tried unsuccessfully to establish her complicity in the assassination of President McKinley. In the opening decades of the new century, Emma became involved in a wide range of activities. As a dynamic and polemical speaker she toured America lecturing on anarchism, the new drama and the revolt of women. In 1906 she and Berkman launched the radical publication of *Mother Earth*, in 1911 she published her book *Anarchism and Other Essays,* and in 1914 she published her drama lectures under the title *The Social Significance of the Modern Drama.* Frequent vigilante attempts to censor her remarks and publications prompted her to wage countless battles for free speech and to further harass those who upheld traditional values by lecturing on free love, voluntary motherhood and family limitation. The government, however, won in the long run. In 1908 they deprived her of her citizenship by denaturalizing her missing husband, and in 1919 she and Berkman were deported to Russia after serving two years in prison for their leadership in the opposition to military conscription. After two years in Russia, Emma expatriated herself and moved to Sweden, then to Germany and finally to England. In 1923 she published *My Disillusionment in Russia* in which she attacked liberals and radicals who cried out against suppression of Civil rights in the west but ignored the much worse suppression in Russia. In 1931 Emma published *Living My Life,* her autobiography and source of income for some time to follow. Emma's last political efforts were waged on behalf of the anti-Franco forces in Spain. In 1939 she travelled to Canada to raise money for the lost cause and in early 1940 she suffered a stroke and died on May 14, 1940 at the age of 71.

The following speech was delivered numerous times in 1915 and was widely circulated as a pamphlet. It also appeared in printed form in the December, 1915 issue of *Mother Earth.*

"Preparedness: The Road to Universal Slaughter"

Ever since the beginning of the European conflagration, the whole human race almost has fallen into the deathly grip of the war anesthesis, overcome by the mad teeming fumes of a blood soaked chloroform, which has obscured its vision and paralyzed its heart. Indeed, with the exception of some savage tribes, who know nothing of Christian religion or of brotherly love, and who also know nothing of dreadnaughts, submarines, munition manufacture and war loans, the rest of the race is under this terrible narcosis. The human mind seems to be conscious of but one thing, murderous speculation. Our whole civilization, our entire cutlure is concentrated in the mad demand for the most perfected weapons of slaughter.

Ammunition! Ammunition! O, Lord, thou who rulest heaven and earth, thou God of love, of mercy and of justice, provide us with enough ammunition to destroy our enemy. Such is the prayer which is ascending daily to the Christian heaven. Just like cattle, panic-stricken in the face of fire, throw themselves into the very flames, so all of the European people have fallen over each other into the devouring flames of the furies of war, and America, pushed to the very brink by unscrupulous politicians, by ranting demagogues, and by military sharks, is preparing for the same terrible feat.

In the face of this approaching disaster, it behooves men and women not yet overcome by the war madness to raise their voice of protest, to call the attention of the people to the crime and outrage which are about to be perpetrated upon them.

America is essentially the melting pot. No national unit composing it is in a position to boast of superior race purity, particular historic mission, or higher culture. Yet the jingoes and war speculators are filling the air with the sentimental slogan of hypocritical nationalism, "America for Americans," "America first, last, and all the time." This cry has caught the popular fancy from one end of the country to another. In order to maintain America, military preparedness must be engaged in at once. A billion dollars of the people's sweat and blood is to be expended for dreadnaughts and submarines for the army and the navy, all to protect this precious America.

The pathos of it all is that the America which is to be protected by a huge military force is not the America of the people, but that of the privileged class; the class which robs and exploits the masses, and controls their lives from the cradle to the grave. No less pathetic is it that so few people realize that preparedness never leads to peace, but that it is indeed the road to universal slaughter.

With the cunning methods used by the scheming diplomats and military cliques of Germany to saddle the masses with Prussian militarism, the American military ring with its Roosevelts, its Garrisons, its Daniels, and lastly its Wilsons, are moving the very heavens to place the militaristic heel upon the necks of the American people, and, if successful, will hurl America into the storm of blood and tears now devastating the countries of Europe.

Forty years ago Germany proclaimed the slogan: "Germany above everything. Germany for the Germans, first, last and always. We want peace; therefore we must prepare for war. Only a well armed and thoroughly prepared nation can maintain peace, can command respect, can be sure of its national integrity." And Germany continued to prepare, thereby forcing the other nations to do the same. The terrible European war is only the culminating fruition of the hydra-headed gospel, military preparedness.

Since the war began, miles of paper and oceans of ink have been used to prove the barbarity, the cruelty, the oppression of Prussian militarism. Conservatives and radicals alike are giving their support to the Allies for no other reason than to help crush that militarism, in the presence of which, they say, there can be no peace or progress in Europe. But though America grows fat on the manufacture of munitions and war loans to the Allies to help crush Prussians the same cry is now being raised in America which, if carried into national action, would build up an American militarism far more terrible than German or Prussian militarism could ever be, and that because nowhere in the world has capitalism become so brazen in its greed and nowhere is the state so ready to kneel at the feet of capital.

Like a plague, the mad spirit is sweeping the country, infesting the clearest heads and staunchest hearts with the deathly germ of militarism. National security leagues, with cannon as their emblem of protection, naval leagues with women in their lead have sprung up all over the country, women who boast of representing the gentler sex, women who in pain and danger bring forth life and yet are ready to dedicate it to the Moloch War. Americanization societies with well known liberals as members, they who but yesterday decried the patriotic clap-trap of to-day, are now lending themselves to befog the minds of the people and to help build up the same destructive institutions in America which they are directly and indirectly helping to pull down in Germany—militarism, the destroyer of youth, the raper of women, the annihilator of the best in the race, the very mower of life.

Even Woodrow Wilson, who not so long ago indulged in the phrase "A nation too proud to fight," who in the beginning of the war ordered prayers for peace, who in his proclamations spoke of the necessity of watchful waiting, even he has been whipped into line. He has now joined his worthy colleagues in the jingo movement, echoing their clamor for preparedness and their howl of "America for Americans." The difference between Wilson and Roosevelt is this: Roosevelt, a born bully, uses the club; Wilson, the historian, the college professor, wears the smooth polished university mask, but underneath it he, like Roosevelt, has but one aim, to serve the big interests, to add to those who are growing phenomenally rich by the manufacture of military supplies.

Woodrow Wilson, in his address before the Daughters of the American Revolution, gave his case away when he said, "I would rather be beaten than ostracized." To stand out against the Bethlehem, du Pont, Baldwin, Remington, Winchester metallic cartridges and the rest of the armament ring means political ostracism and death. Wilson knows that; therefore he betrays his original position, goes back on the bombast of "too proud to fight" and howls as loudly as any other cheap politician for preparedness and national glory, the silly pledge that navy league women intend to impose upon every school child: "I pledge myself to do all in my power to further the interests of my country, to uphold its institutions and to maintain the honor of its name and its flag. As I owe everything in life to my country, I consecrate my heart, mind and body to its service and promise to work for its advancement and security in times of peace and to shrink from no sacrifices or privation in its cause should I be called upon to act in its defence for the freedom, peace and happiness of our people."

To uphold the institutions of our country—that's it—the institutions which protect and sustain a handful of people in the robbery and plunder of the masses, the institutions which drain the blood of the native as well as of the foreigner, and turn it into wealth and power; the institutions which rob the alien of whatever originality he brings with him and in return gives him cheap Americanism, whose glory consists in mediocrity and arrogance.

The very proclaimers of "America first" have long before this betrayed the fundamental principles of real Americanism, of the kind of Americanism that Jefferson had in mind when he said that the best government is that which governs least; the kind of America that David Thoreau worked for when he proclaimed that the best government is the one that doesn't govern at all; or the other truly great Americans who aimed to make of this country a haven of refuge, who hoped that all the disinherited and oppressed people in coming to these shores would give character, quality and meaning to the country. That is not the America of the politician and munition speculators. Their America is powerfully portrayed in the idea of a young New York Sculptor; a hard cruel hand with long, lean, merciless fingers, crushing in over the heart of the immigrant, squeezing out its blood in order to coin dollars out of it and give the foreigner instead blighted hopes and stunted aspirations.

No doubt Woodrow Wilson has reason to defend these institutions. But what an ideal to hold out to the young generation! How is a military drilled and trained people to defend freedom, peace and happiness? This is what Major General O'Ryan has to say of an efficiently trained generation: "The soldier must be so trained that he becomes a mere automaton; he must be so trained that it will destroy his initiative; he must be so trained that he is turned into a machine. The soldier must be forced into the military noose; he must be jacked up; he must be ruled by his superiors with pistol in hand."

This was not said by a Prussian Junker; not by a German barbarian; not by Treitschke or Bernhardi, but by an American Major General. And he is right. You cannot conduct war with equals; you cannot have militarism with free born men; you must have slaves, automatons, machines, obedient disciplined creatures, who will move, act, shoot and kill at the command of their superiors. That is preparedness, and nothing else.

It has been reported that among the speakers before the Navy League was Samuel Gompers. If that is true, it signalizes the greatest outrage upon labor at the hands of its own leaders. Preparedness is not directed only against the external enemy; it aims much more at the internal enemy. It concerns that element of labor which has learned not to hope for anything from our institutions, that awakened part of the working people which has realized that the war of classes underlies all wars among nations, and that if war is justified at all it is the war against economic dependence and political slavery, the two dominant issues involved in the struggle of the classes.

Already militarism has been acting its bloody part in every economic conflict, with the approval and support of the state. Where was the protest of Washington when "our men, women and children" were killed in Ludlow? Where was that high sounding outraged protest contained in the note to Germany? Or is there any difference in killing "our men, women and children" in Ludlow or on the high seas? Yes, indeed. The men, women and children at Ludlow were working people, belonging to the disinherited of the earth, foreigners who had to be given a taste of the glories of Americanism, while the passengers of the *Lusitania* represented wealth and station—therein lies the difference.

Preparedness, therefore, will only add to the power of the privileged few and help them to subdue, to enslave and crush labor. Surely Gompers must know that, and if he joins the howl of the military clique, he must stand condemned as a traitor to the cause of labor.

Just as it is with all the other institutions in our confused life, which were supposedly created for the good of the people and have accomplished the very reverse, so it will be with preparedness. Supposedly, America is to prepare for peace; but in reality it will be the cause of war. It always has been thus—all through bloodstained history, and it will continue until nation will refuse to fight against nation, and until the people of the world will stop preparing for slaughter. Preparedness is like the seed of a poisonous plant; placed in the soil, it will bear poisonous fruit. The European mass destruction is the fruit of that poisonous seed. It is imperative that the American workers realize this before they are driven by the jingoes into the madness that is forever haunted by the spectre of danger and invasion; they must know that to prepare for peace means to invite war, means to unloose the furies of death over land and seas.

That which has driven the masses of Europe into the trenches and to the battlefields is not their inner longing for war; it must be traced to the cut-throat competition for military equipment, for more efficient armies, for larger warships, for more powerful cannon. You cannot build up a standing army and then throw it back into a box like tin soldiers. Armies equipped to the teeth with weapons, with highly developed instruments of murder and backed by their military interests, have their own dynamic functions. We have but to examine into the nature of militarism to realize the truism of this contention.

Militarism consumes the strongest and most productive elements of each nation. Militarism swallows the largest part of the national revenue. Almost nothing is spent on education, art, literature and science compared with the amount devoted to militarism in times of peace, while in times of war everything else is set at naught; all life stagnates, all effort is curtailed; the very sweat and blood of the masses are used to feed this insatiable monster—militarism. Under such circumstances, it must become more arrogant, more aggressive, more bloated with its own importance. If for no other reason, it is out of surplus energy that militarism must act to remain alive; therefore it will seek an enemy or create one artificially. In this civilized purpose and method, militarism is sustained by the state, protected by the laws of the land, fostered by the home and the school, and glorified by public opinion. In other words, the function of militarism is to kill. It cannot live except through murder.

But the most dominant factor of military preparedness and the one which inevitably leads to war, is the creation of group interests, which consciously and deliberately work for the increase of armament whose purposes are furthered by creating the war hysteria. This group interest embraces all those engaged in the manufacture and sale of munitions and in military equipment for personal gain and profit. For instance, the family Krupp, which owns the largest cannon munition plant in the world; its sinister influence in Germany, and in fact in many other countries, extends to the press, the school, the church and to statesmen of highest rank. Shortly before the war, Carl Liebknecht, the one brave public man in Germany now, brought to the attention of the Reichstag that the family Krupp had in its employ officials of the highest military position, not only in Germany, but in France and in other countries. Everywhere its emissaries have been at work, systematically inciting national hatreds and antagonisms. The same investigation brought to light an international war supply trust who care not a hang for patriotism, or for love of the people, but who use both to incite war and to pocket millions of profits out of the terrible bargain.

It is not at all unlikely that the history of the present war will trace its origin to this international murder trust. But is it always necessary for one generation to wade through oceans of blood and heap up mountains of human sacrifice that the next generation may learn a grain of truth from it all? Can we of to-day not profit by the cause which led to the European war, can we not learn that it was preparedness, thorough and efficient preparedness on the part of Germany and the other countries for military aggrandizement and material gain; above all can we not realize that preparedness in America must and will lead to the same result, the same barbarity, the same senseless sacrifice of life? Is America to follow suit, is it to be turned over to the American Krupps, the American military cliques? It almost seems so when one hears the jingo howls of the press, the blood and thunder tirades of bully Roosevelt, the sentimental twaddle of our college-bred President.

The more reason for those who still have a spark of libertarianism and humanity left to cry out against this great crime, against the outrage now being prepared and imposed upon the American people. It is not enough to claim being neutral; a neutrality which sheds crocodile tears with one eye and keeps the other riveted upon the profits from war supplies and war loans is not neutrality. It is a hypocritical cloak to cover the country's crimes. Nor is it enough to join the bourgeois pacifists, who proclaim peace among the nations, while helping to perpetuate the war among the classes, a war which in reality is at the bottom of all other wars.

It is this war of the classes that we must concentrate upon, and in that connection the war against false values, against evil institutions, against all social atrocities. Those who appreciate the urgent need of co-operating in great struggles must oppose military preparedness imposed by the state and capitalism for the destruction of the masses. They must organize the preparedness of the masses for the overthrow of both capitalism and the state. Industrial and economic preparedness is what the workers need. That alone leads to revolution at the bottom as against mass destruction from on top. That alone leads to true internationalism of labor against Kaiserdom, Kingdom, diplomacies, military cliques and bureaucracy. That alone will give the people the means to take their children out of the slums, out of the sweat shops and the cotton mills. That alone will enable them to inculcate in the coming generation a new ideal of brotherhood, to rear them in play and song and beauty; to bring up men and women, not automatons. That alone will enable woman to become the real mother of the race, who will give to the world creative men, and not soldiers who destroy. That alone leads to economic and social freedom, and does away with all wars, all crimes, and all injustice.

Angelina Grimké
(1805–1879)

Angelina Grimké was born on February 20, 1805 in Charleston, South Carolina. The last of fourteen children, she spent her first twenty-four years living on her family's plantation where she experienced both the advantages and disadvantages of an upper-class Southern life style. The advantages included private tutoring and the opportunity to exchange ideas and debate issues with some of the most prominent members of South Carolina political circles. The disadvantages, however, emerged clearer and clearer over the years as she daily encountered the travesties of slavery and as she discovered the hopelessness of influencing change as a lone individual. Hence, in 1829 she joined her older sister Sarah in Philadelphia in hopes that her sister's adopted Quaker religion would also become a source of solace for herself. By 1835 Angelina's impatience with the Quaker conservatism in response to the slavery question prompted her to join the Philadelphia Female Anti-Slavery Society. From that year until 1840 she tirelessly devoted her energies to the anti-slavery movement. In 1836 she wrote and published "An Appeal to the Christian Women of the South," which achieved popular acclaim and led to an invitation to move to New York City to conduct anti-slavery meetings for small groups of interested women. In 1837 she wrote and published "Appeal to the Women of the Nominally Free States," which increased her notoriety in the North and prompted the New England Anti-Slavery Association to ask her and her sister to join them for a lecture tour throughout New England. From 1837 to 1838, Angelina and Sarah toured New England and created a sensation by addressing mixed-sex audiences. The Congregational Ministerial Association of Massachusetts was so disturbed about their lecture tour that they issued a pastoral letter objecting to their "unwomanly behavior" for daring to speak to "promiscuous" audiences from a public platform. This rebuke only served to spark Angelina's interests in the rights of women and her subsequent series of letters in the *Liberator* of 1838, where she spoke out on a woman's right to speak anywhere and to have a voice in the formation of laws. In the same year Angelina demonstrated her woman's rights argument by becoming the first woman to testify before a committee of the Massachusetts Legislature and by delivering a series of lectures in Boston's Odeon Hall to mixed-sex audiences numbered in the thousands. In 1838 she married Theodore Weld, also an active member of the anti-slavery movement, although more conservative than his new wife. Two days after her marriage, Angelina delivered an impassioned hour-long address to a Philadelphia anti-slavery convention while an angry mob demonstrated outside and who later burned down the hall. This particular event led to her decision to cease her lecture career and promote the cause of anti-slavery through petitions and writing. In 1839 she and her husband published *American Slavery As It Is: Testimony of a Thousand Witnesses*, which Harriet Beecher Stowe drew heavily upon when she wrote *Uncle Tom's Cabin*. By 1840 Angelina, her husband and her sister had mostly retired from activity in the anti-slavery movement and, from that time until their deaths, the three of them taught in various schools throughout New Jersey and Massachusetts. In 1873 Angelina suffered a paralytic stroke which partially incapacitated her for the next six years before her death on October 26, 1879 at the age of 74.

The following speech was delivered on May 14, 1863 at the national convention of the Women's National Loyal League in New York City. The speech appears in printed form in *The History of Woman Suffrage*, Vol. II, pp. 54–56.

"The North, Go On! Go On!"

I came here with no desire and no intention to speak; but my heart is full, my country is bleeding, my people are perishing around me. But I feel as a South Carolinian, I am bound to tell the North, go on! go on! Never falter, never abandon the principles which you have adopted. I could not say this if we were now where we stood two years ago. I could not say thus when it was proclaimed in the Northern States that the Union was all that we sought. No, my friends, such a Union as we had then, God be praised that it has perished. Oh, never for one moment consent that such a Union should be re-established in our land. There was a time when I looked upon the Fathers of the Revolution with the deepest sorrow and the keenest reproach. I said to their shadows in another world, "Why did you leave this accursed system of slavery for us to suffer and die under? why did you not, with a stroke of the pen, determine—when you acquired your own independence—that the principles which you adopted in the Declaration of Independence should be a shield of protection to every man, whether he be slave or whether he be free?" But, my friends, the experience of sixty years has shown me that the fruit grows slowly. I look back and see that great Sower of the world, as he traveled the streets of Jerusalem and dropped the precious seed, "Do unto others as ye would that others should do unto you." I look at all the contests of different nations, and see that, whether it were the Patricians of Rome, England, France, or any part of Europe, every battle fought gained something to freedom. Our fathers, driven out by the oppression of England, came to this country and planted that little seed of liberty upon the soil of New England. When our Revolution took place, the seed was only in the process of sprouting. You must recollect that our Declaration of Independence was the very first National evidence of the great doctrine of brotherhood and equality. I verily believe that those who were the true lovers of liberty did all they could at that time. In their debates in the Convention they denounced slavery—they protested against the hypocrisy and inconsistency of a nation declaring such glorious truths, and then trampling them underfoot by enslaving the poor and oppressed, because he had a skin not colored like their own; as though a man's skin should make any difference in the recognition of his rights, any more than the color of his hair or of his eyes. This little blade sprouted as it were from the precious seeds that were planted by Jesus of Nazareth. But, my friends, if it took eighteen hundred years to bring forth the little blade which was seen in our Declaration, are we not unreasonable to suppose that more could have been done than has been done, looking at the imperfections of human nature, looking at the selfishness of man, looking at his desire for wealth and his greed for glory?

Had the South yielded at that time to the freemen of the North, we should have had a free Government; but it was impossible to overcome the long and strong prejudices of the South in favor of slavery. I know what the South is. I lived there the best part of my life. I never could talk against slavery without making my friends angry—never. When they thought the day was far off, and there was no danger of emancipation, they were willing to admit it was an evil; but when God in His providence raised up in this country an Anti-slavery Society, protesting against the oppressions of the colored man, they began to feel that truth which is more powerful than arms—that truth which is the only banner under which we can successfully fight. They were comparatively quiet till they found, in the election of Mr. Lincoln, the scepter had actually departed from them. His election took place on the ground that slavery was not to be extended—that it must not pass into the Territories. This was what alarmed them. They saw that if the National Government should take one such step, it never would stop there; that this principle had never before been acknowledged by those who had any power in the nation.

God be praised. Abolitionists never sought place or power. All they asked was freedom; all they wanted was that the white man should take his foot off the negro's neck. The South determined to resist the election of Mr. Lincoln. They determined if Fremont was elected, they would rebel. And this rebellion is like their own Republic, as they call it; it is founded upon slavery. As I asked one of my friends one day, "What are you rebelling for? The North never made any laws for you that they have not cheerfully obeyed themselves. What is the trouble between us?" Slavery, slavery is the trouble. Slavery is a "divine institution." My friends, it is a fact that the South has incorporated slavery into her religion; that is the most fearful thing in this rebellion. They are fighting, verily believing that they are doing God service. Most of them have never seen the North. They understand very little of the working of our institutions; but their politicians are stung to the quick by the prosperity of the North. They see that the institution which they have established can not make them wealthy, can not make them happy, can not make them respected in the world at large, and their motto is, "Rule or ruin."

Before I close, I would like, however strange it may seem, to utter a protest against what Mrs. Stanton said of colonizing the aristocrats in Liberia. I can not consent to such a thing. Do you know that Liberia has never let a slave tread her soil?—that when, from the interior of the country, the slaves came there to seek shelter, and their heathen masters pursued them, she never surrendered one? She stands firmly on the platform of freedom to all. I am deeply interested in this colony of Liberia. I do not want it to be cursed with the aristocracy of the South, or any other aristocracy, and far less with the Copperheadism of the North (Laughter). If these Southern aristocrats are to be colonized, Mrs. President, don't you think England is the best place for them? England is the country which has sympathized most deeply with them. She has allowed vessels to be built to prey upon our commerce; she has sent them arms and ammunition, and everything she could send through the West India Islands. Shall we send men to Liberia who are ready to tread the black man under their feet? No. God bless Liberia for what she has done, and what she is destined to do. (Applause).

I am very glad to say here, that last summer I had the pleasure of entertaining several times, in our house, a Liberian who was well educated in England. He had graduated at Oxford College, and had a high position there. His health broke down, and he went to Liberia. "When I went to Liberia," said he, "I had a first-rate education, and I supposed, of course, I would be a very superior man there; but I soon found that, though I knew a great deal more Greek and Latin and mathematics than most of the men there, I was a child to them in the science of government and history. "Why," said he, "you have no idea of the progress of Liberia. The men who go there are freemen— citizens; the burdens of society are upon them; and they feel that they must begin to educate themselves, and they are self-educated men. The President of Liberia, Mr. Benson, was a slave about seven years ago on a plantation in this country. He went to Liberia. He was a man of uncommon talents. He educated himself to the duties which he found himself called upon to perform as a citizen. And when Mr. Benson visited England a year ago, he had a perfect ovation. The white ladies and gentlemen of England, those who were really anti-slavery in their feelings—who love liberty—followed him wherever he went. They opened their houses, they had their *soirees,* and they welcomed him by every kind of demonstration of their good wishes for Liberia."

Now, Mrs. President, the great object that I had in view in rising, was to give you a representative from South Carolina. (Applause). I mourn exceedingly that she has taken the position she has. I once had a brother who, had he been there, would have stood by Judge Pettigrew in his protest against the action of the South. He, many years ago, during the time of nullification in 1832, was in the Senate of South Carolina, and delivered an able address, in which he discussed these very points, and showed that the South had no right of secession; that, in becoming an integral part of the United States, they had themselves voluntarily surrendered that right. And he remarked, "If you persist in this contest, you will be like a girdled tree, which must perish and die. You can not stand."

Frances Harper
(1825–1911)

Frances Harper was born on September 24, 1825 in Baltimore, Maryland. The only child of free Negro parents, she became orphaned before she was three years of age and spent most of her childhood with her uncle's family. After attending her uncle's school for free Negroes, she left in 1839 to earn her living by doing domestic work for a Baltimore bookseller where she learned to sew and where she read voraciously in her spare time. In 1850 Frances became a sewing teacher at Union Seminary near Columbus, Ohio and in 1852 she secured a teaching position in Little York, Pennsylvania. During this time period she came into contact with numerous abolitionists and with their encouragement she delivered her first antislavery lecture in New Bedford, Massachusetts in August of 1854. Her immediate success as a speaker launched her career as a reformer. Engaged as lecturer by the Maine Anti-Slavery Society, she traveled throughout the state for two years, and from 1856 to 1860 she lectured in Pennsylvania, New Jersey, New York and Ohio. Frances varied her talks using recitations of her antislavery verse from her book *Poems on Miscellaneous Subjects,* which was published in 1854 and which sold 12,000 copies by 1858. On November 22, 1860 she briefly interrupted her career with her marriage to Fenton Harper, but once again returned to the lecture circuit when he died in 1864. For several years after the Civil War she toured the South addressing both black and racially mixed audiences about the need for education, temperance, and a higher standard of domestic morality among blacks, but she also spoke out strongly against white racial violence. In 1871, Frances settled in Philadelphia and published several works: *Sketches of Southern Life* (1872), *Iola Leroy, or Shadows Uplifted* (1892), and *The Martyr of Alabama and Other Poems* (1894). In her later years, she also turned to other reform causes. From 1883 to 1890 Frances served as head of the Department for Work among Negroes of the National Woman's Christian Temperance Union. She organized several Sunday schools in Philadelphia to help curb delinquency, and in 1894 became a director of the American Association of Education of Colored Youth. In 1896 she became an active organizer of the National Association of Colored Women, an extension of her long-time advocacy of women's rights. On February 22, 1911 Frances died in Philadelphia at the age of eighty-five.

The following speech was delivered before the New York City Anti-Slavery Society on their 4th anniversary, May 13, 1857. It was later printed in the *National Anti-Slavery Standard,* (May 23, 1857), p. 3. According to biographers, this is the only extant anti-slavery speech delivered by Frances Harper.

"Liberty for Slaves"

Could we trace the record of every human heart, the aspirations of every immortal soul, perhaps we would find no man so imbruted and degraded that we could not trace the word liberty either written in living characters upon the soul or hidden away in some nook or corner of the heart. The law of liberty is the law of God, and is antecedent to all human legislation. It existed in the mind of Deity when He hung the first world upon its orbit and gave it liberty to gather light from the central sun.

Some people say, set the slaves free. Did you ever think, if the slaves were free, they would steal everything they could lay their hands on from now till the day of their death—that they would steal more than two thousand millions of dollars? (applause) Ask Maryland, with her tens of thousands of slaves, if she is not prepared for freedom, and hear her answer: "I help supply the coffee-gangs of the South." Ask Virginia, with her hundreds of thousands of slaves, if she is not weary with her merchandise of blood and anxious to shake the gory traffic from her hands, and hear her reply: "Though fertility has covered my soil, though a genial sky bends over my hills and vales, though I hold in my hand a wealth of water-power enough to turn the spindles to clothe the world, yet, with all these advantages, one of my chief staples has been the sons and daughters I send to the human market and human shambles." (applause) Ask the farther South, and all the cotton-growing States chime in, "We have need of fresh supplies to fill the ranks of those whose lives have gone out in unrequited toil on our distant plantations."

A hundred thousand new-born babes are annually added to the victims of slavery; twenty thousand lives are annually sacrificed on the plantations of the South. Such a sight should send a thrill of horror through the nerves of civilization and impel the heart of humanity to lofty deeds. So it might, if men had not found out a fearful alchemy by which this blood can be transformed into gold. Instead of listening to the cry of agony, they listen to the ring of dollars and stoop down to pick up the coin. (applause)

But a few months since a man escaped from bondage and found a temporary shelter almost beneath the shadow of Bunker Hill. Had that man stood upon the deck of an Austrian ship, beneath the shadow of the house of the Hapsburgs, he would have found protection. Had he been wrecked upon an island or colony of Great Britain, the waves of the tempest-lashed ocean would have washed him deliverance. Had he landed upon the territory of vine-encircled France and a Frenchman had reduced him to a thing and brought him here beneath the protection of our institutions and our laws, for such a nefarious deed that Frenchman would have lost his citizenship in France. Beneath the feebler light which glimmers from the Koran, the Bey of Tunis would have granted him freedom in his own dominions. Beside the ancient pyramids of Egypt he would have found liberty, for the soil laved by the glorious Nile is now consecrated to freedom. But from Boston harbour, made memorable by the infusion of three-penny taxed tea, Boston in its proximity to the plains of Lexington and Concord, Boston almost beneath the shadow of Bunker Hill and almost in sight of Plymouth Rock, he is thrust back from liberty and manhood and reconverted into a chattel. You have heard that, down South, they keep bloodhounds to hunt slaves. Ye bloodhounds, go back to your kennels; when you fail to catch the flying fugitive, when his stealthy tread is heard in the place where the bones of the revolutionary sires repose, the ready North is base enough to do your shameful service. (applause)

Slavery is mean, because it tramples on the feeble and weak. A man comes with his affidavits from the South and hurries me before a commissioner; upon that evidence *ex parte* and alone he hitches me to the car of slavery and trails my womanhood in the dust. I stand at the threshold of the Supreme Court and ask for justice, simple justice. Upon my tortured heart is thrown the mocking words, "You are a negro; you have no rights which white men are bound to respect"! (loud and long-continued applause) Had it been my lot to have lived beneath the Crescent instead of the Cross, had injustice and violence been heaped upon my head as a Mohammedan woman, as a member of a common faith, I might have demanded justice and been listened to by the Pasha, the Bey or the Vizier; but when I come here to ask for justice, men tell me, "We have no higher law than the Constitution". (applause)

But I will not dwell on the dark side of the picture. God is on the side of freedom; and any cause that has God on its side, I care not how much it may be trampled upon, how much it may be trailed in the dust, is sure to triumph. The message of Jesus Christ is on the side of freedom, "I come to preach deliverance to the captives, the opening of the prison doors to them that are bound." The truest and noblest hearts in the land are on the side of freedom. They may be hissed at by slavery's minions, their names cast out as evil, their characters branded with fanaticism, but O, *"To side with Truth is noble when we share her humble crust Ere the cause bring fame and profit and it's prosperous to be just."*

May I not, in conclusion, ask every honest, noble heart, every seeker after truth and justice, if they will not also be on the side of freedom. Will you not resolve that you will abate neither heart nor hope till you hear the death-knell of human bondage sounded, and over the black ocean of slavery shall be heard a song, more exulting than the song of Miriam when it floated o'er Egypt's dark sea, the requiem of Egypt's ruined hosts and the anthem of the deliverance of Israel's captive people? (great applause)

Anne Hutchinson
(c. 1591–1643)

Anne Hutchinson was born in the year 1591 in Alford, Lincolnshire, England. As the second of thirteen children, Anne grew up in a rebellious religious household, her father being an Anglican clergyman who was frequently censured and imprisoned for his insistence on capable clergy. In 1605 the family moved to London where Anne remained until she married William Hutchinson in 1612. For the next twenty-two years Anne and her husband resided in Alford where they expanded their family to include twelve children. During her time in Alford Anne came under the influence of John Cotton, vicar of an Anglican church with Puritan leanings. She became so thoroughly immersed in Cotton's conceptions of salvation that when he was compelled to flee to Boston, Massachusetts in 1633 she convinced her family to follow him there in 1634. Anne's husband quickly became a prosperous businessman and the family soon entertained members of the highest level of colonial society. Anne's social gatherings with wives prompted her to hold private conferences in her home to enlighten them about her version of John Cotton's religious views. These small gatherings soon expanded into larger meetings held twice weekly and began to include men as well as women. Anne's meetings escaped critical comment for some time until in 1635 a Puritan clergyman named Wilson began to hear of her critical contrasts between his preachings and Cotton's. For the next two years the town of Boston and the rest of the colony became divided into two warring camps. Finally in March, 1637 the General Court condemned all the errors maintained by Anne, and in November the same court brought her to trial for "traducing the ministers and their ministry," and sentenced her to banishment from the colony. In March of 1638 she was once again brought to trial by the Church of Boston where she was accused of lying and formally excommunicated. Soon thereafter she and her children left for Rhode Island to join her husband and friends in a newly established settlement on the island of Aquidnick in Narragansett Bay. After her husband died in 1642, Anne and her six youngest children moved to the Dutch colony of New Netherland (in what is now Pelham Bay Park in the Bronx). One year later Anne and all but her youngest child were massacred by Indians.

The following testimony is part of the court transcript of "The Examination of Mrs. Anne Hutchinson at the Court at Newtown," November, 1637. It appeared in printed form as an appendix to the second volume of Thomas Hutchinson, *History of the Colony and Province of Massachusetts Bay* (Boston, Ma., 1767).

"The Examination of Mrs. Anne Hutchinson"

Mrs. H. If you please to give me leave I shall give you the ground of what I know to be true. Being much troubled to see the falseness of the constitution of the church of England, I had like to have turned separatist; whereupon I kept a day of solemn humiliation and pondering of the thing; this scripture was brought unto me—he that denies Jesus Christ to be come in the flesh is antichrist—This I considered of and in considering found that the papists did not deny him to be come in the flesh, nor we did not deny him—who then was antichrist? Was the Turk antichrist only? The Lord knows that I could not open scripture; he must by his prophetical office open it unto me. So after that being unsatisfied in the thing, the Lord was pleased to bring this scripture out of the Hebrews. He that denies the testament denies the testator, and in this did open unto me and give me to see that those which did not teach the new covenant had the spirit of antichrist, and upon this he did discover the ministry unto me and ever since. I bless the Lord, he hath let me see which was the clear ministry and which the wrong. Since that time I confess I have been more choice and he hath let me to distinguish between the voice of my beloved and the voice of Moses, the voice of John Baptist and the voice of antichrist, for all those voices are spoken of in scripture. Now if you do condemn me for speaking what in my conscience I know to be truth I must commit myself unto the Lord.

Mr. Nowell. How do you know that that was the spirit?

Mrs. H. How did Abraham know that it was God that bid him offer his son, being a breach of the sixth commandment?

Dep. Gov. By an immediate voice.

Mrs. H. So to me by an immediate revelation.

Dep. Gov. How! an immediate revelation.

Mrs. H. By the voice of his own spirit to my soul. I will give you another scripture, Jer. 46. 27, 28—out of which the Lord shewed me what he would do for me and the rest of his servants.—But after he was pleased to reveal himself to me I did presently like Abraham run to Hagar. And after that he did let me see the atheism of my own heart, for which I begged of the Lord that it might not remain in my heart, and being thus, he did shew me this (a twelvemonth after) which I told you of before. Ever since that time I have been confident of what he hath revealed unto me.

Obliterated another place out of Daniel chap. 7. and he and for us all, wherein he shewed me the sitting of the judgment and the standing of all high and low before the Lord and how thrones and kingdoms were cast down before him. When our teacher came to New-England it was a great trouble unto me, my brother Wheelwright being put by also. I was then much troubled concerning the ministry under which I lived, and then that place in the 30th of Isaiah was brought to my mind. Though the Lord give thee bread of adversity and water of affliction yet shall not thy teachers be removed into corners any more, but thine eyes shall see thy teachers. The Lord giving me this promise and they being gone there was none then left that I was able to hear, and I could not be at rest but I must come hither. Yet that place of Isaiah did much follow me, though the Lord give thee the bread of adversity and water of affliction. This place lying I say upon me then this place in Daniel was brought unto me and did shew me that though I should meet with affliction yet I am the same God that delivered Daniel out of the lion's den, I will also deliver thee.—Therefore I desire you to look to it, for you see this scripture fulfilled this day and therefore I desire you that as you tender the Lord and the church and commonwealth to consider and look what you do. You have power over my body but the Lord Jesus hath power over my body and soul, and assure yourselves thus much, you do as much as in you lies to put the Lord Jesus Christ from you, and if you go on in this course you begin you will bring a curse upon you and your posterity, and the mouth of the Lord hath spoken it.

Dep. Gov. What is the scripture she brings?

Mr. Stoughton. Behold I turn away from you.

Mrs. H. But now having seen him which is invisible I fear not what man can do unto me.

Gov. Daniel was delivered by miracle do you think to be deliver'd so too?

Mrs. H. I do here speak it before the court. I look that the Lord should deliver me by his providence.

Mary Harris "Mother" Jones
(1830?–1930)

Mary Harris Jones was born on May 1, 1830? in Cork, Ireland. The oldest of three children, she moved to Toronto, Canada at the age of eight where she attended public schools and graduated from high school in 1837. From 1847 to 1861, Mary taught public school in Toronto, taught in Saint Mary's Convent in Monroe, Michigan and served for a brief stint as a dressmaker in Chicago. In 1861 she moved to Memphis, Tennessee to assume yet another teaching post, and there she met and married George Jones, an iron molder. After the yellow fever epidemic of 1867 had resulted in the tragic death of her husband and four children, Mary returned to Chicago and opened up a dress shop with the meager funds left to her from her husband's union pension. Four years later the 1871 fire that razed much of Chicago also destroyed her dress shop. Now destitute, Mary managed to find dressmaking jobs with the wealthy families who lived along Lake Michigan. From 1871 to 1891 she attended union meetings in her spare time, suffered the labor panic of 1873, participated in minor ways in the railroad strikes of the late 1870's, and witnessed the Haymarket Square Riot of 1886. In 1891, at the age of 61, Mary travelled to her first coal strike in Virginia, and from that day on she would be known as "Mother Jones." From Virginia Mary moved on to the anthracite strikes in West Virginia and Pennsylvania in the 1890's and early 1900's. From 1903 to 1905 she went back and forth between northern and southern coal strike zones in Colorado and served her first stint in jail as a "labor agitator." Between 1905 and 1912 Mary campaigned for copper miners in Michigan, Arizona and Montana and coal miners in Pennsylvania. The years 1912-13 found her in West Virginia again fighting for coal miners and once again serving time in jail. Then back to Colorado from 1913 to 1915 for the mine wars there and more time spent in jail. In 1915 she travelled back to Michigan to help copper miners once more, and in 1921 she made her third and final trip to the West Virginia coal mines. In between battles for miners, Mary led a 22-day children's march from Pennsylvania to New York City to publicize the need for child labor laws, joined women bottlers on strike in Wisconsin, women shirtwaist makers and dressmakers on strike in New York City, Philadelphia and Chicago, aided striking railroad employees in the West and Pacific Northwest, and fought for steel strikers in Pennsylvania and Ohio. Mary also sold and wrote articles for the Socialist magazine *Appeal to Reason,* helped found the Socialist Labor Party and the International Workers of the World, exerted continuous effort on behalf of Mexican revolutionaries in exile in America, attended the Pan-American Labor Congress in Mexico, and wrote and published a 255-page autobiography. On November 30, 1930 Mary Harris "Mother" Jones finally lay down to rest at the age of one hundred years and six months.

The following speech was delivered on the front steps of the State Capital building in Charleston, West Virginia, on August 15, 1912. It was later reprinted in the U.S. Congressional Hearings, "Conditions in the Paint Creek District, West Virginia," Subcommittee of the Committee on Education and Labor, U.S. Senate, 63rd Congress, 1st Session, September 1913, pp. 2262-2275.

"Appeal to the Cause of Miners in the Paint Creek District"

This, my friends, marks, in my estimation, the most remarkable move ever made in the State of West Virginia. It is a day that will mark history in the long ages to come. What is it? It is an uprising of the oppressed against the master class.

From this day on, my friends, Virginia—West Virginia—shall march in the front of the Nation's States. To me, I think, the proper thing to do is to read the purpose of our meeting here today—why these men have laid down their tools, why these men have come to the statehouse.

To His Excellency WILLIAM E. GLASSCOCK,
  Governor of the State of West Virginia:

It is respectfully represented unto your excellency that the owners of the various coal mines doing business along the valley of Cabin Creek, Kanawha County, W. Va., are maintaining and have at present in their employ a large force of armed guards, armed with Winchesters, a dangerous and deadly weapon; also having in their possession three Gatling guns, which they have stationed at commanding positions overlooking the Cabin Creek Valley, which said weapons said guards use for the purpose of browbeating, intimidating, and menacing the lives of all the citizens who live in said valley, who are not in accord with the management of the coal companies, which guards are cruel, and their conduct toward the citizens is such that it would be impossible to give a detailed account of.

Therefore suffice it to say, however, that they beat, abuse, maim, and hold up citizens without process of law; deny freedom of speech, a provision guaranteed by the Constitution; deny the citizens the right to assemble in a peaceable manner for the purpose of discussing questions in which they are concerned. Said guards also hold up a vast body of laboring men who live at the mines, and so conduct themselves that a great number of men, women, and children live in a state of constant fear, unrest, and dread.

We hold that the stationing of said guards along the public highways and public places is a menace to the general welfare of the State. That such action on the part of the companies in maintaining such guards is detrimental to the best interests of society and an outrage against the honor and dignity of the State of West Virginia. [Loud applause.]

As citizens interested in the public weal and general welfare, and believing that law and order and peace should ever abide, that the spirit of brotherly love and justice and freedom should everywhere exist, we must tender our petition that you would bring to bear all the powers of your office as chief executive of this State for the purpose of disarming said guards and restoring to the citizens of said valley all the rights guaranteed by the Constitution of the United States and said State.

In duty bound, in behalf of the miners of the State of West Virginia.

I want to say, with all due respect to the governor—I want to say to you that the governor will not, can not, do anything, for this reason: The governor was placed in this building by Scott and Elkins and he don't dare oppose them. [Loud applause.] Therefore you are asking the governor of the State to do something that he can not do without betraying the class he belongs to. [Loud applause.]

I remember the governor in a State, when Grover Cleveland was perched in the White House— Grover Cleveland said he would send the Federal troops out, and the governor of that State said, "Will you? If you do, I will meet your Federal troops with the State troops, and we will have it out." Old Grover never sent the troops; he took back water. [Applause and cries of "Yes; he did."]

You see, my friends, how quickly the governor sent his militia when the coal operators got scared to death. [Applause.]

I have no objection to the militia. I would always prefer the militia, but there was no need in this country for the militia; none whatever. They were law-abiding people, and the women and children. They were held up on the highways, caught in their homes, and pulled out like rats and beaten up—some of them. I said, "If there is no one else in the State of West Virginia to protest, I will protest." [Loud applause, and cries of "Yes, she will: 'Mother' will."]

The womanhood of this State shall not be oppressed and beaten and abused by a lot of contemptible, damnable bloodhounds hired by the operators. They wouldn't keep their dog where they keep you fellows. You know that. They have a good place for their dogs and a slave to take care of them. The mine owners' wives will take the dogs up, and say, "I love you, dea-h" [trying to imitate by tone of voice].

My friends the day for petting dogs is gone; the day for raising children to a nobler manhood and better womanhood is here. [Applause and cries of "Amen! Amen!"]

You have suffered; I know you have suffered. I was with you nearly three years in this State. I went to jail; went to the Federal courts; but I never took any back water. I still unfurl the red flag of industrial freedom; no tyrant's face shall you know, and I call you today into that freedom—long perch on the bosom—[Interrupted by applause.]

I am back again to find you, my friends, in a state of industrial peonage—after 10 years' absence I find you in a state of industrial peonage.

The superintendent at Acme—I went up there, and they said we were unlawful—we had an unlawful mob along. Well, I will tell you the truth; we took a couple of guns because we knew we were going to meet some thugs, and by jimminy—[Interrupted by applause.]

We will prepare for the job, just like Lincoln and Washington did. We took lessons from them, and we are here to prepare for the job.

Well, when I came out on the public road the superintendent—you know the poor salary slave—he came out and told me that there were notaries public there and a squire—one had a peg leg—and the balance had pegs in their skulls. [Applause.]

They forbid me speaking on the highway, and said that if I didn't discontinue I would be arrested. Well, I want to tell you one thing, I don't run into jail, but when the bloodhounds undertake to put me in jail I will go there. I have gone there. I would have had the little peg-leg squire arrest me, only I knew this meeting was going to be pulled off to-day, to let the world know what was going on in West Virginia. When I get through with them, by the Eternal God, they will be glad to let me alone.

I am not afraid of jails. We build the jails, and when we get ready we will put them behind the bars. That may happen very soon; things happen overnight.

Now, brothers, not in all the history of the labor movement have I got such an inspiration as I have got from you here to-day. Your banners are history; they will go down to the future ages, to the children unborn, to tell them the slave has risen, children must be free.

The labor movement was not originated by man. The labor movement, my friends, was a command from God Almighty. He commanded the prophets thousands of years ago to go down and redeem the Israelites that were in bondage, and he organized the men into a union and went to work. And they said, "The masters have made us gather straw; they have been more cruel than they were before." "What are we going to do?" The prophet said, "A voice from heaven has come to get you together." They got together and the prophet led them out of the land of bondage and robbery and plunder into the land of freedom. And when the army of the pirates followed them the Dead Sea opened and swallowed them up, and for the first time the workers were free.

And so it is. That can well be applied to the State of West Virginia. When I left Cabin Creek 10 years ago to go to another terrific battle field every man on Cabin Creek was organized—every single miner. The mine owners and the miners were getting along harmoniously; they had an understanding and were carrying it out. But they had some traitors who made a deal with the mine owners and the organization was driven out of Cabin Creek. There were no better miners in the whole State of West Virginia than on Cabin Creek, and no better operators in those days. You got along together. They were trying to make it happy and comfortable for you, but the demon came and tore the organization to pieces and you are at war to-day.

I hope, my friends, that you and the mine owners will put aside the breach and get together before I leave the State. But I want to say, make no settlement until they sign up that every bloody murderer of a guard has got to go. [Loud applause.]

This is done, my friends, beneath the flag our fathers fought and bled for, and we don't intend to surrender our liberty. [Applause.]

I have a document issued 18 years ago telling how they must handle the labor movement—pat them on the back; make them believe that they were your devoted friends. I hold the document, taken from their statement in Washington. It plainly states, "We have got to crucify them, but we have got to do it cunningly." And they have been doing it cunningly. But I want to say, in answer to your statements, that you are dealing with a different class of workers to-day than 18 years ago. We have begun education; we have educated the workers and you can't enslave them. They will come again, and you will either take to the ocean and get out of the Nation and leave us alone or you will settle right with us. [Loud applause.]

It is different now, my friends. It was Mark Hanna who said some years ago—the shrewdest politician America ever had—he said, "I want to tell you that before 1912 the Republican and Democratic Parties will be about to get their deathblow."

Never in the history of the United States was there such an upheaval as there is to-day. The politicians are cutting each other's throats, eating each other up; they are for the offices. Teddy, the monkey chaser, had a meeting in Chicago. He was blowing his skull off his carcass about race suicide. God Almighty, bring him down the C. & O. and he will never say another word about race suicide. The whole population seems to be made up out of "kids." Every woman has three babies in her arms and nine on the floor. So you will see there is no danger of race suicide. When he sees this he will keep his mouth shut on that.

See the condition we are in today. There is a revolution. There is an editorial in one of the papers in your own State showing how little they have done for the workers, that the workers are awakening. The literature is being circulated among them. I myself have circulated millions and millions of pieces of literature in this country and awakened the miners. On the trains they say, "Oh, Mother, you gave us a book that woke us up." As long as you woke up right, it is all right. He says, "I have woke up right." Then, if you woke up right, you are my children.

O you men of wealth! O you preachers! You are going over to China and sending money over there for Jesus. For God's sake, keep it at home; we need it. Let me tell you, them fellows are owned body and soul by the ruling class and they would rather take a year in hell with Elkins than ninety-nine in heaven. [Loud applause.] Do you find a minister preaching against the guards?

[Cries from the audience "They are traitors; moral cowards."]

He will preach about Jesus, but not about the guards.

When we were crossing the bridge at Washington the bloodhounds were at the company store. These bloodhounds might have thrown me into the river and I wouldn't have known it. The men were hollering "Police! Police!" I said, "What is the matter with you?" They said, "O God! Murder! Murder!" Another one came out, and his feet never touched the sidewalk.

My boys came running to me and said, "Oh, Mother, they are killing the boys." The traction car turned the corner. I said, "Call them boys here." Then they went; they thought I had an army with me. Then I picked up a boy streaming with blood where the hounds had beat him.

You are to blame. You have voted for the whole gang of commercial pirates every time you get a chance to free yourselves.

It is time to clean them up.

[Cries of "She is right; she is right!"]

If this Nation is to march onward and upward, the day of change is here.

I had been reading of the *Titanic* when she went down. Did you read of her? The big guns wanted to save themselves, and the fellows that were guiding below took up a club and said, "We will save our people." And then the papers came out and said those millionaires tried to save the women. O, Lord, why don't they give up their millions if they want to save the women and children? Why do they rob them of home; why do they rob millions of women to fill the hell holes of capitalism?

I realize—I remember what they did to me—the Guggenheims—I remember what the Guggenheim bloodhounds did to me one night in Colorado. They went to the hotel after we had organized the slaves. I took the 4 o'clock train for the southern fields, and the bloodhounds, the chief of police, and the whole gang of commercial bloodhounds came up to the hotel and went to the register to find my room, and the hotel keeper said that I had left at 4 o'clock. We had a meeting that night. They took a fellow and drove him down the street barefooted and put him on the train and told him never to come back. And we are very civilized! They don't do that in Russia; it is in America.

They took me and put me in jail—I had the smallpox—I had the Helen Gould smallpox covering me all over. And at 4 o'clock in the morning they came and the bloodhounds—Helen Gould's bloodhounds—and they bound 400 miners in Colorado for gold, and threw their widows and orphans out on the highways in the snow. When I was fighting a battle with those wretches they put me into a pen which you built, a pesthouse, it was burned down before morning, it wasn't worth 50 cents. We went down by a store, and the storekeeper said, "God Almighty, put us down in the cellar and they won't know us, put the dirty clothes on us—when them dirty clothes found out that there was such a lot of rotten carcasses under them, the dirty clothes turned over." [Applause and laughter.]

If your sheriff had done his duty as a citizen of this State and according to his oath, he would have disarmed the guards and then there would have been no more trouble.

(Cries of: "That is right, that is right.")

Just make me governor for one month. I won't ask for a sheriff or policeman, and I will do business, and there won't be a guard stay in the State of West Virginia. [Applause.] The mine owners won't take 69,000 pounds of coal in dockage off of you fellows. Sixty-nine thousand pounds of coal they docket you for, and a few pounds of slate, and then they give to Jesus on Sunday.

They give your missionary women a couple of hundred dollars and rob you under pretense of giving to Jesus. Jesus never sees a penny of it, and never heard of it. They use it for the women to get a jag on and then go and hollow for Jesus.

I wish I was God Almighty, I would throw down something some night from heaven and get rid of the whole blood-sucking bunch. [Laughter and applause.]

I want to show you here that the average wages you fellows get in this country is $500 a year. Before you get a thing to eat there is $20 taken out a month, which leaves about $24 a month.

Then you go to the "pluck-me" stores and want to get something to eat for your wife, and you are off that day, and the child comes back and says, "Papa, I can't get anything." "Why," he says, "There is $4 coming to me." The child says, "They said there was nothing coming to you." And the child goes back crying without a mouthful of anything to eat. The father goes to the "pluck-me" store and says to the manager, "There is $4 coming to me," and the manager says,

"Oh, no; we have kept that for rent." "You charge $6 a month, and there are only three days gone." "Well," he says, "It is a rule that two-thirds of the rent is to be kept if there is only one day."

That is honesty. Do you wonder these women starve? Do you wonder at this uprising? And you fellows have stood it entirely too long. It is time now to put a stop to it. We will give the governor until to-morrow night to take them guards out of Cabin Creek.

(Very loud applause, and cries of: "And no longer.")

Here on the steps of the Capital of West Virginia, I say that if the governor won't make them go then we will make them go.

(Loud applause, and cries of "That we will," "Only one more day," "The guards have got to go.")

We have come to the chief executive, we have asked him, and he couldn't do anything. [Laughter.]

The prosecuting attorney is of the same type—another fellow belonging to the ruling class. [Applause and murmurings in the crowd.] Hush up there, hush up, hush up.

I want to tell you that the governor will get until to-morrow night, Friday night, to get rid of his bloodhounds, and if they are not gone, we will get rid of them. [Loud applause.]

Aye men, aye men, inside of this building, aye women, come with me and see the horrible pictures, see the horrible condition the ruling class has put these women in. Aye, they destroy women. Look at those little children, the rising generation, yes, look at the little ones, yes, look at the women assaulted. Some one said that that place ought to be drained up there. The mine owner's home is drained; the superintendent's home is drained. But I want to ask you, when a man works 10 or 11 hours in the foul gas of the mine day after day, if he is in condition to come out and drain.

[Cries of "Not on your life; no."]

I have worked, boys, I have worked with you for years. I have seen the suffering children, and in order to be convinced I went into the mines on the night shift and day shift and helped the poor wretches to load coal at times. We lay down at noon and we took our lunches and we talked our wrongs over, we gathered together at night and asked "How will we remedy things?" We organized secretly, and after a while held public meetings. We got our people together in those organized States. To-day the mine owners and the miners come together. They meet each other and shake hands, and have no more war in those States, and the workingmen are becoming more intelligent. And I am one of those my friends, I don't care about your woman suffrage and the temperance brigade or any other of your class associations, I want women of the coming day to discuss and find out the cause of child crucifixion, that is what I want to find out.

I have worked in the factories of Georgia and Alabama, and these bloodhounds were tearing the hands off of children and working them 14 hours a day until I fought for them. They made them put up every Saturday money for missionary work in China. I know what I am talking about. I am not talking haphazard, I have the goods.

Go down, men of to-day, who rob and exploit, go down into hell and look at the ruins you have put there, look at the jails. We pay $6,000,000 a year to chain men like demons in a bastile—and we call ourselves civilized. Six million dollars a year we pay for jails, and nothing for education.

I have been in jail more than once, and I expect to go again. If you are too cowardly to fight, I will fight. You ought to be ashamed of yourselves, actually to the Lord you ought, just to see one old woman who is not afraid of all the bloodhounds. How scared those villains are when one woman 80 years old, with her head gray, can come in and scare hell out of the whole bunch.

90

[Laughter.] We didn't scare them? The mine owners run down the street like a mad dog to-day. They ask who started this thing. I started it, I did it, and I am not afraid to tell you if you are here, and I will start more before I leave West Virginia. I started this mass meeting to-day, I had these banners written, and don't accuse anybody else of the job. [Loud applause.]

It is freedom or death, and your children will be free. We are not going to leave a slave class to the coming generation, and I want to say to you that the next generation will not charge us for what we have done; they will charge and condemn us for what we have left undone. [Cries of "That is right."]

You have got your bastile. Yes; we have no fears of them at all. I was put out at 12 o'clock at night—and landed with 5 cents in my pocket—by seven bayonets in the State of Colorado. The governor told me—he is a corporation rat, you know—he told me never to come back. A man is a fool, if he is a governor, to tell a woman not to do a thing. [Loud applause, and cries of "Tell them again; tell them about it."]

I went back next day and I have been back since the fight, and he hasn't bothered me. He has learned it won't do to tamper with women of the right metal. You have a few cats [mocking]— they are not women, they are what you call ladies. There is a difference between women and ladies. The modern parasites made ladies, but God Almighty made women. [Applause and cries of "Tell us one more."]

Now, my boys, you are mine; we have fought together, we have hungered together, we have marched together, but I can see victory in the Heavens for you. I can see the hand above you guiding and inspiring you to move onward and upward. No white flag—we can not raise it; we must not raise it. We must redeem the world.

Go into our factories, see how the conditions are there, see how women are ground up for the merciless money pirates, see how many of the poor wretches go to work with crippled bodies. I talked with a mother who had her small children working. She said to me, "Mother, they are not of age, but I had to say they were; I had to tell them they were of age so they could get a chance to help me to get something to eat." She said after they were there a little while, "I have saved $40, the first I ever saw. I put that into a cow and we had some milk for the little ones." In all the years her husband had put in the earth digging out wealth, he never got a glimpse of $40 until he had to take his infant boys, that ought to go to school, and sacrifice them.

If there was no other reason that should stimulate every man and woman to fight this damnable system of commercial pirates. [Cries of "Right, right."] That alone should do it, my friends.

Is there a committee here? I want to take a committee of the well-fed fellows and well-dressed fellows; I want to present this to the governor. Be very polite. Don't get on your knees. Get off your knees and stand up. None of these fellows are better than you, they are only flesh and blood— that is the truth.

(Committee formed around "Mother" and start into the capitol building.) These fellows all want to go and see the king. [Laughter.]

I will give the press a copy of this resolution and this petition, that was given to the governor.

Now, my boys, guard rule and tyranny will have to go; there must be an end. I am going up Cabin Creek. I am going to hold meetings there. I am going to claim the right of an American citizen. I was on this earth before these operators were. I was in this country before these operators. I have been 74 years under this flag. I have got the right to talk. I have seen its onward march. I have seen the growth of oppression, and I want to say to you, my friends, I am going to claim my right as a citizen of this Nation. I won't violate the law; I will not kill anybody or starve anybody; but I will talk unsparingly of all the corporation bloodhounds we can bring to jail. [Laughter.]

I have no apologies to offer. I have seen your children murdered; I have seen you blown to death in the mines, and there was no redress. A fellow in Colorado says, "Why don't you prop the mines?" The operator said, "Oh, hell; Dagoes are cheaper than props!" Every miner is a Dago with the blood-sucking pirates, and they are cheaper than props, because if they kill a hundred of you, well, it was your fault; there must be a mine inspector kept there.

The night before the little Johnson boys were killed the mine inspector—John Laing is a mine owner; he wouldn't inspect them—the mine inspector went there and said the mines are propped securely. The next morning the little Johnson children went to work, and when they were found their hands were clasped in their dinner buckets with two biscuits.

You work for Laing day after day. He is a mine inspector, but he wouldn't be if I had anything to say about it. He would take a back seat.

Boys, I want to say to you, obey the law. Let me say to the governor and let me say to the mine owners—let me say to all people—that I will guarantee there will be no destruction of property.

In the first place, that is our property. It is inside where our jobs are. We have every reason to protect it. In the mines is where our jobs are. We are not out to destroy property; we are out to preserve and protect property, and I will tell you why. We are going to get more wages and we are going to stop the docking system. Put that down. Your day for docking is done. Stop it. If they don't stop it, we will. [Cries of "Good!" "Good!"]

We'll take care of the property; there will be no property destroyed. [Cries of "Not a bit!"]

Not a bit; and if you want your property protected these miners will protect it for you, and they won't need a gun. [Cries of "It is our interest to do so!"]

We will protect it at the risk of our lives. I know the miners; I have marched with 10,000—20,000—and destroyed no property. We had 20,000 miners in Pennsylvania, but destroyed no property.

They used to do that years ago, but after we have educated them they saw that violence was not the idea. We stopped it; we organized; we brought them to school once again. I will tell you why we are not going to destroy your property, Mr. Governor: Because one of these days we are going to take over the mines. [Loud applause.]

That is what we are going to do; we are going to take over those mines.

The Government has a mine in North Dakota. It works eight hours—not a minute more. There are no guards, no police, no militia. The men make $125 a month, and there is never any trouble at that mine. Uncle Sam is running the job, and he is a pretty good mine inspector. [Cries of "Tell it, mamma; I can't!"]

There used to be, when I was in Illinois before, a bunch of these black brutes down at Arbuckle, and we had them organized. There was a fellow whose name was "Sy." We have them in the miners' union, as well as in the mines. I asked them whether they were grafting in the union—they got $10 a piece each month, $20 in all. I went down and when they came up reading the financial statement and all those $10 were read, I said, "What is the $10 going for?" They told me. I said, "Get out of camp, I have no use for grafters."

We have them in the union. They have learned the lesson from the mine owners. There was a good old darkey there, and said, "Oh," said Sy, "I done talked to the Lord for a week, and the Lord jest come and whispered in my ear last night, and said, 'Sy, Sy, Sy, I have done had a talk with "Mother" about that graft. Come down to-morrow night,' I said, "O, Lord Jesus, don't fail to let 'Mother' come," and I went. He said, "Jesus didn't lie. Jesus said, 'Mother' come here sure, she take care of that money, and wouldn't let them fellows get it for nothing." At once the fellows said Amen.

So we put a stop to the graft. We have a lot of grafters, too. It is a disease. We have learned the game from the fellows above.

I want you to listen a moment. I want the business men to listen. You business men are up against it. There is a great revolution going on in the industrial world. The Standard Oil Co. owns 86 great department stores in this country. The small business man is beginning to be eliminated. He has got to get down, he can't get up. It is like Carnegie said before the Tariff Commission in Washington. "Gentlemen, I am not bothered about tariff on steel rails." He says, "What concerns me and my class is the right to organize."

The day for the small man is gone, and the day to rise is not here. We want the right to organize. Carnegie said that in a few years—he went into the business with five thousand—he took seven thousand five hundred. He said he knew the time was ripe for steel bridges, and they went into it. He closed out his interest for $300,000,000.

Do you wonder that the steel workers are robbed? When one thief alone can take $300,000,000 and give to a library—to educate our skulls because you didn't get a chance to educate them yourselves.

A fellow said, "I don't think we ought to take those libraries." Yes, take them, and let him build libraries in every town in the country. It is your money. Yet he comes and constructs those libraries as living monuments reddened with the blood of men, women, and children that he robbed.

How did he make $300,000,000? Come with me to Homestead, and I will show you the graves reddened with the blood of men, women, and children. That is where we fixed the Pinkertons, and they have never rose from that day to this. And we will fix the Baldwins in West Virginia.

The Pinkertons were little poodle dogs for the operators. We will fix the Baldwins just the same.

Some fellow said, "You are talking on the porch of the statehouse." That is the very place I want to talk, where what I say will not be perverted.

Senator Dick said, when I met him, "I am delighted to see you, 'Mother' Jones." I said, "I am not delighted to see you." He said, "What is the matter?" I said, "You have passed the Dick military bill to shoot my class down, that is why I wouldn't shake hands with you." That is the way to do business with those fellows. All the papers in the country wrote it up, and he was knocked down off his perch. I will knock a few of these Senators down before I die. [Cries of "Tell it, 'Mother'; I heard it."]

I will tell you. I want you all to be good. [A voice, "Yes; I will." "We are always good."]

They say you are not, but I know you better than the balance do.

Be good; don't drink, only a glass of beer. The parasite blood-suckers will tell you not to drink beer, because they want to drink it all, you know. They are afraid to tell you to drink for fear there will not be enough for their carcass. [Cries of "The governor takes champagne!"]

He needs it. He gets it from you fellows. He ought to drink it. You pay for it, and as long as he can get it for nothing, any fellow would be a fool not to drink it.

But I want you to be good. We are going to give the governor until to-morrow night. He will not do anything. He could if he would, but the fellows who put him in won't let him. [Cries of "Take him out."]

I don't want him out, because I would have to carry him around. [Applause.]

I want you to keep the peace until I tell you to move, and when I want you every one will come. [Loud applause.]

Now, be good. I don't tell you to go and work for Jesus. Work for yourselves; work for bread. That is the fight we have got. Work for bread. They own our bread.

This fight that you are in is the great industrial revolution that is permeating the heart of men over the world. They see behind the clouds the star that rose in Bethlehem nineteen hundred years ago, that is bringing the message of a better and nobler civilization. We are facing the hour. We are in it, men, the new day; we are here facing that star that will free men and give to the Nation a nobler, grander, higher, truer, purer, better manhood. We are standing on the eve of that mighty hour when the motherhood of the Nation will rise, and instead of clubs or picture shows or excursions, she will devote her life to the training of the human mind, giving to the Nation great men and great women.

I see that hour. I see the star breaking your chains; your chains will be broken, men. You will have to suffer more and more, but it won't be long. There is an awakening among all the nations of the earth.

I want to say, my friends, as Kipling said: He was a military colonel or general in the British Army, and he said:

> We have fed you all thousands of years,
>   And you hail us yet unfed.
> There is not a dollar of your stolen wealth
>   But what marks the graves of workers dead.
> We have given our best to give you rest;
>   You lie on your silken fold.
> O, God, if that be the price of your stolen wealth
>   We have paid it o'er and o'er.
>
> There is never a mine blown skyward now,
>   But our boys are burned to death for gold;
> There is never a wreck on the ocean
>   But what we are its ghastly crew.
> Go count your dead by the forges rail
>   Of the factories where your children lie;
> O, God, if that be the price of your stolen wealth,
>   We pay it a thousand fold.
>
> We have fed you all for thousands of years;
>   That was our doom, you know,
> Since the days they chained us on the field,
>   Till the fight that is now on over the world.
> Aye, you have beaten our lives, our babies and wives,
>   In chains you naked lie.
> O, God, if that be the price we pay for your stolen wealth,
>   We have paid it o'er and o'er.

We are going to stop payment. I want you to quit electing such judges as you have been. This old judge you had here, he used to be your lawyer. When this fight was on he was owned by the corporations. When you wanted him he went off fishing and got a pain in his back. Elect judges and governors from your own ranks.

A doctor said to me in Cincinnati, "Did you ever graduate from a college, Mother Jones?" I said, "I did." He said, "Would you mind telling me?" "No," I said, "I graduated from the college of hard knocks." That is my college; I graduated from that college—hunger, persecution, and suffering—and I wouldn't exchange that college for all the university dudes on the face of God's earth. [Loud applause.]

I know of the wrongs of humanity; I know your aching backs; I know your swimming heads; I know your little children suffer; I know your wives, when I have gone in and found her dead and found the babe nursing at the dead breast, and found the little girl 11 years old taking care of three children. She said, "Mother, will you wake up, baby is hungry and crying?" When I laid my hand on mamma she breathed her last. And the child of 11 had to become a mother to the children.

Oh, men, have you any hearts? Oh, men, do you feel? Oh, men, do you see the judgment day on the throne above, when you will be asked, "Where did you get your gold?" You stole it from these wretches. You murdered, you assassinated, you starved, you burned them to death, that you and your wives might have palaces, and that your wives might go to the seashore. Oh God, men, when I see the horrible picture, when I see the children with their hands off, when I took an army of babies and walked a hundred and thirty miles with a petition to the President of the United States, to pass a bill in Congress to keep these children from being murdered for profit. He had a secret service then all the way to the palace. And now they want to make a President of that man! What is the American Nation coming to?

Manhood, womanhood, can you stand for it? They put reforms in their platforms, but they will get no reform. He promised everthing to labor. When we had the strike in Colorado he sent 200 guns to blow our brains out. I don't forget. You do, but I don't. And our women were kicked out like dogs at the point of the bayonet. That is America. They don't do it in Russia. Some women get up with $5 worth of paint on their cheeks and have tooth brushes for their dogs and say, "Oh, them horrible miners," "Oh, that horrible old Mother Jones, that horrible old woman."

I am horrible. I admit, and I want to be to you blood-sucking pirates.

I want you, my boys, to buckle on your armor. This is the fighting age; this is not the age for cowards; put them out of the way.

(At this point "Mother" stopped suddenly and said to some one in the crowd: "Say, are you an operator, with that cigar in your grub?")

Take your medicine, because we are going to get after you, no doubt about it. [Cries from the crowd "Give it to them!"] Yes, I will. [Cries again "Give it to them!"]

I want you to be good. Give the governor time until to-morrow night, and if he don't act then it is up to you. We have all day Saturday, all day Sunday, all day Monday, and Tuesday, and Wednesday if we need it.

We are used to living on little, we can take a crust of bread in our hands and go.

When they started that Civic Federation in New York they got women attached to the Morgan and Rockefeller joint, they wanted to revolutionize the mechanics in Washington. One day I went to their dinner. An Irishman, a machinist, rolled up his sleeves and ran into a restaurant and got a piece of bologna as long as my arm—you know it is black. He got some bread. He put a chunk of the bologna into his mouth and put some bread in his mouth and went out eating. One of these women came along and said, "Oh, my man, don't eat that, it will ruin your stomach; it will give you indigestion." He said, "Oh, hell, the trouble with my stomach is I never get enough to digest."

That is the trouble with half our stomachs. We don't get enough to digest, and when we do get something we are afraid to put it in lest it won't digest.

Go to the "pluck-me" store and get all you can eat. Then you say to "Mirandy"—you say, "O, God, I have a pain in my stomach." You wash yourself, and she holds the water. The mine owner's wife don't hold the water. "Oh, Mirandy, bring the linen to take the corporation hump off my back."

I can't get up to you. I would like to be there, I would give you a hump on your back.

Boys, stay quiet until to-morrow night. I think it would be a good thing to work to-morrow, because the mine owners will need it. The mine commissioner will get a pain in his skull to-night and his wife will give him some "dope." The mine owner's wife is away at the seashore. When she finds no more money coming she will say, "Is there any more money coming?" He will say, "Most of the miners are not working." She will say, "Take the guards and shoot them back into the mines, those horrible fellows."

The governor says, if you don't go to work, said he, in the mines or on the railroads I am going to call the militia, and I will shoot you. So we went. I said we can get ready too. What militia can you get to fight us? Those boys on Paint Creek wouldn't fight us if all the governors in the country wanted you to. I was going yesterday to take dinner with them, but I had something else to do. I am going some day to take dinner with them, and I will convert the whole bunch to my philosophy. I will get them all my way.

Now, be good, boys. Pass the hat around, some of these poor devils want a glass of beer. Get the hat. The mine owner robs them. Get a hat, you fellows of the band.

I want to tell you another thing. These little two by four clerks in the company stores, they sell you five beans for a nickle, sometimes three beans for a nickle. I want to tell you, be civil to those. Don't say anything.

Another thing I want you to do: I want you to go in regular parade, three or four together. The moving-picture man wants to get your picture to send over the country.

(Some one in the crowd asks what the collection is being taken for.)

The hat is for miners who came up here broke, and they want to get a glass of beer. [Loud applause.]

And to pay their way back—and to get a glass of beer. I will give you $5. Get a move on and get something in it.

This day marks the forward march of the workers in the State of West Virginia. Slavery and oppression will gradually die. The National Government will get a record of this meeting. They will say, my friends, this was a peaceful, law-abiding meeting. They will see men of intelligence, that they are not out to destroy but to build. And instead of the horrible homes you have got we will build on their ruins homes for you and your children to live in, and we will build them on the ruins of the dog kennels which they wouldn't keep their mules in. That will bring forth better ideas than the world has had. The day of oppression will be gone. I will be with you whether true or false. I will be with you at midnight or when the battle rages, when the last bullet ceases, but I will be in my joy, as an old saint said:

> O, God, of the mighty clan,
>   God grant that the woman who suffered for you,
> Suffered not for a coward, but oh, for a man.
>   God grant that the woman who suffered for you,
> Suffered not for a coward, but oh, for a fighting man.

[Loud applause.]

Bring the hat in. Is that all you got? [As the hat was handed to her.] "That is all I got."

Go and get some more; that is not enough to go on a strike.

Any of you big fellows got any money in your pockets? If you have shell it out or we will take it out.

(A man coming up out of the crowd: "Here is $10. I will go and borrow more. Shake hands with me, an old union miner. My children are able to take care of themselves, and I will take of myself. Fight, fight, right. I have a good rifle, and I will get more money. If I don't have enough to pay my railroad fare I will walk. I don't care if this was the last cent I had, I will give it to 'Mother' and go and get some more.")

Maybe the governor will give something.

(Cries of "Call him out.")

(Governor, governor, governor.)

The governor is sick. He can't come out. [Applause.]

(Cries of "Better stay sick.")

Hand in the money. [From some one, "The governor is sick."]

MOTHER. Yes; he has got a pain in his stomach.

Go over and form a parade, the moving-picture man wants to take a picture. Go ahead and arrange the parade. Get out and get them in line.

(Cries of "Gov. Glasscock.")

Hush up, the poor fellow is sick.

(Cries for "Houston, Houston.")

(Cries of "Gone to the hospital.")

Now, let us go home. Be good boys. I am coming down to the camps and see you.

Florence Kelley
(1859–1932)

Florence Kelley was born on September 12, 1859 in Philadelphia, Pennsylvania. The third of eight children, she grew up in a prosperous political family with a strong Quaker background. Receiving most of her early schooling at home due to frequent illnesses, Florence entered Cornell in 1876 and received her Bachelor of Arts degree in 1882. While traveling and studying in Europe she became intrigued by socialism and translated Engels' *The Condition of the Working Class in England* in 1844, which was eventually published in the United States in 1887. While in Zurich she met a fellow socialist student, Lazare Wischnewetzky, and married him in 1884. In 1886 she and her husband returned to America and resided in New York City. For the next five years the couple raised their three children and actively participated in the local Socialist Labor Party. In 1891, Florence divorced her husband and moved to Chicago to live and work at Jane Addams' Hull House. Her growing concern about child labor and working conditions in general led to her appointment as an Illinois factory inspector in 1893. During this time period she also attended Northwestern University Law School and earned her law degree in 1894. In 1899 Florence returned to New York City to assume the job of general secretary of the newly formed National Consumers' League, a position which she dedicated herself to until her death. During her tenure as general secretary she organized sixty Consumers' Leagues in twenty different states, and planned and implemented two international conferences. Another reform concern which occupied much of Florence's attention was the enactment of wage and hour laws, and by 1913 it was largely due to her efforts that nine states had adopted some form of minimum wage legislation. Other reform causes also drew her attention, including the organizing of the National Association for the Advancement of Colored People in 1909, the founding of the Women's International League for Peace and Freedom in 1919, and serving as president of the Intercollegiate Socialist Society (later the League for Industrial Democracy) during 1918-1920. The 1920's proved disappointing to Florence and, although she continued to be involved in her numerous reform causes, she gradually lost her health and died on February 17, 1932 of acute anemia at the age of seventy-two.

The following lecture was delivered to students at several universities and colleges in Chicago and New York during the years 1893-1904. It was later printed in Florence Kelley, *Some Ethical Gains Through Legislation* (New York, N.Y., 1905), pp. 58-66.

"The Child, the State, and the Nation"

It has been shown that children are working in their homes, in the streets, in commerce, and in manufacture; and it appears that there are divers economic and social causes for their work.

Chief among these causes of child labor is the greed of parents, due largely but not exclusively to poverty. Two cases out of the writer's acquaintance may illustrate the false ideals which underlie much parental exploitation of young children.

An Italian immigrant arrived in this country possessed of nothing beyond his wife, little son and daughter, and railroad fare to Chicago. In that city he rented one dark room in a tenement-house and proceeded to pick rags in the streets. His wife sorted the rags in the court of the tenement-house with the help of the daughter; and the boy became a boot-black as soon as he was strong enough to make leather shine. The children never attended school, the compulsory attendance law being, at that time, wholly illusory. The father prospered, placed money in the savings-bank, and in an incredibly short time began to buy, under a third mortgage, the house in which he lived. The court of the tenement-house becoming too small for his work, he rented a vacant lot on which he stored rags, old iron and junk of all sorts. He never ceased to pick rags, and transferred the labors of his wife and daughter from their court to the new place of business which he surrounded with a high fence. He completed the payments for all the mortgages upon the tenement-house, continuing to the time of his death to live, with all his family, in the dark room which he had occupied on his arrival. He paid for the corner-lot upon which he conducted his business and made other investments. It was his ideal to leave his children a large fortune. But one day he trod upon a rusty nail, and with characteristic niggardliness, bound up his bleeding foot with one of his own rags. Lockjaw followed and he died, leaving to his now grown up, illiterate son and daughter one hundred and forty thousand dollars. The son, by drinking and gambling, dissipated the fortune in a few months, and the daughter disappeared into the sad obscurity of the Levee.

In the case of the second family, a young Bohemian, able-bodied and eager to work, brought his bride to this country, both filled with the hope of earning and owning a home. When the eldest child was eleven years old, the father was killed on the railroad, where he was at work as a section-hand, and the home, half-paid for, was lost by the widow. But she never wavered from the early ideal, and sent her eldest boy at once to work in a cutlery, where he riveted the wooden handles of knives, performing an entirely mechanical task adapted to his feeble intellect. The child was hunchbacked, feeble-minded and consumptive. When the mother was remonstrated with for exposing him to the fatigue and danger attending his work among wood-dust and steel-filings, her reply was: "Him no good. Him work, send Valeria and Bocumil school, buy house, them some good." For years, the factory inspectors of the state, and the local school officer, after the enactment of the compulsory attendance law, endeavored to free the unfortunate boy from his deadly occupation. The mother made whatever affidavits might be necessary from time to time, to enable him to continue, and relentlessly sent his brother and sister to work at the earliest moment possible. When last seen, she was rising at three o'clock in the morning to dig onions for a pickle factory in the outskirts of the city; the daughter Valeria, ten years old, was working from dawn to dark throughout the summer, sorting onions; the cripple was dying of overwork and neglect; and the other boy, Bocumil, originally healthy, had become deformed from beginning too early to carry boards on his back in a furniture factory.

The widow, however, regarded herself and was regarded by her approving pastor as a model of thrift because she had bought and partially paid for a tiny frame cottage, on the prairie, far from any school, in the immediate neighborhood of the pickle-factory. She will never know that she has lost for her children all the best things that America offers to the immigrant child, in the life of the public schools. Fortunately, the recently enacted stringent laws will make it impossible for other children coming to Chicago to be deprived, by the false ideals of their parents, of those precious possessions of child life in America, leisure and school.

A second cause of child-labor is the greed of employers for cheap labor, enhanced by every improvement in machinery of the kind that makes the work of children available; and enhanced, also, by the very cheapness of the children to such an extent as to delay the introduction of new machinery if its installation is costly. This greed is exhibited in its most odious form in the glass industry, the textile industry, and the sweating-system. It knows no restraints except those of effective legislation enforced by enlightened public opinion, as is shown by the action of those Northern cotton mill men who obey the laws of Massachusetts and New York in their mills in those states, but in Georgia fall to the level of their local competitors, employing children ten years old and less, throughout eleven hours a day.

A third cause of child labor is the greed of the community in desiring to keep down the cost of maintenance of its dependent class. This greed disguises itself under the form of solicitude for the moral welfare of the children. Just as the managers of the worst so-called reformatories insist that children must work under the contract system, "because they must be kept busy to keep them from being bad," so this solicitude for childish morals insists that "children must not be habituated to dependence," quite forgetting that dependence is the quality bestowed upon childhood as its distinguishing characteristic.

Any candid person, on being asked, "What virtues may be reasonably expected of children?" must reply that we do not yet know. Our studies of the psychology of childhood are still so imperfect and inconclusive that it is not safe to dogmatize in this field. But by a process of elimination it is possible to arrive at certain conclusions which seem worth at least careful consideration.

Thus, observation of so-called self-made men suggests a serious danger that a child precociously self-respecting in the matter of earning his living may pay a high price, later in life, for his precocity. It is proverbial that the employer who began life as a working boy and through continuous exertions rose to power and responsibility, is apt to be a ruthless employer. The unnatural strain of his own early experience seems to entail this penalty upon his character and consequently upon his unhappy employees. Self-respect due to self-maintenance seems to be a virtue suitable to the later years of adolescence and to adult life,—never to childhood. Moral precocity seems to be quite generally followed by exhaustion or by reaction taking the form of greed, rapacity and calculating self-seeking.

Just as excessive fatigue, or habitual loss of sleep in childhood is punished in later life by the craving for stimulants, and by nervous insufficiency manifesting itself in the most diverse ways,—so the burden of industrial employment borne in early, tender years, disables the boy or girl for enlightened, self-supporting citizenship in later life.

To impute a virtue not normal to childhood and then insist that the children shall live up to adult standards applied to that virtue, is perverted, and injurious alike to the community which follows this course and to the children who suffer under it. If the burden of self-maintenance or the attempted maintenance of others is placed upon young children,—if child labor is tolerated,—the ethical standards of the community are bad. For a task which is normal and right for adults cannot be performed by children without sacrificing in the process their future usefulness to the Republic.

The insistent plea that children must work in order that they may acquire habits of thrift and attain prosperity for themselves and their families is uttered with greatest persistence by the employers who profit by the labor of the children. It is the glass manufacturers who voice this tender solicitude for the moral well-being of the wage-earning children in New Jersey and Pennsylvania, when there is a growing movement in those states for prohibiting night work, as it has been prohibited in Illinois. In the South, it is the cotton-mill owners and their legal advisers who insist that little children from the mountain farms must toil eleven hours a day in the mills of Georgia, working throughout the night whenever it may be useful to their employers to have them do so.

These pleas are heard with willing ears by communities which begrudge money for the maintenance of schools and the assistance of dependent widows and orphans; and not without good reason. No sooner had the new law of New Jersey required children to attend school to the fourteenth birthday, and prohibited boys under that age from working in manufacture, than it became necessary to build a new schoolhouse in a suburb of Millville, to accommodate the boys turned out of the glassworks. In Alton the enforcement of the child labor law of 1893 led to the immediate construction of a new schoolhouse for the children freed from the glassworks, and to the reopening of a building which had long been out of use. Wherever children are freed from work, the community must provide for them schools, teachers, attendance agents, factory inspectors and all those officials and provisions which are essential to the care and defense of childhood under the pressure of the competitive system.

Besides being essentially immoral, the effort to burden young children with the task of self-maintenance is doomed to failure, for under existing conditions a child does not, and cannot achieve complete self-maintenance. The three great series of industries in which children are largely employed,—the textiles, glass-making and the needle-trades,—are parasite trades. They are all protected by tariffs for the advantage of the employers;—and by more or less stringent trade regulations for the advantage of the adult male employees. In the case of the needle-trades, there are lavish subsidies from the public treasury of New York City, the great center of the needle-trades for the western hemisphere. By the help of these subsidies, sewing is done by the inmates of institutions erroneously called private, while maintained by the taxes of the community, at rates with which no private manufacturer can long compete. But more insidious than all these contributions to the parasite industries is the steady contribution of underpaid work from children who carry home wages too small to support them.

Parents become willing to exert themselves less when the eldest boy and girl begin to contribute something towards the family maintenance, and are not strenuous in the demand that the child's wage shall afford self-support. "Every little helps," is the hand-to-mouth consideration with which the hard-worked immigrant withdraws his son or daughter from school on the first day that the law allows.

The unthinking community tends to approve every exertion in the direction of money earning on the part of those who are most nearly at the line of submergence, asking no questions as to the ultimate effect upon the future citizen.

The oncoming generation neither knows nor cares what burden of incapacitated members the present generation is preparing for it. But the burden will have to be borne, just in proportion as the children of to-day are deprived of the right to childhood. And nothing is more surely handed down than the callous indifference of the mass of the people to the *causes* of that destitution which is an intrinsic part of the life of every manufacturing community;—as, for instance, the death or disability of the breadwinner, or the widespread and ever-increasing custom of desertion by the fathers of burdensome young children.

Thus the essentially immoral effort to place upon the children the burden of self-maintenance not only fails at the moment,—it reacts injuriously upon the community, preparing for the next generation an undue share of incapacitated members, bequeathing to the future a large proportion of unfit and incapable citizens, and finally generating, among the people at large, indifference to the causes of death or disability of the breadwinner.

On the other hand, with the growing recognition of the right of the child to maintenance and education throughout a prolonged period, goes a lively interest in the health and welfare and probity of the normal breadwinner, who is theoretically responsible for its support.

In other words, while the demand for child labor is an economic one, the causes of its persistence are moral and social and are rooted in the false ideals of parents, employers, taxpayers, and all those indifferent people who care nothing what citizens are being trained for the future life of the Republic.

Susette LaFlesche
(1854–1903)

Susette LaFlesche was born on May 26, 1854 in a village of the Omaha Indian tribe near the site of present-day Bellevue, Nebraska. The second of five children, Susette grew up on a reservation under the protective watch of her father, Iron Eye, who presided as chief. At the age of eight she started attending a Presbyterian mission school and proved such an eager student that a proprietor of a Presbyterian girl's seminary in New Jersey invited her there as a student. When she graduated from the seminary in 1873 she returned to the reservation to join the teaching staff of one of the government schools. In 1879 Susette initiated her reform career on behalf of Indian rights when she joined Thomas Henry Tibbles and Standing Bear of the Ponca Indian tribe to tour the East lecturing on the plight of resettled Indian tribes. Acting as an interpreter and wearing her Indian costume and using her Indian name Bright Eyes, Susette made a strong impression on Eastern audiences. For the next several years she and Thomas Tibbles, whom she married in 1881, lectured throughout the Eastern and Mid-Atlantic states and testified on several occasions before Congressional committees. In 1886, with the passage of the Dawes Act in sight (which authorized the allotment of reservation land with citizenship rights to individual Indians), Susette and her husband embarked on a ten-month lecture tour of England for the Pond lyceum bureau. Returning from the highly successful English tour in 1887, the Tibbles settled back in Nebraska where Susette gained a reputation as a writer, with her numerous essays and stories published in midwestern journals and magazines. On May 26, 1903 Susette succumbed to years of frail health and died at the young age of forty-nine.

The following speech was delivered in Faneuil Hall in Boston on November 25, 1879. It was printed the following day in the Boston *Daily Advertiser* (November 26, 1879), p. 4.

"The Plight of the Ponca Indians"

I have lived all my life, with the exception of two years, which I spent at school in New Jersey, among my own tribe, the Omahas, and I have had an opportunity, such as is accorded to but few, of hearing both sides of the "Indian question." I have at times felt bitterly toward the white race, yet were it not for some who have shown all kindness, generosity and sympathy toward one who had no claims on them but that of common humanity, I shudder to think what I would now have been. As it is, my faith in justice and God has sometimes almost failed me but, I thank God, only almost. It crushed our hearts when we saw a little handful of poor, ignorant, helpless, but peaceful people, such as the Poncas were, oppressed by a mighty nation, a nation so powerful that it could well have afforded to show justice and humanity if it only would. It was so hard to feel how powerless we were to help those we loved so dearly when we saw our relatives forced from their homes and compelled to go to a strange country at the point of the bayonet. The whole Ponca tribe were rapidly advancing in civilization; cultivated their farms, and their schoolhouses and churches were well filled, when suddenly they were informed that the government required their removal to Indian Territory. My uncle said it came so suddenly upon them that they could not realize it at first, and they felt stunned and helpless. He also said if they had had any idea of what was coming, they might have successfully resisted; but as it was, it was carried rigidly beyond their control. Every objection they made was met by the word "soldier" and "bayonet." The Poncas had always been a peaceful tribe, and were not armed, and even if they had been they would rather not have fought. It was such a cowardly thing for the government to do! They sold the land which belonged to the Poncas to the Sioux, without the knowledge of the owners, and, as the Poncas were perfectly helpless and the Sioux well armed, the government was not afraid to move the friendly tribe.

The tribe has been robbed of thousands of dollars' worth of property, and the government shows no disposition to return what belongs to them. That property was lawfully theirs; they had worked for it; the annuities which were to be paid to them belonged to them. It was money promised by the government for land they had sold to the government. I desire to say that all annuities paid to Indian tribes by the government are in payment for land sold by them to the government, and are not charity. The government never gave any alms to the Indians, and we all know that through the "kindness" of the "Indian ring" they do not get the half of what the government actually owes them. It seems to us sometimes that the government treats us with less consideration than it does even the dogs.

For the past hundred years the Indians have had none to tell the story of their wrongs. If a white man did an injury to an Indian he had to suffer in silence, or being exasperated into revenge, the act of revenge has been spread abroad through the newspapers of the land as a causeless act, perpetrated on the whites just because the Indian delighted in being savage. It is because I know that a majority of the whites have not known of the cruelty practiced by the "Indian ring" on a handful of oppressed, helpless and conquered people, that I have the courage and confidence to appeal to the people of the United States. I have said "a conquered people." I do not know that I have the right to say that. We are helpless, it is true; but at heart we do not feel that we are a conquered people. We are human beings; God made us as well as you; and we are peculiarly his because of our ignorance and helplessness. I seem to understand why Christ came upon the earth and wandered over it, homeless and hated of all men. It brings him so much nearer to us to feel that he has suffered as we suffer, and can understand it all—suffered that we might feel that we belonged to him and were his own.

I will relate a single instance out of many, given me by my father, who knows the individuals concerned in it. I do not select it because it exceeds in horrors others told me by my Indian friends, but because it happens to be freshest in my memory. My father said there was in the Pawnee tribe a warrior holding a prominent position and respected by all the Indians. A white man was given the position on the reservation of government farmer for the Pawnee tribe. The Pawnees expected, of course, that he would go around among them and teach them how to plough and plant. Instead of doing that, he had fenced in a large piece of land, and had that sown and planted with grain and produce of all kinds. The Indians planted it and thought they would receive a part, at least, of the harvest. They never got any of it. The warrior mentioned above was one day in the field killing the blackbirds which had alighted in the field in large numbers. While engaged in doing this the powder gave out. He went to the government farmer's house to ask for more. He saw a jewelled flask hanging up in the outside of the door, and as the farmer came to the door he pointed to his gun to show that it was empty, and motioned to the flask to make known that he wanted some more powder. The government farmer shook his head and refused. The Indian, thinking he had misunderstood, raised his arm to take the flask to show him what he wanted. The government farmer, I suppose, thinking he, the Indian, intended to take the flask without his permission, raised a broadaxe lying on the ground, swung it in the air, and at one blow chopped the man's arm and cut into his side. The farmer then fled. The Pawnee Indians gathered around the dying warrior, and were making preparations for war on the white people in revenge for the deed, but the dying man made them promise him that they would do nothing in return. He said, "I am dying, and when I am dead you cannot bring me back to life by killing others. The government will not listen to you, but will listen to the farmer and send its soldiers and kill many of you, and you will all suffer for my sake. Let me die in peace and know you will not have to suffer for me." They promised him, and none but the indian people ever knew anything about it. It is wrongs such as these which, accumulating, exasperate the Indians beyond endurance and prompt them to deeds of vengeance, which, to those who know only one side of the story, seem savage barbarism, and the Indians are looked upon with horror as beings whose thirst for blood is ever unslaked. I tell you we are human beings, who love and hate as you do. Our affections are as strong, if not stronger, than yours; stronger in that we are powerless to help each other, and can only suffer with each other.

Before the tribal relations were voluntarily broken up by the Omahas, my father was a chief. He helped make some of the treaties with the government. He had been acquainted with the last eighteen agents who have transacted the business for one tribe on the part of the government, and out of those eighteen agents four only were good and honest men. The following instance will show how these agents squandered the money of the tribe: About four years ago one of them, without counselling the tribe, had a large handsome house built at a cost of about five thousand dollars, at the expense of the Omaha tribe. The building was intended by the agent, he said, for an infirmary, but he could not get any Indian to go into it, and it has never been used for anything since. It is of no use to the tribe, but it was a good job for the contractors. The tribe is now endeavoring to have it altered, to use it as a boarding school for the Indian children.

I have been intimately acquainted with the affairs of the Poncas. The Poncas and Omahas speak the same language and have always been friends, and thus I have known all their sorrows and troubles. Being an Indian, I, of course, have a deep interest in them. So many seem to think that Indians fight because they delight in being savage and are bloodthirsty. Let me relate one or two instances which serve to show how powerless we are to help ourselves. Some years ago an Omaha man was missed from one of our tribes. No one could tell what had become of him. Some of our people went to look for him. They found him in a pig-pen, where he had been thrown to the hogs after having been killed by the white men. Another time a man of our tribe went to a settlement about ten miles distant from our reserve to sell potatoes. While he stood sorting them out two young men came along.—they were white men, and one of them had just arrived from the East; he said to his companion, "I should like to shoot that Indian, just to say that I had shot one." His companion badgered him to do it. He raised his revolver and shot him. Four weeks ago, just as we were starting on this trip, a young Indian boy of sixteen was stabbed by a white boy of thirteen. The stabbing took place near my house. The white people in the settlements around wondered that the Indian allowed the white boy to stab him, when he was so much older and stronger. It was because the Indian knew, as young as he was, that if he struck a blow to defend himself, and injured the boy in defending himself, the whole tribe would be punished for his act; that troops might be sent for and war made on the tribe. I think there was heroism in that boy's act. For wrongs like these we have no redress whatever. We have no protection from the law. The Indians all know that they are powerless. Their chiefs and leading men had been to Washington, and have returned to tell their people of the mighty nation which fill the land once theirs. They know if they fight that they will be beaten, and they only fight when they are driven to desperation or are at the last extremity; and when they do at last fight, they have none to tell their side of the story, and it is given as a reason that they fight because they are bloodthirsty.

I have come to you to appeal for your sympathy and help for my people. They are immortal beings, for whom Christ died. They asked me to appeal to the churches, because they had heard that they were composed of God's people, and to the judges because they righted all wrongs. The people who were once owners of this soil ask you for their liberty, and law is liberty.

Mary E. Lease
(1850–1933)

Mary E. Lease was born on September 11, 1850 in Ridgway, Elk County, Pennsylvania. The sixth of eight children, Mary grew up on a farm and attended nearby parochial schools until she was fourteen. After her father's death in Andersonville prison during the Civil War, neighbors helped her continue her education by financing her attendance at St. Elizabeth's Academy in Allegany, New York. Following two years of teaching in rural New York, Mary moved to Kansas in 1870 to teach in the town of Osage Mission. In 1873 she married Charles Lease, a pharmacist and farmer. For the next ten years the Leases tried farming in Kingman County, Kansas and later in Denison, Texas. Finally abandoning farming in 1883, Mary and her husband and four children moved to Wichita, Kansas and set up a pharmacy. Mary's early social actions included the formation of the Hypatia Society for women to discuss current issues, and a speaking tour to raise funds for the recently founded Irish National League. With the emergence of the farmer's revolt in mortgage-ridden Kansas, Mary found a new movement she could heartily endorse. In 1885 her address to the state convention of the farmer-supported Union Labor Party drew wide acclaim and launched her on a speaking tour of the state in the campaign of 1888. In 1889 she joined E. S. Moore in founding a labor paper, the *Colorado Workman,* and in 1891 the largest local assembly of the Knights in Kansas elected her master workman (president). Mary's career as an advocate for farmer's rights achieved the most prominence in the 1890's. As a tempestuous and charismatic speaker for the Farmer's Alliance and the People's (Populist) party, she stumped the state of Kansas in 1890, carried her campaign into Missouri, the Far West and the South in 1891, campaigned for General James B. Weaver for President in 1892, and reported the Bryan campaign for the New York *World* in the 1896 presidential campaign. However, Mary's role in the Populist movement as an agitator rather than as a practical politician led her into frequent altercations with the leadership and ultimately alienated her from the party. Remaining in the East after the campaign of 1896, for the next thirty-plus years she lectured occasionally and supported such reform causes as birth control, woman suffrage and prohibition. On October 29, 1933 at the age of 83, Mary died in Callicoon, New York of a leg infection and chronic nephritis.

The following speech was delivered at a Pupulist rally in Kansas City, Kansas in March, 1891. It was later printed in the Kansas City *Star* (April 1, 1891).

"The Red Dragon of Wall Street Vs. the Farmer"

Wall Street owns this country. It is no longer a government of the people, by the people and for the people, but a government of Wall Street, by Wall Street and for Wall Street. The great common people of this country are slaves, and monopoly is the master. The West and South are bound and prostrated before the manufacturing East. Money rules and our Vice President is a London banker. Our laws are the output of a system which clothes rascals in robes and honesty in rags.

The parties lie to us and the political speakers mislead us. Take Ingalls for example. He waves the "bloody shirt" and he never smelled gunpowder in all his cowardly life. His war record is confined to courtmartialing a chicken thief. In this People's Party we find not only the boys who wore the blue but the boys who wore the grey. The North and South have been kept separated because of the unscrupulous scheming of the leaders of both political parties. Let us today cherish none but sacred and fraternal memories for the boys in blue and the boys in grey. It was only those who skulked at home who all these years have kept up the strife between the North and South. The mortgage indebtedness and the opposition by the money power rests just as heavily on the Southern states as on the Federal states, just as heavily on the Democratic brother as on the Republican brother.

We were told two years ago in Kansas to go to work and raise a big crop, that was all we needed. We went to work and plowed and planted; the rains fell, the sun shone, nature smiled, and we raised the big crop they told us to; and what came of it? Corn 8 cents, oats 10 cents, beef 2 cents. No price at all for butter and eggs. That's what came of it. Then the politicians said we suffered from overproduction. Overproduction, when 10,000 little children starve to death every year in the United States. When over 100,000 shop girls in New York are forced to sell their virtue for the bread their niggardly wages deny them.

Tarriff is not the paramount question. The main question is the money question. Kansas suffers from two great robbers, the Sante Fe railroad and the loan sharks. The common people are robbed to enrich their masters. There are thirty men in the United States whose aggregate wealth is over one and one-half billions of dollars. Go home and figure out how many paupers you must have to make one of those thirty men with the circulation only $10 per capita. There are one-half million tramps; that is, men looking for work.

What the Alliance wants are money, land and cheaper transportation. We want the abolition of national banks and we want power to make loans direct from the government. We want either the amendment or the accursed foreclosure system wiped out. Land equal to a tract thirty miles wide and ninety miles long in Kansas has been foreclosed on and bought in by the loan sharks in a year. We will stand by our homes and stay by our firesides by force if necessary, and we will not pay our debts to the loan shark companies until the government pays its debts to us. The people are at bay; let the bloodhounds of money who dog us beware!

Lucretia Mott
(1793–1880)

Lucretia Mott was born on January 3, 1793 in Nantucket, Massachusetts. The second child of seven, Lucretia grew up in the strong Quaker community of the island, which was largely a woman's world since most of the men were off on whaling and trading voyages for long periods of time. In 1804 the family left behind their isolated island life and moved to Boston where Lucretia attended both private and public schools. When she reached age thirteen, Lucretia attended the Friends' boarding school near Pough-keepsie, New York, where she became an assistant teacher after graduation. In 1809 Lucretia rejoined her family when they moved to Philadelphia, and in 1811 she married James Mott, a fellow Quaker. Between 1812 and 1828 Lucretia gave birth to six children and became an active minister at Quaker meetings. Her transition from speaking at the Friends' meeting house to the public platform was both a natural and easy one and soon she became actively involved in the anti-slavery movement. In 1833 she helped form the Philadelphia Female Anti-Slavery Society, and later served on the executive committee of the National Anti-Slavery Society after they dropped their restriction against female participants. In 1837 Lucretia helped organize the Anti-Slavery Convention of American Women, and in 1840 she was one of several American women chosen as delegates to the World's Anti-Slavery Convention in London. The London convention denied recognition to the women delegates, however, and Lucretia found herself assigned a seat "behind the bar," where she utilized her isolation by joining with Elizabeth Cady Stanton and plotting a woman's rights convention. In 1848 she and Elizabeth carried out their plot by convening the Seneca Falls, New York conference which would launch the Woman's Suffrage Movement. From this time on, woman's rights claimed most of Lucretia's time and energy. In 1850 she published her *Discourse on Woman* and spent the next twenty-plus years addressing and presiding over various state and national woman's rights conventions. During the Civil War and after Lucretia also devoted energy to Quaker causes which provided economic aid and education for freed Negroes in the North and South. In 1866 she was named as the first president of the Equal Rights Association, which would later split into two branches of the woman's suffrage movement despite her efforts to prevent the division. Lucretia remained active in both women's causes and Negro causes in the last years of her life and died peacefully at age 87 on November 11, 1880.

The following address was delivered at the 5th National Woman's Rights Convention in Philadelphia on October 18, 1854. It appeared in printed form in *The History of Woman Suffrage*, Vol. I (Rochester, N.Y., 1881) pp. 368–375.

"Why Should Not Woman Seek to Be a Reformer?"

I have not come here with a view of answering any particular parts of the lecture alluded to, in order to point out the fallacy of its reasoning. The speaker, however, did not profess to offer anything like argument on that occasion, but rather a sentiment. I have no prepared address to deliver to you, being unaccustomed to speak in that way; but I felt a wish to offer some views for your consideration, though in a desultory manner, which may lead to such reflection and discussion as will present the subject in a true light.

Why should not woman seek to be a reformer? If she is to shrink from being such an iconoclast as shall "break the image of man's lower worship," as so long held up to view; if she is to fear to exercise her reason, and her noblest powers, lest she should be thought to "attempt to act the man," and not "acknowledge his supremacy"; if she is to be satisfied with the narrow sphere assigned her by man, nor aspire to a higher, lest she should transcend the bounds of female delicacy; truly it is a mournful prospect for woman. We would admit all the difference, that our great and beneficent Creator has made, in the relation of man and woman, nor would we seek to disturb this relation; but we deny that the present position of woman is her true sphere of usefulness; nor will she attain to this sphere, until the disabilities and disadvantages, religious, civil, and social, which impede her progress, are removed out of her way. These restrictions have enervated her mind and paralyzed her powers. While man assumes that the present is the original state designed for woman, that the existing "differences are not arbitrary nor the result of accident," but grounded in nature; she will not make the necessary effort to obtain her just rights, lest it should subject her to the kind of scorn and contemptuous manner in which she has been spoken of.

So far from her "ambition leading her to attempt to act the man," she needs all the encouragement she can receive, by the removal of obstacles from her path, in order that she may become the "true woman." As it is desirable that man should act a manly and generous part, not "mannish," so let woman be urged to exercise a dignified and womanly bearing, not womanish. Let her cultivate all the graces and proper accomplishments of her sex, but let not these degenerate into a kind of effeminacy, in which she is satisfied to be the mere plaything or toy of society, content with her outward adornings, and the flattery and fulsome adulation too often addressed to her.

Did Elizabeth Fry lose any of her feminine qualities by the public walk into which she was called? Having performed the duties of a mother to a large family, feeling that she owed a labor of love to the poor prisoner, she was empowered by Him who sent her forth, to go to kings and crowned heads of the earth, and ask audience of these, and it was granted her. Did she lose the delicacy of woman by her acts? No. Her retiring modesty was characteristic of her to the latest period of her life. It was my privilege to enjoy her society some years ago, and I found all that belonged to the feminine in woman—to true nobility, in a refined and purified moral nature. Is Dorothea Dix throwing off her womanly nature and appearance in the course she is pursuing? In finding duties abroad, has any "refined man felt that something of beauty has gone forth from her"? To use the contemptuous word applied in the lecture alluded to, is she becoming "mannish"? Is she compromising her womanly dignity in going forth to seek to better the condition of the insane and afflicted? Is not a beautiful mind and a retiring modesty still conspicuous in her?

Indeed, I would ask, if this modesty is not attractive also, when manifested in the other sex? It was strikingly marked in Horace Mann, when presiding over the late National Educational Convention in this city. The retiring modesty of William Ellery Channing was beautiful, as well as of many others who have filled elevated stations in society. These virtues, differing as they may in degree in man and woman, are of the same nature, and call forth our admiration wherever manifested.

The noble courage of Grace Darling is justly honored for risking her own life on the coast of England, during the raging storm, in order to rescue the poor, suffering, shipwrecked mariner.

Woman was not wanting in courage in the early ages. In war and bloodshed this trait was often displayed. Grecian and Roman history have lauded and honored her in this character. English history records her courageous women too, for unhappily we have little but the records of war handed down to us. The courage of Joan of Arc was made the subject of a popular lecture not long ago by one of our intelligent citizens. But more noble, moral daring is marking the female character at the present time, and better worthy of imitation. As these characteristics come to be appreciated in man too, his warlike acts with all the miseries and horrors of the battleground will sink into their merited oblivion, or be remembered only to be condemned. The heroism displayed in the tented field must yield to the moral and Christian heroism which is shadowed in the signs of our times.

The lecturer regarded the announcement of woman's achievements, and the offering of appropriate praise through the press, as a gross innovation upon the obscurity of female life—he complained that the exhibition of attainments of girls in schools was now equal to that of boys, and the newspapers announce that "Miss Brown received the first prize for English grammar," etc. If he objected to so much excitement of emulation in schools, it would be well; for the most enlightened teachers discountenance these appeals to love of approbation and self-esteem. But while prizes continue to be awarded, can any good reason be given why the name of the girl should not be published as well as that of the boy? He spoke with scorn, that "we hear of Mrs. President so and so; and committees and secretaries of the same sex." But if women can conduct their own business, by means of presidents and secretaries of their own sex, can he tell us why they should not? They will never make much progress in any moral movement while they depend upon men to act for them. Do we shrink from reading the announcement that Mrs. Somerville is made an honorary member of a scientific association? That Miss Herschel has made some discoveries, and is prepared to take her equal part in science? Or that Miss Mitchell, of Nantucket, has lately discovered a planet, long looked for? I cannot conceive why "honor to whom honor is due" should not be rendered to woman as well as man; nor will it necessarily exalt her, or foster feminine pride. This propensity is found alike in male and female, and it should not be ministered to improperly in either sex.

In treating upon the affections, the lecturer held out the idea that as manifested in the sexes they were opposite if not somewhat antagonistic, and required a union as in chemistry to form a perfect whole. The simile appeared to me far from a correct illustration of the true union. Minds that can assimilate, spirits that are congenial, attract one another. It is the union of similar, not of opposite affections, which is necessary for the perfection of the marriage bond. There seemed a want of proper delicacy in his representing man as being bold in the demonstration of the pure affection of love. In persons of refinement, true love seeks concealment in man as well as in woman. I will not enlarge upon the subject, although it formed so great a part of his lecture. The contrast drawn seemed a fallacy, as has much, very much, that has been presented in the sickly sentimental strains of the poet from age to age.

The question is often asked, "What does woman want, more than she enjoys? What is she seeking to obtain? Of what rights is she deprived? What privileges are withheld from her?" I answer, she asks nothing as favor, but as right; she wants to be acknowledged a moral, responsible being. She is seeking not to be governed by laws in the making of which she has no voice. She is deprived of almost every right in civil society, and is a cipher in the nation, except in the right of presenting a petition. In religious society her disabilities have greatly retarded her progress. Her exclusion from the pulpit or ministry, her duties marked out for her by her equal brother man, subject to creeds, rules, and disciplines made for her by him, is unworthy her true dignity.

In marriage there is assumed superiority on the part of the husband, and admitted inferiority with a promise of obedience on the part of the wife. This subject calls loudly for examination in order that the wrong may be redressed. Customs suited to darker ages in Eastern countries are not binding upon enlightened society. The solemn covenant of marriage may be entered into without these lordly assumptions and humiliating concessions and promises.

There are large Christian denominations who do not recognize such degrading relations of husband and wife. They ask no aid from magistrate or clergyman to legalize or sanctify this union. But acknowledging themselves in the presence of the Highest and invoking His assistance, they come under reciprocal obligations of fidelity and affection, before suitable witnesses. Experience and observation go to prove that there may be as much harmony, to say the least, in such a union, and as great purity and permanence of affection, as can exist where the common ceremony is observed.

The distinctive relations of husband and wife, of father and mother of a family, are sacredly preserved, without the assumption of authority on the one part, or the promise of obedience on the other. There is nothing in such a marriage degrading to woman. She does not compromise her dignity or self-respect; but enters married life upon equal ground, by the side of her husband. By proper education, she understands her duties, physical, intellectual, and moral; and fulfilling these, she is a helpmeet in the true sense of the word.

I tread upon delicate ground in alluding to the institutions of religious associations; but the subject is of so much importance that all which relates to the position of woman should be examined apart from the undue veneration which ancient usage receives.

> "Such dupes are men to custom, and so prone
> To reverence what is ancient, and can plead
> A course of long observance for its use,
> That even servitude, the worst of ills,
> Because delivered down from sire to son,
> Is kept and guarded as a sacred thing."

So with woman. She has so long been subject to the disabilities and restrictions with which her progress has been embarrassed, that she has become enervated, her mind to some extent paralyzed; and like those still more degraded by personal bondage, she hugs her chains. Liberty is often presented in its true light, but it is liberty for man. I would not go so far, either as regards the abject slave or woman; for in both cases they may be so degraded by the crushing influences around them, that they may not be sensible of the blessings of freedom. Liberty is not less a blessing, because oppression has so long darkened the mind that it can not appreciate it. I would, therefore, urge that woman be placed in such a situation in society, by the recognition of her rights, and have such opportunities for growth and development, as shall raise her from this low, enervated, and paralyzed condition, to a full appreciation of the blessing of entire freedom of mind.

It is with reluctance that I make the demand for the political rights of women, because this claim is so distasteful to the age. Woman shrinks, in the present state of society, from taking any interest in politics. The events of the French Revolution, and the claim for woman's rights, are held up to her as a warning. Let us not look at the excesses of women alone, at that period; but remember that the age was marked with extravagances and wickedness in men as well as women. Political life abounds with these excesses and with shameful outrage. Who knows but that if woman acted her part in governmental affairs, there might be an entire change in the turmoil of political life? It becomes man to speak modestly of his ability to act without her. If woman's judgment were exercised, why might she not aid in making the laws by which she is governed? Lord Brougham remarked that the works of Harriet Martineau upon Political Economy were not excelled by those of any political writer of the present time. The first few chapters of her "Society in America," her views of a Republic, and of government generally, furnish evidence of woman's capacity to embrace subjects of universal interest.

Far be it from me to encourage women to vote, or to take an active part in politics in the present state of our government. Her right to the elective franchise, however, is the same, and should be yielded to her, whether she exercise that right or not. Would that man, too, would have no participation in a government recognizing the life-taking principle; retaliation and the sword. It is unworthy a Christian nation. But when in the diffusion of light and intelligence a Convention shall be called to make regulations for self-government on Christian principles, I can see no good reason why women should not participate in such an assemblage, taking part equally with man.

Professor Walker, of Cincinnati, in his "Introduction to American Law," says: "With regard to political rights, females form a positive exception to the general doctrine of equality. They have no part or lot in the formation or administration of government. They cannot vote or hold office. We require them to contribute their share in the way of taxes to the support of government, but allow them no voice in its direction. We hold them amenable to the laws when made, but allow them no share in making them. This language applied to males would be the exact definition of political slavery; applied to females custom does not teach us so to regard it." Woman, however, is beginning so to regard it.

He further says: "The law of husband and wife, as you gather it from the books, is a disgrace to any civilized nation. The theory of the law degrades the wife almost to the level of slaves. When a woman marries, we call her condition coverture, and speak of her as a *femme covert*. The old writers call the husband baron, and sometimes in plain English, lord. . . . The merging of her name in that of her husband is emblematic of the fate of all her legal rights. The torch of Hymen serves but to light the pile on which these rights are offered up. The legal theory is, that marriage makes the husband and wife one person, and that person is the husband. On this subject, reform is loudly called for. There is no foundation in reason or expediency for the absolute and slavish subjection of the wife to the husband, which forms the foundation of the present legal relations. Were woman, in point of fact, the abject thing which the law in theory considers her to be when married, she would not be worthy the companionship of man."

I would ask if such a code of laws does not require change? If such a condition of the wife in society does not claim redress? On no good ground can reform be delayed. Blackstone says: "The very being and legal existence of woman is suspended during marriage; incorporated or consolidated into that of her husband under whose protection and cover she performs everything." Hurlbut, in his Essay upon Human Rights, says: "The laws touching the rights of women are at variance with the laws of the Creator. Rights are human rights, and pertain to human beings without distinction of sex. Laws should not be made for man or for woman, but for mankind. Man was not born to command, nor woman to obey. . . . The law of France, Spain, and Holland, and one of our own States, Louisiana, recognizes the wife's right to property, more than the common law of England. . . . The laws depriving woman of the right of property are handed down to us from dark and feudal times, and are not consistent with the wiser, better, purer spirit of the age. The wife is a mere pensioner on the bounty of her husband. Her lost rights are appropriated to himself. But justice and benevolence are abroad in our land awakening the spirit of inquiry and innovation; and the Gothic fabric of the British law will fall before it, save where it is based upon the foundation of truth and justice."

May these statements lead you to reflect upon this subject, that you may know what woman's condition is in society, what her restrictions are, and seek to remove them. In how many cases in our country the husband and wife begin life together, and by equal industry and united effort accumulate to themselves a comfortable home. In the event of the death of the wife the household remains undisturbed, his farm or his workshop is not broken up or in any way molested. But when the husband dies he either gives his wife a portion of their joint accumulation, or the law apportions to her a share; the homestead is broken up, and she is dipossessed of that which she earned equally with him; for what she lacked in physical strength she made up in constancy of labor and toil, day and evening. The sons then coming into possession of the property, as has been the custom until of later time, speak of having to keep their mother, when she in reality is aiding to keep them. Where is the justice of this state of things? The change in the law of this State and of New York in relation to the property of the wife, goes to a limited extent toward the redress of these wrongs which are far more extensive and involve much more than I have time this evening to point out.

On no good ground can the legal existence of the wife be suspended during marriage, and her property surrendered to her husband. In the intelligent ranks of society the wife may not in point of fact be so degraded as the law would degrade her; because public sentiment is above the law. Still, while the law stands, she is liable to the disabilities which it imposes. Among the ignorant classes of society, woman is made to bear heavy burdens, and is degraded almost to the level of the slave. There are many instances now in our city, where the wife suffers much from the power of the husband to claim all that she can earn with her own hands. In my intercourse with the poorer class of people, I have known cases of extreme cruelty from the hard earnings of the wife being thus robbed by the husband, and no redress at law.

An article in one of the daily papers lately presented the condition of needle-women in England. There might be a presentation of this class in our own country which would make the heart bleed. Public attention should be turned to this subject in order that avenues of more profitable employment may be opened to women. There are many kinds of business which women, equally with men, may follow with respectability and success. Their talents and energies should be called forth, and their powers brought into the highest exercise. The efforts of women in France are sometimes pointed to in ridicule and sarcasm, but depend upon it, the opening of profitable employment to women in that country is doing much for the enfranchisement of the sex. In England and America it is not an uncommon thing for a wife to take up the business of her deceased husband and carry it on with success.

Our respected British Consul stated to me a circumstance which occurred some years ago, of an editor of a political paper having died in England; it was proposed to his wife, an able writer, to take the editorial chair. She accepted. The patronage of the paper was greatly increased, and she a short time since retired from her labors with a handsome fortune. In that country, however, the opportunities are by no means general for woman's elevation.

In visiting the public school in London a few years since, I noticed that the boys were employed in linear drawing, and instructed upon the black-board in the higher branches of arithmetic and mathematics; while the girls, after a short exercise in the mere elements of arithmetic, were seated during the bright hours of the morning, stitching wristbands. I asked why there should be this difference made; why the girls too should not have the black-board? The answer was, that they would not probably fill any station in society requiring such knowledge.

The demand for a more extended education will not cease until girls and boys have equal instruction in all the departments of useful knowledge. We have as yet no high-school in this State. The normal school may be a preparation for such an establishment. In the late convention for general education, it was cheering to hear the testimony borne to woman's capabilities for head teachers of the public schools. A resolution there offered for equal salaries to male and female teachers when equally qualified, as practiced in Louisiana, I regret to say, was checked in its passage by Bishop Potter; by him who has done so much for the encouragement of education, and who gave his countenance and influence to that Convention. Still, the fact of such a resolution being offered, augurs a time coming for woman which she may well hail. At the last examination of the public schools in this city, one of the alumni delivered an address on Woman, not as is too common in culogistic strains, but directing the attention to the injustice done to woman in her position in society in a variety of ways, the unequal wages she receives for her constant toil, etc., presenting facts calculated to arouse attention to the subject.

Women's property has been taxed equally with that of men's to sustain colleges endowed by the States; but they have not been permitted to enter those high seminaries of learning. Within a few years, however, some colleges have been instituted where young women are admitted upon nearly equal terms with young men; and numbers are availing themselves of their long denied rights. This is among the signs of the times, indicative of an advance for women. The book of knowledge is not opened to her in vain. Already is she aiming to occupy important posts of honor and profit in our country. We have three females editors in our State and some in other States of the Union. Numbers are entering the medical profession; one received a diploma last year; others are preparing for a like result.

Let woman then go on, not asking favors, but claiming as right, the removal of all hindrances to her elevation in the scale of being; let her receive encouragement for the proper cultivation of all her powers, so that she may enter profitably into the active business of life; employing her own hands in ministering to her necessities, strengthening her physical being by proper exercise and observance of the laws of health. Let her not be ambitious to display a fair hand and to promenade the fashionable streets of our city, but rather, coveting earnestly the best gifts, let her strive to occupy such walks in society as will befit her true dignity in all the relations of life. No fear that she will then transcend the proper limits of female delicacy. True modesty will be as fully preserved in acting out those important vocations, as in the nursery or at the fireside ministering to man's self-indulgence. Then in the marriage union, the independence of the husband and wife will be equal, their dependence mutual, and their obligations reciprocal.

In conclusion, let me say, with Nathaniel P. Willis: "Credit not the old-fashioned absurdity that woman's is a secondary lot, ministering to the necessities of her lord and master! It is a higher destiny I would award you. If your immortality is as complete, and your gift of mind as capable as ours of increase and elevation, I would put no wisdom of mine against God's evident allotment. I would charge you to water the undying bud, and give it healthy culture, and open its beauty to the sun; and then you may hope that when your life is bound up with another, you will go on equally and in a fellowship that shall pervade every earthly interest."

Carry Nation
(1846–1911)

Carry Nation was born on November 25, 1846 in Garrand County, Kentucky. The oldest of six children, Carry moved with her family several times within Kentucky and later to Missouri and Texas before they finally settled permanently in Missouri in 1862. Carry's childhood was plagued by her mother's severe mental disorders and her own semi-invalid state during most of her early years. As a consequence, Carry had but a few years of schooling, including both public and private and occasional private tutoring. In 1867 Carry married a former boarder, Charles Gloyd, and moved to Holden, Missouri. Within two years her husband had died from alcohol abuse and Carry and her young daughter moved in with her mother-in-law. For the next four years she taught school in Holden until she married David Nation in 1877. In 1879 the Nations moved to Texas, but after several unsuccessful business ventures they moved to Medicine Lodge, Kansas in 1889. It was during her first years in Kansas that Carry formed her individualized religious tenets, which included her Messianic role to wage war against liquor traffic. In 1892 she helped found the county chapter of the Women's Christian Temperance Union, and in 1899 staged her first invasion of a local saloon by singing temperance songs until a crowd closed the place down. Repeat performances shortly dried up the whole town and she moved in to Kiowa to close down that town as well, this time brandishing her soon-to-be famous hatchet. After several more forays in Wichita and Topeka, Carry was jailed by the anti-temperance forces while simultaneously the state temperance convention awarded her a gold medal inscribed "To the Bravest Woman in Kansas." In 1901, penniless after a term in jail, she undertook an East Coast lecture tour for the Furlong Lyceum Bureau of Rochester. For the next several years Carry lectured from coast to coast while at the same time selling her autobiography and thousands of miniature hatchets engraved "Carry Nation, Joint Smasher." Much of her income went to pay fines for disturbing the peace or court costs for destroying property, but what was left over she used to finance a series of prohibition magazines (*Smasher's Mail, Home Defender,* and the *Hatchet)* and to support her home for drunkards' wives and mothers in Kansas City. By 1905 Carry only lectured sporadically and on June 9, 1911, she died in Leavenworth, Kansas after a lengthy illness.

The following address was delivered throughout the country in the years 1903–1905. It appeared in printed form in Carry Nation, *The Use and Need of the Life of Carry A. Nation* (Topeka, Ks., 1908), pp. 254–59.

"Prohibition or Abolition—What It Means"

God is a politician; so is the devil. God's politics are to protect and defend mankind, bringing to them the highest good and finally heaven. The devil's politics are to deceive, degrade and to make miserable, finally ending in hell. The Bible fully explains this. The two kinds of seed started out from Abel and Cain, then Ishmael and Isaac, Esau and Jacob. There are but these two kinds of people. God's crowd and the Devil's crowd. The first law given and broken in Eden was a prohibition law. God said: "Thou shalt not." The devil tempted and persuaded the first pair to disobey. He did it by deceiving the woman. The fact of redemption now is to bring them back to the law of God. What is law? God says that sin is a transgression of law. Blackstone says: "Law commands that which is right and prohibits that which is wrong." Law is one, as truth is one. It is not possible to make a bad law. If it is bad, it is not a law. We have bad statutes. Law is always right. Nothing is wrong that is legal, and wrong may be licensed, but never legalized. I find lawyers who do not understand this. I often hear the term "legalized saloon." When I was passing the building of the supreme court in New York City, on Madison Avenue, I read an inscription on one of the marble statues representing a judge with a book on either side of the door: "Every law not based on wisdom is a menace to the state." This is a false, misleading sentence for all law is wisdom. It might have read: "All statutes not based on wisdom, are a menace to the state." Then at the base of the statue of a soldier, on the other side of the entrance, was this statement: "We do not use force until good laws are defied." Which ought to read: "We do not use force until laws are defied." Such ideas as these are corrupting courts, and biasing the public mind, and the injury is more than apparent to the observer. If law is not a standard, what standard can we have? We must have one. We repeat again: "Law commands that which is right and prohibits that which is wrong." Any statute that does this is lawful. Any that does not, is anarchy.

God is truly the author of law. The theocratic form of government was perfect and the only perfect government that ever existed, we need no other statutes than those that God gave. He said: "We must not kill a bird sitting on her young; must not see our enemy's beast fall under his burden and not help him rise." And the refinement of mercy was taught in the statute that said, "You must not kill the mother and lamb in one day; must not seethe a kid in its mother's milk; must not muzzle the ox that treadeth out the corn." The use, and the only use, of law is to prevent and punish for sin. All law has a penalty for those who violate it. Governments that are the greatest blessing to its citizens are those who can prohibit, or abolish the most sin or crime. Crime is not prevented by toleration, but by prohibition. Nine of the ten commandments are prohibitive and begin with, "Thou shalt not."

The success of life, the formation of character, is in proportion to the courage one has to say to one's ownself: "Thou shalt not." (Exod. 20.) It is not the man or woman who has no temptation to sin, who has the strong character, but the man or woman who has the desire but will not yield to sin. Some people ask: Why did God make the Devil? the Devil is God's fire. Like an alchemist God is purifying souls. The Devil is an agent in salvation. Every Devil in hell is harnessed up to push every saint into heaven.

Those who are counted worthy to enter into the delights of that heavenly land are those who have had their "fiery trials," (I Pet. 4:12) tried and made white. Man would have no credit and could not hear, "Good and faithful servant" if he had no temptations to do otherwise, man would be but a mere machine.

God has never used for his work, any but those who prohibit evil. The Pilgrim Fathers were forced from the mother country because this principle of prohibition burned in their hearts. When England would oppose the colonies, it was prohibition that smashed the tea, over in Boston harbor. George Washington was put at the head of the colonial armies that prohibited, by much bloodshed and suffering, the oppression from the mother country. Our Civil War was the result of the principle to abolish or prohibit the slavery of the colored race. Now we have a worse slavery than England threatened us with or the poor blacks suffered at the hands of their taskmasters. This slavery of soul and body, is one that leads to eternal death. The forces of darkness and death are with those who are willing to be led captive by the Devil at his will, and to lead others under this grievous yoke of those who are trying to perpetuate the cause of evil.

There are men who desire to be loyal, who are voting for license or in license parties, because they do not stop to think. The people are generally right on all questions. They go wrong more for lack of thought, than for lack of heart. Edmund Burke, the greatest English statesman, said: "The people have as good government as they deserve." Because the people have always had the power, and in America especially, they are sovereign. The president and all others in office, are but servants of the people. In another chapter I have given what the supreme court says about the impossibility of licensing wrong by law, or according to law.

Hear the language of the Declaration of Independence: "We hold these truths to be self evident, that all men are created free and equal, that they are endowed by their creator, with certain inalienable rights, that among these are life, liberty, and the pursuit of happiness, that to secure these rights, governments are instituted among men deriving their just powers from the consent of the governed." The licensing of intoxicating drink results in suicide and murder, whether or not the saloon-keeper or state be held responsible. Some one is. Who? The man who consents to or aids by his vote is most criminal. It is said that drink kills a man a minute. Suppose that we had a war that killed a man every five minutes. Would there not be howling for an end of bloodshed. This is more than ten times worse, for the soul is more valuable than the body.

Freedom or liberty in animals is following instinct and underlying appetite. Not so with man; to the reverse. It is the freedom of conscience and will, from the bondage of ignorance of the person, the gratification of appetite and passion. The body is a good servant, but a tyrant when it is master. A man must be master or slave. One must first, like Daniel, "Purpose in his heart that he will not defile himself." (Dan. 1:8.) Liberty or freedom is only attained by prohibition of opportunity to do wrong to ourselves or allow any one else to do so. Citizenship not only requires one to obey law but must see that others do so also.

The principles of government are founded on liberty and self-control. Drunkenness is a loss of self-control. Anything that animalizes men, is a menace to the life of the state and prevents the purpose of government. Thus placing the weapon of destruction in the hands of its foes and the danger is great, because so many citizens are under the domination of their own will and passion. This class is being multiplied by this licensed crime. These willing classes are an integral part of the nation. By licensing rum, we are fostering a power that is increasing the weakness, and preventing the self-control of its citizens. This is conspiracy, treason, black as night. Some plead the revenue of our wealth. Our wealth is in our citizens. The state cannot add to its treasury at the expense of its manhood without punishing herself. The state must guard the character of its citizens. It can not make them honest, but it must punish dishonesty; cannot make them humane, but it must prohibit an act of inhumanity; and should oppose and forbid every license that man would desire or try to obtain that which would allow such gratification of the animal over the moral.

The nation is what its homes are. The family first, then the nation. Nothing can injure an individual or a family that is not an injury to the state. The fight for firesides means a fight for our national life. Our revolutionary sires fought for this. This is the fight that Carry A. Nation is making. It is the heart of love, liberty and peace. Some of these thoughts I have copied from an article I read on a few leaves of a torn pamphlet, no name. But the writer has the true meaning of government. I am a prohibitionist because I am a christian. I want to get to heaven. None but prohibitionists ever do. Hell is made for those who take license to sin.

Kate Richards O'Hare
(1876–1948)

Kate Richards O'Hare was born on March 26, 1876 in Ottawa County, Kansas. The fourth child of five, she grew up on a farm in her early youth before the family settled in Kansas City to begin a new business in machinery. After attending schools in Ottawa and Kansas City, Kate became a machinist's apprentice in her father's shop in 1894. During this time she also worked for temperance causes and the Florence Crittenton Mission for "fallen women" in Kansas City. In 1901 Kate attended a training school for Socialist party workers in Girard, Kansas, and for the next twenty years devoted much of her talents to the Socialist Party. In 1902 she married a fellow Socialist, Francis O'Hare, and they travelled together agitating for socialism on the Great Plains by specializing in the Socialist "encampment," a mixture of Chautauqua, religious camp meeting, and Socialist convention that proved effective in attracting farmers to the party. In 1912 Kate and her husband became editors of the *National Rip-Saw* (later renamed the *Socialist Revolution* in 1917 and the *American Vanguard* in 1923), a Socialist weekly newspaper. In the years before World War I the O'Hares campaigned actively against United States participation in the war, and in 1917 Kate was indicted under the wartime Espionage Act for reportedly making a seditious comment in one of her speeches. Denying the charge and fighting against the indictment Kate, nevertheless, was found guilty and sentenced to five years in prison. On April 15, 1919, she entered prison and remained there until an amnesty campaign successfully commuted her sentence on May 29, 1920 (President Coolidge later granted her a full pardon). Upon her release Kate campaigned actively for the release of other political prisoners and for the Socialist presidential campaign of Eugene Debs, then a prisoner in Atlanta. In 1922 she and her husband were the primary organizers of the Children's Crusade, a march on Washington by children of opponents of war who were still in prison. In late 1922 the O'Hares moved to Leesville, Louisiana, and joined in the Llano Co-operative Colony where they published their newspaper and Kate taught in their Commonwealth College, an institution for workers' education. In 1928 Kate divorced her husband and married Charles Cunningham and moved to California. From that time on she devoted most of her energies to prison reform and campaigning for Upton Sinclair's "End Poverty in California" movement. In 1939 Governor Olsen appointed her assistant director of the Department of Penology and she proceeded to transform California's backward penal system into one of the most progressive ones in the nation. On January 10, 1948, Kate died of a coronary thrombosis at the age of seventy.

The following address was delivered to audiences in Miller's Hall, La Touraine Hall and the East Side Labor Lyceum in Buffalo, New York on April 8, 9, 10, 1919. Kate was on her way to be incarcerated at the Missouri State Prison on April 15, 1919. It appeared in printed form in the Oakland *World* (April 25, 1919).

"Farewell Address of a Socialist"

I would not if I could have one day different, one hour unlived, one deed undone, one word unspoken. I have nothing to regret, nothing to retract, nothing for which to apologize. I am willing to leave my life as I have lived it and let the future judge between me and my judges.

For eighteen months the very atmosphere of the nation has been surcharged with the roaring, shrieking shouts of Americanism, then in a single day a thunderous silence descended upon us and we felt the stunned scene of unreality that fell upon the soldiers in the trenches when the signing of the armistice suddenly stopped the roar and bedlam of war.

Like the toper suddenly separated from his bottle, or the "coke" fiend from his "snuff," we felt a growing desire for the exhilaration of the intoxicant of rampant Americanism. We resented the gray, colorless, sordid aspects of the life robbed of the rosy glow of patriotism. When the armistice spread the black pall of silence over fervid oratory and burning editorials, we felt a deep sense of personal loss; something was missing from our lives.

And there is another cry—vague, and shrouded in mystery. Sometimes used to express the superlative of disorder and lawlessness—sometimes to indicate in a mild and academic way, a hoped for refuge from the social tornado—the word "Socialism."

And, as the word "Americanism" goes into eclipse, and the word "Socialism" no longer evokes terror, comes another word—"Bolshevism."

Max Eastman, one of the foremost writers and teachers of the country, went to Fargo, North Dakota, to deliver a lecture on "Democracy." A great crowd evidently interested in the thing we were fighting to make the world safe for, gathered in the court to listen to what he had to say. A drunken mob, led by a judge and a "very respectable" attorney, invaded the "temple of justice" and would have murdered Max Eastman but for the sublime heroism and unflinching courage of a woman. An attempted murder of Max Eastman was flaunted as an exhibition of the "spirit of Americanism."

During the time when "Americanism" was so very rampant, I went to Erie, Pennsylvania, to deliver a lecture on "Christ Before Pilate." As I sat at the dinner table in the hotel, a dining room girl, shaking with fear and hysterical with excitement, came to me and begged that I would not leave the hotel that evening and would not attempt to do my work. When I pressed her for a reason, she gave me a copy of the Erie Times, and in a box on the front page, in glaring type, was an invitation for all good Americans to be at the court house at eight o'clock that evening with their guns to murder me, as proof of their burning "Americanism."

Then there was written into the history of our country the most shameful story of abject cowardice on the part of elected officials that has ever blackened the pages of human history—the so-called "espionage act." In the future our grandchildren will read in their school histories the names of the men responsible for that law with exactly the same feeling that we school children felt when we read the name of Judge Taney, of the Dred Scott decision fame.

Was this Americanism?

By the enactment of certain parts of this one act a way was opened by which we as people lost rights secured by hundreds of years of ceaseless struggle, rights that had been bought and paid for in the blood and suffering of our fathers, religious liberty, the very ideal that sent the Puritan forefathers to this savage land, was destroyed overnight. In the land whose constitution guarantees religious liberty, by the misuse of this act, scores of men were sent to prison for ten and twenty years for circulating a book that stated in the mildest, gentlest language that wars were contrary to the teaching of Jesus. Thousands of young men whose religious convictions made it impossible for them to bear arms or kill their fellow men were forced by the most brutal methods into uniforms, dragged like felons to training camps, subjected to tortures that vie with the horrors of the Inquisition, and that sent many of them to an untimely grave.

Free Speech Crushed

In all modern history there has never been such a flagrant violation of the very spirit of free speech. Not even in Russia under the bloody czars were such brutal laws enacted to curb natural expression of opinions, and not even by the czar's henchmen were they so ruthlessly and unfairly enforced. Under the operation of the "espionage act" it was not necessary to really commit the crime of having an opinion of the administration; it was not necessary to do anything at all, or to be responsible for any results. Hundreds of people are now behind prison bars whom the administration never charged with any overt act; they merely were found guilty for having an "intent," and that "intent" was sufficient to call down upon their heads punishment far more severe than is dealt out to thieves, bank wreckers, white slaves and murderers. No white slaver who has made traffic in human flesh for the profits of vice in this country has ever been sentenced to five, ten or twenty years in prison, as Rose Pastor Stokes, Eugene V. Debs and others have been sentenced for having an "intent" that never accomplished any purpose whatever.

Jailed for "Intent"

And an "intent" need not be proven, if such a thing could be. All that was necessary to draw a long prison sentence was to have a reputation in the labor movement for loyalty and service to the working class, a couple of nondescript witnesses and a jury hand picked by the "Council of Defense" and the trick was done. I saw in the tombs in New York City a tiny, half-starved scrap of girlhood that should have been in a grade school, who was sentenced to twenty years at hard labor for saying that President Wilson was a hypocrite, and that girl is now serving this monstrous sentence with Stars and Stripes the emblem of freedom, justice, and democracy, flying over the hell-hole in which she is imprisoned.

Hypocritical Cry of "Disloyalty"

Then all over this country came a reign of terror, a prostitution of courts and a violation of constitutional rights by elected officials for which our children and our children's children will blush in shame. Soon the country was overrun by spies, seeking not German vandals but Americans who held ideas and beliefs differing from the administration. Soon every vicious element in our society was hot on the trail of every man or woman who had ever stood for social justice and industrial democracy, and found it an easy matter to railroad them to prison. It was only necessary to cry "disloyal," "seditious," "pro-German," "un-American," and like the witches of old the leaders of the working class were hounded, imprisoned and murdered.

The New World "Bolshevism"

What is the strange, new force that is sweeping over the world—this fearsome Bolshevism?

If we place the slightest dependence on the truthlessness of our newspapers and other censored sources of public information, we well might shudder before its danger and fear the Bolshevist reign of terror, its orgy of rapine, lust, free-love, robbery, bloodshed, and wholesale murder. But, in spite of all the shouts and groans and cries of the "press," we remain quite calm, serene and unafraid. We have learned by long and bitter experience that when the "kept press" assails a thing, that it must be something very beneficial to the working class; that when the newspapers slander and villify an individual or movement may be serving the masses and endangering the privileged classes.

Bolshevism is a new word, but the charges brought against it and its supporters have a strangely familiar sound—we seem to remember them of old. Privilege is so sterile of ideas; so barren of imagination, that it has not been able to think of one new lie; to concoct one fresh slander; to turn one new trick or say one new thing about Bolshevism that has not already been worn to tatters in the assaults upon abolition of slavery, trade unionism, woman's suffrage, Socialism, the Non-Partisan League and the I. W. W.

The scarecrows that it dangles before our eyes have ceased to alarm us; familiarity has bred contempt. Bolshevism may cause the goose-flesh of abject terror to prickle the spine of the "powers that prey," but it has no terrors for the working class. We know that robbery, rapine, free-love, and murder have just as much relation to Bolshevism as mob violence, thuggery, and murder have to Americanism.

Socialism Hastened by World War

Socialism is coming, and it seems poetic justice that it should be thrust upon the world by its most bitter enemies. Industrial and political autocracy run mad plunged the whole world into war, and then the world, in order to save itself from utter destruction, was compelled to turn to Socialism for salvation. The warring nations did not make the long strides towards industrial democracy because they loved the Socialists, or wanted Socialism, but because it is the only thing that can meet the situation and save the world from utter chaos and ruin.

For twenty years the Socialists have been trying vainly to give you "great" American sovereign voting kings'—Socialism. We tried so hard to make you understand—we wanted you to take Socialism in peace and intelligence, by the sane, sober use of your ballots, but you would have none of it. You were good Democrats or Republicans and we were a lot of crazy fanatics, and you refused to take Socialism in peace, by lawful, constitutional means.

Now, you dear old mossbacks, rock-ribbed, hidebound Democrats and Republicans have had a little Socialism thrust into you on the end of a bayonet, and it wasn't a Socialist bayonet, either. Well, if you like it better that way, we must be content. We did our best, there is no blood on our hands and no guilt on our skirts, and if you have been compelled to learn your lesson and take your Socialism in the bloodshed and agony, the hell and horror of war, you and you alone are to blame.

Danger of Insane Revolt

Friends! I know, and you know, if you have the moral courage to face the facts, that we are on the verge of social revolution. A social revolution that is coming, not because Socialists have preached the gospel of industrial democracy, but because you have turned a deaf ear to it. The streets of this city, and of every other city may run red with the blood spilled in mad revolt; in wild, unrestrained and insane revolution, before the snow falls again unless there is more breadth of vision, more real statesmanship displayed by our elected officials than has yet been displayed.

And that red revolution will not be stayed by a Supreme Court decision that sends a thousand Socialists to prison by sustaining the "espionage" act. That decision of the United States Supreme Court handed down on the third day of March, 1919, may be but another Dred Scott decision, that decides nothing but the sublime stupidity of the ruling class. Judge Taney and his associates, by that memorable decision in 1857, sent one poor, humble negro back to slavery, but he also sent one million of the pick and flower of American manhood to death on the battle fields of the Civil War, and he sent three million negroes to final freedom.

That red revolution that threatens will not be stayed by passing laws making it a crime to display a red flag. Revolution can come under a pink flag, or a green one, or a blue, or under the Stars and Stripes, or under no flag at all. The want of a biscuit, a beefsteak and a job has caused more revolutions than all the flags that ever waved, and when red revolution comes in this country, it will not be because of the bitter want for bread, meat, labor and love.

Has No Regrets

Comrades, I am closing now. This may be the last message that I shall ever give you, for in a few short days I, too, will be one of the political prisoners shut behind steel bars.

For myself I have no regrets, and only a deep sense of humility and thankfulness if I may be counted worthy to take my place at the very bottom of that illustrious list of those who have died for the love of their fellow-men.

Looking back over twenty years, I am content. I gave to the service of the working class all that I had and all that I was, and no one can do more. I gave my girlhood, my young womanhood, my wifehood and my motherhood. I have taken babies unborn into the thick of the class war; I have served in the trenches with a nursing baby at my breast; I leave my children now without my care and protection, but I know that I have only done my duty.

I would not, if I could, have one day different; one hour unlived; one deed undone; one word unspoken. I have nothing to regret, nothing to retract, nothing for which to apologize. I am willing to leave my life as I have lived it; and let the future judge between me and my judges.

I want you to know that I am calm, serene and unafraid, and face my ordeal without hate in my heart and without fear for the future. Nothing that I may find behind prison walls can injure me. I can and will rise above it all. And I will not be idle there; my work will not end, there is a bigger and more urgent work for me to do in prison than I ever found outside. I have tried to serve the workers because I felt they needed service, but the thousands of helpless victims of our stupid, outworn penal system need me more. If there is any institution in our social organism which needs the light of intelligent study, rational understanding and sane revolution, it is our criminal laws; their administration and systems of punishment.

When I go to prison, I leave four children outside: a boy of fifteen, a girl of twelve, and twins, boys ten years of age.

And to my children, I know no one can take a mother's place, but they, too, come of good fighting stock, and they will face the loss of their mother with courage worthy of their ancestry. When they are old enough to understand, they will rather have had a mother inside prison walls true to her ideals and principles, then outside, a craven coward who dared not protest when our rights were wrested from us and when grievous wrongs were thrust upon us.

It is not my fate or the fate of my children that I tremble for, it is the fate of my country. It is not a prison cell that I dread, but blind, insane, unintelligently directed revolution. It is not the nightmare of gray stone walls that fills my dreams, but the picture of gutters of our cities running red with the blood of our people.

Leonora O'Reilly
(1870–1927)

Leonora O'Reilly was born on February 16, 1870 in New York City. The youngest of two children, Leonora grew up in grim poverty on New York's East Side. After a few years of public school, she went to work in a collar factory at the age of eleven to help her widowed mother support the family. In 1886 Leonora joined a local assembly of the Knights of Labor and in the same year organized a club called the Working Women's Society. For the next several years her labor reform activities expanded the number of her acquaintances to include many upper-middle-class reformers who offered her guidance in her program of self-education. In 1894 Leonora joined the Social Reform Club of Lillian Wald's Henry Street Settlement and three years later was elected vice-president. Throughout this time period she continued working a ten-hour day in a shirtwaist factory on Third Avenue where she had become forewoman. In 1897 Leonora helped organize a women's local of the United Garment Workers of America and found herself in great demand as a speaker to reform groups. Returning to school in 1898 and graduating in 1900, she became head worker at Asacoz House, a Brooklyn settlement. In 1902 Leonora began teaching at the Manhattan Trade School for Girls, where she served until 1909. The founding of the National Women's Trade Union League in 1903 opened further doors for Leonora. For two years she served on the board, and in 1909 became vice-president of the New York branch and received a lifetime annuity from Mary Dreier so that she could devote full time to the League. For the next several years Leonora travelled throughout the country speaking on behalf of the League when she was not actively involved in strikes and demonstrations in New York. During this same time period she also devoted time to other reform causes. She helped to found the National Association for the Advancement of Colored People and served on its first General Committee. In 1910 Leonora became an active member in the Socialist party in New York, and in 1912 she added women's suffrage to her concerns when she became chairman of the industrial committee for the New York City Woman Suffrage Party. After the outbreak of war, the League appointed Leonora its delegate to the International Congress of Women at The Hague in 1915. In 1919 she served as a delegate to the International Congress of Working Women in Washington, D.C. Leonora's many commitments, however, severely strained her health, and on April 3, 1927 she died of heart disease at the early age of 57.

The following speech was read before the National Society of Women Workers in Buffalo, New York, on Thursday, August 29, 1901. A typescript of the speech is located in the Leonora O'Reilly Papers, Brown University Library (microfilm edition of "Papers of the Women's Trade Union League and Its Principal Leaders," O'Reilly Papers, Reel 9), Providence, Rhode Island.

"Women's Opportunities in the Civil Service"

Perhaps no one subject today is exciting more wide spread interest among medical men, if not among all thinking people, than that of the part insects play in the spread of disease. Says a leading New York newspaper referring to the subject: "The spraying of ponds and puddles with oil is after all a temporary expedient and only commendable as the most convenient method of minimizing the effects of causes which it does nothing to destroy." What is needed in Staten Island as everywhere else where mosquitoes threaten human health and temper, is not the occasional or even frequent use of petroleum or other insect-destroyers, but a thorough utilization of the means which modern sanitary science provides for improving general health conditions.

Now, I think I hear you asking, "What have mosquitoes to do with civil government or Civil Service Reform, especially with woman's opportunities in Civil Service Reform?"

Mosquitoes? Nothing, perhaps, save for the common sense conclusion arrived at by the intelligence of the medical men, that the spread of disease can be most effectively controlled by measures directed to the destruction of the cause of the disease. With this homely example before us let us see what is the disease which threatens our body social today, and what we as women can do to destroy the germ of that disease.

Our present social ailment, one which has affected every department of the government, has grown out of what is known as the "spoils system;" a system based on the old barbaric principle that "to the victor belong the spoils." Let us not waste time discussing whether this principle could ever have been right, but, rather, granting that possibly it may have had its uses in times past, let us acknowledge that today, in the twentieth century, we have outgrown such war-like methods in civil government at least.

In the early days of our Republic the questions asked of each office seeker were, "Is he honest? Is he capable? Is he faithful to the constitution?" In our present diseased state, the one question asked of an office seeker is, "Is he faithful to the party?" Now parties are not bad things in themselves; they are good institutions where they represent the collective aspirations of a group of people for what they believe to be the best interest of the body politic. But just so soon as a party loses sight of the good of the whole and works for "party" right or wrong, it becomes a menace to the community and must be dealt with accordingly.

Loyalty is one of the cardinal virtues. But it must be loyalty to a worthy end. We must change the spirit which blandly cries "my party right or wrong" to one which shall more truly express the sentiment of intelligent free men.

Now, what can we non-voting women do toward this end?

A great deal, sisters mine. Those are not idle words which say, the hand that rocks the cradle sways the world. If all state secrets were uncovered, don't you think in these days as well as in the days of old, many Heads of Departments would disappear behind female figures and faces? But, be that as it may, wisdom tells us we should always make use of the opportunity at hand today, as a preparation for the larger duty of tomorrow which is sure to come as a reward for today's work well done.

First and foremost, we are home-makers and possibly home-keepers, and it is in the home and school that the nation is trained. In our local organizations we stand as united home-keepers; in this national organization, as the nation's home-keepers.

The United States is our home. What we can do for the health and happiness of these States, our home, is as much a part of our daily concern as how to make the special home we happen to be born into happier and more comfortable.

In this national organization, without political affiliation or pledge to any party, we stand free and unhampered, able to take a broad outlook upon our national home. Each club and each individual is a part of the patriotic conscience which must actually guide the better life of America. Can we not in our organized, national capacity take some united action which aims at the uplifting of our national life?

For twenty years we have had an agitation going on in the country known as The Civil Service Reform. It has no partisan significance; it seeks to lift all parties to a higher conception of public duty. Its ultimate object is to take away from the political parties the great bulk of appointments in the purely executive or business part of the Government. This desired change has been called the Merit System. Positions under it can be obtained only by those qualified to fill the offices. There is no consideration given to anything but special fitness. It is designed to secure the right of any well equipped citizen, man or woman, irrespective of party, wealth or influence, to serve the people in public office whether in town, state or nation. Civil Service Reform is not a cure for all our woes; it is a relief for the time being. Some day some one will come wise enough to tell us how to thoroughly purify our social life for all time.

Civil Service Reform is not a matter of politics alone; it concerns our moral life, our moral responsibilities. Through our club life, as we enter more and more into the work of the betterment of the world,—and take a more intelligent interest in philanthropic, industrial, educational and corrective measures, we face the spoils system everywhere. Our first step as women, as citizens, as part of the civil government, is to protest against the system which has packed our institutions and public departments with inefficient employees. What one among us but has known of some institution or asylum where the unfortunate classes have been in charge of the miserably unfit? Great public works have miscarried or been ruined as a result of poor construction; in the large cities the police corruption is proverbial; the public health has suffered and hordes of mercenaries have often been maintained in the place of trained public servants.

Laws may be passed from time to time, but a mightier force even than law itself must be brought to bear upon the question. Public sentiment is the power behind the throne in all democratic government. As a moral force put into vigorous action it is irresistible. The first step is to enlighten this public sentiment. The process is largely individual. When each man and each woman sees the truth and does what he or she can do to promote it, the ideals of this nation can be realized, but not until then. That we see the truth, and see it more clearly every day, is indisputable, but to see and not to act is criminal if not fatal. Women, lacking the direct power of the ballot, forget their possible share in the mighty engine of public opinion.

The most important factor in the forming of this public opinion is the training of the young. This is primarily woman's function. Good citizenship must be taught in the home and the common schools. No opportunity should be lost to impress upon the child his or her future share in the government. For a Democracy is not necessarily a perfect government; it is a continuous growth, a long slow education where each individual man or woman learns his or her personal responsibility for the well being of all. And let us not forget that one of the strongest arguments for Civil Service Reform is that it stimulates education. In a government founded upon the intelligence and integrity of every citizen the foundation stone must be education.

It may be that through this very reform we will learn that all have not equal opportunities to get an education. Let this not frighten or discourage us. Like the spraying of the ponds, we are doing our best for the time being. When we as a people become thoroughly convinced that ignorance is the cause of all our woes, have no fear but that there is hand, head and heart enough in this land of ours to wipe out the pest for all time.

But I have been talking a long time on the ethical side of Woman's Opportunity in Civil Service Reform to a very practical body of women. The truth is, sisters mine, I am convinced that if we get right ethically we can't go far wrong practically, so I've left the practical part of my speech for the close, so that if you cut me off before the finish I shall have said my say and you may guess the statistics.

When women have had an opportunity in Civil Service what has been the result? The same as every where else. She has not failed. Says the Hon. John R. Proctor, United States Civil Service Commissioner: "Three distinct benefits have accrued to the women of the United States by reason of the introduction of the merit system.

First;—They may obtain employment in the government service without political influence.

Second;—they may continue in the public service without fear of dismissal by reason of changes occurring in the administration.

Third;—no restriction is placed upon women's rising to any position in the classified service which their education and adaptability will permit them to fill."

"And how does this law work?" I think I hear my practical sister ask. Thiswise: from July 16th, 1883, to June 30th, 1900, there were appointed to the classified service in the department of Washington, through competitive examination, two thousand and forty-four women. This number includes one thousand two hundred and sixty printers' assistants in the Bureau of Engraving and Printing at a compensation of a dollar and a quarter a day, which is the lowest salary paid in the classified service. About one-third of all the employees in the department of Washington are women. They are employed in ordinary clerical capacity although many technical positions are filled by them.

Three women employees receive $1800 a year; about fifty receive $1600 a year; one hundred receive $1400; four hundred and fifty receive $1200; three hundred receive $1000; and the remainder receive from $660 to $900 per year.

A fair comparison of the progress made by women in government employ since the enactment of the Civil Service Law of 1883, is shown in the State Department, office of the Secretary. In 1883 there were ten women employed and the highest salary received was $1400, there being but one who received that. In 1889, in the same office, there were seventeen, the highest salary being $1600; there were several employed at $1400, and others at $1200 a year.

Of the total number of women taking the competitive examinations during the past ten years, over seventy-seven per cent have successfully passed and there are fifty-seven kinds of examinations which are open alike to men and women. At the present time the proportion of women to men being appointed is about one-sixth in the departments at Washington.

Appointments of women winning their places through open competition will continue as the women continue to offer superior qualifications for doing public work. And with this last word I will leave you, fellow working women. Offer superior qualifications for doing public work. Glorious as woman's record has been, there is still a beyond; there are many departments to be opened up to us; there is still room for a greater liberality on the part of those who decide whether men or women shall have these positions. Remember, this government is not outside of us. It is we who are the government. What we want it to be it shall be. With this thought in mind let every one of the clubs represented here make a study of our own government. Let some clubs study Civil Service Reform Movement, others the meaning of Constitutional Government, still others learn what it means to be born into a Republic or a Democracy. Such studies would not be without the field of woman's club work; therefore, take it up, fellow working women, and encourage that intelligence which maintains it to be a duty for us to leave our country in a healthier state than that in which we found it. No citizen can do more nor should he do less than that. When we have done this much, be sure the next generation will pick up the work where we leave off and carry it still farther along toward that city of the future where man shall live with man as brother.

Alice Paul
(1885–   )

Alice Paul was born on January 11, 1885 in Moorestown, New Jersey. The only child of a prosperous Quaker family, she attended private Friends' schools in New Jersey before entering Swarthmore College in 1901. After graduating in 1905, she did graduate work at the New York School of Social Work for a year and also resided at the New York College Settlement. In 1906 Alice embarked for England to participate in the British settlement movement and to pursue post-graduate work at Birmingham and London universities. During her three years abroad she became actively involved in the British Suffrage Movement and served time in prison on three different occasions for disorderly conduct at suffragist demonstrations. In 1912 Alice returned to the United States to receive a M.A. degree and Ph.D. degree from the University of Pennsylvania, based largely on her graduate work completed in England. In the same year she became chairperson of the Congressional Committee of the American Woman Suffrage Association. A year later she led a group of militant suffragists in seceding from the parent organization and forming the Congressional Union for Woman Suffrage. Alice served as national chairperson of the Congressional Union until 1917 when it merged with the Woman's Party to form the National Woman's Party. Once again her militant suffragist demonstrations during this time period led to three prison sentences. After women won the vote in 1920 Alice resumed her education, obtaining three law degrees— a LL.B. from Washington College of Law (1922), and a LL.M. (1927) and a D.C.L. (1928) from American University. During this same time period she succeeded in introducing the Equal Rights Amendment for the first time in Congress (1923) and assumed the chair of the Women's Research Foundation (1927). In the 1930's Alice's work expanded to the international scene: from 1930–33 she chaired the nationality committee of the Inter-American Commission of Women; as a member of the executive committee of the Equal Rights International she lobbied for complete equality for women throughout the world; and in the late 1930's she founded the World Party for Equal Rights for Women. Throughout the 1940's and 1950's, Alice continued to lobby in the United States Congress for passage of the E.R.A. while simultaneously continuing her international lobbying before the United Nations for a World Equal Rights Amendment. Since the 1960's Alice Paul has largely retired from active public life due to frail health, but her dedication to equal rights for women remains her guiding principle.

The following speech was delivered at the "Little White House" (Cameron House) in Washington, D.C. on April 9, 1916, at a conference of national officers, state officers and members of the advisory council of the Congressional Union. It was later printed in Inez Haynes Irwin, *The Story of the Woman's Party* (New York, N.Y., 1921), pp. 149–151.

"Forming the Woman's Party"

This is the third time we have called together the members of our Advisory Council and our state and national officers to lay before them a new project. The first time was at Newport when we proposed a campaign against all Democratic candidates for Congress in the Suffrage States. The second time was a year ago in New York when we proposed to convert the Congressional

Union into a national organization with branches in the different States. Today we want to lay another plan before you for your consideration—that is the organization of a political Party of women voters who can go into this next election, if it is necessary to go into it, as an independent Party.

I think we are all agreed on certain essential points. First—from what source our opposition comes. We are agreed that it comes from the Administration. We do not have to prove that. Second—we are agreed as to where our power lies—that is in the Suffrage States. Third—we are agreed as to the political situation. We know that the two Parties are about equal, that both want to win. We know that the Suffrage States are doubtful States and that every one of those States is wanted by the political Parties. We know that many of the elections will be close. The State of Nevada was won by only forty votes in the last Senatorial election. In Utah it was a week before the campaign was decided. In Colorado, the same. Going back over a period of twenty years it would have been necessary to have changed only nine per cent of the total vote cast in the presidential elections in order to have thrown the election to the other Party. This gives us a position of wonderful power, a position that we have never held before and that we cannot hope to hold again for at least four years, and which we may not hold then.

We have been working for two years to effect an organization in the Suffrage States and have finally completed such an organization. Our last branch was formed about ten days ago in the State of Washington. We now have to demonstrate to the Administration, to the majority Party in Congress, that the organization in the Suffrage States does exist and that it is a power to be feared. There are many months still remaining, probably, before Congress will adjourn. If in these months we can build up so strong an organization there that it really will be dangerous to oppose it, and if we can show Congress that we have such an organization, then we will have the matter in our hands.

We have sent a request to our branches in the East to select one or more representative women who will go out to the West and make a personal appeal to the women voters to stand by us even more loyally than they have before—to form a stronger organization than has ever before existed.

Today we must consider what concrete plan we shall ask these envoys who go out to the West to propose to the voting women. I do not think it will do very much good to go through the voting States and simply strengthen our Suffrage organizations. That will not be enough to terrify the men in Congress. Suffrage organizations, unfortunately, have come to stand for feebleness of action and supineness of spirit. What I want to propose is that when we go to these women voters we ask them to begin to organize an independent political Party that will be ready for the elections in November. They may not have to go into these elections. If they prepare diligently enough for the elections they won't have to go into them. The threat will be enough. We want to propose to you that we ask the women voters to come together in Chicago at the time that the Progressives and Republicans meet there in June, to decide how they will use these four million votes that women have, in the next election.

Now, if women who are Republicans simply help the Republican Party, and if women who are Democrats help the Democratic Party, women's votes will not count for much. But if the political Parties see before them a group of independent women voters who are standing together to use their vote to promote Suffrage, it will make Suffrage an issue—the women voters at once become a group which counts; whose votes are wanted. The Parties will inevitably have to go to the women voters if the latter stand aloof and do not go to the existing political Parties. The political Parties will have to offer them the thing which will win their votes. To count in an election you do not have to be the biggest Party; you have to be simply an independent Party that will stand for one object and that cannot be diverted from that object.

Four years ago there was launched a new Party, the Progressive Party. It really did, I suppose, decide the last Presidential election. We can be the same determining factor in this coming election. And if we can make Congress realize that we can be the determining factor, we won't have to go into the election at all.

What I would like to propose, in short, is that we go to the women voters and ask them to hold a convention in Chicago the first week in June, and that we spend these next two months in preparation. We could not have a better opportunity for preparation than this trip of the envoys through every one of the Suffrage States, calling the women together to meet in Chicago, the place where the eyes of the whole country will be turned in June.

We want very much to know what you think about this plan and whether you will help us in carrying it through. It is not an easy thing to launch a new Party and have it stand competition with the Republican and Democratic Parties. If we undertake it, we must make it a success. We must make it worthy to stand beside these great Parties. That is the biggest task that we have ever dreamed of since we started the Congressional Union.

Ernestine Rose
(1810–1892)

Ernestine Rose was born on January 13, 1810 in the ghetto of Piotrkow, Russian Poland. An only child and daughter of the town Rabbi, Ernestine grew up with more freedom and more education than was typical for girls of her background. At age fourteen she rejected all Jewish dogma relating to women, and two years later, in 1826, contested her father's right to arrange for her marriage in order to pass on an inheritance left to her by her mother. Having won her claim in court, Ernestine turned most of the inheritance over to her father in return for her freedom to leave Poland. The next several years she lived in Germany, Holland and France before settling in England in 1831. While in England Ernestine joined Robert Owen in 1835 to found the Association of All Classes of All Nations. In the following year she met and married William Rose, a disciple of Owen's. Immediately after her marriage she and her husband left for the United States and settled in New York City. Soon after arriving Ernestine became active in working for the married women's property bill and became acquainted with Elizabeth Cady Stanton. She also became active in the free-thought movement and lectured frequently for the Society for Moral Philanthropists. For the next thirty years Ernestine devoted most of her time to the cause of women's rights and she missed few of the national conventions and delivered addresses at most of them. In addition, she lectured in more than twenty states and addressed legislative bodies interweaving the issues of women's rights, temperance, antislavery and freedom of thought. During the Civil War she worked with Elizabeth Cady Stanton and Susan B. Anthony in the Women's Loyal National League and later in the American Equal Rights Association. In 1869, Ernestine returned to England with her husband where she occasionally delivered speeches for various reform causes. At the age of 82, she died on August 4, 1892 in Brighton, England.

The following speech was delivered on May 14, 1863 at the national convention of the Women's National Loyal League in new York City. The speech appears in printed form in *The History of Woman Suffrage*, Vol. II, pp. 73-78.

"The Necessity for the Utter Extinction of Slavery"

Louis Kossuth told us it is not well to look back for regret, but only for instruction. I therefore intend slightly to cast my mind's eye back for the purpose of enabling us, as far as possible, to contemplate the present and foresee the future. It is unnecessary to point out the cause of this war. It is written on every object we behold. It is but too well understood that the primary cause is Slavery; and it is well to keep that in mind, for the purpose of gaining the knowledge how ultimately to be able to crush that terrible rebellion which now desolates the land. Slavery being the cause of the war, we must look to its utter extinction for the remedy. (Applause).

We have listened this evening to an exceedingly instructive, kind and gentle address, particularly that part of it which tells how to deal with the South after we have brought them back. But I think it would be well, at first, to consider how to bring them back!

Abraham Lincoln has issued a Proclamation. He has emancipated all the slaves of the rebel States with his pen, but that is all. To set them really and thoroughly free, we will have to use some other instrument than the pen. (Applause). The slave is not emancipated; he is not free. A gentleman once found himself of a sudden, without, so far as he knew, any cause, taken into prison. He sent for his lawyer, and told him. "They have taken me to prison." "What have you done?" said the lawyer. "I have done nothing," he replied. "Then, my friend, they can not put you in prison." "But I am in prison." "Well, that may be; but I tell you, my dear friend, they can not put you in prison." "Well," said he, "I want you to come and take me out, for I tell you, in spite of all your lawyer logic, I am in prison, and I shall be until you take me out." (Great laughter). Now the poor slave has to say, "Abraham Lincoln, you have pronounced me free; still I am a slave, bought and sold as such, and I shall remain a slave till I am taken out of this horrible condition." Then the question is, *How?* Have not already two long years passed over more than a quarter of a million of the graves of the noblest and bravest of the nation? Is that not enough? No; it has proved not to be enough. Let us look back for a moment. Had the Proclamation of John C. Fremont been allowed to have its effect; had the edict of Hunter been allowed to have its effect, the war would have been over. (Applause). Had the people and the Government, from the very commencement of the struggle, said to the South, "You have openly thrown down the gauntlet to fight for Slavery; we will accept it, and fight for Freedom," the rebellion would long before now have been crushed. (Applause). You may blame Europe as much as you please, but the heart of Europe beats for freedom. Had they seen us here accept the terrible alternative of war for the sake of freedom, the whole heart of Europe would have been with us. But such has not been the case. Hence the destruction of over a quarter of a million of lives and ten millions of broken hearts that have already paid the penalty; and we know not how many more it needs to wipe out the stain of that recreancy that did not at once proclaim this war a war for freedom and humanity.

And now we have got here all around us Loyal Leagues. Loyal to what? What does it mean? I have read that term in the papers. A great many times I have heard that expression to-day. I know not what others mean by it, but I will give you my interpretation of what I am loyal to. I speak for myself. I do not wish any one else to be responsible for my opinions. I am loyal only to justice and humanity. Let the Administration give evidence that they too are for justice to all, without exception, without distinction, and I, for one, had I ten thousand lives, would gladly lay them down to secure this boon of freedom to humanity. (Applause). But without this certainty, I am not unconditionally loyal to the Administration. We women need not be, for the law has never yet recognized us. (Laughter). Then I say to Abraham Lincoln, "Give us security for the future, for really when I look at the past, without a guarantee, I can hardly trust you." And then I would say to him, "Let nothing stand in your way; let no man obstruct your path."

Much is said in the papers and in political speeches about the Constitution. Now, a good constitution is a very good thing; but even the best of constitutions need sometimes to be amended and improved, for after all there is but one constitution which is infallible, but one constitution that ought to be held sacred, and that is the human constitution. (Laughter). Therefore, if written constitutions are in the way of human freedom, suspend them till they can be improved. If generals are in the way of freedom, suspend them too; and more than that, suspend their money. We have got here a whole army of generals who have been actually dismissed from the service, but not from pay. Now, I say to Abraham Lincoln, if these generals are good for anything, if they are fit to take the lead, put them at the head of armies, and let them go South and free the slaves you have announced free. If they are good for nothing, dispose of them as of anything else that is useless. At all events, cut them loose from the pay. (Applause). Why, my friends, from July, 1861, to October, 1862—for sixteen long months—we have been electrified with the name of our great little Napoleon! And what has the great little Napoleon done? (Laughter). Why, he has done just enough to prevent anybody else from doing anything. (Great applause). But I have no quarrel with him. I don't know him. I presume none of you do. But I ask Abraham Lincoln—I like to go to headquarters, for where the greatest power is assumed, there the greatest responsibility rests, and in accordance with that principle I have nothing to do with menials, even though they are styled Napoleons—but I ask the President why McClellan was kept in the army so long after it was known—for there never was a time when anything else was known—that he was both incapable and unwilling to do anything? I refer to this for the purpose of coming, by and by, to the question, "What ought to be done?" He was kept at the head of the army on the Potomac just long enough to prevent Burnside from doing anything, and not much has been done since that time. Now, McClellan may be a very nice young man—I haven't the slightest doubt of it—but I have read a little anecdote of him. Somebody asked the president of a Western railroad company, in which McClellan was an engineer, what he thought about his abilities. "Well," said the president, "he is a first-rate man to build bridges; he is very exact, very mathematical in measurement, very precise in adjusting the timber; he is the best man in the world to build a good, strong, sound bridge, but after he has finished it, he never wishes anybody to cross over it." (Great laughter). Well, we have disposed of him partially, but we PAY him yet, and you and I are taxed for it. But if we are to have a new general in his place, we may ask, what has become of Sigel? Why does that disinterested, noble-minded, freedom-loving man in vain ask of the Administration to give him an army to lead into the field?

A VOICE: Ask Halleck.

Halleck! If Halleck is in the way, dispose of him. (Applause). Do you point me to the Cabinet? If the Cabinet is in the way of freedom, dispose of the Cabinet—(applause) some of them, at least. The magnitude of this war has never yet been fully felt or acknowledged by the Cabinet. The man at its head—I mean Seward—has hardly yet woke up to the reality that we have a war. He was going to crush the rebellion in sixty days. It was a mere *bagatelle!* Why, he could do it after dinner, any day, as easy as taking a bottle of wine! If Seward is in the way of crushing the rebellion and establishing freedom, dispose of him. From the cause of the war, learn the remedy, decide the policy, and place it in the hands of men capable and willing to carry it out. I am not unconditionally loyal, until we know to what principle we are to be loyal. Promise justice and freedom, and all the rest will follow. Do you know, my friends, what will take place if something decisive is not soon done? It is high time to consider it. I am not one of those who look on the darkest side of things, but yet my reason and reflection forbid me to hope against hope. It is only eighteen months more before another Presidential election—only one year before another President will be nominated. Let the present administration remain as indolent, as inactive, and, apparently, as indifferent as they have done; let them keep generals that are inferior to many of their private soldiers: let them keep the best generals there are in the country—Sigel and Fremont—unoccupied—(applause); let them keep the country in the same condition in which it has been the last two years, and is now, and what would be the result, if, at the next election, the Democrats succeed—I mean the sham Democrats? I am a democrat, and it is because I am a democrat that I go for human freedom. Human freedom and true democracy are identical. Let the Democrats, as they are now called, get into office, and what would be the consequence? Why, under this hue-and-cry for Union, *Union,* UNION, which is like a bait held out to the mass of the people to lure them on, they will grant to the South the meanest and the most contemptible compromises that the worst slaveholders in the

South can require. And if they really accept them and come back—my only hope is that they will not—but if the South should accept these compromises, and come back, slavery will be fastened, not only in the South, but it will be nationally fastened on the North. Now, a good Union, like a good Constitution, is a most invaluable thing; but a false Union is infinitely more despicable than no Union at all; and for myself, I would vastly prefer to have the South remain independent, than to bring them back with that eternal curse nationalized in the country. It is not enough for Abraham Lincoln to proclaim the slaves in the South free, nor even to continue the war until they shall be really free. There is something to be done at home; for justice, like charity, must begin at home. It is a mockery to say that we emancipate the slaves we can not reach and pass by those we can reach. First, free the slaves that are under the flag of the Union. If that flag is the symbol of freedom, let it wave over free men only. The slaves must be freed in the Border States. Consistency is a great power. What are you afraid of? That the Border States will join with the now crippled rebel States? We have our army there, and the North can swell its armies. But we can not afford to fight without an object. We can not afford to bring the South back with slavery. We can not compromise with principle. What has brought on this war? Slavery, undoubtedly. Slavery was the primary cause of it. But the great secondary cause was the fact that the North, for the sake of the Union, has constantly compromised. Every demand that the South made of the North was acceded to, until the South came really to believe that they were the natural and legitimate masters, not only of the slaves, but of the North too.

Now, it is time to reverse all these things. This rebellion and this war have cost too dear. The money spent, the vast stores destroyed, the tears shed, the lives sacrificed, the hearts broken are too high a price to be paid for the mere *name* of Union. I never believed we had a Union. A true Union is based upon principles of mutual interest, of mutual respect and reciprocity, none of which ever existed between the North and South. They based their institutions on slavery; the North on freedom.

I care not by what measure you end the war, if you allow one single germ, one single seed of slavery to remain in the soil of America, whatever may be your object, depend upon it, as true as effect follows cause, that germ will spring up, that noxious weed will thrive, and again stifle the growth, wither the leaves, blast the flowers, and poison the fair fruits of freedom. Slavery and freedom can not exist together. Seward proclaimed a truism, but he did not appreciate its import. There is an irrepressible conflict between freedom and slavery. You might as well say that light and darkness can exist together as freedom and slavery. We, therefore, must urge the Government to do something, and that speedily to secure the boon of freedom, while they yet can, not only in the rebel States, but in our own States too, and in the Border States. It is just as wrong for us to keep slaves in the Union States as it ever was in the South. Slavery is as great a curse to the slaveholder as it is a wrong to the slaves; and yet while we free the rebel slaveholder from the curse, we allow it to continue with our Union-loving men in the Border States. Free the slaves in the Border States, in Western Virginia, in Maryland, and wherever the Union flag floats, and then there will be a consistency in our actions that will enable us to go to work earnestly with heart and hand united, as we move forward to free all others and crush the rebellion. We have had no energy yet in the war, for we have fought only for the purpose of reuniting, what has never been united, restoring the old Union—or rather the shadow as it was. A small republic, a small nation, based upon the eternal principle of freedom, is great and powerful. A large empire based upon slavery, is weak and without foundation. The moment the light of freedom shines upon it, it discloses its defects, and unmasks its hideous deformities. As I said before, I would rather have a small republic without the taint and without the stain of slavery in it, than to have the South brought back by compromise. To avert such calamity, we must work. And our work must mainly be to watch and criticise and urge the Administration to do its whole duty to freedom and humanity.

Deborah Sampson
(1760–1827)

Deborah Sampson was born on December 17, 1760 in Plympton, Massachusetts, near Plymouth. The oldest child of six, Deborah was bound out as a servant at the age of ten and worked in this capacity until the age of 18. Her part time attendance at the Middleborough public school, supplemented by instruction from the family she worked for, enabled her to teach school for half a year in 1779. But Deborah's penchant for adventure prompted her to resign her teaching post and walk to Boston, and from there to Bellingham, Massachusetts, where on May 20, 1782, she enlisted in the Continental forces under the alias of Robert Shurtleff. As a member of the Fourth Massachusetts Regiment she participated in several skirmishes before she was wounded near Tarrytown, New York. Deborah's hospitalization resulted in her exposure as a member of the female sex and on October 25, 1784, she was discharged by General Henry Knox at West Point. Upon returning to Massachusetts she met Benjamin Gannet, a farmer in Sharon, and married him in 1785. Three children and several years later, Deborah achieved notoriety when Herman Mann published a romanticized biography about her entitled *The Female Review* (1797). In 1802, under Mann's supervision, she toured various New England and New York towns delivering speeches which recounted her adventures as a revolutionary soldier. This tour provided some financial assistance for Deborah and her destitute family and also assisted her in gaining support to obtain a pension from the United States government. In 1804 a letter from Paul Revere greatly abetted her cause, and in 1805 she began receiving a pension. After Deborah's death in 1827 at the age of 66, her husband successfully petitioned the government to continue the pension to compensate for the many years he had paid heavy medical bills for his wife, whose sickness and suffering, he contended, were occasioned by her military service.

The following address was delivered in Massachusetts, Rhode Island and New York in 1802. A copy of the address as delivered in Boston, Massachusetts on March 22, 1802 is printed as a pamphlet entitled "An Address by Deborah Sampson Gannett" (Dedham, Ma., 1802) and located in the Sharon, Massachusetts Historical Society archives.

"An Address on Life as a Female Revolutionary Soldier"

Not unlike the example of the patriot and philanthropist, though perhaps perfectly so in effect, do I awake from the tranquil slumbers of retirement, to active, public scenes of life, like those which now surround me. That genius which is the prompter of *curiosity,* and that spirit which is the support of *enterprize,* early drove, or, rather illured me, from the corner of humble obscurity— their cheering aspect has again prevented a torpid rest.

Secondary to these are the solicitations of a number of worthy characters and friends, too persuasive and congenial with my own disposition to be answered with indifference, or to be rejected, have induced me thus to advance and bow submissive to an audience, simply and concisely to rehearse a *tale of truth;* which, though it took its rise, and finally terminated in the splendor of public life, I was determined to repeat only as the soliloquy of a hermit, or to the visionary phantoms, which hover through the glooms of solitude.

A tale—the truth of which I was ready to say, but which, perhaps, others have already said for me, ought to expel me from the enjoyment of society, from the acknowledgment of my own sex, and from the endearing friendship of the other. But this, I venture to pronounce, would be saying too much: For as I should thus not respect *myself,* should be entitled to none from *others.*

I indeed recollect it as a foible, an error and presumption, into which, perhaps, I have too inadvertantly and precipitately run; but which I now retrospect with anguish and amazement—recollect it, as a THOMSON, or any other moralizing naturalist, susceptible to the like fine feelings of nature, recollects the howling blasts of *winter,* at a period when *Flora* has strewed the earth with all her profusion of delicacies, and whose zephyrs are wasting their fragrance to heighten our sensations of tranquility and pleasure;—or, rather, perhaps, I ought to recollect it, as a mariner, having regained his native shore of serenity and peace, looks back on the stormy billows which, so long and so constantly had threatened to ingulph him in the bowels of the deep! And yet I must frankly confess, I recollect it with a kind of satisfaction, which no one can better conceive and enjoy than him, who, recollecting the *good intentions* of a *bad deed,* lives to see and to correct any indecorum of his life.

But without further preliminary apologies, yet with every due respect towards this brilliant and polite circle, I hasten to a review of the most conspicuous parts of that path, which led to achievements, which some have believed, but which many still doubt. Their accomplishment once seemed to me as impossible, as that I am author of them, is now incredible to the incredulous, or wounding to the ear of more refined delicacy and taste. They are a breach in the decorum of my sex, unquestionably; and, perhaps, too unfortunately ever irreconcilable with the rigid maxims of the moralist; and a sacrifice, which, while it may seem perfectly incompatible with the requirements of virtue—and which of course must ring discord in the ear, and disgust to the bosom of sensibility and refinement, I must be content to leave to time and the most scrutinizing enquiry to disclose.

Unlettered in any scholastic school of erudition, you will not expect, on this occasion, the entertainment of the soft and captivating sounds of eloquence; but rather a narration of facts in a mode as uncouth as they are unnatural. *Facts*—which, though I once experienced, and of which memory has ever been painfully retentive, I cannot now make you feel, or paint to the life.

Know then, that my juvenile mind early became inquisitive to understand—not merely whether the principles, or rather the seeds of *war* are analogous to the genuine nature of *man*—not merely to know why he should forego every trait of *humanity,* and to assume the character of a *brute;* or, in plainer language, why he should march out tranquilly, or in a paroxism of rage against his fellow-man, to butcher, or be butchered?—for these, alas! were too soon horribly verified by the massacres in our streets, in the very streets which encompass this edifice—in yonder adjacent villas, on yonder memorable eminence, where now stand living monuments of the atrocious, the heart-distracting, mementous scenes, that followed in rapid succession!

This I am ready to affirm, though it may be deemed unnatural in my sex, is not a demoralization of human nature. The sluices, both of the blood of *freemen* and of *slaves,* were first opened here. And those hills and vallies, once the favorite resort, both of the lover and philosopher, have been drunk with their blood! A new subject was then opened to the most pathetic imagination, and to the rouzing of every latent spark of humanity, one should think, in the bosoms of the *wolves,* as well as in those of the *sheep,* for whose blood they were so thirsty.

But most of all, my mind became agitated with the enquiry—why a nation, separated from us by an ocean more than three thousand miles in extent, should endeavor to enforce on us plans of subjugation, the most unnatural in themselves, unjust, inhuman, in their operations, and unpractised even by the uncivilized savages of the wilderness? Perhaps nothing but the critical juncture of the times could have excused such a philosophical disquisition of politics in woman, notwithstanding it was a theme of universal speculation and concern to man. We indeed originated from her, as from a parent, and had, perhaps, continued to this period in subjection to her mandates, had we not discovered, that this, her romantic, avaricious and cruel disposition extended to *murder,* after having bound the *slave!*

Confirmed by this time in the justness of a defensive war on the one side, from the most aggravated one on the other—my mind ripened with my strength; and while our beds and our roses were sprinkled with the blood of indiscriminate youth, beauty, innocence and decrepit old age, I only seemed to want the *license* to become one of the severest *avengers* of the wrong.

For several years I looked on these scenes of havoc, rapacity and devastation, as one looks on a drowning man, on the conflagration of a city—where are not only centered his coffers of gold, but with them his choicest hopes, friends, companions, his all—without being able to extend the rescuing hand to either.

Wrought upon at length, you may say, by an enthusiasm and phrenzy, that could brook no control—I burst the tyrant bands, which *held my sex in awe,* and clandestinely, or by stealth, grasped an opportunity, which custom and the world seemed to deny, as a natural priviledge. And whilst poverty, hunger, nakedness, cold and disease had dwindled the *American Armies* to a handful—whilst universal terror and dismay ran through our camps, ran through our country—while even WASHINGTON himself, at their head, though like a god, stood, as it were, on a pinacle tottering over the abyss of destruction, the last prelude to our falling a wretched prey to the yawning jaws of the monster aiming to devour—not merely for the sake of gratifying a fecetious curiosity, like that of my reputed Predecessor, in her romantic excursions through the garden of bliss—did I throw off the soft habiliments of *my sex,* and assume those of the *warrior,* already prepared for battle.

Thus I became an actor in that important drama, with an inflexible resolution to persevere through the last scene; when we might be permitted and acknowledged to enjoy what we had so nobly declared we would possess, or lose with our lives—FREEDOM and INDEPENDENCE!— When the philosopher might resume his researches unmolested—the statesman be disembarrassed by his distracting theme of national politics—the divine find less occasion to invoke the indignation of heaven on the usurpers and cannibals of the inherent rights and even existence of man—when the son should again be restored to the arms of his disconsolate parent, and the lover to the bosom of her, for whom indeed he is willing to jeopard his life, and for whom alone he wishes to live!

A new scene, and, as it were, a new world now opened to my view; the objects of which now seemed as important, as the transition before seemed unnatural. It would, however, here be a weakness in me to mention the tear of repentence, or of that of temerity, from which the stoutest of my sex are, or ought not to be, wholly exempt on extreme emergencies, which many times involuntarily stole into my eye, and fell unheeded to the ground: And that too before I had reached the embattled field, the ramparts, which protected its internal resources—which shielded youth, beauty, and the delicacy of that sex at home, which perhaps I had forfeited in turning volunteer in their defence. *Temeritis*—when reflections on my former situation, and this new kind of being, were daggers more frightful, than all the implements of war—when the rustling of every leaf was an omen of danger, the whisper of each wind, a tale of woe! If then the poignancy of thought stared me thus haggardly in the face, found its way to the inmost recesses of my heart, thus forcibly, in the commencement of my career—what must I not have anticipated before its close!

The curtain is now up—a scene opens to your view; but the objects strike your attention less forcibly, and less interestingly, than they then did, not only my own eyes, but every energetic sensation of my soul. What shall I say further? Shall I not stop short, and leave to your imaginations to pourtray the tragic deeds of war? Is it not enough, that I here leave it even to unexperience to fancy the hardships the anxieties, the dangers, even of the best life of a soldier? And were it not improper, were it not unsafe, were it not indelicate, and were I certain I should be entitled to a pardon, I would appeal to the soft bosom of my own sex to draw a parallel between the perils and sexual inconveniences of a girl in her teens, and not only in the armour, but in the capacity, at any rate, obliged to perform the duties in the field—and those who go to the camp without a masquerade, and consequently subject only to what toils and sacrifices they please: Or, will a conclusion be more natural from those who sometimes take occasion to complain by their own domestic fire-sides; but who, indeed, are at the same time in affluence, cherished in the arms of their companions, and sheltered from the storms of war by the rougher sex in arms?

Many have seen, and many can contemplate, in the field of imagination, battles and victories amidst garments rolled in blood: but it is only one of my own sex, exposed to the storm, who can conceive of my situation.

We have all heard of, many have doubtless seen, the meteor streaming through or breaking in the horizon—the terrific glare of the comet, in its approach towards, or in its declension from us, in its excentric orbit—the howling of a tempest—the electric fluid, which darts majesty and terror through the clouds—its explosion and tremendous effects!—BOSTONIANS, and you who inhabit its environs, you who have known from experience your houses and your hills tremble from the cannonade of *Charlestown,*—your ears are yet wounded by the shrieks of her mangled and her distressed—your eyes swimming in a deluge of anguish at the sight of our butchered, expiring relatives and friends; while the conflagration of the town added the last solemnity to the scene!

This idea must assimulate with the progress of this horrid delusion of war. Hence you can behold the parched soil of *White-Plains* drink insatiate the blood of her most peaceful and industrious proprietors—of *freemen,* and of *slaves!* I was there! The recollection makes me shudder!—A dislocated limb draws fresh anguish from my heart!

You may have heard the thunderings of a volcano—you may have contemplated, with astonishment and wonder, the burial of a city by its eruption. Your ears then are yet deafened from the thunderings of the invasion of *York Town*—your eyes dazzled, your imaginations awfully sublimed, by the fire which belched from its environs, and towered, like that from an eruption of *Etna,* to the clouds! Your hearts yet bleed, from every principle of humanity, at the recollection of the havoc, carnage and death that reigned there!

Three successive weeks, after a long and rapid march, found me amidst this storm.—But, happy for AMERICA, happy for EUROPE, perhaps for the WORLD, when, on the delivery of CORNWALLIS'S sword to the illustrious, the immoral WASHINGTON, or rather by his order, to the brave LINCOLN, the sun of *Liberty* and *Independence* burst through a sable cloud, and his benign influence was, almost instantaneously, felt in our remotest corners! The phalanx of war was thus broken through, and the palladium of peace blossoming on its ruins.

I will not hence urge you to retrace with me (tranquilly you surely cannot) all the footsteps of our valient heroic LEADERS through the distraction both of elements and of war. I will not even pourtray an attempt to reinforce the brave SCHUYLER, then on the borders of Canada; where, if the *war-whoop* of infernals should not strike you with dismay, the *tommahawk* would soon follow!

138

Nor need I point you to the death-like doors of the hospital in Philadelphia, whose avenues were crouded with the sick, the dying and the dead; though myself made one of the unhappy croud!

You have now but the shade of a picture; which neither time nor my abilities will permit me to show you to the life. The haggard fiend, despair, may have stared you in the face, when giving over the pursuit of a favorite, lost child: And it is only in this torture of suspense that we can rightly conceive of its situation.

Such is my experience—not that I ever mourned the loss of a child, but that I considered myself as lost! For, on the one hand, if I fell not a victim to the infuriate rabble of a mob, or of a war not yet fully terminated—a disclosure of my peculiar situation seemed infinitely worse than either. And if from stratagem and perseverance, I may acquire as great knowledge in every respect as I have of myself in this, my knowledge, at least of human nature, will be as complete as it is useful.

But we will now hasten from the field, from the embattled entrenchments, built for the destruction of man, from a long, desolating war, to contemplate more desirable and delightful scenes. And notwithstanding curiosity may prompt any to retrace the climax of our revolution, the means, under a smiling, superintending providence, by which we have outrode the storms of danger and distress—what heart will forget to expand with joy and gratitude, to beat in unison, at the propitious recollection? And I enquire, what infant tongue can ever forget or cease being taught to lisp the praises of WASHINGTON, and those of that bright constellation of WORTHIES, who swell the list of COLUMBIAN fame—those, by whose martial skill and philanthropic labors, we were first led to behold, after a long and stormy night, the smiling sun of *Peace* burst on our benighted WORLD! And while we drop a tear over the flowery turf of those patriots and sages, may she unrivalled enjoy and encrease her present bright sunshine of happiness! May agriculture and commerce, industry and manufactures, arts and sciences, virtue and decorum, union and harmony—those richest sources of our worth, and strongest pillars of our strength, become stationary, like fixed stars in the firmament, to flourish in her clime!

> Hail dearest LIBERTY! thou source sublime!
> What rays refulgent dart upon our clime!
> For thee the direful contest has been waged,
> Our hope, and all that life held dear engaged.
> Thee the prime offspring which my thoughts employ,
> Once sought with grief—now turns that grief to joy.
> Your beatific influence extend
> O'er AFRICA, whose sable race befriend.
> May EUROPE, as our sister-empire, join,
> To hail thee rising with your power divine,
> From the lone cottage to the tyrant's throne,
> May LIBERTY, ethereal guest, be known!
> Be thou preserved for nations yet unborn,
> Fair as the shining Star that decks the morn.

But the question again returns—*What particular inducement could she have thus to elope from the soft sphere of her own sex, to perform a deed of valor by way of sacrilege on unhallowed ground—voluntarily to face the storms both of elements and war, in the character of him, who is more fitly made to brave and endure all danger?*

AND dost thou ask what fairy hand inspired
A *Nymph* to be with martial glory fired?
Or, what from art, or yet from nature's laws,
Has join'd a *Female* to her country's cause?
Why on great Mar's theatre she drew
Her *female* pourtrait, though in soldier's hue?

THEN ask—why *Cincinnatus* left his farm?
Why science did old PLATO'S bosom warm?
Why HECTOR in the Trojan war should dare?
Or why should HOMER trace his actions there?
Why NEWTON in philosophy has shown?
Or CHARLES, for solitude, has left his throne?
Why LOCKE in metaphysics should delight—
Precisian sage, to set false reason right?
Why ALBION'S SONS should kindle up a war?
Why JOVE or VULCAN hurried on the car?
Perhaps the same propensity you use,
Has prompted her a martial course to choose.
Perhaps to gain refinements where she could,
This rare achievement for her country's good.
Or was some hapless *lover* from her torn—
As EMMA did her valient HAMMON mourn?
Else he must tell, who would this truth attain,
Why one is formed for pleasure—one for pain:
Or, boldly, why our MAKER made us such—
Why *here* he gives too *little—there* too *much!*

I would not purposely evade a a pertinent answer; and yet I know not, at present, how to give a more particular one than has already been suggested.

I am indeed willing to acknowledge what I have done, an error and presumption. I will call it an *error* and *presumption,* because I swerved from the accustomed flowry paths of *female delicacy,* to walk upon the heroic precipice of feminine perdition!—I indeed left my morning pillow of roses, to prepare a couch of brambles for the night; and yet I awoke from this refreshed, to gather nought but the thorns of anguish for the next night's repose—and in the precipitancy of passion, to prepare a moment for repentance at leisure!

Had all this been achieved by the rougher hand, more properly assigned to wield the sword in duty and danger in a defensive war, the most cruel in its measures, though important in its consequences; these thorns might have been converted into wreaths of immoral glory and fame. I therefore yield every claim of honor and distinction to the hero and patriot, who met the foe in his own name; though not with more heartfelt satisfaction, with the trophies, which were most to redound to the future grandeur and importance of the country in which he lives.

But *repentance* is a sweet solace to conscience, as well as the most complete atonement to the Supreme JUDGE of our offences: notwithstanding the tongue of malevolence and scurrility may be continually preparing its most poisonous ingredients for the punishment of a crime which has already received more than half a pardon.

Yet if even this be deemed too much of an extenuation of a breach in the modesty of the *female world*—humilized and contented will I sit down inglorious, for having unfortunately performed an important part assigned for another—like a bewildered star traversing out of its accustomed orbit, whose twinkling beauty at most has become totally obscured in the presence of the sun.

But as the rays of the sun strike the eye with the greatest lustre when emerging from a thick fog, and as those actions which have for their objects the extended hand of charity to the indigent and wretched—to restore a bewildered traveller to light—and, to reform in ourselves any irregular and forlorn course of life; so, allowing myself to be one or the greatest of these, do I still hope for some claim on the indulgence and patronage of the public; as in such case I might be conscious of the approbation of my GOD.

I cannot, contentedly, quit this subject or this place, without expressing, more emphatically, my high respect and veneration for my own SEX. The indulgence of this respectable circle supercedes my merit, as well as my most sanguine expectations. You receive at least in return my warmest gratitude. And though you can neither have, or perhaps need, from me the instructions of the sage, or the advice of the counsellor; you surely will not be wholly indifferent to my most sincere declaration of friendship for that sex, for which this checkered flight of my life may have rendered me the least ornamental example; but which, neither in adversity or prosperity, could I ever learn to forget or degrade.

I take it to be from the greatest extremes both in virtue and in vice, that the uniformly virtuous and reformed in life can derive the greatest and most salutary truths and impressions.—Who, for example, can contemplate for a moment, the *prodigal*—from the time of his revelry with harlots, to that of his eating husks with swine, and to his final return to his father—without the greatest emotion of disgust, pity and joy? And is it possible to behold the effects of the unprincipled conduct of the *libertine,* the *bacchanalian,* the *debauchee,* and what is more wretched of all, of the emaciated, haggard form of a modern *baggage* in the streets, without bringing into exercise every passion of abhorrence and commisseration? And yet, happy, those, who at the same time receive a monitor which fixes a resolve, never to embark on such a sea of perdition; where we see shipwreck of all that is enobling to the dignity of *man*—all that is lovely and amiable in the character of *woman!*

I cannot, indeed bring the adventures, even of the worst part of my own life, as parallels with this black catalogue of crimes. But in whatever I may be thought to have been unnatural, unwise and indelicate, it is now my most fervent desire it may have a suitable impression on you—and on me, a penitent for every wrong thought and step. The rank you hold in the scale of beings is, in many respects, superior to that of man. *Nurses* of his growth, and invariable models of his habits, he becomes a suppliant at your shrine, emulous to please, assiduous to cherish and support, to live and to die for you! *Blossoms* from your very birth, you become his admiration, his joy, his eden companions in this world.—How important then is it, that these *blossoms* bring forth such *fruit,* as will best secure your own delights and felicity, and those of him, whose every enjoyment, and even his very existence, is so peculiarly interwoven with your own!

On the whole, as we readily acquiesce in the acknowledgment, that the *field* and the *cabinet* are the proper spheres assigned to our MASTERS and our LORDS; may *we,* also, deserve the dignified title and encomium of MISTRESS and LADY, in our *kitchens* and in our *parlours.* And as an overruling providence may succeed our wishes—let us rear an offspring in every respect worthy to fill the most illustrious stations of their predecessors.

Margaret Sanger
(1879–1966)

Margaret Sanger was born on September 14, 1879 in Corning, New York. The sixth of eleven children from a working class family, she was unusually fortunate to extend her education beyond the requisite eight years of public school. After three years of attending a private coeducational prep school in the Catskills, she taught the first grade in a Little Falls, New Jersey school before returning to Nursing school for two years in White Plains, New York. In 1902 she married and moved to New York City where she lived and worked for most of the next forty years. For the first ten years she worked as a home nurse in Manhattan and in her spare time became active in labor movements attempting to organize textile workers in the East. Both of these experiences dramatically influenced her future reform efforts: her nursing experiences with poor and immigrant women convinced her of the necessity for planned parenthood and birth control, and her contacts with Emma Goldman and Elizabeth Gurley Flynn in Industrial Workers of the World activities inspired her to become a political activist for sexual reform. The repression of her publications on female sexuality in the socialist weekly "The Call" in 1912–1913 only sparked her determination to challenge Federal postal laws. After a trip to Europe in 1914 where she gathered information on birth control devices, she began publishing her militantly feminist journal "The Woman Rebel." Once again the post office ruled that the material was "unmailable," but Margaret continued defying their mandates until she was finally indicted. To avoid imprisonment she escaped to Europe, leaving behind her "Family Limitation" pamphlet which provided the most detailed information available on birth control. In 1915 she returned to New York after the government had dropped charges against her. Still undaunted, in 1916 she and her sister opened a clinic on birth control in Brooklyn, which the police closed after ten days. Her trial and subsequent jail term brought both notoriety to her as a reformer and to the birth control movement she so courageously championed and, not long after this, the laws were expanded to allow birth control information to be distributed. In 1921 Margaret organized the American Birth Control League, which in 1942 was renamed Planned Parenthood. In 1923 she realized one of her most important achievements when she opened the Birth Control Clinical Research Bureau in New York City staffed by doctors. By 1938, 300 such birth control clinics had been established throughout the country by Margaret and her followers. In 1938 she moved to Arizona to semi-retire, but emerged once again in 1952 to found the International Planned Parenthood Federation and to serve as its first President. Her final accomplishment was bringing research information to the attention of the eventual inventor of the birth control pill (Catherine McCormick). On September 6, 1966 she died peacefully at the age of 86.

The following address was delivered numerous times for the American Birth Control League during 1921–22. It was later reprinted as a chapter in Margaret Sanger, *The Pivot of Civilization* (New York, N.Y., 1922), pp. 190–219.

"A Moral Necessity for Birth Control"

> I went to the Garden of Love,
>   And saw what I never had seen;
> A Chapel was built in the midst,
>   Where I used to play on the green.
>
> And the gates of this Chapel were shut,
>   And "Thou shalt not" writ over the door;
> So I turned to the Garden of Love
>   That so many sweet flowers bore.
>
> And I saw it was filled with graves,
>   And tombstones where flowers should be;
> And priests in black gowns were walking their rounds,
>   And binding with briars my joys and desires.
>
>   *William Blake*

Orthodox opposition to Birth Control is formulated in the official protest of the National Council of Catholic Women against the resolution passed by the New York State Federation of Women's Clubs which favored the removal of all obstacles to the spread of information regarding practical methods of Birth Control. The Catholic statement completely embodies traditional opposition to Birth Control. It affords a striking contrast by which we may clarify and justify the ethical necessity for this new instrument of civilization as the most effective basis for practical and scientific morality. "The authorities at Rome have again and again declared that all positive methods of this nature are immoral and forbidden," states the National Council of Catholic Women. "There is no question of the lawfulness of birth restriction through abstinence from the relations which result in conception. The immorality of Birth Control as it is practised and commonly understood, consists in the evils of the particular method employed. These are all contrary to the moral law because they are unnatural, being a perversion of a natural function. Human faculties are used in such a way as to frustrate the natural end for which these faculties were created. This is always intrinsically wrong—as wrong as lying and blasphemy. No supposed beneficial consequence can make good a practice which is, in itself, immoral. . . .

"The evil results of the practice of Birth Control are numerous. Attention will be called here to only three. The first is the degradation of the marital relation itself, since the husband and wife who indulge in any form of this practice come to have a lower idea of married life. They cannot help coming to regard each other to a great extent as mutual instruments of sensual gratification, rather than as cooperators with the Creator in bringing children into the world. This consideration may be subtle but it undoubtedly represents the facts.

"In the second place, the deliberate restriction of the family through these immoral practices deliberately weakens self-control and the capacity for self-denial, and increases the love of ease and luxury. The best indication of this is that the small family is much more prevalent in the classes that are comfortable and well-to-do than among those whose material advantages are moderate or small. The theory of the advocates of Birth Control is that those parents who are comfortably situated should have a large number of children *(sic!)* while the poor should restrict their off-spring to a much smaller number. This theory does not work, for the reason that each married couple have their own idea of what constitutes unreasonable hardship in the matter of bearing and rearing children. A large proportion of the parents who are addicted to Birth Control practices are sufficiently provided with worldly goods to be free from apprehension on the economic side; nevertheless, they have small families because they are disinclined to undertake the other burdens involved in bringing up a more numerous family. A practice which tends to produce such exaggerated notions of what constitutes hardship, which leads men and women to cherish such a degree of ease, makes inevitably for inefficiency, a decline in the capacity to endure and to achieve, and for a general social decadence.

"Finally, Birth Control leads sooner or later to a decline in population. . . ." (The case of France is instanced.) But it is essentially the moral question that alarms the Catholic women, for the statement concludes: "The further effect of such proposed legislation will inevitably be a lowering both of public and private morals. What the fathers of this country termed indecent and forbade the mails to carry, will, if such legislation is carried through, be legally decent. The purveyors of sexual license and immorality will have the opportunity to send almost anything they care to write through the mails on the plea that it is sex information. Not only the married but also the unmarried will be thus affected; the ideals of the young contaminated and lowered. The morals of the entire nation will suffer.

"The proper attitude of Catholics . . . is clear. They should watch and oppose all attempts in state legislatures and in Congress to repeal the laws which now prohibit the dissemination of information concerning Birth Control. Such information will be spread only too rapidly despite existing laws. To repeal these would greatly accelerate this deplorable movement."

The Catholic position has been stated in an even more extreme form by Archbishop Patrick J. Hayes of the archdiocese of New York. In a "Christmas Pastoral" this dignitary even went to the extent of declaring that "even though some little angels in the flesh, through the physical or mental deformities of their parents, may appear to human eyes hideous, misshapen, a blot on civilized society, we must not lose sight of this Christian thought that under and within such visible malformation, lives an immortal soul to be saved and glorified for all eternity among the blessed in heaven."

With the type of moral philosophy expressed in this utterance, we need not argue. It is based upon traditional ideas that have had the practical effect of making this world a vale of tears. Fortunately such words carry no weight with those who can bring free and keen as well as noble minds to the consideration of the matter. To them the idealism of such an utterance appears crude and cruel. The menace to civilization of such orthodoxy, if it be orthodoxy, lies in the fact that its powerful exponents may be for a time successful not merely in influencing the conduct of their adherents but in checking freedom of thought and discussion. To this, with all the vehemence of emphasis at our command, we object. From what Archbishop Hayes believes concerning the future blessedness in Heaven of the souls of those who are born into this world as hideous and misshapen beings he has a right to seek such consolation as may be obtained; but we who are trying to better the conditions of this world believe that a healthy, happy human race is more in keeping with the laws of God, than disease, misery and poverty perpetuating itself generation after generation. Furthermore, while conceding to Catholic or other churchmen full freedom to preach their own doctrines, whether of theology or morals, nevertheless when they attempt to carry these ideas into legislative acts and force their opinions and codes upon the non-Catholics, we consider such action an interference with the principles of democracy and we have a right to protest.

Religious propaganda against Birth Control is crammed with contradiction and fallacy. It refutes itself. Yet it brings the opposing views into vivid contrast. In stating these differences we should make clear that advocates of Birth Control are not seeking to attack the Catholic church. We quarrel with that church, however, when it seeks to assume authority over non-Catholics and to dub their behavior immoral because they do not conform to the dictatorship of Rome. The question of bearing and rearing children we hold is the concern of the mother and the potential mother. If she delegates the responsibility, the ethical education, to an external authority, that is her affair. We object, however, to the State or the Church which appoints itself as arbiter and dictator in this sphere and attempts to force unwilling women into compulsory maternity.

When Catholics declare that "the authorities at Rome have again and again declared that all positive methods of this nature are immoral and forbidden," they do so upon the assumption that morality consists in conforming to laws laid down and enforced by external authority, in submission to decrees and dicta imposed from without. In this case, they decide in a wholesale manner the conduct of millions, demanding of them not the intelligent exercise of their own individual judgment and discrimination, but unquestioning submission and conformity to dogma. The Church thus takes the place of all-powerful parents, and demands of its children merely that they should obey. In my belief such a philosophy hampers the development of individual intelligence. Morality then becomes a more or less successful attempt to conform to a code, instead of an attempt to bring reason and intelligence to bear upon the solution of each individual human problem.

But, we read on, Birth Control methods are not merely contrary to "moral law," but forbidden because they are "unnatural," being "the perversion of a natural function." This, of course, is the weakest link in the whole chain. Yet "there is no question of the lawfulness of birth restriction through abstinence"—as though abstinence itself were not unnatural! For more than a thousand years the Church was occupied with the problem of imposing abstinence on its priesthood, its most educated and trained body of men, educated to look upon asceticism as the finest ideal; it took one thousand years to convince the Catholic priesthood that abstinence was "natural" or practicable. Nevertheless, there is still this talk of abstinence, self-control, and self-denial, almost in the same breath with the condemnation of Birth Control as "unnatural."

If it is our duty to act as "cooperators with the Creator" to bring children into the world, it is difficult to say at what point our behavior is "unnatural." If it is immoral and "unnatural" to prevent an unwanted life from coming into existence, is it not immoral and "unnatural" to remain unmarried from the age of puberty? Such casuistry is unconvincing and feeble. We need only point out that rational intelligence is also a "natural" function, and that it is as imperative for us to use the faculties of judgment, criticism, discrimination of choice, selection and control, all the faculties of the intelligence, as it is to use those of reproduction. It is certainly dangerous "to frustrate the natural ends for which these faculties were created." This, also, is always intrinsically wrong—as wrong as lying and blasphemy—and infinitely more devastating. Intelligence is as natural to us as any other faculty, and it is fatal to moral development and growth to refuse to use it and to delegate to others the solution of our individual problems. The evil will not be that one's conduct is divergent from current and conventional moral codes. There may be every outward evidence of conformity, but this agreement may be arrived at, by the restriction and suppression of subjective desires, and the more or less successful attempt at mere conformity. Such "morality" would conceal an inner conflict. The fruits of this conflict would be neurosis and hysteria on the one hand; or concealed gratification of suppressed desires on the other, with a resultant hypocrisy and cant. True morality cannot be based on conformity. There must be no conflict between subjective desire and outward behavior.

To object to these traditional and churchly ideas does not by any means imply that the doctrine of Birth Control is anti-Christian. On the contrary, it may be profoundly in accordance with the Sermon on the Mount. One of the greatest living theologians and most penetrating students of the problems of civilization is of this opinion. In an address delivered before the Eugenics Education

Society of London, William Ralph Inge, the Very Reverend Dean of St. Paul's Cathedral, London, pointed out that the doctrine of Birth Control was to be interpreted as of the very essence of Christianity.

"We should be ready to give up all our theories," he asserted, "if science proved that we were on the wrong lines. And we can understand, though we profoundly disagree with, those who oppose us on the grounds of authority. . . . We know where we are with a man who says, 'Birth Control is forbidden by God; we prefer poverty, unemployment, war, the physical, intellectual and moral degeneration of the people, and a high death rate to any interference with the universal command to be fruitful and multiply'; but we have no patience with those who say that we can have unrestricted and unregulated propagation without those consequences. It is a great part of our work to press home to the public mind the alternative that lies before us. Either rational selection must take the place of the natural selection which the modern State will not allow to act, or we must go on deteriorating. When we can convince the public of this, the opposition of organized religion will soon collapse or become ineffective." Dean Inge effectively answers those who have objected to the methods of Birth Control is "immoral" and in contradiction and inimical to the teachings of Christ. Incidentally he claims that those who are not blinded by prejudices recognize that "Christianity aims at saving the soul—the personality, the nature, of man, not his body or his environment. According to Christianity, a man is saved, not by what he has, or knows, or does, but by what he is. It treats all the apparatus of life with a disdain as great as that of the biologist; so long as a man is inwardly healthy, it cares very little whether he is rich or poor, learned or simple, and even whether he is happy, or unhappy. It attaches no importance to quantitative measurements of any kind. The Christian does not gloat over favorable trade-statistics, nor congratulate himself on the disparity between the number of births and deaths. For him . . . the test of the welfare of a country is the quality of the human beings whom it produces. Quality is everything, quantity is nothing. And besides this, the Christian conception of a kingdom of God upon earth teaches us to turn our eyes to the future, and to think of the welfare of posterity as a thing which concerns us as much as that of our own generation. This welfare, as conceived by Christianity, is of course something different from external prosperity; it is to be the victory of intrinsic worth and healthiness over all the false ideals and deep-seated diseases which at present spoil civilization."

"It is not political religion with which I am concerned," Dean Inge explained, "but the convictions of really religious persons; and I do not think that we need despair of converting them to our views."

Dean Inge believes Birth Control is an essential part of Eugenics, and an essential part of Christian morality. On this point he asserts: "We do wish to remind our orthodox and conservative friends that the Sermon on the Mount contains some admirably clear and unmistakable eugenic precepts. 'Do men gather grapes of thorns, or figs of thistles? A corrupt tree cannot bring forth good fruit, neither can a good tree bring forth evil fruit. Every tree which bringeth not forth good fruit is hewn down, and cast into the fire.' We wish to apply these words not only to the actions of individuals, which spring from their characters, but to the character of individuals, which spring from their inherited qualities. This extension of the scope of the maxim seems to me quite legitimate. Men do not gather grapes of thorns. As our proverb says, you cannot make a silk purse out of a sow's ear. If we believe this, and do not act upon it by trying to move public opinion towards giving social reform, education and religion a better material to work upon, we are sinning against the light, and not doing our best to bring in the Kingdom of God upon earth."

As long as sexual activity is regarded in a dualistic and contradictory light,—in which it is revealed either as the instrument by which men and women "cooperate with the Creator" to bring children into the world, on the one hand; and on the other, as the sinful instrument of self-gratification, lust and sensuality, there is bound to be an endless conflict in human conduct, producing ever increasing misery, pain and injustice. In crystallizing and codifying this contradiction, the Church not only solidified its own power over men but reduced women to the most abject and prostrate slavery. It was essentially a morality that would not "work." The sex instinct in the human race is too strong to be bound by the dictates of any church. The church's failure, its century after century of failure, is now evident on every side: for, having convinced men and women that only in its baldly propagative phase is sexual expression legitimate, the teachings of the Church have driven sex under-ground, into secret channels, strengthened the conspiracy of silence, concentrated men's thoughts upon the "lusts of the body," have sown, cultivated and reaped a crop of bodily and mental diseases, and developed a society congenitally and almost hopelessly unbalanced. How is any progress to be made, how is any human expression or education possible when women and men are taught to combat and resist their natural impulses and to despise their bodily functions?

Humanity, we are glad to realize, is rapidly freeing itself from this "morality" imposed upon it by its self-appointed and self-perpetuating masters. From a hundred different points the imposing edifice of this "morality" has been and is being attacked. Sincere and thoughtful defenders and exponents of the teachings of Christ now acknowledge the falsity of the traditional codes and their malignant influence upon the moral and physical well-being of humanity.

Ecclesiastical opposition to Birth Control on the part of certain representatives of the Protestant churches, based usually on quotations from the Bible, is equally invalid, and for the same reason. The attitude of the more intelligent and enlightened clergy has been well and succinctly expressed by Dean Inge, who, referring to the ethics of Birth Control, writes: *"This is emphatically a matter in which every man and woman must judge for themselves, and must refrain from judging others."* We must not neglect the important fact that it is not merely in the practical results of such a decision, not in the small number of children, not even in the healthier and better cared for children, not in the possibility of elevating the living conditions of the individual family, that the ethical value of Birth Control alone lies. Precisely because the practice of Birth Control does demand the exercise of decision, the making of choice, the use of the reasoning powers, is it an instrument of moral education as well as of hygienic and racial advance. It awakens the attention of parents to their potential children. It forces upon the individual consciousness the question of the standards of living. In a profound manner it protects and reasserts the inalienable rights of the child-to-be.

Psychology and the outlook of modern life are stressing the growth of independent responsibility and discrimination as the true basis of ethics. The old traditional morality, with its train of vice, disease, promiscuity and prostitution, is in reality dying out, killing itself off because it is too irresponsible and too dangerous to individual and social well-being. The transition from the old to the new, like all fundamental changes, is fraught with many dangers. But it is a revolution that cannot be stopped.

The smaller family, with its lower infant mortality rate, is, in more definite and concrete manner than many actions outwardly deemed "moral," the expression of moral judgment and responsibility. It is the assertion of a standard of living, inspired by the wish to obtain a fuller and more expressive life for the children than the parents have enjoyed. If the morality or immorality of any course of conduct is to be determined by the motives which inspire it, there is evidently at the present day no higher morality than the intelligent practice of Birth Control.

The immorality of many who practise Birth Control lies in not daring to preach what they practise. What is the secret of the hypocrisy of the well-to-do, who are willing to contribute generously to charities and philanthropies, who spend thousands annually in the upkeep and sustenance of the delinquent, the defective and the dependent; and yet join the conspiracy of silence that prevents the poorer classes from learning how to improve their conditions, and elevate their standards of living? It is as though they were to cry: "We'll give you anything except the thing you ask for—the means whereby you may become responsible and self-reliant in your own lives."

The brunt of this injustice falls on women, because the old traditional morality is the invention of men. "No religion, no physical or moral code," wrote the clear-sighted George Drysdale, "proposed by one sex for the other, can be really suitable. Each must work out its laws for itself in every department of life." In the moral code developed by the Church, women have been so degraded that they have been habituated to look upon themselves through the eyes of men. Very imperfectly have women developed their own self-consciousness, the realization of their tremendous and supreme position in civilization. Women can develop this power only in one way; by the exercise of responsibility, by the exercise of judgment, reason or discrimination. They need ask for no "rights." They need only assert power. Only by the exercise of self-guidance and intelligent self-direction can that inalienable, supreme, pivotal power be expressed. More than ever in history women need to realize that nothing can ever come to us from another. Everything we attain we must owe to ourselves. Our own spirit must vitalize it. Our own heart must feel it. For we are not passive machines. We are not to be lectured, guided and molded this way or that. We are alive and intelligent, we women, no less than men, and we must awaken to the essential realization that we are living beings, endowed with will, choice, comprehension, and that every step in life must be taken at our own initiative.

Moral and sexual balance in civilization will only be established by the assertion and expression of power on the part of women. This power will not be found in any futile seeking for economic independence or in the aping of men in industrial and business pursuits, nor by joining battle for the so-called "single standard." Woman's power can only be expressed and make itself felt when she refuses the task of bringing unwanted children into the world to be exploited in industry and slaughtered in wars. When we refuse to produce battalions of babies to be exploited; when we declare to the nation; "Show us that the best possible chance in life is given to every child now brought into the world, before you cry for more! At present our children are a glut on the market. You hold infant life cheap. Help us to make the world a fit place for children. When you have done this, we will bear you children,—then we shall be true women." The new morality will express this power and responsibility on the part of women.

"With the realization of the moral responsibility of women," writes Havelock Ellis, "the natural relations of life spring back to their due biological adjustment. Motherhood is restored to its natural sacredness. It becomes the concern of the woman herself, and not of society nor any individual, to determine the conditions under which the child shall be conceived. . . ."

Moreover, woman shall further assert her power by refusing to remain the passive instrument of sensual self-gratification on the part of men. Birth Control, in philosophy and practice, is the destroyer of that dualism of the old sexual code. It denies that the sole purpose of sexual activity is procreation; it also denies that sex should be reduced to the level of sensual lust, or that woman should permit herself to be the instrument of its satisfaction. In increasing and differentiating her love demands, woman must elevate sex into another sphere, whereby it may subserve and enhance the possibility of individual and human expression. Man will gain in this no less than woman; for in the age-old enslavement of woman he has enslaved himself; and in the liberation of womankind, all of humanity will experience the joys of a new and fuller freedom.

On this great fundamental and pivotal point new light has been thrown by Lord Bertrand Dawson, the physician of the King of England. In the remarkable and epoch-making address at the Birmingham Church Congress (referred to in my introduction), he spoke of the supreme morality of the mutual and reciprocal joy in the most intimate relation between man and woman. Without this reciprocity there can be no civilization worthy of the name. Lord Dawson suggested that there should be added to the clauses of marriage in the Prayer Book "the complete realization of the love of this man and this woman one for another," and in support of his contention declared that sex love between husband and wife—apart from parenthood—was something to prize and cherish for its own sake. The Lambeth Conference, he remarked, "envisaged a love invertebrate and joyless," whereas, in his view, natural passion in wedlock was not a thing to be ashamed of or unduly repressed. The pronouncement of the Church of England, as set forth in Resolution 68 of the Lambeth Conference seems to imply condemnation of sex love as such, and to imply sanction of sex love only as a means to an end,—namely, procreation. The Lambeth Resolution stated:

"In opposition to the teaching which under the name of science and religion encourages married people in the deliberate cultivation of sexual union as an end in itself, we steadfastly uphold what must always be regarded as the governing considerations of Christian marriage. One is the primary purpose for which marriage exists—namely, the continuation of the race through the gift and heritage of children; the other is the paramount importance in married life of deliberate and thoughtful self-control."

In answer to this point of view Lord Dawson asserted:

"Sex love has, apart from parenthood, a purport of its own. It is something to prize and to cherish for its own sake. It is an essential part of health and happiness in marriage. And now, if you will allow me, I will carry this argument a step further. If sexual union is a gift of God it is worth learning how to use it. Within its own sphere it should be cultivated so as to bring physical satisfaction to both, not merely to one. . . . The real problems before us are those of sex love and child love; and by sex love I mean that love which involves intercourse or the desire for such. It is necessary to my argument to emphasize that sex love is one of the dominating forces of the world. Not only does history show the destinies of nations and dynasties determined by its sway— but here in our every-day life we see its influence, direct or indirect, forceful and ubiquitous beyond aught else. Any statesmanlike view, therefore, will recognize that here we have an instinct so fundamental, so imperious, that its influence is a fact which has to be accepted; suppress it you cannot. You may guide it into healthy channels, but an outlet it will have, and if that outlet is inadequate and unduly obstructed irregular channels will be forced. . . .

"The attainment of mutual and reciprocal joy in their relations constitutes a firm bond between two people, and makes for durability of the marriage tie. Reciprocity in sex love is the physical counterpart of sympathy. More marriages fail from inadequate and clumsy sex love than from too much sex love. The lack of proper understanding is in no small measure responsible for the unfulfilment of connubial happiness, and every degree of discontent and unhappiness may, from this cause, occur, leading to rupture of the marriage bond itself. How often do medical men have to deal with these difficulties, and how fortunate if such difficulties are disclosed early enough in married life to be rectified. Otherwise how tragic may be their consequences, and many a case in the Divorce Court has thus had its origin. To the foregoing contentions, it might be objected, you are encouraging passion. My reply would be, passion is a worthy possession—most men, who are any good, are capable of passion. You all enjoy ardent and passionate love in art and literature. Why not give it a place in real life? Why some people look askance at passion is because they are confusing it with sensuality. Sex love without passion is a poor, lifeless thing. Sensuality, on the other hand, is on a level with gluttony—a physical excess—detached from sentiment, chivalry, or tenderness. It is just as important to give sex love its place as to avoid its over-emphasis. Its real and effective restraints are those imposed by a loving and sympathetic companionship, by the privileges of parenthood, the exacting claims of career and that civic sense which prompts men to do social service. Now that the revision of the Prayer Book is receiving consideration, I should like to suggest with great respect an addition made to the objects of marriage in the Marriage Service, in these terms, 'The complete realization of the love of this man and this woman, the one for the other.' "

Turning to the specific problem of Birth Control, Lord Dawson declared, "that Birth Control is here to stay. It is an established fact, and for good or evil has to be accepted. Although the extent of its application can be and is being modified, no denunciations will abolish it. Despite the influence and condemnations of the Church, it has been practised in France for well over half a century, and in Belgium and other Roman Catholic countries is extending. And if the Roman Catholic Church, with its compact organization, its power of authority and its disciplines, cannot check this procedure, it is not likely that Protestant Churches will be able to do so, for Protestant religions depend for their strength on the conviction and esteem they establish in the heads and hearts of their people. The reasons which lead parents to limit their offspring are sometimes selfish, but more often honorable and cogent."

A report of the Fabian Society on the morality of Birth Control, based upon a census conducted under the chairmanship of Sidney Webb, concludes: "These facts—which we are bound to face whether we like them or not—will appear in different lights to different people. In some quarters it seems to be sufficient to dismiss them with moral indignation, real or simulated. Such a judgment appears both irrelevant and futile. . . . If a course of conduct is habitually and deliberately pursued by vast multitudes of otherwise well-conducted people, forming probably a majority of the whole educated class of the nation, we must assume that it does not conflict with their actual code of morality. They may be intellectually mistaken, but they are not doing what they feel to be wrong."

The moral justification and ethical necessity of Birth Control need not be empirically based upon the mere approval of experience and custom. Its morality is more profound. Birth Control is an ethical necessity for humanity to-day because it places in our hands a new instrument of self-expression and self-realization. It gives us control over one of the primordial forces of nature, to which in the past the majority of mankind have been enslaved, and by which it has been cheapened and debased. It arouses us to the possibility of newer and greater freedom. It develops the power, the responsibility and intelligence to use this freedom in living a liberated and abundant life. It permits us to enjoy this liberty without danger of infringing upon the similar liberty of our fellow men, or of injuring and curtailing the freedom of the next generation. It shows us that we need not seek in the amassing of worldly wealth, nor in the illusion of some extra-terrestrial Heaven or earthly Utopia of a remote future the road to human development. The Kingdom of Heaven is in a very definite sense within us. Not by leaving our body and our fundamental humanity behind us, not by aiming to be anything but what we are, shall we become ennobled or immortal. By knowing ourselves, by expressing ourselves, by realizing ourselves more completely than has ever before been possible, not only shall we attain the kingdom ourselves but we shall hand on the torch of life undimmed to our children and the children of our children.

Rose Schneiderman
(1882–1972)

Rose Schneiderman was born on April 6, 1882 in the small village of Saven in Russian Poland. In 1890 she migrated to New York City with her parents and three siblings where they resided in a poor immigrant section of the lower East Side. Rose's education consisted of two years of traditional Hebrew school and two years in Russian public schools before arriving in America, where she eventually finished the 9th grade after frequent interruptions. At the tender age of 13, Rose began work as a department store cash girl and sales clerk. After moving on to a better job in a cap factory, she launched her union career in 1903 when she organized her shop into the first female local of the Jewish Socialist United Cloth Hat and Cap Makers' Union. Two years later their local had reached several hundred and, as its secretary, Rose was instrumental in leading them in a successful thirteen week strike against open shop policies. In the same year (1905) she joined the Women's Trade Union League (a coalition of workers and middle-and-upper-class reformers), which was dedicated to unionizing working women and lobbying for protective legislation. In 1906 she began receiving a stipend from the League as a full time organizer and from that time on she and Mary Dreier became the New York City League's most important leaders. Under League auspices, Rose played a key role in organizing the International Ladies Garment Workers' Union, served as a leader of the Shirtwaistmaker's strike "The Uprising of the Twenty Thousand," and helped lead the White Goods Workers in its 1913 strike. In 1918 she became President of the New York Women's Trade Union League where she reigned until 1949; and in 1926 she became President of the National Women's Trade Union League, where she served until 1950. As a delegate for the WTUL to the Paris Peace Conference in 1919 she also helped organize the International Congress of Working Women. Her reputation as a labor organizer also brought her in contact with the suffrage movement and she committed her spare time to campaigning for the vote in Ohio in 1913 and in the 1915 and 1917 New York state campaigns. Her labor experience eventually won her governmental attention as well when Franklin Delano Roosevelt appointed her to serve on the Labor Advisory Board of the National Recovery Administration from 1933 to 1935, and the Governor of New York appointed her to serve as Secretary of the New York State Department of Labor from 1937 to 1943. After further successful organizing efforts for laundry workers and hotel workers and helping to set the 8-hour day and minimum wage laws, Rose retired in 1955 at the age of 73. She died at the age of 90 in the New York Jewish Home and Hospital for the Aged on August 11, 1972.

The following lecture was delivered before the "Suffrage School" in Washington, D.C. on December 16, 1913. A typescript of the lecture is located in the Rose Schneiderman Papers, Brown University Library (microfilm edition of "Papers of the Women's Trade Union League and Its Principal Leaders," Schneiderman Papers, Reel 2), Providence, Rhode Island.

"Under What Conditions Women Work"

Yesterday I spoke on the question of men in industry and tried to show that even in this enlightened state of New York there is much room for improvement. Recently the Anti-suffragists made a statement showing how superior the legislation for women was in this great state where the women do not vote, to the legislation in those states where they do vote, and how unnecessary, therefore, Votes for Women are. I have tried to show that at least where men are concerned very little has been done except by their own efforts in trade organization. Let us today consider under what conditions women work.

There are about 800,000 working women in this state, where according to the anti-suffragists, men's chivalry toward women has made votes for women an unnecessary demand.

The fire hazards which I mentioned yesterday, and which still prevail, apply to women as well as men of course, as do sanitary conditions, cleanliness and comfort in factories. I wish you could have been with me while employers showed me with great pride their dressing rooms for their employees, bare and barren rooms of varied sizes, sometimes so full of lockers there was scarcely room to turn round, sometimes so empty of all furniture—even chairs—that you wondered what the room was meant for; sometimes indeed with a solitary couch and chair in factories where hundreds of women were employed. I have yet to find a man who had any kind of an apology to offer for any kind of a thing he showed. They open the door with a grand sweep of the arm and as you enter the desolate comfortless rooms have announced with great satisfaction, "Here are the dressing rooms."

There are many factories and trades where women stand all day where there are even no chairs, though those are called for by the law. There are many kinds of work at which girls could sit instead of stand if the pressure of work were not so intense, if they were not speeded up to the highest point of endurance.

If you go into a tobacco, or canning factory you will frequently find little boxes, or low slabs of wood with boxes underneath, used as seats; and I've gone into a laundry and seen girls sitting on the raised platform upon which the machine rested, eating luncheon because there were no seats whatsoever. When the commission proposed a law requiring backs to chairs wherever possible, the idea seemed so preposterous that one of the prominent senators got upon the floor and protested vigorously against such a law, declaring that this law was simply a fore-runner, of course, for the demand for velvet cushions and velvet cushioned backs with a spread eagle on the top! He made an eloquent plea and the law was not passed by the illustrious senators of New York State for the comfort of young working women. And though this law has been passed since, many girls are found standing because it takes too much time to sit down, and many girls in different stores keep standing because the rule of the store is to stand, though the state requires seats.

A mercantile inspector found some girls standing in a store when they were not busy and asked the reason of this. One of the girls had the temerity to say that the rule of the store did not allow her to sit down. The inspector went to the manager who asked the inspector which department this was and said he would fix it. On his return the manager said, "I have settled that," and on being asked how, he informed the inspector that he had dismissed the girl. The mercantile department was trying to get the girl to testify before the court that she had not been permitted to sit down, but she refused, for the simple reason that she was afraid of not finding work elsewhere. But what an absurd law, to require employees to testify against their employer before action can be taken. I mention this particularly because the effect of standing upon women is detrimental to their health. Dr. George W. Golar, commissioner of health for Rochester, stated before the commission, "I have a photograph of the feet and legs of women who stand and the great tortuous varicose veins upon those legs could make one expend as much pity on those women as upon the horse that was being whipped in the street." Also he expresses himself in no uncertain terms upon bad ventilation saying "The general effect, of course, is to lower the health of the worker and with that lowering health there comes ansemis, and the diseases of the lungs and when you couple the bad ventilation with low wages and the increased cost of living, it simply means that you are going to interfere with the proper support of their families."

When you go to a factory as I have done, and see young girls in the first flush of womanhood bending their backs to the machine, or sitting crouched upon a chair putting stitches into men's hats; or standing with the stench of dead beasts in their nostrils in packing houses, putting sausages into sausage skins, standing on slime-soaked floors with wet feet; or when you see them in the laundries in steam filled rooms because there is no adequate hood over the machine, you marvel at the courage, or buoyancy of youth. And then when you see middle aged women with their drawn faces, still at the same kind of work they were doing as young girls, with evidently the life, buoyancy and hope crushed out; or when you see the old, old women who should be tenderly treated because of their age, we marvel at the tragedy of life which held such promise and gave so little fulfillment.

I shall never forget a woman coming before the State Factory Investigation Commission in Troy. She was an old woman somewhere in the sixties, she was frail and delicate, dressed all in black which emphasized more than anything else could have done the palor of her face, the only color of which was in the red-rimmed eyes. She was timid and in her testimony it was quite clear that she did not want to offend her employer. She had worked in that factory for some twenty-six years, and when she was asked by the counsel what time she came to work she said that her employer was very good to her, and that while they opened at seven, she did not have to get there until 7:30; and while they closed at six she left at 5:30. When asked how much she made a week she said,—of course she could not make as much now as she had made; she had made as much as $11.00 but now she could not make more than $4.00 a week, but her employer was good to her in allowing her to come! A little while ago they had changed their machine and so she had to buy a new one and she was very fortunate in getting one second-hand from a girl who was going to be married, but she had to pay $35.00 for it! Thirty-five dollars for a machine, the worker of which made not over four dollars a week! Eight and a half week's wages as price of the machine without which she had not even made those $4.00. I think that if that frail and delicate woman could be taken through the state just to tell her story as she did before the commission the people might realize the need of an old age pension.

But today there is no hope for any woman who is forced to labor to have any respite even in her remotest old age. It is said, of course, that her children should take care of her; but what of the woman who does not marry, or who, having married, has lost her children and husband? Or of the old mother who is too proud to be a burden upon her young son who himself is supporting his family with difficulty?

There are thousands of girls and men working in the textile mills of this state under conditions which are almost a guarantee for tuberculosis, and yet there are not only these external conditions which are detrimental; there is even a more menacing problem, more menacing because we are at least recognizing the necessity of having cleanliness in factories, and certain sanitary conditions. The thing I mean is the sub-division of work as the result of the extraordinary mechanical inventions. Do you realize that ninety-nine people take part in making a shoe? That corsets are made by about thirteen hands, a man's coat by twenty-nine people? We have machinery running at the rate of 450 stitches a minute, and many machines running anywhere from two to seven needles, and the young workers behind these machines must feed the cloth into them as fast as steam power, or electric power demands. There are girls working at piece-work rates which act like a whip over them demanding the highest possible speed to make any sort of a wage. We have women pressing petticoats at the rate of 72 dozen a day; girls seaming 1500 yards a day (or tucking), and what we are asking is that the delicate human machine shall follow the pace of the electric power which is ruthless in its demand.

This question of nerve exhaustion as the result of modern inventions has practically not been studied by anybody except that the workers themselves have struck against intolerable conditions. It is perfectly clear that the eye-strain upon girls watching four or seven needles is greater than if she only watched one. And yet we limit hours not according to nerve exhausting work but simply by rule of thumb. We have with great difficulty managed to establish in the New York State a 54 hour week and a 9 or 10 hour day, according as we get a half holiday on Saturday.

A few years ago there was a strike of the telephone operators in Toronto. A Royal Commission to investigate conditions among telephone operators was appointed. Twenty-six physicians testified for this commission. Without a dissenting voice they said that the exacting demand of the telephone business was such that it caused nerve exhaustion very soon. Some testified that in their judgment, no woman could work at the telephone business for more than three years without so shattering her nervous system that she could never regain her health. Some went so far as to say that if women worked so long it was impossible for them to be normal, or to bear normal children, and at least one physician stated that he had known of cases of sterility among telephone operators and that in his judgment it was due to the kind of work they had done. In the United States there is one strong telephone girls union—namely in Boston, they organized there for self-preservation. We do not realize the nerve strain—eye, ear, voice and hand are in constant use. In some exchanges girls have to answer in busy time 200 calls an hour. The girls in Boston tried to avoid a strike but were finally forced into it, and then the telephone company in Boston hurried 500 girls there from other parts of the state and from Washington, Philadelphia, and New York, put them up at the swellest hotel, the Copley House, and promised them $25.00 wages in order to break the strike. No amount of money is saved to break strikes and every possible means are used to continue to pay young women such wages upon which it is almost impossible for them to live.

The State Factory Investigating Commission had some interesting hearings on home work. They came to the conclusion that all home work should be abolished eventually, but they started by only prohibiting the making or preparing of all food stuffs, children's clothes and children's toys in the home. The investigation showed that New York City was not the only offender, but that all smaller towns like Utica, Little Falls, Gloversville, Rochester, Niagara Falls, Syracuse, etc. indulged in home work. It was very demonstrated that licensing tenement houses was utterly inadequate to insure either sanitation or other conditions of work which were not health destroying. Of course, the advantage to the manufacturers in having home work is very apparent. He saves rest, there is no limitation of hours, no limitation as to the ages, no expense as to machinery, light or heat. Our investigator states that in a "Large majority of cases home-work is done to augment the family income, the small addition being not only welcome but necessary and constitutes the margin which saves the family from destruction, or often application for relief."

The great menace to society from home work is not so much a danger of transmitting disease, although this is constant, as it is the menace which results from exploited childhood and womanhood. It is impossible to guard children from being exploited in their homes. Here is little Giovanna who says "I get up at five o'clock in the morning and then I work with my mother; at nine o'clock I go to school, I have no time for play, I must work by feathers; at ten o'clock I go to bed." Little nine year old Antoinette says "I earn money for my mother after school and on Saturdays

154

and half a day Sunday; no, I do not play, I must work, I get up to work at four o'clock and go to bed at nine o'clock."

Now we could report one story after another showing how the children are forced to work. Of course the moment an opportunity offers for them to enter the factory they do it, their vitality and vigor already sapped. Is this an intelligent way we have of dealing with the citizens of our Republic? Yet for a few children who go to school and work after school, we have thousands and thousands who escape school; and when at fourteen they leave school to go to work, what do we find? Here is a young caramel wrapper whose business it is to wrap caramels from 8 a.m. till 5 p.m. with one hour for luncheon—she is paid $3.50 a week. Here is another who weighs the candy, she gets $3.50; and here is one who makes flowers, the kind women wear on their hats, and she gets $3.00. And so you can enumerate many trades where our young children of 14 spend eight hours of their day, forty-eight hours a week at such intelligent work as wrapping caramels. We think we have a wonderful law in New York limiting the hours to eight, but I would like to ask you if it is common sense for democracy to allow its children to wrap caramels at $3.50 a week instead of training and educating them in industrial schools so that when they are mature they may be intelligent citizens, and when they are married become intelligent mothers.

Of course eight hours a day is very much better than twelve, but let me quote to you from one of the leading educators in New York, Director of Technical Education at Teacher's College. He says this, "One half of our school children leave school at seventh grade. Of those over 16 years, 17% are not in school. This is in cities of 25,000 population and over. The years in which the majority enter occupation are 14 and 15 mostly, they are entering casual occupations or drifting here and there into crime." This is testimony abundantly substantiated.

To come back to our older factory working girls anywhere from 16 to 25 or 30 years of age. We have in recent years experienced a tremendous awakening on the part of these young women who have risen up and struck against conditions. We have had some very picturesque strikes in New York, picturesque enough to arouse public interest though a perfectly plain, simple, necessary strike of a few hundreds; When nothing particular happens except suffering on the part of those who are striking it does not arouse any particular interest or enthusiasm, or any support. Girls who are working for $3.50 or $4.50 a week,—women with families to support earning six to seven or eight dollars a week, and yet employers spend many thousands of dollars on private detectives and so-called thugs, to break those strikes, and nothing but endurance on the part of the workers have brought about a change of conditions. We expect very heroic action on little bread and butter. My sister went into the home of one woman whose husband was working in one of the big garment trades. She had a new-born baby by her side and three or four other young children, cowed because they had had nothing to eat. Yet she urged her husband to stick and not go back to work, and when asked how she found courage to do it she replied, "We do not live by bread alone, and I would rather see them starve and die than for us to betray our faith."

We certainly do not have to go far afield to find heroism; our industrial life calls for it constantly, not only of men, nor only of women who are grown, but ask it of little children and young delicate girls. From the point of view of spirit, this heroism is magnificient and it is well perhaps for us to know that we have it, and yet how wasteful from the point of view of democracy and how dangerous! Because we cannot continue repeatedly to ask this sort of heroism without losing it.

Bread and butter, shelter and clothes and adequate food are absolutely necessary to people, and more than that we need time for other things,—of the spirit and mind—and, what is more, we need money for it, and when they talk of minimum wages and say that a girl can live on six or eight dollars a week they take nothing into account except bare necessities; and when they say that eight or nine hours a day is reasonable they take nothing into account except work, and they do not for one moment consider the needs of the mind and spirit and the right of every individual to have leisure for the development of the higher qualities of man.

Then with 800,000 women working in our own state alone, we are told that in this state conditions are so good, that so much has been done that we women as a whole should be satisfied or content.

I want to say to you suffragists, especially to some of you who are saying that the working women are not taking part in this great suffrage movement, and that they are not coming to the fore as they should, how can they? Working nine, ten hours a day and then on their return home attending to their home duties, where is the time for them to take active part in even a suffrage movement? Many times they have to stay in the factory and work through the evening, they cannot make engagements without the reservation that they can break them if work calls. And when these women join their union, attend their meetings and pay their dues they are doing more for social betterment than any other group that we know of. They are getting their suffrage training. It is no easy task for a girl to be chairman of her shop of 30 or 100 or 200 girls. They adjust the difficulties, wisely advise and lead and in conference with their employer get splendid training. Many times they have special assessment to help their fellow workers, either in their own city or in a remote state, to better their conditions through organization; and the sinews of war in times of strikes have been carried by thousands and thousands of women as well as men who, out of their limited wage, have accepted an assessment of fifteen or twenty-five cents a week. In their own Trade Union organization they work side by side with men; they confer side by side with them, voting on the questions in the union on the same terms as men. There they discuss what affects not only their own organization, but what is affecting their own community or state; matters which could only be met through the ballot they hear discussed and form their judgment upon, and they decide in their own organization, for instance, whether it should stand for the initiative referendum or recall, which kind of workman's compensation it wants, or what other law may be of advantage to the state or nation. Yet when they leave the Trade Union meeting place, they are disenfranchised working women unable to use their judgment for the benefit of society as a whole. Woman suffrage will only accomplish the results we expect of it and hope of it if women develop into an intelligent electorate, and I would like to impress upon you the need of becoming familiar with industrial conditions so that when we get the power we can change them; and it seems to me that it is up to the women of leisure who are working in some way in the suffrage movement not to cry out or protest against the working woman's indifference to suffrage but to recognize her distinct contribution as an organized worker and to be ready to stand by her in her heavily handicapped struggle to better her conditions. Some of the leaders of the New York State have done this magnificently, but there are thousands who have not and who stand aloof and indifferent to the great struggle.

On the other hand, the great number of working women who have not yet been aroused to the necessity of organization nor to the need of the vote should be reached by suffrage in an intelligent and sympathetic way. They could do this by making them see the relation of the vote to the conditions of labor; the relation of the vote to the life of the working woman who has to pump up water instead of drawing it from a faucet because of the indifference of the politician to her comfort; the relation of her vote to the milk and food with which her children are fed; the relation of the vote to the warmth of the so-called wool with which she has to cover her children; and then the relation of her vote to the enforcement of the law for the protection of her children in the street, in the factory or in the shop.

In this way the suffragists have a great opportunity to lay before a group of over worked women the power of their vote; in this way an intelligent electorate would be developed who knows before it has it, what it can do with the vote, and who will use it effectively. It is as we suffragists make ourselves intelligent upon the problems which we will have to solve that the vote will be of any use to us or to the community or nation.

I do not deny for one moment the natural right that women have to the ballot and perhaps we shall have to do the same as the men have done,—suffer for our own ignorance before we make the right use of it as a class. I hope not, I hope that we have learned by experience that men have had, that it is a blunt instrument unless intelligence is behind it; and that we may not have to spend many years in acquiring knowledge that could be ours now because of the many men and women who have labored to bring the great problems of the country before the people. One of the great problems of our time is the industrial problem and it has many angles.

If the women of leisure and opportunity would do as that young and extraordinary woman Carala Voerishoffer did we would more quickly get results. She, a daughter of privilege, born to a great fortune with the privilege of student years behind her, served her city and state as no other young woman of privilege has done. Unsatisfied with learning of conditions through others, she herself went into factories to get first hand knowledge. As a worker in a laundry through one hot summer, she learned the conditions of that trade and the hardships of the workers. Through following up the young immigrant women, going on the trains with them as an immigrant woman direct from Ellis Island, entering the city of Chicago and other cities as an immigrant, she learned to know the conditions and difficulties that confront the young brave immigrant girls who come to this country because of their great dream of opportunities for work. As inspector in the labor camps of New York State she learned from her own experience of the exploitations of the simple hearted immigrant who comes here believing he has come to the land of freedom, and, knowing these conditions intimately she labored to change them and allied herself with the movements that are making for fundamental democracy, and so too, she allied herself with the Trade Union movement because she realized that through it could be obtained democracy in the workshop. In her death New York State as well as New York City, and the cause that makes for democracy, lost a staunch friend and fighter, because she not only recognized evils but fought hard to right them.

So, for instance, in the shirt-waist strike in New York where thousands of girls were arrested she went bail. She went to the day court, she was at hand in the night court giving bail for those who were arrested; she did it so modestly, simply as a matter of course that only a few except those who benefitted by her knew of it, and she did it in this way because she believed more than anything else that only that as people proved themselves in service on an equality with other people would they be of any value. There may not be many who can do like her, who are so situated or gifted in such a way as she was, and yet there are many who can ally ourselves to the great forces that make for righteousness and be adherents of them while working for woman suffrage. Political democracy will not do us much good unless we have industrial democracy; and industrial democracy can only come through intelligent workers participating in the business of which they are a part, and working out the best methods for all.

So once more I call upon you women to stand ready to help the working woman. Not to ask her to come out and help you get woman suffrage but to go to her and offer her your help to win woman suffrage. Show her that you understand her difficulties, are in sympathy with her struggle, eager to help her when the opportunity offers; that you want woman suffrage to give the working woman the much needed weapon to the end that all women together may work for the common good of mankind.

Anna Howard Shaw
(1847–1919)

Anna Howard Shaw was born on February 14, 1847 in Newcastle-on-Tyne, England. The sixth of seven children, she and her family migrated to the United States in 1851 and lived in New Bedford, Massachusetts for a year before moving to Lawrence, Massachusetts where the family home served as a station on the Underground Railroad for runaway slaves. In 1859 the family moved to the territory of Michigan where Anna and her younger brother largely ran the wilderness home while their father returned to New England to earn money and their mother suffered bouts of mental incapacitation. Despite the constant moving, Anna persisted in obtaining whatever education she could. She went to public school for a few years in Lawrence, resumed schooling in a frontier schoolhouse in Michigan, and later finished high school in Big Rapids. Upon the completion of high school, Anna's interest in religion drew her to the ministry. In 1870 she began preaching in Michigan and in 1871 she became a licensed preacher. This early experience prompted her to apply to Boston University's theology school in 1876, where she received a certificate in the ministry in 1878 as the only woman in the class. Since the university provided financial support only for male students, Anna served as the pastor for two churches on Cape Cod to support herself while attending school. She applied for ordination with one of the churches (Methodist Episcopal Church), but was denied, and her license to preach was revoked as well. But the Methodist Protestant Church ordained her as the first woman minister and she continued her pastorate at this church until she resigned in 1885. In 1883 Anna decided to change professions, and she returned to Boston University to study medicine and received her M.D. degree in 1886. With two professional degrees achieved, Anna turned her attention to reform causes. From 1885 to 1887 she worked as a paid lecturer and organizer with the Massachusetts Woman Suffrage Association. From 1888 to 1892 the Women's Christian Temperance Union hired her as their Superintendent of Franchise to work for the suffrage movement. By this time the National American Women Suffrage Association had learned of her great skills as an orator and they appointed her as a national lecturer in 1891. From 1892 to 1904 Anna served as Vice President of NAWSA, and from 1904 to 1915 as President, both experiences revealing her superb talents as a speaker but also exposing her weaknesses as an administrator. With the recall of Carrie Chapman Catt to the Presidency of NAWSA, Anna spent the last years of her life involved in World War I events. She served as Chairperson of the Women's Committee of the United States Council of National Defense from 1918 to 1919 and received the "Distinguished Service Medal" for her efforts. While engaged in an exhausting U.S. tour to campaign for the League of Nations, Anna died on July 2, 1919 at the age of 73.

The following sermon was delivered before the International Council of Women in Washington, D.C. on March 24, 1888. It appeared in printed form in *The History of Woman Suffrage*, Vol. IV (Rochester, N.Y., 1902) pp. 128–133.

"The Heavenly Vision"

"Whereupon, O, King Agrippa, I was not disobedient unto the heavenly vision." Acts, xxvi:19.

In the beauty of his Oriental home the Psalmist caught the vision of the events in the midst of which you and I are living to-day. And though he wrought the vision into the wonderful prophecy of the 68th Psalm, yet so new and strange were the thoughts to men, that for thousands of years they failed to catch its spirit and understand its power.

The vision which appeared to David was a world lost in sin. He heard its cry for deliverance, he saw its uplifted hands. Everywhere the eyes of good men were turned toward the skies for help. For ages had they striven against the forces of evil; they had sought by every device to turn back the flood-tide of base passion and avarice, but to no purpose. It seemed as if all men were engulfed in one common ruin. Patient, sphinx-like, sat woman, limited by sin, limited by social custom, limited by false theories, limited by bigotry and by creeds, listening to the tramp of the weary millions as they passed on through the centuries, patiently toiling and waiting, humbly bearing the pain and weariness which fell to her lot.

Century after century came forth from the divine life only to pass into the great eternity— and still she toiled and still she waited. At last, in the mute agony of despair, she lifted her eyes above the earth to heaven and away from the jarring strifes which surrounded her, and that which dawned upon her gaze was so full of wonder that her soul burst its prison-house of bondage as she beheld the vision of true womanhood. She knew then it was not the purpose of the Divine that she should crouch beneath the bonds of custom and ignorance. She learned that she was created not from the side of man, but rather by the side of man. The world had suffered because she had not kept her divinely-appointed place. Then she remembered the words of prophecy, that salvation was to come to the race not through the man, but through the descendant of the woman. Recognizing her mission at last, she cried out: "Speak now, Lord, for thy servant heareth thee." And the answer came: "The Lord giveth the Word, and the women that publish the tidings are a great host."

To-day the vision is a reality. From every land the voice of woman is heard proclaiming the word which is given her, and the wondering world, which for a moment stopped its busy wheel of life that it might smite and jeer her, has learned at last that wherever the intuitions of the human mind are called into special exercise, wherever the art of persuasive eloquence is demanded, wherever heroic conduct is based upon duty rather than impulse, wherever her efforts in opening the sacred doors for the benefit of truth can avail—in one and all these respects woman greatly excels man. Now the wisest and best people everywhere feel that if woman enters upon her tasks wielding her own effective armor, if her inspirations are pure and holy, the Spirit Omnipotent, whose influence has held sway in all movements and reforms, whose voice has called into its service the great workmen of every age, shall, in these last days, fall especially upon woman. If she venture to obey, what is man that he should attempt to abrogate her sacred and divine mission? In the presence of what woman has already accomplished, who shall say that a true woman—noble in her humility, strong in her gentleness, rising above all selfishness, gathering up her varied gifts and accomplishments to consecrate them to God and humanity—who shall say that such an one is not in a position to do that for which the world will no longer rank her other than among the first in the work of human redemption? Then, influenced by lofty motives, stimulated by the wail of humanity and the glory of God, woman may go forth and enter into any field of usefulness which opens up before her. . . .

In the Scripture from which the text is taken we recognize a universal law which has been the experience of every one of us. Paul is telling the story of a vision he saw, which became the inspiration of his life, the turning point where his whole existence was changed, when, in obedience to that vision, he put himself in relation with the power to which he belonged, and recognizing in that One which appeared to him on his way from Jerusalem to Damascus his Divine Master, he also recognized that the purpose of his life could be fulfilled only when, in obedience to that Master, he caught and assimilated to himself the nature of Him, whose servant he was. . . .

Every reformer the world has ever seen has had a similar experience. Every truth which has been taught to humanity has passed through a like channel. No one of God's children has ever gone forth to the world who has not first had revealed to him his mission, in a vision.

To this Jew, bound by the prejudices of past generations, weighed down by the bigotry of human creeds, educated in the schools of an effete philosophy, struggling through the darkness and gloom which surrounded him, when as a persecutor he sought to annihilate the disciples of a new faith, there came this vision into his life; there dawned the electric light of a great truth, which found beneath the hatred and pride and passion which filled his life and heart, the divine germ that is implanted in the soul of each one of God's children. . . .

Then came crowding through his mind new queries: "Can it be that my fathers were wrong, and that their philosophy and religion do not contain all there is of truth? Can it be that outside of all we have known, there lies a great unexplored universe to which the mind of man can yet attain?" And filled with the divine purpose, he opened his heart to receive the new truth that came to him from the vision which God revealed to his soul.

All down through the centuries God has been revealing in visions the great truths which have lifted the race, step by step, until to-day womanhood, in this sunset hour of the nineteenth century, is gathered here from the East and the West, the North and the South, women of every land, of every race, of all religious beliefs. But diverse and varied as are our races, our theories, our religions, yet we come together here with one harmonious purpose—that of lifting humanity into a higher, purer, truer life.

To one has come the vision of political freedom. She saw how the avarice and ambition of one class with power made them forget the rights of another. She saw how the unjust laws embittered both—those who made them and those upon whom the injustice rested. She recognized the great principles of universal equality, seeing that all alike must be free; that humanity everywhere must be lifted out of subjection into the free and full air of divine liberty.

To another was revealed the vision of social freedom. She saw that sin which crushed the lives of one class, rested lightly on the lives of the other. She saw its blighting effect on both, and she lifted up her voice and demanded that there be recognized no sex in sin.

Another has come hither, who, gazing about her, saw men brutalized by the rum fiend, the very life of a nation threatened, and the power of the liquor traffic, with its hand on the helm of the Ship of State, guiding it with sails full spread straight upon the rocks to destruction. Then, looking away from earth, she beheld a vision of what the race and our nation might become, with all its possibility of wealth and power, if freed from this burden, and forth upon her mission of deliverance she sped her way.

Another beheld a vision of what it is to be learned, to explore the great fields of knowledge which the Infinite has spread before the world. And this vision has driven her out from the seclusion of her own quiet life that she might give this great truth to womanhood everywhere. . . .

And so we come, each bearing her torch of living truth, casting over the world the light of the vision that has dawned upon her soul.

But there is still another vision which reaches above earth, beyond time—a vision which has dawned upon many, that they are here not to do their own work, but the will of Him who sent them. And the woman who sees the still higher truth, recognizes the great power to which she belongs and what her life may become when, in submission to that Master, she takes upon herself the nature of Him whom she serves.

We will notice in the second place the purpose of all these visions which have come to us. Paul was not permitted to dwell on the vision of truth which came to him. God had a purpose in its manifestation, and that purpose was revealed when He said to the wonder-striken servant, "Arise; for I have appeared unto thee for this purpose, not that thou behold the truth for thyself, but to make thee a minister and a witness both of that which thou hast already seen and of other truths which I shall reveal unto thee. Go unto the Gentiles. Give them the truth which thou shalt receive that their eyes may be opened, and that they may be turned from darkness to light; that they, too, may receive a like inheritance with thyself. . . ."

This, then, is God's lesson to you and to me. He opens before our eyes the vision of a great truth and for a moment He permits our wondering gaze to rest upon it; then He bids us go forth. Jacob of old saw the vision of God's messengers ascending and descending, but none of them standing still.

Herein, then, lies the secret of the success of the reformer. First the vision, then the purpose of the vision. "I was not disobedient unto the heavenly vision." This is the manly and noble confession of one of the world's greatest reformers, and in it we catch a glimpse of the secrets of the success of his divinely-appointed mission. The difference between the Saul of Tarsus and Paul the Prisoner of the Lord was measured by his obedience. This, too, is a universal law, true of the life of every reformer, who, having had revealed to him a vision of the great truth, has in obedience to that vision carried it to humanity. Though at first he holds the truth to himself, and longs to be lifted up by its power, he soon learns that there is a giving forth of that which one possesses which enriches the giver, and that the more he gives of his vision to men the richer it becomes, the brighter it grows, until it illuminates all his pathway. . . .

Yet Paul's life was not an idle dream; it was a constant struggle against the very people whom he tried to save; his greatest foes were those to whom he was sent. He had learned the lesson all reformers must sooner or later learn, that the world never welcomes its deliverers save with the dungeon, the fagot or the cross. No man or woman has ever sought to lead his fellows to a higher and better mode of life without learning the power of the world's ingratitude; and though at times popularity may follow in the wake of a reformer, yet the reformer knows popularity is not love. The world will support you when you have compelled it to do so by manifestations of power, but it will shrink from you as soon as power and greatness are no longer on your side. This is the penalty paid by good people who sacrifice themselves for others. They must live without sympathy; their feelings will be misunderstood; their efforts will be uncomprehended. Like Paul, they will be betrayed by friends; like Christ in the agony of Gethsemane, they must bear their struggle alone.

Our reverence for the reformers of the past is posterity's judgment of them. But to them, what is that now? They have passed into the shadows where neither our voice of praise or of blame disturbs their repose.

This is the hardest lesson the reformer has to learn. When, with soul aglow with the light of a great truth, she, in obedience to the vision, turns to take it to the needy one, instead of finding a world ready to rise up and receive her, she finds it wrapped in the swaddling clothes of error, eagerly seeking to win others to its conditions of slavery. She longs to make humanity free; she listens to their conflicting creeds, and yearns to save them from the misery they endure. She knows that there is no form of slavery more bitter or arrogant than error, that truth alone can make man free, and she longs to bring the heart of the world and the heart of truth together, that the truth may exercise its transforming power over the life of the world. The greatest test of the reformer's courage comes when, with a warm, earnest longing for humanity, she breaks for it the bread of truth and the world turns from this life-giving power and asks instead of bread a stone.

It is just here that so many of God's workmen fail, and themselves need to turn back to the vision as it appeared to them, and to gather fresh courage and new inspiration for the future. This, my sisters, we all must do if we would succeed. The reformer may be inconsistent, she may be stern or even impatient, but if the world feels that she is in earnest she can not fail. Let the truth which she desires to teach first take possession of herself. Every woman who to-day goes out into the world with a truth, who has not herself become possessed of that truth, had far better stay at home.

Who would have dreamed, when at that great anti-slavery meeting in London, some years ago, the arrogance and pride of men excluded the women whom God had moved to lift up their voices in behalf of the baby that was sold by the pound—who would have dreamed that that very exclusion would be the keynote of woman's freedom? That out of the prejudice of that hour God should be able to flash upon the crushed hearts of those excluded the grand vision which we see manifested here to-day? That out of a longing for the liberty of a portion of the race, God should be able to show to women the still larger vision of the freedom of all human kind?

Grand as is this vision which meets us here, it is but the dawning of a new day; and as the first beams of morning light give promise of the radiance which shall envelop the earth when the sun shall have arisen in all its splendor, so there comes to us a prophecy of that glorious day when the vision which we are now beholding, which is beaming in the soul of one, shall enter the hearts and transfigure the lives of all.

Elizabeth Cady Stanton
(1815–1902)

Elizabeth Cady Stanton was born on November 12, 1815 in Johnstown, New York. The fourth of six children, she grew up in a political family. Her father served in the State Legislature, in Congress and as a judge of the Supreme Court of New York, and her mother's family played major roles in the State Legislature. Elizabeth studied the classics at home and later attended the Johnstown Academy. In 1832 she graduated from Emma Willard's famous Troy Female Seminary. In 1840 Elizabeth married Henry Stanton, a noted abolitionist, and joined him in attending the World's Anti-Slavery Convention in London. While there she met Lucretia Mott (one of the spurned female delegates) and they talked of planning a woman's convention. Eight years later she and Lucretia carried out their plans when they held the infamous 1848 Woman's Rights Convention in Seneca Falls, New York. There they presented their "Declaration of Sentiments," which included the first resolution to give woman the vote. During the next several years Elizabeth wrote numerous articles on women and temperance for Horace Greeley's *New York Tribune* and actively participated in women's conferences. In 1850 Elizabeth met Susan B. Anthony, and from that time on their personal and political collaboration influenced and inspired generations of feminists. In the 1850's Elizabeth focused most of her energies on broadening women's property laws and in 1854 she spoke before the New York Legislature, an unprecedented event for a woman. In the early 1860's she and Susan joined other abolitionists to fight for Negro suffrage, touring New York in 1861 and in 1863 organizing the Women's Loyal National League, which eventually presented 300,000 signatures to the U.S. Senate demanding the immediate abolition of slavery. After the Civil War Elizabeth and Susan toured Kansas to campaign for state suffrage in 1867, launched the woman's rights weekly paper *Revolution* in 1868, and formed the National Women's Suffrage Association in 1869 which Elizabeth presided over for the next twenty years. In 1870 Elizabeth also began a twelve year lecture tour for the lyceum movement, her favorite lectures being "Our Girls," "Our Boys," "Coeducation," and "Marriage and Divorce." During this same decade she and Susan also campaigned for suffrage in the far west and framed the "Women's Declaration of Rights" for the Philadelphia Centennial Exposition. In the 1880's she and Susan and Mathilda Joslyn Gage started work on the invaluable first three volumes of *The History of Woman Suffrage* and helped organize the International Council of Women. In 1890 the two separate women's suffrage associations reunited into one association and elected Elizabeth as the first president. In 1895 Elizabeth published her version of religious observance in *The Woman's Bible*, which scandalized many suffragists who thought it was too radical. In 1898 her reminiscences appeared in published form in *Eighty Years or More*. On October 26, 1902 Elizabeth died in her sleep at the age of 86 soon after having written Theodore Roosevelt urging him to declare support for woman suffrage.

The following speech was delivered at the National Convention of the American Equal Rights Association at the Church of Puritans in New York City on May 9, 1867. It appeared in printed form in *The History of Woman Suffrage*, Vol. II (Rochester, N.Y., 1881) PP. 185-190.

"The Case for Universal Suffrage"

Resolved, That government, of all sciences, is the most exalted and comprehensive, including, as it does, all the political, commercial, religious, educational, and social interests of the race.

Resolved, That to speak of the ballot as an "article of merchandise," and of the science of government as the "muddy pool of politics," is most demoralizing to a nation based on universal suffrage.

In considering the question of suffrage, there are two starting points: one, that this right is a gift of society, in which certain men, having inherited this privilege from some abstract body and abstract place, have now the right to secure it for themselves and their privileged order to the end of time. This principle leads logically to governing races, classes, families; and, in direct antagonism to our idea of self-government, takes us back to monarchies and despotisms, to an experiment that has been tried over and over again, 6,000 years, and uniformly failed.

Ignoring this point of view as untenable and anti-republican, and taking the opposite, that suffrage is a natural right—as necessary to man under government, for the protection of person and property, as are air and motion to life—we hold the talisman by which to show the right of all classes to the ballot, to remove every obstacle, to answer every objection, to point out the tyranny of every qualification to the free exercise of this sacred right. To discuss this question of suffrage for women and negroes, as women and negroes, and not as citizens of a republic, implies that there are some reasons for demanding this right for these classes that do not apply to "white males."

The obstinate persistence with which fallacious and absurd objections are pressed against their enfranchisement—as if they were anomalous beings, outside all human laws and necessities—is most humiliating and insulting to every black man and woman who has one particle of healthy, high-toned self-respect. There are no special claims to propose for women and negroes, no new arguments to make in their behalf. The same already made to extend suffrage to all white men in this country, the same John Bright makes for the working men of England, the same made for the emancipation of 22,000,000 Russian serfs, are all we have to make for black men and women. As the greater includes the less, an argument for universal suffrage covers the whole question, the rights of all citizens. In thus relaying the foundations of government, we settle all these side issues of race, color, and sex, and class legislation, and remove forever the fruitful cause of the jealousies, dissensions, and revolutions of the past. This is the platform of the American Equal Rights Association. "We are masters of the situation." Here black men and women are buried in the citizen. As in the war, freedom was the key-note of victory, so now is universal suffrage the key-note of reconstruction.

"Negro suffrage" may answer as a party cry for an effete political organization through another Presidential campaign; but the people of this country have a broader work on hand to-day than to save the Republican party, or, with some abolitionists, to settle the rights of races. The battles of the ages have been fought for races, classes, parties, over and over again, and force always carried the day, and will until we settle the higher, the holier question of individual rights. This is our American idea, and on a wise settlement of this question rests the problem whether our nation shall live or perish.

The principle of inequality in government has been thoroughly tried, and every nation based on that idea that has not already perished, clearly shows the seeds of death in its dissensions and decline. Though it has never been tried, we know an experiment on the basis of equality would be safe; for the laws in the world of morals are as immutable as in the world of matter. As the Astronomer Leverrier discovered the planet that bears his name by a process of reason and calculation through the variations of other planets from known laws, so can the true statesman, through the telescope of justice, see the genuine republic of the future amid the ruins of the mighty nations that have passed away. The opportunity now given us to make the experiment of self-government should be regarded by every American citizen as a solemn and a sacred trust. When we remember that a nation's life and growth and immortality depend on its legislation, can we exalt too highly the dignity and responsibility of the ballot, the science of political economy, the sphere of government? Statesmanship is, of all sciences, the most exalted and comprehensive, for it includes all others. Among men we find those who study the laws of national life more liberal and enlightened on all subjects than those who confine their researches in special directions. When we base nations on justice and equality, we lift government out of the mists of speculation into the dignity of a fixed science. Everything short of this is trick, legerdemain, sleight of hand. Magicians may make nations seem to live, but they do not. The Newtons of our day who should try to make apples stand in the air or men walk on the wall, would be no more puerile in their experiments than are they who build nations outside of law, on the basis of inequality.

What thinking man can talk of *coming down* into the arena of politics? If we need purity, honor, self-sacrifice and devotion anywhere, we need them in those who have in their keeping the life and prosperity of a nation. In the enfranchisement of woman, in lifting her up into this broader sphere, we see for her new honor and dignity, more liberal, exalted and enlightened views of life, its objects, ends and aims, and an entire revolution in the new world of interest and action where she is soon to play her part. And in saying this, I do not claim that woman is better than man, but that the sexes have a civilizing power on each other. The distinguished historian, Henry Thomas Buckle, says: "The turn of thought of women, their habits of mind, their conversation, invariably extending over the whole surface of society, and frequently penetrating its intimate structure, have, more than all other things put together, tended to raise us into an ideal world, and lift us from the dust into which we are too prone to grovel." And this will be her influence in exalting and purifying the world of politics. When woman understands the momentous interests that depend on the ballot, she will make it her first duty to educate every American boy and girl into the idea that to vote is the most sacred act of citizenship—a religious duty not to be discharged thoughtlessly, selfishly or corruptly; but conscientiously, remembering that, in a republican government, to every citizen is entrusted the interests of the nation. Would you fully estimate the responsibility of the ballot, think of it as the great regulating power of a continent, of all our interests, political, commercial, religious, educational, social and sanitary!

To many minds, this claim for the ballot suggests nothing more than a rough polling-booth where coarse, drunken men, elbowing each other, wade knee-deep in mud to drop a little piece of paper two inches long into a box—simply this and nothing more. The Poet Wordsworth, showing the blank materialism of those who see only with their outward eyes, says of his Peter Bell:

> "A primrose on the river's brim
> A yellow primrose was to him,
> And it was nothing more."

So our political Peter Bells see the rough polling-booth in this great right of citizenship, and nothing more. In this act, so lightly esteemed by the mere materialist, behold the realization of that great idea struggled for in the ages and proclaimed by the Fathers, the right of self-government.

That little piece of paper dropped into a box is the symbol of equality, of citizenship, of wealth, of virtue, education, self-protection, dignity, independence and power—the mightiest engine yet placed in the hand of man for the uprooting of ignorance, tyranny, superstition, the overturning of thrones, altars, kings, popes, despotisms, monarchies and empires. What phantom can the sons of the Pilgrims be chasing, when they make merchandise of a power like this? Judas Iscariot, selling his Master for thirty pieces of silver, is a fit type of those American citizens who sell their votes, and thus betray the right of self-government. Talk not of the "muddy pool of politics," as if such things must need be. Behold, with the coming of woman into this higher sphere of influence, the dawn of the new day, when politics, so called, are to be lifted into the world of morals and religion; when the polling-booth shall be a beautiful temple, surrounded by fountains and flowers and triumphal arches, through which young men and maidens shall go up in joyful procession to ballot for justice and freedom; and when our election days shall be kept like the holy feasts of the Jews at Jerusalem. Through the trials of this second revolution shall not our nation rise up, with new virtue and strength, to fulfill her mission in leading all the peoples of the earth to the only solid foundation of government, "equal rights to all." . . .

Our danger lies, not in the direction of despotism, in the one-man power, in centralization; but in the corruption of the people. . . .

It is in vain to look for a genuine republic in this country until the women are baptized into the idea, until they understand the genius of our institutions, until they study the science of government, until they hold the ballot in their hands and have a direct voice in our legislation. What is the reason, with the argument in favor of the enfranchisement of women all on one side, without an opponent worthy of consideration—while British statesmen, even, are discussing this question—the Northern men are so dumb and dogged, manifesting a studied indifference to what they can neither answer nor prevent? What is the reason that even abolitionists who have fearlessly claimed political, religious and social equality for women for the last twenty years, should now, with bated breath, give her but a passing word in their public speeches and editorial comments— as if her rights constituted but a side issue of this grave question of reconstruction? All must see that this claim for *male* suffrage is but another experiment in class legislation, another violation of the republican idea. With the black man we have no new element in government, but with the education and elevation of women we have a power that is to develop the Saxon race into a higher and nobler life, and thus, by the law of attraction, to lift all races to a more even platform than can ever be reached in the political isolation of the sexes. Why ignore 15,000,000 women in the reconstruction? The philosophy of this silence is plain enough. The black man crowned with the rights of citizenship, there are no political Ishmaelites left but the women. This is the last stronghold of aristocracy in the country. Sydney Smith says: "There always has been, and always will be, a class of men in the world so small that, if women were educated, there would be nothing left below them."

It is a consolation to the "white male," to the popinjays in all our seminaries of learning, to the ignorant foreigner, the boot-black and barber, the idiot—for a "white male" may vote if he be not more than nine-tenths a fool—to look down on women of wealth and education, who write books, make speeches, and discuss principles with the savans of their age. It is a consolation for these classes to be able to say, "well, if woman can do these things, they can't vote after all." I heard some boys discoursing thus not long since. I told them they reminded me of a story I heard of two Irishmen the first time they saw a locomotive with a train of cars. As the majestic fire-horse, with all its grace and polish, moved up to a station, stopped, and snorted, as its mighty power was curbed, then slowly gathered up its forces again and moved swiftly on— "be jabers," says Pat, "there's muscle for you. What are we beside that giant?" They watched it intently till out of sight, seemingly with real envy, as if oppressed with a feeling of weakness and poverty before this unknown power; but rallying at last, one says to the other: "No matter, Pat; let it snort and dash on—it can't vote, after all."

Poor human nature wants something to look down on. No privileged order ever did see the wrongs of its own victims, and why expect the "white male citizen" to enfranchise woman without a struggle—by a scratch of the pen to place themselves on a dead level with their lowest order? And what a fall would that be, my countrymen. In none of the nations of modern Europe is there a class of women so degraded politically as are the women of these Northern States. In the Old World, where the government is the aristocracy, where it is considered a mark of nobility to share its offices and powers—there women of rank have certain hereditary rights which raise them above a majority of the men, certain honors and privileges not granted to serfs or peasants. In England women may be Queen, hold office, and vote on some questions. In the Southern States even the women were not degraded below their working population, they were not humiliated in seeing their coachmen, gardeners, and waiters go to the polls to legislate on their interests; hence there was a pride and dignity in their bearing not found in the women of the North, and pluck in the chivalry before which Northern doughfaceism has ever cowered. But here, where the ruling class, the aristocracy, is "male," no matter whether washed or unwashed, lettered or unlettered, rich or poor, black or white, here in this boasted northern civilization, under the shadow of Bunker Hill and Faneuil Hall, which Mr. Phillips proposes to cram down the throat of South Carolina—here women of wealth and education, who pay taxes and are amenable to law, who may be hung, even though not permitted to choose the judge, the juror, or the sheriff who does the dismal deed, women who are your peers in art, science, and literature—already close upon your heels in the whole world of thought—are thrust outside the pale of political consideration with traitors, idiots, minors, with those guilty of bribery, larceny, and infamous crime. What a category is this in which to place your mothers, wives, and daughters. "I ask you, men of the Empire State, where on the footstool do you find such a class of citizens politically so degraded? Now, we ask you, in the coming Constitutional Convention, to so amend the Second Article of our State Constitution as to wipe out this record of our disgrace.

"But," say you, "women themselves do not make the demand." Mr. Phillips said on this platform, a year ago, that "the singularity of this cause is, that it has to be carried on against the wishes and purposes of its victims," and he has been echoed by nearly every man who has spoken on this subject during the past year. Suppose the assertion true, is it a peculiarity of this reform? . . . Ignorant classes always resist innovations. Women looked on the sewing-machine as a rival for a long time. Years ago the laboring classes of England asked bread; but the Cobdens, the Brights, the Gladstones, the Mills have taught them there is a power behind bread, and to-day they ask the ballot. But they were taught its power first, and so must woman be. Again, do not those far-seeing philosophers who comprehend the wisdom, the beneficence, the morality of free trade urge this law of nations against the will and wishes of the victims of tariffs and protective duties? If you can prove to us that women do not wish to vote, that is no argument against our demand. There are many duties in life that ignorant, selfish, unthinking women do not desire to do, and this may be one of them.

"But," says Rev. O. B. Frothingham, in a recent sermon on this subject, "they who first assume political responsibilities must necessarily lose something of the feminine element." In the education and elevation of woman we are yet to learn the true manhood and womanhood, the true masculine and feminine elements. Dio Lewis is rapidly changing our ideas of feminine beauty. In the large waists and strong arms of the girls under his training, some dilettante gentleman may mourn a loss of feminine delicacy. So in the wise, virtuous, self-supporting, common-sense women we propose as the mothers of the future republic, the reverend gentleman may see a lack of what he considers the feminine element. In the development of sufficient moral force to entrench herself on principle, need a woman necessarily lose any grace, dignity, or perfection of character? Are not those who have advocated the rights of women in this country for the last twenty years as delicate and refined, as moral, high-toned, educated, just, and generous as any women in the land? I have seen women in many countries and classes, in public and private; but have found none more pure and noble than those I meet on this platform. I have seen our venerable President in converse with the highest of English nobility, and even the Duchess of Sutherland did not eclipse her in grace, dignity, and conversational power. Where are there any women, as wives and mothers, more beautiful in their home life than Lucretia Mott and Lucy Stone, or Antoinette Brown Blackwell? Let the freedmen of the South Sea Islands testify to the faithfulness, the devotion, the patience, and tender mercy of Frances D. Gage, who watched over their interests, teaching them to read and work for two long years. Some on our platform have struggled with hardship and poverty— been slaves even in "the land of the free and the home of the brave," and bear the scars of life's battle. But is a self-made woman less honorable than a self-made man? Answer our arguments. When the Republic is in danger, no matter for our manners. When our soldiers came back from the war, wan, weary, and worn, maimed, halt, blind, wrinkled, and decrepit—their banners torn, their garments stained with blood—who, with a soul to feel, thought of anything but the glorious work they had done? What if their mothers on this platform be angular, old, wrinkled, and gray? They, too, have fought a good fight for freedom, and proudly bear the scars of the battle. We alone have struck the key-note of reconstruction. While man talks of "equal, impartial, manhood suffrage," we give the certain sound, "universal suffrage." While he talks of the rights of races, we exalt the higher, the holier idea proclaimed by the Fathers, and now twice baptized in blood, "individual rights." To woman it is given to save the Republic.

Maria Stewart
(c. 1803–1879)

Maria Stewart was born sometime in the year 1803 in Hartford, Connecticut. Orphaned at the age of five, Maria was bound to a clergyman until the age of fifteen. Her education limited to what she learned in "Sabbath Schools" and gleaned from the clergyman's private library, Maria nevertheless managed to learn to read and write at a fairly sophisticated level for black females in her time period. In 1826 she moved to Boston to marry James W. Stewart, who shortly thereafter died from yellow fever. Maria achieved notoriety in the years 1832–33 by delivering four public addresses on slavery at a time when no women except Frances Wright and women in Quaker meetings were speaking from a public platform. Public pressure and the fact that others in the black community began to hold her in contempt for speaking publicly as a female, probably explains why she only delivered these four speeches before ceasing her campaign and moving to New York City in 1833. Maria devoted the next thirty years to teaching: from 1833 to 1852 she taught in public schools in New York; from 1852 to 1861 she taught black children in her own school in Baltimore; and from 1861 to the end of the Civil War she taught at her own school in Washington, D.C. In her last few years she worked as a Matron at a Freedman's Hospital in Washington and opened a Sunday School for black children in 1871. In 1879 she published the second edition of her speeches and writings (the first in 1835) with an introductory letter by William Lloyd Garrison. On December 17, 1879 Maria died peacefully in Washington, D.C., at the age of 76.

The following speech was delivered at the African Masonic Hall in Boston on February 27, 1833. It was later printed in the *Liberator* (April 27, 1833).

"African Rights and Liberty"

African rights and liberty is a subject that ought to fire the breast of every free man of color in these United States, and excite in his bosom a lively, deep, decided and heart-felt interest. When I cast my eyes on the long list of illustrious names that are enrolled on the bright annals of fame amongst the whites, I turn my eyes within, and ask my thoughts, "Where are the names of our illustrious ones?" It must certainly have been for the want of energy on the part of the free people of color that they have been long willing to bear the yoke of oppression. It must have been the want of ambition and force that has given the whites occasion to say, that our natural abilities are not as good, and our capacities by nature inferior to theirs. They boldly assert, that, did we possess a natural independence of soul, and feel a love for liberty within our breasts, some one of our sable race, long before this, would have testified it, notwithstanding the disadvantages under which we labor. We have made ourselves appear altogether unqualified to speak in our own defence, and are therefore looked upon as objects of pity and commiseration. We have been imposed upon, insulted and derided on every side; and now, if we complain, it is considered as the height of impertinence. We have suffered ourselves to be considered as dastards, cowards, mean, faint-hearted wretches; and on this account, (not because of our complexion,) many despise us and would gladly spurn us from their presence.

These things have fired my soul with a holy indignation, and compelled me thus to come forward, and endeavor to turn their attention to knowledge and improvement; for knowledge is power. I would ask, is it blindness of mind, or stupidity of soul, or the want of education, that has caused our men who are 60 or 70 years of age, never to let their voices be heard nor their hands be raised in behalf of their color? Or has it been for the fear of offending the whites? If it has, O ye fearful ones, throw off your fearfulness, and come forth in the name of the Lord, and in the strength of the God of Justice, and make yourselves useful and active members in society; for they admire a noble and patriotic spirit in others—and should they not admire it in us? If you are men, convince them that you possess the spirit of men; and as your day, so shall your strength be. Have the sons of Africa no souls? feel they no ambitious desires? shall the chains of ignorance forever confine them? shall the insipid appellation of "clever negroes," or "good creatures," any longer content them? Where can we find amongst ourselves the man of science, or a philosopher, or an able statesman, or a counsellor at law? Show me our fearless and brave, our noble and gallant ones. Where are our lecturers on natural history, and our critics in useful knowledge? There may be a few such men amongst us, but they are rare. It is true, our fathers bled and died in the revolutionary war, and others fought bravely under the command of Jackson, in defence of liberty. But where is the man that has distinguished himself in these modern days by acting wholly in the defence of African rights and liberty? There was one—although he sleeps, his memory lives.

I am sensible that there are many highly intelligent gentlemen of color in these United States, in the force of whose arguments, doubtless, I should discover my inferiority; but if they are blest with wit and talent, friends and fortune, why have they not made themselves men of eminence, by striving to take all the reproach that is cast upon the people of color, and in endeavoring to alleviate the woes of their brethren in bondage? Talk, without effort, is nothing; you are abundantly capable, gentlemen, of making yourselves men of distinction; and this gross neglect, on your part, causes my blood to boil within me. Here is the grand cause which hinders the rise and progress of the people of color. It is their want of laudable ambition and requisite courage.

Individuals have been distinguished according to their genius and talents, ever since the first formation of man, and will continue to be whilst the world stands. The different grades rise to honor and respectability as their merits may deserve. History informs us that we sprung from one of the most learned nations of the whole earth—from the seat, if not the parent of science; yes, poor, despised Africa was once the resort of sages and legislators of other nations, was esteemed the school for learning, and the most illustrious men in Greece flocked thither for instruction. But it was our gross sins and abominations that provoked the Almighty to frown thus heavily upon us, and give our glory unto others. Sin and prodigality have caused the downfall of nations, kings and emperors; and were it not that God in wrath remembers mercy, we might indeed despair; but a promise is left us; "Ethiopia shall again stretch forth her hands unto God."

But it is of no use for us to boast that we sprung from this learned and enlightened nation, for this day a thick mist of moral gloom hangs over millions of our race. Our condition as a people has been low for hundreds of years, and it will continue to be so, unless, by the true piety and virtue we strive, to regain that which we have lost. White Americans, by their prudence, economy and exertions, have sprung up and become one of the most flourishing nations in the world, distinguished for their knowledge of the arts and sciences, for their polite literature. Whilst our minds are vacant and starving for want of knowledge, theirs are filled to overflowing. Most of our color have been taught to stand in fear of the white man from their earliest infancy, to work as soon as they could walk, and call "master" before they scarce could lisp the name of mother. Continual fear and laborious servitude have in some degree lessened in us that natural force and energy which belong to man; or else, in defiance of opposition, our men, before this would have nobly and boldly contended for their rights. But give the man of color an equal opportunity with the white, from the cradle to manhood, and from manhood to the grave, and you would discover the dignified statesman, the man of science, and the philosopher. But there is no such opportunity for the sons of Africa, and I fear that our powerful ones are fully determined that there never shall be. Forbid, ye Powers on High, that it should any longer be said that our men possess no force. O ye sons of Africa, when will your voices be heard in our legislative halls, in defiance of your enemies, contending for equal rights and liberty? How can you, when you reflect from what you have fallen, refrain from crying mightily unto God, to turn away from us the fierceness of his anger, and remember our transgressions against us no more forever. But a God of infinite purity will not regard the prayers of those who hold religion in one hand, and prejudice, sin and pollution in the other; he will not regard the prayers of self-righteousness and hypocrisy. Is it possible, I exclaim, that for the want of knowledge, we have labored for thousands of years to support others, and been content to receive what they chose to give us in return? Cast your eyes about—look as far as you can see—all, all is owned by the lordly white, except here and there a lowly dwelling which the man of color, midst deprivations, fraud and opposition, has been scarce able to procure. Like king Solomon, who put neither nail nor hammer to the temple, yet received the praise; so also have the white Americans gained themselves a name, like the names of the great men who are in the earth, whilst in reality we have been their principal foundation and support. We have pursued the shadow, they have obtained the substance; we have performed the labor, they have received the profits; we have planted the vines, they have eaten the fruits of them.

I would implore our men, and especially our rising youth, to flee from the gambling board and the dance hall; for we are poor, and have no money to throw away. I do not consider dancing as criminal in itself, but it is astonishing to me that our young men are so blind to their own interest and the future welfare of their children, as to spend their hard earnings for this frivolous amusement; for it has been carried on among us to such an unbecoming extent that it has become absolutely disgusting. "Faithful are the wounds of a friend, but the kisses of an enemy are deceitful." Had those men amongst us, who have had an opportunity, turned their attention as assiduously to mental and moral improvement as they have to gambling and dancing, I might have remained quietly at home, and they stood contending in my place. These polite accomplishments will never enroll your names on the bright annals of fame, who admire the belle void of intellectual knowledge, or applaud the dandy that talks largely on politics, without striving to assist his fellow in the revolution, when the nerves and muscles of every other man forced him into the field of action. You have a right to rejoice, and to let your hearts cheer you in the days of your youth; yet remember that for all these things God will bring you into judgment. Then, O ye sons of Africa, turn your mind from these perishable objects, and contend for the cause of God and the rights of man. Form yourselves into temperance societies. There are temperate men amongst you; then why will you any longer neglect to strive, by your example, to suppress vice in all its abhorrent forms? You have been told repeatedly of the glorious results arising from temperance, and can you bear to see the whites arising in honor and respectability, without endeavoring to grasp after that honor and respectability also?

But I forbear. Let our money, instead of being thrown away as heretofore, be appropriated for schools and seminaries of learning for our children and youth. We ought to follow the example of the whites in this respect. Nothing would raise our respectability, add to our peace and happiness and reflect so much honor upon us, as to be ourselves the promoters of temperance, and the supporters, as far as we are able, of useful and scientific knowledge. The rays of light and knowledge have been hid from our view; we have been taught to consider ourselves as scarce superior to the brute creation; and have performed the most laborious part of American drudgery. Had we as people received one half the early advantages the whites have received, I would defy the government of these United States to deprive us any longer of our rights.

I am informed that the agent of the Colonization Society has recently formed an association of young men, for the purpose of influencing those of us to go to Liberia who may feel disposed. The colonizationalists are blind to their own interest, for should the nations of the earth make war with America, they would find their forces much weakened by our absence; or should we remain here, can our "brave soldiers" and "fellow citizens," as they were termed in time of calamity, condescend to defend the rights of the whites, and be again deprived of their own, or sent to Liberia in return? O, if the colonizationists are real friends to Africa, let them expend the money which they collect in erecting a college to educate her injured sons in this land of gospel light and liberty; for it would be most thankfully received on our part, and convince us of the truth of their professions, and save time, expense and anxiety. Let them place before us noble objects, worthy of pursuit, and see if we prove ourselves to be those unambitious negores they term us. But ah! methinks their hearts are so frozen towards us, they had rather their money should be sunk in the ocean than to administer it to our relief; and I fear, if they dared, like Pharaoh king of Egypt, they would order every male child amongst us to be drowned. But the most high God is still as able to subdue the lofty pride of these white Americans, as He was the heart of that ancient rebel. They say though we are looked upon as things, yet we sprang from a scientific people. Had our men the requisite force and energy, they would soon convince them, by their efforts both in public and private, that they were men, or things in the shape of men. Well may the colonizationists laugh us to scorn for our negligence; well may they cry, "Shame to the sons of Africa." As the burden of the Israelites was too great for Moses to bear, so also is our burden too great for our noble advocate to bear. You must feel interested, my brethren, in what he undertakes, and hold up his hands by your good words, or in spite of himself his soul will become discouraged, and his heart will die within him; for he has, as it were, the strong bulls of Bashan to contend with.

It is of no use for us to wait any longer for a generation of well educated men to arise. We have slumbered and slept too long already; the day is far spent; the night of death approaches; and you have sound sense and good judgment sufficient to begin with, if you feel disposed to make a right use of it. Let every man of color throughout the United States, who possesses the spirit and principles of a man, sign a petition to Congress to abolish slavery in the District of Columbia, and grant you the rights and privileges of common free citizens; for if you had had faith as a grain of mustard seed, long before this the mountains of prejudice might have been removed. We are all sensible that the Anti-Slavery Society has taken hold of the arm of our whole population, in order to raise them out of the mire. Now all we have to do is, by a spirit of virtuous ambition to strive to raise ourselves; and I am happy to have it in my power thus publicly to say that the colored inhabitants of this city, in some respects, are beginning to improve. Had the free people of color in these United States nobly and boldly contended for their rights, and showed a natural genius and talent, although not so brilliant as some; had they held up, encouraged and patronized each other; nothing could have hindered us from being a thriving and flourishing people. There has been a fault amongst us. The reason why our distinguished men have not made themselves more influential is, because they fear that the strong current of opposition through which they must pass, would cause their downfall and prove their overthrow. And what gives rise to this opposition? Envy. And what has it amounted to? Nothing. And who are the cause of it? Our whited sepulchres, who want to be great, and don't know how; who love to be called of men "Rabbi, Rabbi," who put on false sanctity, and humble themselves to their brethren, for the sake of acquiring the highest place in the synagogue, and the uppermost seats at the feast. You, dearly beloved, who are the genuine followers of our Lord Jesus Christ, the salt of the earth and the light of the world, are not so culpable. As I told you, in the very first of my writing, I tell you again, I am but as one drop in the bucket—as one particle of the small dust of the earth. God will surely raise up those amongst us who will plead the cause of virtue, and the pure principles of morality, more eloquently than I am able to do.

It appears to me that America has become like the great city of Babylon, for she has boasted in her heart,— "I sit a queen, and am no widow, and shall see no sorrow." She is indeed a seller of slaves and the souls of men; she has made the Africans drunk with the wine of her fornication; she has put them completely beneath her feet, and she means to keep them there; her right hand supports the reins of government, and her left hand the wheel of power, and she is determined not to let go her grasp. But many powerful sons and daughters of Africa will shortly arise, who will put down vice and immorality amongst us, and declare by Him that sitteth upon the throne, that they will have their rights; and if refused, I am afraid they will spread horror and devastation around. I believe that the oppression of injured Africa has come up before the majesty of Heaven; and when our cries shall have reached the ears of the Most High, it will be a tremendous day for the people of this land; for strong is the arm of the Lord God Almighty.

Life has almost lost its charms for me; death has lost its sting and the grave its terrors; and at times I have a strong desire to depart and dwell with Christ, which is far better. Let me entreat my white brethren to awake and save our sons from dissipation, and our daughters from ruin. Lend the hand of assistance to feeble merit, and plead the cause of virtue amongst our sable race; so shall our curses upon you be turned into blessings; and though you shall endeavor to drive us from these shores, still we will cling to you the more firmly; nor will we attempt to rise above you; we will presume to be called equals only.

The unfriendly whites first drove the native American from his much loved home. Then they stole our fathers from their peaceful and quiet dwellings, and brought them hither and made bond men and bond women of them and their little ones; they have obliged our brethren to labor, kept them in utter ignorance, nourished them in vice and raised them in degradation; and now that we have enriched their soil, and filled their coffers, they say that we are not capable of becoming like white men, and that we never can rise to respectability in this country. They would drive us to a strange land. But before I go, the bayonet shall pierce me through. African rights and liberty is a subject that ought to fire the breast of every free man of color in these United States, and excite in his bosom a lively, deep, decided and heartfelt interest.

Lucy Stone
(1818–1893)

Lucy Stone was born on August 13, 1818 in Coy's Hill, about three miles from West Brookfield, Massachusetts. The eighth of nine children, Lucy grew up on a prosperous farm and attended public school until age 16. For the next several years Lucy taught in a district school and with her earnings studied for brief periods at Quabong Seminary in Warren, at Wesleyan Academy in Wilbraham, and in 1839 at Mount Holyoke Female Seminary in South Hadley. In 1843, at age 25, Lucy enrolled at Oberlin College, where she graduated with honors in 1847 as the first Massachusetts woman to receive a college degree. Not long after graduation, the American Anti-Slavery Society appointed her as a lecturer, largely due to the influence of William Lloyd Garrison and Abby Kelley Foster. However, Lucy's concerns also included the status of women and she worked out a compromise with the society which would allow her to speak for them on the weekends and devote the weekdays to lectures on woman's rights. In 1850 she helped to organize the first national woman's rights convention in Worcester, Massachusetts, where she delivered an address which reportedly converted Susan B. Anthony to the cause and eventually, in printed form, inspired John Stuart Mill's classic "The Enfranchisement of Women." Until her marriage in 1855 to Henry Blackwell, Lucy travelled extensively; lecturing on woman suffrage in Canada, as far west as Missouri, and into parts of the South. After her marriage, Lucy gave up an active career until the end of the Civil War. In 1866, she resumed her reform efforts and helped to organize and provide leadership for the American Equal Rights Association, designed to press for both Negro and woman suffrage. After serving as president of the New Jersey Woman Suffrage Association, Lucy and her husband were persuaded to move to Boston so she could assume leadership in the New England movement. In 1869 Lucy parted company with Elizabeth Cady Stanton and Susan B. Anthony, primarily due to conflicts concerning passage of the 15th Amendment minus woman suffrage, and helped to found the American Woman Suffrage Association. One of her greatest contributions to the woman's movement was the founding in 1870 of the weekly newspaper, the *Woman's Journal,* which she and her husband assumed editorship of in 1872. The Journal, which ran for forty-seven years, achieved wide acclaim for its excellent scholarship and the caliber of its contributors and served as a major voice in the women's movement. After 1887 Lucy's voice failed and she seldom spoke in public. Her last lectures were delivered at the World's Columbian Exposition in Chicago in 1893. Several months later, Lucy died at the age of 75 on October 18, 1893.

The following speech was delivered at the National Woman's Rights Convention at the Broadway Tabernacle in New York City on November 25, 1856. It appeared in printed form in *The History of Woman Suffrage,* Vol. I (Rochester, N.Y., 1881) pp. 650–653.

"Nature and Revelation and Woman's Right to Vote"

If we were living in New Zealand where there is no revelation and nobody has ever heard of one, there would yet be an everlasting truth or falsehood on this question of woman's rights, and the inhabitants of that island would settle it in some way, without revelation. The true test of every

174

question is its own merits. What is true will remain. What is false will perish like the leaves of autumn when they have served their turn.

But in regard to this question of Nature and Revelation, we found our claim on both. By Revelation I suppose the gentleman means Scripture. I find it there, "He who spake as never man spake" held up before us all radiant with God's own sunlight the great truth, "All things whatsoever ye would that men should do to you, do ye even so to them"; and that revelation I take as the foundation of our claim, and tell the gentleman who takes issue with us, that if he would not take the position of woman, denied right of access to our colleges, deprived of the right of property, compelled to pay taxes, to obey laws that he never had a voice in making, and be defrauded of the children of his love, then, according to the revelation which he believes in, he must not be thus unjust to me.

The gentleman says he believes in Paul. So do I. When Paul declares that there is neither Jew nor Greek, neither bond nor free, male nor female in Christ, I believe he meant what he said. The gentleman says he believes in Paul more than in the Anglo-Saxon blood. I believe in both. But when Paul tells us to "submit ourselves to every ordinance of man for the Lord's sake," and to "fear God and honor the king," the heavy tread of the Anglo-Saxon blood walks over the head of Paul and sweeps away from this republic the possibility of a king. And the gentleman himself, I presume, would not assent to the sway of a crowned monarch, Paul to the contrary, notwithstanding. Just as the people have outgrown the injunction of Paul in regard to a king, so have the wives his direction to submit themselves to their husbands. The gentleman intimates that wives have no right to vote against their husbands, because the Scriptures command submission, and he fears that it would cause trouble at home if they were to do so. Let me give him the reply of an old lady, gray with the years which bring experience and wisdom. She said that when men wanted to get their fellow-men to vote in the way they desire, they take especial pains to please them, they smile upon them, ask if their wives and children are well, and are exceedingly kind. They do not expect to win their vote by quarreling with them—that would be absurd. In the same way, if a man wanted his wife to vote for his candidate he will be sure to employ conciliatory means.

The golden rule settles this whole question. We claim it as ours, and whatever is found in the Bible contradictory to it, never came from God. If men quote other texts in conflict with this, it is their business, not mine, to make them harmonize. I did not quite understand the gentleman's definition of what is natural. But this I do know, that when God made the human soul and gave it certain capacities, He meant these capacities should be exercised. The wing of the bird indicates its right to fly; and the fin of the fish the right to swim. So in human beings, the existence of a power, presupposes the right to its use, subject to the law of benevolence. The gentleman says the voice of woman can not be heard. I am not aware that the audience finds any difficulty in hearing us from this platform. All Europe and America have listened to the voice of Madam Rachel and Jenny Lind. The capacity to speak indicates the right to do so, and the noblest, highest, and best thing that any one can accomplish, is what that person ought to do, and what God holds him or her accountable for doing, nor should we be deterred by the senseless cry, "It is not our proper sphere."

As regards woman's voting, I read a letter from a lady traveling in the British provinces, who says that by a provincial law of Nova Scotia and New Brunswick, women were actually voters for members of Parliament; and still the seasons come and go, children are born, and fish flock to that shore. The voting there is *viva voce*. In Canada it is well known that women vote on the question of schools. A friend told me when the law was first passed giving women who owned a certain amount of property, or who paid a given rental, a right to vote, he went trembling to the polls to see the result. The first woman who came was a large property holder in Toronto; with marked respect the crowd gave way as she advanced. She spoke her vote and walked quietly away, sheltered by her womanhood. It was all the protection she needed. In face of all the arguments in favor of the incapacity of woman to be associated in government, stood the fact that women had sat on thrones and governed as successfully as men. England owes more to Queen Elizabeth than to any other sovereign except Alfred the Great. We must not always be looking for precedents. New ideas are born and old ones die. Ideas that have prevailed a thousand years have been at last exploded. Every new truth has its birth-place in a manger, lives thirty years, is crucified, and then deified. Columbus argued through long years that there must be a western world. All Europe laughed at him. Five crowned heads rejected him, and it was a woman at last who sold her jewels and fitted out his ships. So, too, the first idea of applying steam to machinery was met with the world's derision. But its triumphs are recognized now. What we need is to open our minds wide and give hospitality to every new thought, and prove its truth.

I want to say a word upon the resolutions. The present time, just after a presidential election, is most appropriate to consider woman's demand for suffrage. The Republican party claims especially to represent the principles of freedom, and during the last campaign has been calling upon women for help. One of the leaders of that party went to Elizabeth Cady Stanton and said he wanted her help in this campaign, and before she told me what answer she made, she asked me how I would have felt if the same had been asked of me. I told her I should have felt as Samson did when the Philistines put out his eyes, and then asked that he should make merriment for them. The Republican party are a part of those who compel us to obey laws we never had a voice in making—to pay taxes without our consent; and when we ask for our political and legal rights, it laughs in our face, and only says: "Help *us* to places of power and emolument, and *we* will rule over you." I know there are men in the Republican party who, like our friend Mr. Higginson, take a higher stand, and are ready to recognize woman as a co-sovereign; but they are the exceptions. There is but one party—that of Gerrit Smith—that makes the same claim for woman that it does for man. But while the Republican and Democratic parties deny our political existence, they must not expect that we shall respond to their calls for aid.

Madame de Staël said to Bonaparte, when asked why she meddled with politics: "Sire, when women have their heads cut off, it is but just they should know the reason." Whatever political influence springs into being, woman is affected by it. We have the same rights to guard that men have; we shall therefore insist upon our claims. We shall go to your meetings, and by and by we shall meet with the same success that the Roman women did, who claimed the repeal of the Appian law. War had emptied the treasury, and it was still necessary to carry it on; women were required to give up their jewels, their carriages, etc. But by and by, when the war was over, they wished to resume their old privileges. They got up a petition for the repeal of the law; and when the senators went to their places, they found every avenue to the forum thronged by women, who said to them as they passed, "Do us justice." And notwithstanding Cato, the Censor, was against them, affirming that men must have failed in their duty or women would not be clamorous for their rights, yet the obnoxious law was repealed.

In that story of Mr. Higginson's, of the heroic woman in Kansas whose left arm was cut off, there is a lesson for us to learn. I tell you, ladies, though we have our left hand cut off by unjust laws and customs, we have yet the right hand left; and when we once demand the ballot with as much firmness as that Kansas daughter did her horse, believe me, it will not be in the power of men to withhold it—even the border ruffians among them will hasten to restore it. After all, the fault is our own. We have sat to

"Suckle fools, and chronicle small beer;"

and, in inglorious ease, have forgotten that we are integral parts in the fabric of human society—that all that interests the race, interests us. We have never once, as a body, claimed the practical application of the principles of our government. It is our own fault. Let it be so no longer. Let us say to men: "Government is just only when it obtains the consent of the governed": we are governed, *surrender to us our ballot*. If they deride, still answer: Surrender our ballot! *and they will give it up*. "It is not in our stars that we are underlings, but in ourselves." Woman has sat, like Mordecai at the king's gate, hoping that her silent presence would bring justice; but justice has not come. The world has talked of universal suffrage; but it has made it universal only to man. It is time we spoke and acted. It is time we gave man faith in woman—and, still more, woman faith in herself. It is time both men and women knew that whatever has been achieved by woman in the realm of mind or matter, has been achieved by right womanly women. Let us then work, and continue to work, until the world shall assent to our right to do whatever the capacities God has given us enable us to do.

Ida Tarbell
(1857–1944)

Ida Tarbell was born on November 5, 1857 in Erie County, Pennsylvania. The eldest of three children, Ida grew up in various rural communities surrounding Erie, Pennsylvania. After attending local public schools, she entered Allegheny College in 1876 and graduated in 1880 as one of only five women students. Two years of teaching English at the Poland (Ohio) Union Seminary interested Ida in writing, and in 1883 she joined the staff of the *Chautauquan* magazine where she remained for eight years. In 1891 she travelled to Paris to study the role of women in the French Revolution and to take classes at the Sorbonne and the College de France. Occasional articles she published in *Scribner's* to earn her expenses brought Ida to the attention of S. S. McClure of *McClure's* magazine. Beginning in 1892 she published feature articles with the magazine, including interviews with such noted Frenchmen as Pasteur, Zola, Daudet and Dumas. In 1894 the magazine convinced Ida to join the staff and return to New York. Several articles on Napoleon brought her wide popular acclaim and resulted in a book entitled *A Short Life of Napoleon Bonaparte* (1895). Ida's next series of articles on Abraham Lincoln increased her fame and also resulted in a book, *The Life of Abraham Lincoln* (1900). But it was Ida's third series of articles which created the most sensation and which became the principal work upon which her reputation rested: her powerful indictment of the Standard Oil Company, collected in book form as *The History of the Standard Oil Company* (1904). In 1906, Ida joined other noted "muckraker" journalists (Lincoln Steffens, Ray Stannard Baker, David Graham Phillips and others) in purchasing and cooperatively editing the *American Magazine.* With the sale of the magazine in 1915, she became a lecturer on the Chautauqua circuit until 1932, except for wartime interruptions, speaking on American business, unemployment, the Versailles Treaty, the League of Nations, and disarmament. Other activities also engaged Ida's talents as a speaker and writer during this time period: she served as a member of the Women's Committee of the U.S. Council of National Defense during World War I, as a delegate to the Industrial Conference in 1919, as a delegate to the Conference on Unemployment in 1921, and as a reporter for *McCall's* magazine in 1926 to cover Mussolini's reign of Italy. She remained active in her old age by giving special courses on the methods of biographies at several colleges and published her autobiography *All in the Day's Work* in 1939 at the age of 82. On January 6, 1944, Ida died of pneumonia on her Connecticut farm where she had spent most of her time since 1906.

The following lecture first appeared as an article in *McClure's Magazine* (January, 1903), but was later delivered several times under the auspices of the Lyceum Movement in the years 1903-04.

"The History of the Standard Oil Company: The Oil War of 1872"

For several days an uneasy rumor had been running up and down the Oil Regions. Freight rates were going up. Now, an advance in a man's freight bill may ruin his business; more, it may mean the ruin of a region. Rumor said that the new rate meant just this; that is, that it more than covered the margin of profit in any branch of the oil business. There was another feature to the report; the railroads were not going to apply the proposed tariffs to everybody. They had agreed to give to a company unheard of until now—the South Improvement Company—a special rate considerably lower than the new open rate. It was only a rumor and many people discredited it. *Why* should the railroads ruin the Oil Regions to build up a company of outsiders?

On the morning of February 26, 1872, the oil men read in their morning papers that the rise which had been threatened had come; moreover, that all members of the South Improvement Company were exempt from the advance. At the news all Oildom rushed into the streets. Nobody waited to find out his neighbor's opinion. On every lip there was but one word, and that was "conspiracy." In the vernacular of the region, it was evident that "a torpedo was filling for that scheme."

In twenty-four hours after the announcement of the increase in freight rates a mass meeting of three thousand excited, gesticulating oil men was gathered in the Opera House at Titusville. Producers, brokers, refiners, drillers, pumpers were in the crowd. Their temper was shown by the mottoes on the banners which they carried: "Down with the conspirators"— "No compromise"— "Don't give up the ship!" Three days later, as large a meeting was held at Oil City, its temper more warlike if possible; and so it went. They organized a Petroleum Producers' Union, pledged themselves to reduce their production by starting no new wells for sixty days and by shutting down on Sundays, to sell no oil to any person known to be in the South Improvement Company, but to support the Creek refiners and those elsewhere who had refused to go into the combination, to boycott the offending railroads, and to build lines which they would own and control themselves. They sent a committee to the Legislature asking that the charter of the South Improvement Company be repealed, and another to Congress demanding an investigation of the whole business on the ground that it was an interference with trade. They ordered that a history of the conspiracy, giving the names of the conspirators and the designs of the company, should be prepared, and 30,000 copies sent to "judges of all courts, Senators of the United States, members of Congress and of State Legislatures, and to all railroad men and prominent businessmen of the country, *to the end that enemies of the freedom of trade may be known and shunned by all honest men.*"

They prepared a petition ninety-three feet long, praying for a free pipe-line bill, something which they had long wanted, but which, so far, the Pennsylvania Railroad had prevented their getting, and sent it by a committee to the Legislature; and for days they kept a thousand men ready to march on Harrisburg at a moment's notice if the Legislature showed signs of refusing their demands. In short, for weeks the whole body of oil men abandoned regular business and surged from town to town intent on destroying the "Monster," the "Forty Thieves," the "Great Anaconda," as they called the mysterious South Improvement Company. Curiously enough, it was chiefly against the combination from the railroads—not the railroads which had granted it—that their fury was directed. They expected nothing but robbery from the railroads, they said. They were used to that; but they would not endure it from men in their own business.

When they began the fight, the mass of the oil men knew nothing more of the South Improvement Company than its name and the fact that it had secured from the railroads advantages in rates which were bound to ruin all independent refiners of oil and to put all producers at its mercy. Their tempers were not improved by the discovery that it was a secret organization, and had been at work under their very eyes for some weeks without their knowing it. At the first public meeting this fact came out, leading refiners of the region relating their experience with the "Anaconda." According to one of these gentlemen, Mr. J. D. Archbold—the same who afterward became vice-president of the Standard Oil Company, which office he now holds—he and his partners had heard of the scheme some months before. Alarmed by the rumor, a committee of independent refiners had attempted to investigate, but could learn nothing until they had given a promise not to reveal what was told them. When convinced that a company had been formed actually strong enough to force or persuade the railroads to give to it special rates and refuse them to all persons outside, Mr. Archbold said that he and his colleagues had gone to the railway kings to remonstrate, but all to no effect. The South Improvement Company by some means had convinced the railroads that they owned the Oil Regions, producers and refiners both, and that hereafter no oil of any account would be shipped except as they shipped it. Mr. Archbold and his partners had been asked to join the company, but had refused, declaring that the whole business was iniquitous, that they would fight it to the end, and that in their fight they would have the backing of the oil men, as a whole. They excused their silence up to this time by citing the pledge exacted from them before they were informed of the extent and nature of the South Improvement Company.

Naturally the burning question throughout the Oil Region, convinced as it was of the iniquity of the scheme, was: who are the conspirators? Whether the gentlemen concerned regarded themselves in the light of "conspirators" or not, they seem from the first to have realized that it would be discreet not to be identified publicly with the scheme, and to have allowed one name alone to appear in all signed negotiations. This was the name of the president, Peter H. Watson. However anxious the members of the South Improvement Company were that Mr. Watson should combine the honors of the president with the trials of scapegoat, it was impossible to keep their names concealed. The *Oil City Derrick,* at that time one of the most vigorous, witty, and daring newspapers in the country, began a blacklist at the head of its editorial columns the day after the raise in freights was announced, and it kept it there until it was believed complete. It stood finally as follows:

THE BLACKLIST

P. H. Watson, Pres. S.I. Co.
Charles Lockhart
W. P. Logan
R. S. Waring
A. W. Bostwick
W. G. Warden
John Rockefeller
Amasa Stone

These seven are given as the Directors of the Southern Improvement Company. They are refiners for merchants of petroleum.

Atlantic & Gt. Western Railway,
L. S. & M. S. Railway,
Philadelphia & Erie Railway,
Pennsylvania Central Railway,
New York Central Railway,
Erie Railway.

Behold "The Anaconda" in all his hideous deformity!

This list was not exact, but it was enough to go on, and the oil blockade, to which the Petroleum Producers' Union had pledged itself, was now enforced against the firms listed, and as far as possible against the railroads. All of these refineries had their buyers on the Creek, and although several of the buyers were young men generally liked for their personal and business qualities, no mercy was shown them. They were refused oil by everybody, though they offered from seventy-five cents to a dollar more than the market price. They were ordered at one meeting "to desist from their nefarious business or leave the Oil Region," and when they declined they were invited to resign from the Oil Exchanges of which they were members. So strictly, indeed, was the blockage enforced that in Cleveland the refineries were closed and meetings for the relief of the workmen were held. In spite of the excitement there was little vandalism, the only violence at the opening of the war being at Franklin, where a quantity of the oil belonging to Mr. Watson was run on the ground.

The sudden uprising of the Oil Regions against the South Improvement Company did not alarm its members at first. The excitement would die out, they told one another. All that they needed to do was to keep quiet, and stay out of the oil country. But the excitement did not die out. Indeed, with every day it became more intense and more widespread. When Mr. Watson's tanks were tapped he began to protest in letters to a friend, F. W. Mitchell, a prominent banker and oil man of Franklin. The company was misunderstood, he complained. "Have a committee of leading producers appointed," he wrote, and "we will show that the contracts with the railroad are as favorable to the producing as to other interests; that the much-denounced rebate will enhance the price of oil at the wells, and that our entire plan in operation and effect will promote every legitimate American interest in the oil trade." Mr. Mitchell urged Mr. Watson to come openly to the Oil Regions and meet the producers as a body. A mass meeting was never a "deliberative body," Mr. Watson replied, but if a few of the leading oil men would go to Albany or New York, or any place favorable to calm investigation and deliberation, and therefore outside of the atmosphere of excitement which enveloped the Oil Country, he would see them. These letters were read to the producers, and a motion to appoint a committee was made. It was received with protests and jeers. Mr. Watson was afraid to come to the Oil Regions, they said. The letters were not addressed to the association, they were private—an insult to the body. "We are lowering our dignity to treat with this man Watson," declared one man. "He is free to come to these meetings if he wants to." "What is there to negotiate about?" asked another. "To open a negotiation is to concede that we are wrong. Can we go halves with these middlemen in their swindle?" "He has set a trap for us," declared another. "We cannot treat him without guilt," and the motion was voted down.

The stopping of the oil supply finally forced the South Improvement Company to recognize the Producers' Union officially, by asking that a committee of the body be appointed to confer with them, on a compromise. The producers sent back a pertinent answer. They believed the South Improvement Company meant to monopolize the oil business. If that was so they could not consider a compromise with it. If they were wrong, they would be glad to be enlightened, and they asked for information. First: the charter under which the South Improvement Company was organized. Second: the articles of association. Third: the officers' names. Fourth: the contracts with the railroads and who signed them. Fifth: the general plan of management.

Until we know these things, the oil men declared, we can no more negotiate with you than we could sit down to negotiate with a burglar as to his privileges in our house.

The Producers' Union did not get the information they asked from the company at that time, but it was not long before they did, and much more, too. The committee which they had appointed to write a history of the South Improvement Company reported on March 20, and in April the Congressional Committee appointed at the insistence of the oil men made its investigation. The former report was published broadcast, and is readily accessible today. The Congressional investigation was not published officially, and no trace of its work can now be found in Washington, but while it was going on, reports were made in the newspapers of the Oil Regions, and at its close the Producers' Union published in Lancaster, Pennsylvania, a pamphlet called the "Rise and Fall of the South Improvement Company," which contains the full testimony taken by the committee. This pamphlet is rare, the writer never having been able to find a copy save in three or four private collections. The most important part of it is the testimony of Peter H. Watson, the president, and W. G. Warden, the secretary of the South Improvement Company. It was in these documents that the oil men found full justification for the war they were carrying on and for the losses they had caused themselves and others. Nothing, indeed, could have been more damaging to a corporation than the publication of the charter of the South Improvement Company. As its president told the Congressional Investigating Committee, when he was under examination, "this charter was a sort of clothes-horse to hang a scheme upon." As a matter of fact, it was a clothes-horse big enough to hang the earth upon. It granted powers practically unlimited. There really was no exaggeration in the summary of its powers made and scattered broadcast by the irate oil men in their "History of the South Improvement Company":

The South Improvement Company can own, contract or operate any work, business or traffic (save only banking); may hold and transfer any kind of property, real or personal; hold and operate on any leased property (oil territory, for instance); make any kind of contract; deal in stocks, securities and funds; loan its credit; guarantee anyone's paper; manipulate any industry; may seize upon the lands of other parties for railroading or any other purpose; may absorb the improvements, property or franchises of any other company, ad infinitum; may fix the fares, tolls or freights to be charged on lines of transit operated by it, or on any business it gives to any other company or line, without limit.

Its capital stock can be expanded or "watered" at liberty; it can change its name and location at pleasure; can go anywhere and do almost anything. It is not a Pennsylvania corporation, only; it can, so far as these enactments are valid, or are confirmed by other legislatures, operate in any state or territory; its directors must be only citizens of the United States—not necessarily of Pennsylvania. It is responsible to no one; its stockholders are only liable to the amount of their stock in it; its directors, when wielding all the princely powers of the corporation, are also responsible only to the amount of their stock in it; it may control the business of the continent and hold and transfer millions of property and yet be rotted to the core. It is responsible to no one; makes no reports of its acts or financial condition; its records and deliberations are secret; its capital illimitable; its object unknown. It can be here today, tomorrow away. Its domain is the whole country; its business everything. Now it is petroleum it grasps and monopolizes; next year it may be iron, coal, cotton or breadstuffs. They are landsmen granted perpetual letters of marque to prey upon all commerce everywhere.

When the course of this charter through the Pennsylvania Legislature came to be traced, it was found to be devious and uncertain. The company had been incorporated in 1870, and vested with all the "powers, privileges, duties, and obligations" of two earlier companies—the Continental Improvement Company and the Pennsylvania Company, both of which were children of that interesting body known as the "Tom Scott Legislature." The act incorporating the company was never published, the name of the member introducing it was never known, and no votes on it are recorded. The origin of the South Improvement Company has always remained in darkness. It was one of thirteen "improvement" companies chartered in Pennsylvania at about the same time, and enjoying the same commercial carte blanche.

Bad as the charter was in appearance, the oil men found that the contracts which the new company had made with the railroads were worse. These contracts advanced the rates of freight from the Oil Regions over 100 per cent, but it was not the railroad that got the greater part of this advance; it was the South Improvement Company. Not only did it ship its own oil at fully a dollar a barrel cheaper on an average than anybody else could, but it received fully a dollar a barrel "rake-off" on a very barrel its competitors shipped. It was computed and admitted by the members of the company who appeared before the investigating committee of Congress that this discrimination would have turned over to them fully $6,000,000 annually on the carrying trade. It is hardly to be wondered at that when the oil men had before them the full text of these contracts they refused absolutely to accept the repeated assertions of the members of the South Improvement Company that their scheme was intended only for "the good of the oil business." The committee of Congress could not be persuaded to believe it either. "Your success meant the destruction of every refiner who refused for any reason to join your company, or whom you did not care to have in, and it put the producers entirely in your power. It would make a monopoly such as no set of men are fit to handle," the chairman of the committee declared. Mr. Warden, the secretary of the company, protested again and again that they meant to take in all the refiners, though he had to admit that the contracts with the railroads were not made on this condition. Mr. Watson affirmed and reaffirmed before the committee that it was the intention of the company to take care of the producers. "It was an essential part of this contract that the producers should join it," he declared. But no such condition was embodied in the contract. It was verbal only, and, besides, it had never been submitted to the producers themselves in any form until after the trouble in the Oil Region began. The committee, like the oil men, insisted that under the circumstances no such verbal understanding was to be trusted.

No part of the testimony before the committee made a worse impression than that showing that one of the chief objects of the combination was to put up the price of refined oil. "Under your arrangement," said the chairman, "the public would have been put to an additional expense of $7,500,000 a year." "What public?" said Mr. Warden. "They would have had to pay it in Europe." "But to keep up the price abroad you would have to keep up the price at home," said the chairman. Mr. Warden conceded the point: "You could not get a better price for that exported without having a better price here." Thirty-two cents a gallon was the ideal price they had in view, though refined had not sold for that since 1869, the average price in 1870 being 26 ⅜ and in 1871 24 ¼. The average price of crude in 1870 was $3.90 a barrel; in 1871, $4.40. The Congressional Committee claimed that any combination formed for the purpose of putting up the price of an article of general consumption was an injury to the public, but the members of the company would not admit it as such. Everybody in the business should make more money, they argued; the profits were too small—the consumer ought to be willing to pay more.

It did not take the full exposition of the objects of the South Improvement Company, brought out by the Congressional Investigating Commmittee, with the publication of charters and contracts, to convince the country at large that the Oil Regions were right in their opposition. From the first the sympathy of the press and the people was with the oil men. It was evident to everybody that if the railroads had made the contracts as charged (and it daily became more evident they had done so), nothing but an absolute monopoly of the whole oil business by this combination could result. It was robbery, cried the newspapers all over the land. "Under the thin guise of assisting in the development of oil refining in Pittsburg and Cleveland," said the New York *Tribune*, "this corporation has simply laid its hand upon the throat of the oil traffic with a demand to 'stand and deliver.' " And if this could be done in the oil business, what was to prevent its being done in any other industry? Why should not a company be formed to control wheat or beef or iron or steel, as well as oil? If the railroads would do this for one company, why not for another? The South Improvement Company, men agreed, was a menace to the free trade of the country. If the oil men yielded now, all industries must suffer from their weakness. The railroads must be taught a lesson as well as would-be monopolists.

The oil men had no thought of yielding. With every day of the war their backbones grew stiffer. The men were calmer, too, for their resistance had found a moral ground which seemed impregnable to them, and arguments against the South Improvement Company now took the place of denunciations. The country so buzzed with discussion on the duties of the railroads that reporters sent from the eastern newspapers commented on it. Nothing was commoner, indeed, on the trains which ran the length of the region, and were its real forums, than to hear a man explaining that the railways derived their existence and power from the people, that their charters were contracts with the people, that a fundamental provision of these contracts was that there should be no discriminating in favor of one person or one town, that such a discrimination was a violation of charter, that therefore the South Improvement Company was founded on fraud, and the courts must dissolve it if the railways did not abandon it.

They now met the very plausible reasons given by the members of the company for their combination more intelligently than at first. There were grave abuses in the business, they admitted; there was too great refining capacity; but this they argued was a natural development in a new business whose growth had been extraordinary and whose limits were by no means defined. Time and experience would regulate it. Give the refiners open and regular freights, with no favors to any one, and the stronger and better equipped would live, the others die—but give all a chance. In fact, time and energy would regulate all the evils of which they complained if there was fair play.

The oil men were not only encouraged by public opinion and by getting their minds clear on the merits of their case; they were upheld by repeated proofs of aid from all sides; even the women of the region were asking what they could do, and offering to wear their "black velvet bonnets" all summer if necessary. Solid support came from the independent refiners and shippers in other parts of the country, who were offering to stand in with them in their contest. New York was already one of the chief refining centers of the country, and the South Improvement Company had left it entirely out of its combination. As incensed as the Creek itself, the New York interests formed an association and about the middle of March sent a committee of three, with H. H. Rogers of Charles Pratt & Company at its head, to Oil City, to consult with the Producers' Union. Their arrival in the Oil Regions was a matter of great satisfaction. What made the oil men most exultant, however, was their growing belief that the railroads—the crux of the whole scheme—were weakening.

However fair the great scheme may have appeared to the railroad kings in the privacy of the council chamber, it began to look dark as soon as it was dragged into the open, and signs of a scuttle soon appeared. General G. B. McClellan, president of the Atlantic and Great Western, sent to the very first mass meeting this telegram:

New York, February 27, 1872

Neither the Atlantic and Great Western, or any of its officers, are interested in the South Improvement Company. Of course, the policy of the road is to accommodate the petroleum interest.

G. B. McClellan

A great applause was started, only to be stopped by the hisses of a group whose spokesman read the following:

> Contract with South Improvement Company signed by Geo. B. McClellan, president, for the Atlantic and Great Western Railroad. I only signed it after it was signed by all the other parties.
>
> Jay Gould

The railroads tried in various ways to appease the oil men. They did not enforce the new rates. They had signed the contracts, they declared, only after the South Improvement Company had assured them that all the refineries and producers were to be taken in. Indeed, they seem to have realized within a fortnight that the scheme was doomed, and to have been quite ready to meet cordially a committee of oil men which went east to demand that the railroads revoke their contracts with the South Improvement Company. This committee, which was composed of twelve persons, three of them being the New York representatives already mentioned, began its work by an interview with Colonel Scott at the Colonial Hotel in Philadelphia. With evident pride the committee wrote back to the Producers' Union that: "Mr. Scott differing in this respect from the railroad representatives whom we afterwards met, notified us that he would call upon us at our hotel." An interesting account of their interview was given to the Hepburn Committee in 1879 by Mr. W. T. Schiede, one of the number:

> We saw Mr. Scott on the 18th of March, 1872, in Philadelphia, and he said to us that he was very much surprised to hear of this agitation in the Oil Regions; that the object of the railroads in making this contract with the South Improvement Company was to obtain an evener to pool the freight—pool the oil freights among the different roads; that they had been cutting each other on oil freights for a number of years, and had not made any money out of it, although it was a freight they should have made money from; that they had endeavored to make an arrangement among themselves, but had always failed; he said that they supposed that the gentlemen representing the South Improvement Company represented the petroleum trade, but as he was now convinced they did not, he would be very glad to make an arrangement with this committee, who undoubtedly did represent the petroleum trade; the committee told him that they could not make any such contract; that they had no legal authority to do so; he said that could be easily fixed, because the Legislature was then in session, and by going to Harrisburg a charter could be obtained in a very few days; the committee still said that they would not agree to any such arrangement, that they did not think the South Improvement Company's contract was a good one, and they were instructed to have it broken, and so they did not feel that they could accept a similar one, even if they had the power.

Leaving Colonel Scott, the committee went on to New York, where they stayed for about a week, closely watched by the newspapers, all of which treated the "Oil War" as a national affair. Various conferences were held, leading up to a final all-important one on March 25, at the Erie offices. Horace Clark, president of the Lake Shore and Michigan Southern Railroad, was chairman of this meeting, and, according to H. H. Rogers's testimony before the Hepburn Committee, in 1879, there were present, besides the oil men, Colonel Scott, General McClellan, Director Diven, William H. Vanderbilt, Mr. Stebbins, and George Hall.

The meeting had not been long in session before Mr. Watson, president of the South Improvement Company, and Mr. John D. Rockefeller, presented themselves for admission. Up to this time Mr. Rockefeller had kept well out of sight in the affair. He had given no interviews, offered no explanations. He had allowed the president of the company to wrestle with the excitement in his own way, but things were now in such critical shape that he came forward in a last attempt to save the organization by which he had been able to concentrate in his own hands the refining interests of Cleveland. With Mr. Watson, he knocked for admission to the council going on in the

Erie offices. The oil men flatly refused to let them in. A dramatic scene followed, Mr. Clark, the chairman, protesting in agitated tones against shutting out his "life-long friend, Watson." The oil men were obdurate. They would have nothing to do with anybody concerned with the South Improvement Company. So determined were they that although Mr. Watson came in, he was obliged at once to withdraw. A *Times* reporter who witnessed the little scene between the two supporters of the tottering company after its president was turned out of the meeting remarks sympathetically that Mr. Rockefeller soon went away, "looking pretty blue."

The acquiescence of the "railroad kings" in the refusal of the oil men to recognize representatives of the South Improvement Company was followed by an unwilling promise to break the contracts with the company. A strong effort was made to persuade the independents to make the same contracts on condition that they shipped as much oil, but they would not hear of it. They demanded open rates, with no rebates to anyone. The Vanderbilts particularly stuck for this arrangement, but were finally obliged to consent to revoke the contracts and to make a new one embodying the views of the Oil Regions. The contract finally signed at this meeting by H. F. Clark for the Lake Shore Road, O. H. P. Archer for the Erie, W. H. Vanderbilt for the Central, George B. McClellan for the Atlantic and Great Western, and Thomas A. Scott for the Pennsylvania, agreed that all shipping of oil should be made on "a basis of perfect equality to all shippers, producers, and refiners, and that no rebates, drawbacks, or other arrangements of any character shall be made or allowed that will give any party the slightest difference in rates or discriminations of any character whatever."

The same rate was put on refined oil from Cleveland, Pittsburg, and the Creek, to eastern shipping points; that is, Mr. Rockefeller could send his oil from Cleveland to New York at $1.50 per barrel; so could his associates in Pittsburg, and this was what it cost the refiner on the Creek; but the latter had this advantage: he was at the wells. Mr. Rockefeller and his Pittsburg allies were miles away, and it cost them, by the new contract, fifty cents to get a barrel of crude to their works. The Oil Regions meant that geographical position should count. Unless there was some way to get around this contract, it looked at that moment very much as if Mr. Rockefeller had bought a white elephant when he swept up the refineries of Cleveland.

This contract was the first effective thrust into the great bubble. Others followed in quick succession. On the 28th, the railroads officially annulled their contracts with the company. About the same time the Pennsylvania Legislature repealed the charter. On March 30, the committee of oil men sent to Washington to be present during the Congressional investigation, now about to begin, spent an hour with President Grant. They wired home that on their departure he said: "Gentlemen, I have noticed the progress of monopolies, and have long been convinced that the National Government would have to interfere and protect the people against them." The President and the members of Congress of both parties continued to show the greatest interest in the investigation, and there was little or no dissent from the final judgment of the committee, given early in May, that the South Improvement Company was the "most gigantic and daring conspiracy" a free country had ever seen. This decision finished the work. The "monster" was slain, the Oil Regions proclaimed exultantly.

And now came the question: what should they do about the blockade established against the members of the South Improvement Company? The railroads they had forgiven; should they forgive the members of the South Improvement Company? This question came up immediately on the repeal of the charter. The first severe test to which their temper was put was early in April, when a firm of Oil City brokers sold some 20,000 barrels of oil to the Standard Oil Company. The moment the sale was noised a perfect uproar burst forth. Indignant telegrams came from every direction condemning the brokers. "Betrayal," "infamy," "mercenary achievement," "the most unkindest cut of all," was the gist of them. From New York, Porter and Archbold telegraphed annulling all their contracts with the guilty brokers. The Oil Exchange passed votes of censure, and the Producers' Union turned them out. A few days later it was learned that a dealer on the Creek was preparing to ship 5,000 barrels to the same firm. A mob gathered about the cars and refused to let them leave. It was only by stationing a strong guard that the destruction of the oil was prevented.

But something had to be done. The cooler heads argued that the blockade, which had lasted now forty days, and from which the region had, of course, suffered enormous loss, should be entirely lifted. The objects for which it had been established had been accomplished—that is, the South Improvement Company had been destroyed; now let free trade be established. If anybody wanted to sell to "conspirators," it was his lookout. A long and excited meeting of men from the entire oil country was held at Oil City to discuss the question. At this meeting telegrams to the president of the Petroleum Producers' Union, Captain William Hasson, from officials of the railroads were read, declaring that the contracts with the South Improvement Company were canceled. Also the following from the Standard Oil Company was read:

CLEVELAND, OHIO, April 8, 1872

To Captain William Hasson: In answer to your telegram, this company holds no contract with the railroad companies or any of them, or with the South Improvement Company. The contracts between the South Improvement Company and the railroads have been canceled, and I am informed you have been so advised by telegram. I state unqualifiedly that reports circulated in the Oil Region and elsewhere, that this company, or any member of it, threatened to depress oil, are false.

JOHN D. ROCKEFELLER, *President*

It was finally decided that "inasmuch as the South Improvement Company contracts were annulled, and the Pennsylvania Legislature had taken pains to safeguard the interests of the trade, and Congress was moving on the same line, after the 15th trade should be free to all." This resolution put an official end to the "oil war."

But no number of resolutions could wipe out the memory of the forty days of terrible excitement and loss which the region had suffered. No triumph could stifle the suspicion and the bitterness which had been sown broadcast through the region. Every particle of independent action had been outraged. Their sense of fair play, the saving force of the region in the days before law and order had been established, had been violated. These were things which could not be forgotten. There henceforth could be no trust in those who had devised a scheme which, the producers believed, was intended to rob them of their business.

It was inevitable that under the pressure of their indignation and resentment some person or persons should be fixed upon as responsible, and should be hated accordingly. Before the lifting of the embargo this responsibility had been fixed. It was the Standard Oil Company of Cleveland, so the Oil Regions decided, which was at the bottom of the business, and the "Mephistopheles of the Cleveland Company," as they put it, was John D. Rockefeller. Even the Cleveland *Herald* acknowledged this popular judgment. "Whether justly or unjustly," the editor wrote, "Cleveland has the odium of having originated the scheme." This opinion gained ground as the days passed. The activity of the president of the Standard in New York, in trying to save the contracts with the railroads, and his constant appearance with Mr. Watson, and the fact brought out by the Congressional investigation that a larger block of the South Improvement Company's stock was owned in the Standard than in any other firm, strengthened the belief. But what did more than anything else to fix the conviction was what they had learned of the career of the Standard Oil Company in Cleveland. Before the oil war the company had been known simply as one of several successful firms in that city. It drove close bargains, but it paid promptly, and was considered a desirable customer. Now the Oil Regions learned for the first time of the sudden and phenomenal expansion of the company. Where there had been at the beginning of 1872 twenty-six refining firms in Cleveland, there were but six left. In three months before and during the oil war the Standard had absorbed twenty plants. It was generally charged by the Cleveland refiners that Mr. Rockefeller had used the South Improvement scheme to persuade or compel his rivals to sell to him. "Why," cried the oil men, "the Standard Oil Company has done already in Cleveland what the South Improvement Company set out to do for the whole country, and it has done it by the same means."

By the time the blockade was raised, another unhappy conviction was fixed on the Oil Regions—the Standard Oil Company meant to carry out the plans of the exploded South Improvement Company. The promoters of the scheme were partly responsible for the report. Under the smart of their defeat they talked rather more freely than their policy of silence justified, and their remarks were quoted widely. Mr. Rockefeller was reported in the *Derrick* to have said to a prominent oil man of Oil City that the South Improvement Company could work under the charter of the Standard Oil Company, and to have predicted that in less than two months the gentleman would be glad to join him. The newspapers made much of the following similar story reported by a New York correspondent:

A prominent Cleveland member of what was the South Improvement Company had said within two days: "The business *now* will be done by the Standard Oil Company. We have a rate of freight by water from Cleveland to New York at seventy cents. No man in the trade shall make a dollar this year. We propose so manipulating the market as to run the price of crude on the Creek as low as two and a half. We mean to show the world that the South Improvement Company was organized for business and means business in spite of opposition." The same thing has been said in substance by the leading Philadelphia member.

"The trade here regards the Standard Oil Company as simply taking the place of the South Improvement Company as being ready at any moment to make the attempt to control the trade as its progenitors did," said the New York *Bulletin* about the middle of April. And the Cleveland *Herald* discussed the situation under the heading, "South Improvement Company *alias* Standard Oil Company." The effect of these reports in the Oil Regions was most disastrous. Their open war became a kind of guerrilla opposition. Those who sold oil to the Standard were ostracized, and its president was openly scorned.

If Mr. Rockefeller had been an ordinary man, the outburst of popular contempt and suspicion which suddenly poured on his head would have thwarted and crushed him. But he was no ordinary man. He had the powerful imagination to see what might be done with the oil business if it could be centered in his hands—the intelligence to analyze the problem into its elements and to find the key to control. He had the essential element to all great achievement, a steadfastness to a purpose which once conceived nothing can crush. The Oil Regions might rage, call him a conspirator and those who sold him oil traitors; the railroads might withdraw their contracts and the legislature annul his charter; undisturbed and unresting he kept at his great purpose. Even if his nature had not been such as to forbid him to abandon an enterprise in which he saw promise of vast profits, even if he had not had a mind which, stopped by a wall, burrows under or creeps around, he would nevertheless have been forced to desperate efforts to save his business. He had increased his refining capacity in Cleveland to 10,000 barrels on the strength of the South Improvement Company contracts. These contracts were annulled, and in their place was one signed by officials of all the oil-shipping roads refusing rebates to everybody. His geographical position was such that it cost him under these new contracts fifty cents more to get oil from the wells to New York than it did his rivals on the Creek. What could he do?

He got a rebate. In spite of the binding nature of the contracts signed in New York on March 25 by representatives of all the railroads, before the middle of April the Standard Oil Company was shipping oil eastward from Cleveland for $1.25–this by the sworn testimony of Mr. H. M. Flagler before a commission of the Ohio State Legislature, in March 1879. How much less a rate than $1.25 Mr. Rockefeller had before the end of April the writer does not know. Of course the rate was secret, and he probably understood now, as he had not two months before, how essential it was that he keep it secret. His task was more difficult now, for he had an enemy active, clamorous, contemptuous, whose suspicions had reached that acute point where they could believe nothing but evil of him—the producers and independents of the Oil Regions. It was utterly impossible that he should ever silence this enemy, for their points of view were diametrically opposed.

They believed in independent effort—every man for himself and fair play for all. They wanted competition, loved open fight. They considered that all business should be done openly—that the railways were bound as public carriers to give equal rates—that any combination which favored one firm or one locality at the expense of another was unjust and illegal.

Mr. Rockefeller's point of view was different. He believed that the "good of all" was in a combination which would control the business as the South Improvement Company proposed to control it. Such a combination would end at once all the abuses the business suffered. As rebates and special rates were essential to this control, he favored them. Of course Mr. Rockefeller knew that the railroad was a public carrier, and that its charter forbade discrimination. But he knew that the railroads did not pretend to obey the laws governing them, that they regularly granted special rates and rebates to those who had large amounts of freight. That is, you could bargain with the railroads as you could with a man carrying on a strictly private business depending in no way on a public franchise. Moreover, Mr. Rockefeller knew that if he did not get rebates, somebody else would; that they were for the wariest, the shrewdest, the most persistent. If somebody was to get rebates, why not he? This point of view was no uncommon one. Many men held it and felt a sort of scorn, as practical men always do for theorists, when it was contended that the shipper was as wrong in taking rates as the railroads in granting them.

Thus, on one hand there was an exaggerated sense of personal independence, on the other a firm belief in combination; on one hand a determination to root out the vicious system of rebates practiced by the railway, on the other a determination to keep it alive and profit by it. Those theories which the body of oil men held as vital and fundamental Mr. Rockefeller and his associates either did not comprehend or were deaf to. This lack of comprehension by many men of what seems to other men to be the most obvious principles of justice is not rare. Many men who are widely known as good, share it. Mr. Rockefeller was "good." There was no more faithful Baptist in Cleveland than he. Every enterprise of that church he had supported liberally from his youth. He gave to its poor. He visited its sick. He wept with its suffering. Moreover, he gave unostentatiously to many outside charities of whose worthiness he was satisfied. He was simple and frugal in his habits. He never went to the theater, never drank wine. He was a devoted husband, and he gave much time to the training of his children, seeking to develop in them his own habits of economy and of charity. Yet he was willing to strain every nerve to obtain for himself special and illegal privileges from the railroads which were bound to ruin every man in the oil business not sharing them with him. Religious emotion and sentiments of charity, propriety and self-denial seem to have taken the place in him of notions of justice and regard for the rights of others.

Unhampered, then, by any ethical consideration, undismayed by the clamor of the Oil Regions, believing firmly as ever that relief for the disorders in the oil business lay in combining and controlling the entire refining interest, this man of vast patience and foresight took up his work. The day after the newspapers of the Oil Regions printed the report of the Congressional Committee on Commerce denouncing the South Improvement Company as "one of the most gigantic and dangerous conspiracies ever attempted," and declaring that if it had not been checked in time it "would have resulted in the absorption and arbitrary control of trade in all the great interests of the country," Mr. Rockefeller and several other members of the South Improvement Company appeared in the Oil Regions. They had come, they explained, to present a new plan of cooperation, and to show the oil men that it was to their interest to go into it. Whether they would be able to obtain by persuasion what they had failed to obtain by assault was now an interesting uncertainty.

Mary Church Terrell
(1863–1954)

Mary Church Terrell was born on September 23, 1863 in Memphis, Tennessee. The oldest of two children, she spent her early years in a comfortable black neighborhood on the outskirts of Memphis. After her parent's divorce in the late 1860's, Mary boarded with a black family in Yellow Springs, Ohio, where she attended the model school on the Antioch College campus for two years and public school for two years. In 1875 she moved to Oberlin, Ohio, where she graduated from both high school (1879) and Oberlin College (1884). After college, Mary taught at Wilberforce University in Xenia, Ohio until 1887 when she moved to Washington, D.C. to teach Latin at the M Street High School. A year later she accepted an offer from her wealthy father to travel and study in Europe. For over two years she toured western Europe, perfecting her skill in various languages and enjoying the diverse cultural opportunities of all the major capitals. In 1890, Mary returned to her teaching post in Washington for the sole purpose of "promoting the welfare of her race." However, a year later she married Robert Terrell, who had been her supervisor at the school, and for the next several years she suffered through the tragic loss of three children, all who died shortly after birth. But in 1895, Mary resumed her noble cause and would tirelessly dedicate herself to it for the remainder of her life. For eleven years (1895-1901, 1906-11) she served on the District of Columbia Board of Education, the first black woman to receive such an appointment. In 1896 she became president of the newly organized National Association of Colored Women, and served for three terms before being voted honorary president for life. As an ardent feminist, she addressed the National American Woman Suffrage Association, travelled as a delegate to the International Council of Women, and served on the executive committee of the Women's International League for Peace and Freedom. As a lecturer she toured the country campaigning against lynching, disfranchisement and discrimination and highlighting black achievements. Between lectures she wrote on black history and life for numerous newspapers and liberal magazines, and in 1940 published her autobiography, *A Colored Woman in a White World*. In the last years of her life she fought vigorously against the segregated restaurants in Washington, urged clemency for Ethel Rosenberg, and pleaded for the life of Rosa Lee Ingram, a Georgia sharecropper who had killed a white man. It was while planning a second trip on behalf of Ingram that Mary Church Terrell died of cancer on July 24, 1954 at the age of 90.

The following speech was delivered before the Washington, D.C. United Women's Club on October 10, 1906. It later appeared in printed form in *The Independent* (January 24, 1907), pp. 181-186.

"What It Means to Be Colored in the Capital of the United States"

Washington, D.C., has been called "The Colored Man's Paradise." Whether this sobriquet was given to the national capital in bitter irony by a member of the handicapped race, as he reviewed some of his own persecutions and rebuffs, or whether it was given immediately after the war by an ex-slave-holder who for the first time in his life saw colored people walking about like freemen, minus the overseer and his whip, history saith not. It is certain that it would be difficult to find a worse misnomer for Washington than "The Colored Man's Paradise" if so prosaic a consideration as veracity is to determine the appropriateness of a name.

For fifteen years I have resided in Washington, and while it was far from being a paradise for colored people, when I first touched these shores it has been doing its level best ever since to make conditions for us intolerable. As a colored woman I might enter Washington any night, a stranger in a strange land, and walk miles without finding a place to lay my head. Unless I happened to know colored people who live here or ran across a chance acquaintance who could recommend a colored boarding-house to me, I should be obliged to spend the entire night wandering about. Indians, Chinamen, Filipinos, Japanese and representatives of any other dark race can find hotel accommodations, if they can pay for them. The colored man alone is thrust out of the hotels of the national capital like a leper.

As a colored woman I may walk from the Capitol to the White House, ravenously hungry and abundantly supplied with money with which to purchase a meal, without finding a single restaurant in which I would be permitted to take a morsel of food, if it was patronized by white people, unless I were willing to sit behind a screen. As a colored woman I cannot visit the tomb of the Father of this country, which owes its very existence to the love of freedom in the human heart and which stands for equal opportunity to all, without being forced to sit in the Jim Crow section of an electric car which starts from the very heart of the city—midway between the Capitol and the White House. If I refuse thus to be humiliated, I am cast into jail and forced to pay a fine for violating the Virginia laws. Every hour in the day Jim Crow cars filled with colored people, many of whom are intelligent and well to do, enter and leave the national capital.

As a colored woman I may enter more than one white church in Washington without receiving that welcome which as a human being I have a right to expect in the sanctuary of God. Sometimes the color blindness of the usher takes on that peculiar form which prevents a dark face from making any impression whatsoever upon his retina, so that it is impossible for him to see colored people at all. If he is not so afflicted, after keeping a colored man or woman waiting a long time, he will ungraciously show these dusky Christians who have had the temerity to thrust themselves into a temple where only the fair of face are expected to worship God to a seat in the rear, which is named in honor of a certain personage, well known in this country, and commonly called Jim Crow.

Unless I am willing to engage in a few menial occupations, in which the pay for my services would be very poor, there is no way for me to earn an honest living, if I am not a trained nurse or a dressmaker or can secure a position as teacher in the public schools, which is exceedingly difficult to do. It matters not what my intellectual attainments may be or how great is the need of the services of a competent person, if I try to enter many of the numerous vocations in which my white sisters are allowed to engage, the door is shut in my face.

From one Washington theater I am excluded altogether. In the remainder certain seats are set aside for colored people, and it is almost impossible to secure others. I once telephoned to the ticket seller just before a matinee and asked if a neat-appearing colored nurse would be allowed to sit in the parquet with her little white charge, and the answer rushed quickly and positively thru the receiver—NO. When I remonstrated a bit and told him that in some of the theaters colored nurses were allowed to sit with the white children for whom they cared, the ticket seller told me that in Washington it was very poor policy to employ colored nurses, for they were excluded from many places where white girls would be allowed to take children for pleasure.

If I possess artistic talent, there is not a single art school of repute which will admit me. A few years ago a colored woman who possessed great talent submitted some drawings to the Cor-

coran Art School, of Washington, which were accepted by the committee of awards, who sent her a ticket entitling her to a course in this school. But when the committee discovered that the young woman was colored they declined to admit her, and told her that if they had suspected that her drawings had been made by a colored woman they would not have examined them at all. The efforts of Frederick Douglass and a lawyer of great repute who took a keen interest in the affair were unavailing. In order to cultivate her talent this young woman was forced to leave her comfortable home in Washington and incur the expense of going to New York. Having entered the Woman's Art School of Cooper Union, she graduated with honor, and then went to Paris to continue her studies, where she achieved signal success and was complimented by some of the greatest living artists in France.

With the exception of the Catholic Unversity, there is not a single white college in the national capital to which colored people are admitted, no matter how great their ability, how lofty their ambition, how unexceptionable their character or how great their thirst for knowledge may be.

A few years ago the Columbian Law School admitted colored students, but in deference to the Southern white students the authorities have decided to exclude them altogether.

Some time ago a young woman who had already attracted some attention in the literary world by her volume of short stories answered an advertisement which appeared in a Washington newspaper, which called for the services of a skilled stenographer and expert typewriter. It is unnecessary to state the reasons why a young woman whose literary ability was so great as that possessed by the one referred to should decide to earn money in this way. The applicants were requested to send specimens of their work and answer certain questions concerning their experience and their speed before they called in person. In reply to her application the young colored woman, who, by the way, is very fair and attractive indeed, received a letter from the firm stating that her references and experience were the most satisfactory that had been sent and requesting her to call. When she presented herself there was some doubt in the mind of the man to whom she was directed concerning her racial pedigree, so he asked her point-blank whether she was colored or white. When she confessed the truth the merchant expressed great sorrow and deep regret that he could not avail himself of the services of so competent a person, but frankly admitted that employing a colored woman in his establishment in any except a menial position was simply out of the question.

Another young friend had an experience which, for some reasons, was still more disheartening and bitter than the one just mentioned. In order to secure lucrative employment she left Washington and went to New York. There she worked her way up in one of the largest dry goods stores till she was placed as saleswoman in the cloak department. Tired of being separated from her family she decided to return to Washington, feeling sure that, with her experience and her fine recommendation from the New York firm, she could easily secure employment. Nor was she overconfident, for the proprietor of one of the largest dry goods stores in her native city was glad to secure the services of a young woman who brought such hearty credentials from New York. She had not been in this store very long, however, before she called upon me one day and asked me to intercede with the proprietor in her behalf, saying that she had been discharged that afternoon because it had been discovered that she was colored. When I called upon my young friend's employer he made no effort to avoid the issue, as I feared he would. He did not say he had discharged the young saleswoman because she had not given satisfaction, as he might easily have done. On the contrary, he admitted without the slightest hesitation that the young woman he had just discharged was one of the best clerks he had ever had. In the cloak department, where she had been assigned, she had been a brilliant success, he said. "But I cannot keep Miss Smith in my employ," he concluded. "Are you not master of your own store?" I ventured to inquire. The proprietor of this store was a Jew, and I felt that it was particularly cruel, unnatural and cold-blooded for the representative of one oppressed and persecuted race to deal so harshly and unjustly with a member of another. I had intended to make this point when I decided to intercede for my young friend, but when I thought how a reference to the persecution of his own race would wound his feelings, the words froze on my lips. "When I first heard your friend was colored," he explained, "I did not believe it and said so to the clerks who made the statement. Finally, the girls who had been most pronounced in their opposition to working in a store with a colored girl came to me in a body and threatened to strike. 'Strike away,' said I, 'your places will be easily filled.' Then they started on another tack. Delegation after delegation began to file down to my office, some of the women my very best customers, to protest against my employing a colored girl. Moreover, they threatened to boycott my store if I did not discharge her at once. Then it became a question of bread and butter and I yielded to the inevitable—that's all. Now," said he, concluding, "if I lived in a great, cosmopolitan city like New York, I should do as I pleased, and refuse to discharge a girl simply because she was colored." But I thought of a similar incident that happened in New York. I remembered that a colored woman, as fair as a lily and as beautiful as a Madonna, who was the head saleswoman in a large department store in New York, had been discharged, after she had held this position for years, when the proprietor accidentally discovered that a fatal drop of African blood was percolating somewhere thru her veins.

Not only can colored women secure no employment in the Washington stores, department and otherwise, except as menials, and such positions, of course, are few, but even as customers they are not infrequently treated with discourtesy both by the clerks and the proprietor himself. Following the trend of the times, the senior partner of the largest and best department store in Washington, who originally hailed from Boston, once the home of Wm. Lloyd Garrison, Wendell Phillips and Charles Sumner, if my memory serves me right, decided to open a restaurant in his store. Tired and hungry after her morning's shopping a colored school teacher, whose relation to her African progenitors is so remote as scarcely to be discernible to the naked eye, took a seat at one of the tables in the restaurant of this Boston store. After sitting unnoticed a long time the colored teacher asked a waiter who passed her by if she would not take her order. She was quickly informed that colored people could not be served in that restaurant and was obliged to leave in confusion and shame, much to the amusement of the waiters and the guests who had noticed the incident. Shortly after that a teacher in Howard University, one of the best schools for colored youth in the country, was similarly insulted in the restaurant of the same store.

In one of the Washington theaters from which colored people are excluded altogether, members of the race have been viciously assaulted several times, for the proprietor well knows that colored people have no redress for such discriminations against them in the District courts. Not long ago a colored clerk in one of the departments who looks more like his paternal ancestors who fought for the lost cause than his grandmothers who were victims of the peculiar institution, bought a ticket for the parquet of this theater in which colored people are nowhere welcome, for himself and mother, whose complexion is a bit swarthy. The usher refused to allow the young man to take the seats for which his tickets called and tried to snatch from him the coupons. A scuffle ensued and both mother and son were ejected by force. A suit was brought against the proprietor and the damages awarded the injured man and his mother amounted to the munificent sum of one cent. One of the teachers in the Colored High School received similar treatment in the same theater.

Not long ago one of my little daughter's bosom friends figured in one of the most pathetic instances of which I have ever heard. A gentleman who is very fond of children promised to take six little girls in his neighborhood to a matinee. It happened that he himself and five of his little friends were so fair that they easily passed muster, as they stood in judgment before the ticket-seller and the ticket taker. Three of the little girls were sisters, two of whom were very fair and the other a bit brown. Just as this little girl, who happened to be last in the procession, went by the ticket taker, that argus-eyed sophisticated gentleman detected something which caused a deep, dark frown to mantle his brow and he did not allow her to pass. "I guess you have made a mistake," he called to the host of this theater party. "Those little girls," pointing to the fair ones, "may be admitted, but this one," designating the brown one, "can't." But the colored man was quite equal to the emergency. Fairly frothing at the mouth with anger he asked the ticket taker what he meant, what he was trying to insinuate about that particular little girl. "Do you mean to tell me," he shouted in rage, "that I must go clear to the Philippine Islands to bring this child to the United States and then I can't take her to the theater in the National Capital?" The little ruse succeeded brilliantly, as he knew it would. "Beg your pardon," said the ticket taker, "don't know what I was thinking about. Of course she can go in."

"What was the matter with me this afternoon? mother," asked the little brown girl innocently, when she mentioned the affair at home. "Why did the man at the theater let my two sisters and the other girls in and try to keep me out?" In relating this incident, the child's mother told me her little girl's question which showed such blissful ignorance of the depressing, cruel conditions which confronted her, completely unnerved her for a time.

Altho white and colored teachers are under the same Board of Education and the system for the children of both races is said to be uniform, prejudice against the colored teachers in the public schools is manifested in a variety of ways. From 1870 to 1900 there was a colored superintendent at the head of the colored schools. During all that time the directors of the cooking, sewing, physical culture, manual training, music and art departments were colored people. Six years ago a change was inaugurated. The colored superintendent was legislated out of office and the directorships, without a single exception, were taken from colored teachers and given to the whites. There was no complaint about the work done by the colored directors no more than is heard about every officer in every school. The directors of the art and physical culture departments were particularly fine. Now, no matter how competent or superior the colored teachers in our public schools may be, they know that they can never rise to the height of a directorship, can never hope to be more than an assistant and receive the meager salary therefore, unless the present regime is radically changed.

Not long ago one of the most distinguished kindergartners in the country came to deliver a course of lectures in Washington. The colored teachers were eager to attend, but they could not buy the coveted privilege for love or money. When they appealed to the director of kindergartens, they were told that the expert kindergartners had come to Washington under the auspices of private individuals, so that she could not possibly have them admitted. Realizing what a loss colored teachers had sustained in being deprived of the information and inspiration which these lectures afforded, one of the white teachers volunteered to repeat them as best she could for the benefit of her colored co-laborers for half the price she herself had paid, and the proposition was eagerly accepted by some.

Strenuous efforts are being made to run Jim Crow street cars in the national capital. "Resolved, that a Jim Crow law should be adopted and enforced in the District of Columbia," was the subject of a discussion engaged in last January by the Columbian Debating Society of the George Washington University in our national capital, and the decision was rendered in favor of the affirmative. Representative Heflin, of Alabama, who introduced a bill providing for Jim Crow street cars in the District of Columbia last winter, has just received a letter from the president of the East Brookland Citizens' Association "indorsing the movement for separate street cars and sincerely hoping that you will be successful in getting this enacted into a law as soon as possible." Brookland is a suburb of Washington.

The colored laborer's path to a decent livelihood is by no means smooth. Into some of the trades unions here he is admitted, while from others he is excluded altogether. By the union men this is denied, altho I am personally acquainted with skilled workmen who tell me they are not admitted into the unions because they are colored. But even when they are allowed to join the unions they frequently derive little benefit, owing to certain tricks of the trade. When the word passes round that help is needed and colored laborers apply, they are often told by the union officials that they have secured all the men they needed, because the places are reserved for white men, until they have been provided with jobs, and colored men must remain idle, unless the supply of white men is too small.

I am personally acquainted with one of the most skillful laborers in the hardware business in Washington. For thirty years he has been working for the same firm. He told me he could not join the union, and that his employer had been almost forced to discharge him, because the union men threatened to boycott his store if he did not. If another man could have been found at the time to take his place he would have lost his job, he said. When no other human being can bring a refractory chimney or stove to its senses, this colored man is called upon as the court of last appeal. If he fails to subdue it, it is pronounced a hopeless case at once. And yet this expert workman receives much less for his services than do white men who cannot compare with him in skill.

And so I might go on citing instance after instance to show the variety of ways in which our people are sacrificed on the altar of prejudice in the Capital of the United States and how almost insurmountable are the obstacles which block his path to success. Early in life many a colored youth is so appalled by the helplessness and the hopelessness of his situation in this country that in a sort of stoical despair he resigns himself to his fate. "What is the good of our trying to acquire an education? We can't all be preachers, teachers, doctors and lawyers. Besides those professions there is almost nothing for colored people to do but engage in the most menial occupations, and we do not need an education for that." More than once such remarks, uttered by young men and women in our public schools who possess brilliant intellects, have wrung my heart. It is impossible for any white person in the United States, no matter how sympathetic and broad, to realize what life would mean to him if his incentive to effort were suddenly snatched away. To the lack of incentive to effort, which is the awful shadow under which we live, may be traced the wreck and ruin of scores of colored youth. And surely nowhere in the world do oppression and persecution based solely on the color of the skin appear more hateful and hideous than in the capital of the United States, because the chasm between the principles upon which this Government was founded, in which it still professes to believe, and those which are daily practiced under the protection of the flag, yawns so wide and deep.

Sojourner Truth
(c. 1797–1883)

Sojourner Truth was born around 1797 in Hurley, Ulster County, New York. The next to the youngest of several children born to slave parents, she passed through the hands of several owners from the time she was old enough to work. From 1810 to 1827 she worked in a household in New Paltz, New York, where she bore at least five children by a fellow slave named Thomas. In 1827 she fled from the New Paltz household and found refuge with a nearby religious group which helped her locate and free two of her children sold into slavery. In 1829 Sojourner and her two children moved to New York City where she secured employment as a domestic and became active in various churches and religious movements. One particular religious cause which attracted her interest was the Retrenchment Society, a cult which supported a church and asylum for New York prostitutes. Joining this cause around 1830, she preached in the church and helped run the asylum until 1833. After a scandal which unjustly implicated her in the mysterious death of a leader in a similar religious cult, Sojourner spent the next ten years maintaining a quiet home and earning her living as a cook, maid and laundress. In 1843, when "the voices" commanded her to take the name of "Sojourner Truth," she started out on a long preaching tour. Until 1850 Sojourner travelled around the New England area preaching about love and the evils of slavery, sleeping where she could and working whenever she needed food. In 1850 she headed west where she drew great crowds in Ohio, Indiana, Missouri, and Kansas and maintained herself financially by selling the *Narrative of Sojourner Truth* (1850), written for her by Olive Gilbert. In the late 1850's Sojourner settled in Battle Creek, Michigan, and tramped throughout the state soliciting gifts of food and clothing for Negro volunteer regiments preparing for the Civil War. In 1864 she travelled to Washington, D.C., to receive recognition for her efforts from President Lincoln. After the Civil War Sojourner campaigned for several years for a "Negro State" in the West, her unplanned speaking tours taking her all over the East and midwest. Interwoven in her central message were appeals for black rights, woman suffrage and temperance. In 1875 Sojourner returned to Michigan where she received hundreds of admiring visitors until her death on November 26, 1883.

The first speech was recorded at the State Woman's Rights Convention in Akron, Ohio on May 28, 1851. It appeared in printed form in *The History of Woman Suffrage,* Vol. I (Rochester, N.Y., 1881) pp. 116-17. The second speech was recorded at the National Convention of the American Equal Rights Association at the Church of Puritans in New York City on May 9, 1867. It later appeared in *The History of Woman Suffrage,* Vol. II (Rochester, N.Y., 1881) pp. 193-94. The contrast in language style is no doubt due to the peculiarities of each recorder.

"Ain't I a Woman?"

(The tumult subsided at once, and every eye was fixed on this almost Amazon form, which stood nearly six feet high, head erect, and eyes piercing the upper air like one in a dream. At her first word there was a profound hush. She spoke in deep tones, which, though not loud, reached every ear in the house, and away through the throng at the doors and windows.)

"Wall, chilern, whar dar is so much racket dar must be somethin' out o' kilter. I tink dat 'twixt de niggers of de Souf and de womin at de Norf, all talkin' 'bout rights, de white men will be in a fix pretty soon. But what's all dis here talkin' 'bout?

"Dat man ober dar say dat womin needs to be helped into carriages, and lifted ober ditches, and to hab de best place everywhar. Nobody eber helps me into carriages, or ober mud-puddles, or gibs me any best place!" (And raising herself to her full height, and her voice to a pitch like rolling thunder, she asked) "And a'n't I a woman? Look at me! Look at my arm! (and she bared her right arm to the shoulder, showing her tremendous muscular power). I have ploughed, and planted, and gathered into barns, and no man could head me! And a'n't I a woman? I could work as much and eat as much as a man—when I could get it—and bear de lash as well! And a'n't I a woman? I have borne thirteen chilern, and seen 'em mos' all sold off to slavery, and when I cried out with my mother's grief, none but Jesus heard me! And a'n't I a woman?

"Den dey talks 'bout dis ting in de head; what dis dey call it?" ("Intellect," whispered some one near.) "Dat's it, honey. What's dat got to do wid womin's rights or nigger's rights? If my cup won't hold but a pint, and yourn holds a quart, wouldn't ye be mean not to let me have my little half-measure full?" (And she pointed her significant finger, and sent a keen glance at the minister who had made the argument. The cheering was long and loud.)

"Den dat little man in black dar, he say women can't have as much rights as men, 'cause Christ wasn't a woman! Whar did your Christ come from?" (Rolling thunder couldn't have stilled that crowd, as did those deep, wonderful tones, as she stood there with outstretched arms and eyes of fire. Raising her voice still louder, she repeated), "Whar did your Christ come from? From God and a woman! Man had nothin' to do wid Him." (Oh, what a rebuke that was to that little man.)

(Turning again to another objector, she took up the defense of Mother Eve. I can not follow her through it all. It was pointed, and witty, and solemn; eliciting at almost every sentence deafening applause; and she ended by asserting:) "If de fust woman God ever made was strong enough to turn de world upside down all alone, dese women togedder (and she glanced her eye over the platform) ought to be able to turn it back, and get it right side up again! And now dey is asking to do it, de men better let 'em." (Long-continued cheering greeted this.) " 'Bleeged to ye for hearin' on me, and now ole Sojourner han't got nothin' more to say."

(Amid roars of applause, she returned to her corner, leaving more than one of us with streaming eyes, and hearts beating with gratitude. She had taken us up in her strong arms and carried us safely over the slough of difficulty turning the whole tide in our favor. I have never in my life seen anything like the magical influence that subdued the mobbish spirit of the day, and turned the sneers and jeers of an excited crowd into notes of respect and admiration. Hundreds rushed up to shake hands with her, and congratulate the glorious old mother, and bid her God-speed on her mission of "testifyin' agin concerning the wickedness of this 'ere people.")

"Equal Rights for All"

My friends, I am rejoiced that you are glad, but I don't know how you will feel when I get through. I come from another field—the country of the slave. They have got their liberty—so much good luck to have slavery partly destroyed; not entirely. I want it root and branch destroyed. Then we will all be free indeed. I feel that if I have to answer for the deeds done in my body just as much as a man, I have a right to have just as much as a man. There is a great stir about colored men getting their rights, but not a word about the colored women; and if colored men get their rights, and not colored women theirs, you see the colored men will be masters over the women, and it will be just as bad as it was before. So I am for keeping the thing going while things are stirring; because if we wait till it is still, it will take a great while to get it going again. White women are a great deal smarter, and know more than colored women, while colored women do not know scarcely anything. They go out washing, which is about as high as a colored woman gets, and their men go about idle, strutting up and down; and when the women come home, they ask for their money and take it all, and then scold because there is no food. I want you to consider on that, chil'n. I call you chil'n; you are somebody's chil'n, and I am old enough to be mother of all that is here. I want women to have their rights. In the courts women have no right, no voice; nobody speaks for them. I wish woman to have her voice there among the pettifoggers. If it is not a fit place for women, it is unfit for men to be there.

I am above eighty years old; it is about time for me to be going. I have been forty years a slave and forty years free, and would be here forty years more to have equal rights for all. I suppose I am kept here because something remains for me to do; I suppose I am yet to help to break the chain. I have done a great deal of work; as much as a man, but did not get so much pay. I used to work in the field and bind grain, keeping up with the cradler; but men doing no more, got twice as much pay; so with the German women. They work in the field and do as much work, but do not get the pay. We do as much, we eat as much, we want as much. I suppose I am about the only colored woman that goes about to speak for the rights of the colored women. I want to keep the thing stirring, now that the ice is cracked. What we want is a little money. You men know that you get as much again as women when you write, or for what you do. When we get our rights we shall not have to come to you for money, for then we shall have money enough in our own pockets; and may be you will ask us for money. But help us now until we get it. It is a good consolation to know that when we have got this battle fought we shall not be coming to you any more. You have been having our rights so long, that you think, like a slave-holder, that you own us. I know that it is hard for one who has held the reins for so long to give up; it cuts like a knife. It will feel all the better when it closes up again. I have been in Washington about three years, seeing about these colored people. Now colored men have the right to vote. There ought to be equal rights now more than ever, since colored people have got their freedom. I am going to talk several times while I am here; so now I will do a little singing. I have not heard any singing since I came here.

(Accordingly, suiting the action to the word, Sojourner sang, "We are going home.") "There, children," said she, "in heaven we shall rest from all our labors; first do all we have to do here. There I am determined to go, not to stop short of that beautiful place, and I do not mean to stop till I get there, and meet you there, too."

Lillian Wald
(1867–1940)

Lillian Wald was born on March 10, 1867 in Cincinnati, Ohio. The third of four children, Lillian grew up in a prosperous family whose financial success took them to Rochester, New York early in her life. After graduating at age 16 from Miss Crittenden's English-French Boarding and Day School in Rochester, she entered the New York Hospital training school for nurses in 1889. After graduation and one unhappy year of nursing, Lillian enrolled in the Woman's Medical College in New York. Early in 1893, while attending medical school, she went out on a nursing call to tend a poor woman in a tenement house and the next day left medical school to devote her lifework as a public health nurse. Believing that public health nurses should live as well as work among the poor, Lillian located a sponsor and in 1895 set up a "Nurses' Settlement" at 265 Henry Street. By 1913 the Henry Street Nursing Settlement had grown from eleven nurses to ninety-two nurses, making approximately 200,000 visits annually to poor tenement homes on the East Side, in upper Manhattan and in the Bronx. During this same time period the settlement expanded its services to include civic, educational, social and philanthropic work, and expanded its cite to include seven houses on Henry Street. Lillian, herself, took a leading role in civic campaigns to eradicate tuberculosis, improve housing, establish more parks and playgrounds and provide scholarships to help boys and girls remain in school until age sixteen. At the turn of the century she and Florence Kelley moved to the forefront of the child welfare movement and in 1904 the two of them founded the National Child Labor Committee. At the outbreak of World War I, Lillian, as president of the American Union Against Militarism, sought by letter and petition to win the Wilson administration to her point of view. When the United States entered the war, she turned her attention to wartime encroachments on civil liberties and served as head of the committee on home nursing of the Council of National Defense. After the war she helped found the League of Free Nations Association and continued her work at Henry Street to expand services. In 1933, shortly after Henry Street's fortieth anniversary, Lillian resigned as head worker and retired to Westport, Connecticut, where she published a sequel to an earlier anecdotal autobiography (*The House on Henry Street* in 1915), which she entitled *Windows on Henry Street* (1934). On September 1, 1940, Lillian died after a long illness brought on by a cerebral hemorrhage.

The following lecture was delivered at the International Congress of Nurses in Buffalo, New York in 1901. It was later printed in *The American Journal of Nursing*, Vol. II, No. 2 (May, 1902), pp. 567–574.

"The Nurses' Settlement in New York"

ABOUT eight years ago tenement-house life in its most pitiable aspect was presented to me. I had been giving a course of lessons in home nursing to a group of proletariats from the older world,—people who find a renewal of hope in New York, if not for themselves, at least for their children. One morning one of the women of the class was not present, and her little daughter came to ask me to call upon her mother, as she was ill. Despite my experience in a large metropolitan hospital, and the subsequent knowledge gained through a year's residence in a reformatory and asylum for the waifs of New York, the exposure of that rear tenement in the lower East Side was a most terrible shock,—a shock that was at first benumbing. A picture was presented of human creatures, moral, and, in so far as their opportunities allowed them, decent members of society, in rooms reached through a court that held open closets to be used by men and women, from some of which the doors had been torn away; up dirty steps into a sick-room where there was no window, the one opening leading into a small, crowded room where husband, children, and boarders were gathered together,—impossible conditions under which to attempt to establish a home and bring up children.

Upon further acquaintance with the house and neighborhood I learned that kindly intention from the outside had not been wholly absent. The visitor from a medical dispensary had called, and, touched by the poverty of the place, had sent a bottle of beef extract with directions for use printed upon it, but there was no one in the house who could read English. Other charitable persons had sent coal; but my nurse's instinct revolted at the knowledge that nobody had washed the woman, made her bed, or performed any of the offices that every human creature should feel entitled to in like condition. I will not take time now to describe all of the circumstances, nor my reflections on the responsibilities of the community, as they appeared to me, to this one family; to me personally it was a call to live near such conditions; to use what power an individual may possess as a citizen to help them, and to give to all of my world, wherever it might be, such information as I could regarding conditions that seemed to be generally unknown.

To a friend the plan was revealed: "Let us two nurses move into that neighborhood; let us give our services as nurses, and let us contribute our sense of citizenship to what seems an alien community in a so-called democratic country." Having formulated some necessary details of the plan, we proceeded to look for suitable quarters, and in the search discovered the "settlement." In the stress of hospital training neither of us had learned that men and women, moved by some personal experience or by theoretical training, had arrived at the same impulse to action and had established themselves in the crowded quarters of cities and called themselves "settlement workers." The idea was identical with our own, and though many activities have grown from that idea, the fundamental principle remains: that people shall take up their residence in industrial communities, giving what they may have of public spirit, and partaking of the life about them; preserving their identity as individuals and endeavoring to keep the settlement free from the institutional form of philanthropic work.

For the first two months of our experiment we two nurses lived at the College Settlement. After that the top floor of a tenement that gave reasonable comfort was our home for two years, and that was practically the beginning of the present association of workers known as the "Nurses' Settlement." The life possible through making our home among the people in a simple, informal way led us easily and naturally into all the questions that affected them.

Through our visits to the children and our interest in their general welfare we learned of the unsatisfactory school conditions, and of the absurdity of a compulsory school law when there was not adequate school accommodation for the children. Such knowledge as came to our notice, such effective protest as would illustrate the conditions of our neighborhood, was brought before a suitable public, individuals, or societies especially concerned whenever occasion could be found or made.

The women on the lower floors in the tenement where we lived were employed in the needle trades, and unbearable treatment at the hands of a foreman had moved them and their fellow-workers to agitate for trade organization. In the search for some one of their own sex who could speak for them in what they called "better English" they came to us, and that was our first introduction to the protest of the workers which is expressed in Trades-Unionism.

A semi-official recognition by the Board of Health gave us the privilege of inspection of the tenements, and valuable information was thus stored up on the housing problem. The experience thus gained had its share of influence in the general education of the public which later led to the Tenement-House Exhibit; to the appointment of a Tenement-House Commission under Governor Roosevelt, and the final creation of a separate department for the city of New York. One of the members of the settlement took active part in the movement, and was one of the two women on the jury of awards for plans for model tenement-houses. Through her efforts to obtain a legacy that had been bequeathed for a fountain somewhere in the city, the Schiff fountain was erected in the neighborhood of the settlement, and was the strong influence in having an adjacent site selected for a park and public playground, to make place for which no more congested and unsightly rookeries could have been demolished.

The movement for public playgrounds is now well known. They have been valiantly fought for and their need wonderfully told by Mr. Jacob A. Riis, that best friend of, and most lovable fighter for, the children of the poor. His efforts have been assisted by the Nurses' Settlement for years.

To meet the rightful demand of the children for play, we conducted in our back yards one of the first playgrounds in the city. It was an experimental station, in a way, as well as an enlightenment of the general public, and was instrumental in helping to develop public feeling in the matter. After a time the interests of the residents of the settlement were directed to the "Out-Door Recreation League," share being taken in its executive work, and coöperation given to Mr. Charles B. Stover, the apostle of New York of out-door play places for the children of crowded districts.

The workers of the settlement can look with gratification upon the increasing interest in public-school matters affecting their neighborhood as in part the result of their efforts to bring public attention to the lack of room for the children in the schools, and in other ways to bring the interests of their localities directly to the School Boards. One of the household was for a time a school inspector, but whether in official relationship or not, the members have been frequently consulted by those in authority on the Board of Education.

I have passed over the steps of growth of the settlement, and to understand how it has attained its present status I should go back to that first beginning in the tenement, when it was apparent that not only were the nurses' services needed for the sick, but that, likewise, their friendly offices were needed as interpreters for bringing to the proper sources the larger and more general matters that affected the life of the people they were in contact with.

Mr. Jacob H. Schiff, who from the very beginning had made us feel his support, encouragement, and confidence, suggested the change from the tenement quarters to a house, arguing that a more permanent basis would be established for these personal services if it were made possible for others to join us. The desire of others to coöperate with us had been for some time apparent, and therefore this most generous and public-spirited citizen's offer was accepted. A house near the tenements, once the property of the fashionable and well-to-do who had inhabited Henry Street half a century earlier, was purchased by him. Necessary changes were made in it, and almost immediately the house was filled with residents and the nursing was extended. The clubs and social features of the house then began to assume organized form.

The next year another house was given for the use of the settlement by a new member, a laywoman, who came into residence, fitted up the second house, and contributed the means to carry it on, and who has taken charge of much of the social work among the young people. Not long after that offers of money and suitable workers came, and fresh opportunities to extend presented themselves.

The needs of an uptown district having been urged, a house was selected there and purchased by Mrs. Butler Duncan for the use of the settlement, and workers were placed in it who had served an apprenticeship in the down-town house. A little later also one floor of a house in still another locality was given by the family of one of the residents, and several nurses are accommodated there. Finally, a dream of the nursing staff was realized in the gift, received from a young married woman, of a charming home in the country, where all the year round, and without restrictions or conditions save those imposed by the circumstances of the patients, the convalescents and tired-out people who need rest are entertained and where, in the summer, many delightful outings for the young people are planned.

From the needs of the neighborhood has sprung the service that we call the "First Aid Room" in three very crowded quarters. In each one a nurse is in attendance at certain hours a day, and cases that require dressings, fresh cuts, old wounds, simple eye cases, eczemas, etc., are treated. These are such nursing cases as might be attended to by the members of the families if the mothers had sufficient leisure or sufficient intelligence. Many of them are sent by the physicians of the large dispensaries, who have not confidence that the parents will apply ointments, dress wounds, or syringe ears daily and in a cleanly way. These are often school-children, and the nurse is thus able to care for a far greater number than would be possible if she went to them.

This work has also a direct bearing on the school attendance of the children, and though many of the cases are not important from a medical point of view, they are of the utmost importance from the educational stand-point, as the children are sent home by the medical school inspectors, and, not being allowed to reënter while the trouble continues, often miss much precious school time, for it must be remembered that few of these children can attend school after fourteen; at that age they all begin wage-earning. As an illustration, I knew of a lad of twelve years who had never been in school because of eczema of the scalp. True, the mother had gone to the dispensaries and obtained ointments, but the overdriven, wornout woman said they did no good. Careful epilation, systematic disinfection, and careful application of the medicament was so successful that when school opened in the fall I had the pleasure of placing the boy there for the first time in his life.

The settlement in coöperation with the New York Kindergarten Association maintains a kindergarten. The children upon graduating from the kindergarten and entering the public schools are invited to come back as members of clubs. They are the youngest club members, and when the first one was called "The Alumnæ Association of the Nurses' Settlement Kindergarten" the name seemed longer than some of the members.

Probably the boys' clubs connected with the settlement hold the most intimate place. The first one organized, of which I have the honor of being a member, undertook the study of the lives of American heroes. We took the term "hero" broadly, and men or women who by fearless living had made the world a better place to live in were counted as such. Thus we had the biographies of those who had contributed as statesmen, soldiers, philanthropists, and writers to the realization of the highest hopes of the country, and living members of the family under discussion often came to contribute personal reminiscences or family history. Since then as this club matured it has taken up the study of civil government and other similar study, and is but a type of what all the clubs are doing. Some of the girls' clubs combine study with the boys and young men, and interesting debates on important topics of the day are held in their meeting-rooms.

In the interests of a considerable number of boys not responsive to the more intellectual stimulus of study, rooms have been set apart for manual work, and with the coöperation of the Children's Aid Society carpentry, wood-carving, and basket work are carried on. The large dancing-school classes, gymnasium work, etc., are possible through the courtesy of this society—it gives us the privilege of using its large and roomy floors after school hours and in the evenings. Our dancing-school has led us to the same conclusion that experience with young people anywhere would bring: that the desire to dance and to meet their kind socially is a wholesome and healthy one, and that it is a dangerous thing not to recognize and meet the want wholesomely, lest innocent desires be diverted wrongly.

The dancing-classes are refined gatherings, properly chaperoned, and with no other restrictions than the ordinary ones of good manners. They are successful rivals to the public dances that are over or back of the saloons, and also provide opportunities for those young people whose careful parents would not allow them to go elsewhere.

We have a penny provident bank, and habits of thrift are inculcated by making it easy to save the pennies. When the deposit reaches the sum of one dollar, an account may be opened in the savings-bank in the locality.

All of such work is not done by the nurses, for besides our valued lay members who share in the social and educational work, a large staff of non-residents take part in the classes and clubs.

The kindergarten teachers are, of course, trained for that purpose. Leaders for clubs and teachers for the various classes are recruited from the outside, and among them are distinguished lecturers who find their students responsive and their audiences sympathetic. Musicales, private theatricals, and the varied undertakings that bring gayety and zest into the social life are successful with us. We are fond of saying that next to nursing typhoid fever we love to give a ball!

Our nusing work is the "raison d'etre" of our existence, from which all our other activities have had their natural and unforced growth, but the papers at this Congress have dwelt upon the detail and method of district nursing, and our methods do not differ sufficiently to warrant my taking up time and space to enlarge upon it. We conceive the underlying thought of the district nurse to be that of neighborliness, and plan to have each nurse work in a small district in close touch with the settlement house that she belongs to, that recourse may be had to it in emergency as quickly as possible.

We hope that the nurse, with her knowledge of hygiene and sanitation and the care of the body in health and illness, will be an educator, and we lay much stress upon this, that she should not have too large a district or too many patients to look after. We believe she should have time to give the bath, and if necessary to make the second and even the third visit in the day, and not be adviser and instructor only, not forgetting her charity organization tenets of the dangers of doing for people what they ought to do for themselves, yet holding to the ideals of the nurse in her work.

With this in mind, though we do not undertake night nursing as a rule, yet we would have a night nurse obtained through a registry if in our opinion this was the only thing to be done for the patient. We also send women to scrub and clean in the homes that the nurses go to, if there is no one who should rightfully perform these services, as we consider it a part of good nursing to have the rooms kept clean.

The various needs of the patient are kept vividly in mind. From what we call the settlement point of view we believe that the patients should know the nurse as a social being rather than as an official visitor, and that all legitimate relationships which may follow from her introduction as a nurse shall be allowed to take place.

It is good from this point of view that the patient should know the home of the nurse, and that the nurse should be intelligent about the housing conditions, the educational provisions, and the social life of the neighborhood in which she works and lives.

From this motive has come the opportunity for the settlement to show where the neighborhood has been neglected, and to bring into communication the different elements of society that go to make up a great city. We think and feel sincerely that the relationship is reciprocal, that we are partaking of the larger life, that society in general has closed the avenues that lead to this knowledge, and that the different elements of society need one another.

The well-meaning employer needs his interpreter, and the people of such neighborhoods as our own should have their point of view considered and given dignified place in the councils of the public-spirited. This is the ideal of democracy, the best "Spirit of the Times," and in its accomplishment we have responsibility and privilege,—our share in speeding the realization of the unity of society, the brotherhood of man.

The numerical record of work done through the settlement for one year was:

NURSING WORK

Three thousand nine hundred and ninety-one calls for nurses to the homes of the sick; twenty-six thousand six hundred nursing visits made; twelve thousand six hundred and ninety-four cases treated in three First Aid Rooms; two hundred and twenty-five convalescents entertained in the Country Home.

SOCIAL WORK

Thirty-five clubs, from kindergarten classes to clubs of married women; dancing school, four classes; singing classes; private theatricals; concerts; gymnasium; fresh air work.

EDUCATIONAL WORK

Kindergarten; reference library; sewing, crotcheting, etc.; basketry; carpentry; carving; housekeeping classes (including cooking, laundry, etc.); home nursing; civics—municipal and national government.

Ida Wells-Barnett
(1862–1931)

Ida Wells-Barnett was born on July 16, 1862 in Holly Springs, Mississippi. The oldest of eight children, she spent her early years as a slave child until the Civil War freed her parents. After completing school at a freedmen's high school and industrial school, Ida, a mere fourteen years of age, convinced a rural school committee that she was eighteen and got a job teaching at the school. In 1884 she moved to Memphis, Tennessee, where she continued to teach while attending summer classes at Fisk University. Encouraged by a local minister, Ida began writing articles under the pen name of "Iola." Because her articles criticized the inadequate schools available to black children, the Memphis school board did not renew her contract in 1891, which prompted her to turn her attention full-time to journalism. By 1892, Ida had become half-owner of the *Memphis Free Speech* and had begun to investigate and report lynchings occurring around Memphis. After a mob had destroyed the paper's offices in late 1892 while she was on a trip to New York, it became impossible for her to return and so she stayed in New York to devote her full time to a one-woman crusade against lynching. For the next several years Ida lectured in cities in the East and founded anti-lynching societies and Negro Woman's Clubs. In 1895 Ida married Ferdinand Lee Barnett, a lawyer and assistant state attorney for the state of Illinois, and moved to Chicago. In the same year she published *A Red Record*, an account of three years' lynchings in the South. Because of the demands of raising four children, Ida traveled less frequently, but she became actively involved with Chicago's black population. Among her many accomplishments, she helped to organize a Negro Woman's Club, took the initiative in founding the Negro Fellowship League, served as secretary of the National Afro-American Council, participated in the creation of the NAACP, founded the first black woman suffrage organization (Alpha Suffrage Club in Chicago), worked with Jane Addams in the successful attempt to block separate schools for black children, and helped to found and direct the Cook County League of Women's Clubs. On March 25, 1931 Ida died of uremia at age sixty-nine.

The following address was delivered at Lyric Hall in New York City on October 5, 1892. It was later printed as a pamphlet, *Southern Horrors: Lynch Law in All Its Phases*, by New York Age Print in November, 1892.

"Southern Horrors: Lynch Law in All Its Phases"

The Offense

Wednesday evening May 24th, 1892, the city of Memphis was filled with excitement. Editorials in the daily papers of that date caused a meeting to be held in the Cotton Exchange Building; a committee was sent for the editors of the "Free Speech" an Afro-American journal published in that city, and the only reason the open threats of lynching that were made were not carried out because they could not be found. The cause of all this commotion was the following editorial published in the "Free Speech" May 21st, 1892, the Saturday previous.

"Eight negroes lynched since last issue of the 'Free Speech' one at Little Rock, Ark., last Saturday morning where the citizens broke (?) into the penitentiary and got their man; three near Anniston, Ala., one near New Orleans; and three at Clarksville, Ga., the last three for killing a white man, and five on the same old racket—the new alarm about raping white women. The same programme of hanging, then shooting bullets into the lifeless bodies was carried out to the letter.

Nobody in this section of the country believes the old thread bare lie that Negro men rape white women. If Southern white men are not careful, they will over-reach themselves and public sentiment will have a reaction; a conclusion will then be reached which will be very damaging to the moral reputation of their women."

"The Daily Commercial" of Wednesday following, May 25th, contained the following leader:

"Those negroes who are attempting to make the lynching of individuals of their race a means for arousing the worst passions of their kind are playing with a dangerous sentiment. The negroes may as well understand that there is no mercy for the negro rapist and little patience with his defenders. A negro organ printed in this city, in a recent issue publishes the following atrocious paragraph: 'Nobody in this section of the country believes the old thread-bare lie that negro men rape white women. If Southern white men are not careful they will over-reach themselves, and public sentiment will have a reaction; and a conclusion will be reached which will be very damaging to the moral reputation of their women.'

The fact that a black scoundrel is allowed to live and utter such loathsome and repulsive calumnies is a volume of evidence as to the wonderful patience of Southern whites. But we have had enough of it.

There are some things that the Southern white man will not tolerate, and the obscene intimations of the foregoing have brought the writer to the very outermost limit of public patience. We hope we have said enough."

The "Evening Scimitar" of same date, copied the "Commercial's" editorial with these words of comment: "Patience under such circumstances is not a virtue. If the negroes themselves do not apply the remedy without delay it will be the duty of those whom he has attacked to tie the wretch who utters these calumnies to a stake at the intersection of Main and Madison Sts., brand him in the forehead with a hot iron and perform upon him a surgical operation with a pair of tailor's shears."

Acting upon this advice, the leading citizens met in the Cotton Exchange Building the same evening, and threats of lynching were freely indulged, not by the lawless element upon which the deviltry of the South is usually saddled—but by the leading business men, in their leading business centre. Mr. Fleming, the business manager and owning a half interest in the Free Speech, had to leave town to escape the mob, and was afterwards ordered not to return; letters and telegrams sent me in New York where I was spending my vacation advised me that bodily harm awaited my return. Creditors took possession of the office and sold the outfit, and the "Free Speech" was as if it had never been.

The editorial in question was prompted by the many inhuman and fiendish lynchings of Afro-Americans which have recently taken place and was meant as a warning. Eight lynched in one week and five of them charged with rape! The thinking public will not easily believe freedom and education more brutalizing than slavery, and the world knows that the crime of rape was unknown during four years of civil war, when the white women of the South were at the mercy of the race which is all at once charged with being a bestial one.

Since my business has been destroyed and I am an exile from home because of that editorial, the issue has been forced, and as the writer of it I feel that the race and the public generally should have a statement of the facts as they exist. They will serve at the same time as a defense for the Afro-Americans Sampsons who suffer themselves to be betrayed by white Delilahs.

The whites of Montgomery, Ala., knew J. C. Duke sounded the keynote of the situation—which they would gladly hide from the world, when he said in his paper, "The Herald," five years ago: "Why is it that white women attract negro men now more than in former days? There was a time when such a thing was unheard of. There is a secret to this thing, and we greatly suspect it is the growing appreciation of white Juliets for colored Romeos." Mr. Duke, like the "Free Speech" proprietors, was forced to leave the city for reflecting on the "honah" of white women and his paper suppressed; but the truth remains that Afro-American men do not always rape (?) white women without their consent.

Mr. Duke, before leaving Montgomery, signed a card disclaiming any intention of slandering Southern white women. The editor of the "Free Speech" has no disclaimer to enter, but asserts instead that there are many white women in the South who would marry colored men if such an act would not place them at once beyond the pale of society and within the clutches of the law. The miscegnation laws of the South only operate against the legitimate union of the races; they leave the white man free to seduce all the colored girls he can, but it is death to the colored man who yields to the force and advances of a similar attraction in white women. White men lynch the offending Afro-American, not because he is a despoiler of virtue, but because he succumbs to the smiles of white women.

The Black and White of It.

The "Cleveland Gazette" of January 16, 1892, publishes a case in point. Mrs. J. S. Underwood, the wife of a minister of Elyria, Ohio, accused an Afro-American of rape. She told her husband that during his absence in 1888, stumping the State for the Prohibition Party, the man came to the kitchen door, forced his way in the house and insulted her. She tried to drive him out with a heavy poker, but he overpowered and chloroformed her, and when she revived her clothing was torn and she was in a horrible condition. She did not know the man but could identify him. She pointed out William Offett, a married man, who was arrested and, being in Ohio, was granted a trial.

The prisoner vehemently denied the charge of rape, but confessed he went to Mrs. Underwood's residence at her invitation and was criminally intimate with her at her request. This availed him nothing against the sworn testimony of a minister's wife, a lady of the highest respectability. He was found guilty, and entered the penitentiary, December 14, 1888, for fifteen years. Some time afterwards the woman's remorse led her to confess to her husband that the man was innocent.

These are her words: "I met Offett at the Post Office. It was raining. He was polite to me, and as I had several bundles in my arms he offered to carry them home for me, which he did. He had a strange fascination for me, and I invited him to call on me. He called, bringing chestnuts and candy for the children. By this means we got them to leave us alone in the room. Then I sat on his lap. He made a proposal to me and I readily consented. Why I did so, I do not know, but that I did is true. He visited me several times after that and each time I was indiscreet. I did not care after the first time. In fact I could not have resisted, and had no desire to resist."

When asked by her husband why she told him she had been outraged, she said: "I had several reasons for telling you. One was the neighbors saw the fellow here, another was, I was afraid I had contracted a loathsome disease, and still another was that I feared I might give birth to a

Negro baby. I hoped to save my reputation by telling you a deliberate lie." Her husband horrified by the confession had Offett, who had already served four years, released and secured a divorce.

There are thousands of such cases throughout the South, with the difference that the Southern white men in insatiate fury wreak their vengeance without intervention of law upon the Afro-Americans who consort with their women. A few instances to substantiate the assertion that some white women love the company of the Afro-American will not be out of place. Most of these cases were reported by the daily papers of the South.

In the winter of 1885–6 the wife of a practicing physician in Memphis, in good social standing whose name has escaped me, left home, husband and children, and ran away with her black coachman. She was with him a month before her husband found and brought her home. The coachman could not be found. The doctor moved his family away from Memphis, and is living in another city under an assumed name.

In the same city last year a white girl in the dusk of evening screamed at the approach of some parties that a Negro had assaulted her on the street. He was captured, tried by a white judge and jury, that acquitted him of the charge. It is needless to add if there had been a scrap of evidence on which to convict him of so grave a charge he would have been convicted.

Sarah Clark of Memphis loved a black man and lived openly with him. When she was indicted last spring for miscegenation, she swore in court that she was *not* a white woman. This she did to escape the penitentiary and continued her illicit relation undisturbed. That she is of the lower class of whites, does not disturb the fact that she is a white woman. "The leading citizens" of Memphis are defending the "honor" of *all* white women, *demi-monde* included.

Since the manager of the "Free Speech" has been run away from Memphis by the guardians of the honor of Southern white women, a young girl living on Poplar St., who was discovered in intimate relations with a handsome mulatto young colored man, Will Morgan by name, stole her father's money to send the young fellow away from that father's wrath. She has since joined him in Chicago.

The Memphis "Ledger" for June 8th has the following: "If Lillie Bailey, a rather pretty white girl seventeen years of age, who is now at the City Hospital, would be somewhat less reserved about her disgrace there would be some very nauseating details in the story of her life. She is the mother of a little coon. The truth might reveal fearful depravity or it might reveal the evidence of a rank outrage. She will not divulge the name of the man who has left such black evidence of her disgrace, and, in fact, says it is a matter in which there can be no interest to the outside world. She came to Memphis nearly three months ago and was taken in at the Woman's Refuge in the southern part of the city. She remained there until a few weeks ago, when the child was born. The ladies in charge of the Refuge were horified. The girl was at once sent to the City Hospital, where she has been since May 30th. She is a country girl. She came to Memphis from her father's farm, a short distance from Hernando, Miss. Just when she left there she would not say. In fact she says she came to Memphis from Arkansas, and says her home is in that State. She is rather good looking, has blue eyes, a low forehead and dark red hair. The ladies at the Woman's Refuge do not know anything about the girl further than what they learned when she was an inmate of the institution; and she would not tell much. When the child was born an attempt was made to get the girl to reveal the name of the Negro who had disgraced her, she obstinately refused and it was impossible to elicit any information from her on the subject."

Note the wording. "The truth might reveal fearful depravity or rank outrage." If it had been a white child or Lillie Bailey had told a pitiful story of Negro outrage, it would have been a case of woman's weakness or assault and she could have remained at the Woman's Refuge. But a Negro child and to withhold its father's name and thus prevent the killing of another Negro "rapist." A case of "fearful depravity."

The very week the "leading citizens" of Memphis were making a spectacle of themselves in defense of all white women of every kind, an Afro-American, M. Stricklin, was found in a white woman's room in that city. Although she made no outcry of rape, he was jailed and would have been lynched, but the woman stated she bought curtains of him (he was a furniture dealer) and his business in her room that night was to put them up. A white woman's word was taken as absolutely in this case as when the cry of rape is made, and he was freed.

What is true of Memphis is true of the entire South. The daily papers last year reported a farmer's wife in Alabama had given birth to a Negro child. When the Negro farm hand who was plowing in the field heard it he took the mule from the plow and fled. The dispatches also told of a woman in South Carolina who gave birth to a Negro child and charged three men with being its father, *every one of whom has since disappeared.* In Tuscumbia, Ala., the colored boy who was lynched there last year for assaulting a white girl told her before his accusers that he had met her there in the woods often before.

Frank Weems of Chattanooga who was not lynched in May only because the prominent citizens became his body guard until the doors of the penitentiary closed on him, had letters in his pocket from the white woman in the case, making the appointment with him. Edward Coy who was burned alive in Texarkana, January 1, 1892, died protesting his innocence. Investigation since as given by the Bystander in the Chicago Inter-Ocean, October 1, proves:

"1. The woman who was paraded as a victim of violence was of bad character; her husband was a drunkard and a gambler.

2. She was publicly reported and generally known to have been criminally intimate with Coy for more than a year previous.

3. She was compelled by threats, if not by violence, to make the charge against the victim.

4. When she came to apply the match Coy asked her if she would burn him after they had 'been sweethearting' so long.

5. A large majority of the 'superior' white men prominent in the affair are the reputed fathers of mulatto children.

These are not pleasant facts, but they are illustrative of the vital phase of the so-called 'race question,' which should properly be designated an earnest inquiry as to the best methods by which religion, science, law and political power may be employed to excuse injustice, barbarity and crime done to a people because of race and color. There can be no possible belief that these people were inspired by any consuming zeal to vindicate God's law against miscegnationists of the most practical sort. The woman was a willing partner in the victim's guilt, and being of the 'superior' race must naturally have been more guilty."

In Natchez, Miss., Mrs. Marshall, one of the *creme de la creme* of the city, created a tremendous sensation several years ago. She has a black coachman who was married, and had been in her employ several years. During this time she gave birth to a child whose color was remarked, but traced to some brunette ancestor, and one of the fashionable dames of the city was its godmother. Mrs. Marshall's social position was unquestioned, and wealth showered every dainty on this child which was idolized with its brothers and sisters by its white papa. In course of time another child appeared on the scene, but it was unmistakably dark. All were alarmed, and "rush of blood, strangulation" were the conjectures, but the doctor, when asked the cause, grimly told them it was a Negro child. There was a family conclave, the coachman heard of it and leaving his own family went West, and has never returned. As soon as Mrs. Marshall was able to travel she was sent away in deep disgrace. Her husband died within the year of a broken heart.

Ebenzer Fowler, the wealthiest colored man in Issaquena County, Miss., was shot down on the street in Mayersville, January 30, 1885, just before dark by an armed body of white men who filled his body with bullets. They charged him with writing a note to a white woman of the place, which they intercepted and which proved there was an intimacy existing between them.

Hundreds of such cases might be cited, but enough have been given to prove the assertion that there are white women in the South who love the Afro-American's company even as there are white men notorious for their preference for Afro-American women.

There is hardly a town in the South which has not an instance of the kind which is well-known, and hence the assertion is reiterated that "nobody in the South believes the old thread bare lie that negro men rape white women." Hence there is a growing demand among Afro-Americans that the guilt or innocence of parties accused of rape be fully established. They know the men of the section of the country who refuse this are not so desirous of punishing rapists as they pretend. The utterances of the leading white men show that with them it is not the crime but the *class*. Bishop Fitzgerald has become apologist for lynchers of the rapists of *white* women only. Governor Tillman, of South Carolina, in the month of June, standing under the tree in Barnwell, S.C., on which eight Afro-Americans were hung last year, declared that he would lead a mob to lynch a *negro* who raped a *white* woman." So say the pulpits, officials and newspapers of the South. But when the victim is a colored woman it is different.

Last winter in Baltimore, Md., three white ruffians assaulted a Miss Camphor, a young Afro-American girl, while out walking with a young man of her own race. They held her escort and outraged the girl. It was a deed dastardly enough to arouse Southern blood, which gives its horror of rape as excuse for lawlessness, but she was an Afro-American. The case went to the courts, an Afro-American lawyer defended the men and they were acquitted.

In Nashville, Tenn., there is a white man, Pat Hanifan, who outraged a little Afro-American girl, and, from the physical injuries received, she has been ruined for life. He was jailed for six months, discharged, and is now a detective in that city. In the same city, last May, a white man outraged an Afro-American girl in a drug store. He was arrested, and released on bail at the trial. It was rumored that five hundred Afro-Americans had organized to lynch him. Two hundred and fifty white citizens armed themselves with Winchesters and guarded him. A cannon was placed in front of his home, and the Buchanan Rifles (State Militia) ordered to the scene for his protection. The Afro-American mob did not materialize. Only two weeks before Eph. Grizzard, who had only been *charged* with rape upon a white woman, had been taken from the jail, with Governor Buchanan and the police and militia standing by, dragged through the streets in broad daylight, knives plunged into him at every step, and with every fiendish cruelty a frenzied mob could devise, he was at last swung out on the bridge with hands cut to pieces as he tried to climb up the stanchions. A naked, bloody example of the blood-thirstiness of the nineteenth century civilization of the Athens of the South! No cannon or military was called out in his defense. He dared to visit a white woman.

At the very moment these civilized whites were announcing their determination "to protect their wives and daughters," by murdering Grizzard, a white man was in the same jail for raping eight-year-old Maggie Reese, an Afro-American girl. He was not harmed. The "honor" of grown women who were glad enough to be supported by the Grizzard boys and Ed Coy, as long as the liaison was not known, needed protection; they were white. The outrage upon helpless childhood needed no avenging in this case; she was black.

A white man in Guthrie, Oklahoma Territory, two months ago inflicted such injuries upon another Afro-American child that she died. He was not punished, but an attempt was made in the same town in the month of June to lynch an Afro-American who visited a white woman.

In Memphis, Tenn., in the month of June, Ellerton L. Dorr, who is the husband of Russell Hancock's widow, was arrested for attempted rape on Mattie Cole, a neighbor's cook; he was only prevented from accomplishing his purpose, by the appearance of Mattie's employer. Dorr's friends say he was drunk and not responsible for his actions. The grand jury refused to indict him and he was discharged.

The New Cry

The appeal of Southern whites to Northern sympathy and sanction, the adroit, insiduous plea made by Bishop Fitzgerald for suspension of judgment because those "who condemn lynching express no sympathy for the *white* woman in the case," falls to the ground in the light of the foregoing.

From this exposition of the race issue in lynch law, the whole matter is explained by the well-known opposition growing out of slavery to the progress of the race. This is crystalized in the oft-repeated slogan: "This is a white man's country and the white man must rule." The South resented giving the Afro-American his freedom, the ballot box and the Civil Rights Law. The raids of the Ku-Klux and White Liners to subvert reconstruction government, the Hamburg and Ellerton, S. C., the Copiah County Miss., and the Layfayette Parish, La., massacres were excused as the natural resentment of intelligence against government by ignorance.

Honest white men practically conceded the necessity of intelligence murdering ignorance to correct the mistake of the general government, and the race was left to the tender mercies of the solid South. Thoughtful Afro-Americans with the strong arm of the government withdrawn and with the hope to stop such wholesale massacres urged the race to sacrifice its political rights for sake of peace. They honestly believed the race should fit itself for government, and when that should be done, the objection to race participation in politics would be removed.

But the sacrifice did not remove the trouble, nor move the South to justice. One by one the Southern States have legally (?) disfranchised the Afro-American, and since the repeal of the Civil Rights Bill nearly every Southern State has passed separate car laws with a penalty against their infringement. The race regardless of advancement is penned into filthy, stifling partitions cut off from smoking cars. All this while, although the political cause has been removed, the butcheries of black men at Barnwell, S. C., Carrolton, Miss., Waycross, Ga., and Memphis, Tenn., have gone on; also the flaying alive of a man in Kentucky, the burning of one in Arkansas, the hanging of a fifteen year old girl in Louisiana, a woman in Jackson, Tenn., and one in Hollendale, Miss., until the dark and bloody record of the South shows 728 Afro-Americans lynched during the past 8 years. Not 50 of these were for political causes; the rest were for all manner of accusations from that of rape of white women, to the case of the boy Will Lewis who was hanged at Tullahoma, Tenn., last year for being drunk and "sassy" to white folks.

These statistics compiled by the Chicago "Tribune" were given the first of this year (1892). Since then, not less than one hundred and fifty have been known to have met violent death at the hands of cruel bloodthirsty mobs during the past nine months.

To palliate this record (which grows worse as the Afro-American becomes intelligent) and excuse some of the most heinous crimes that ever stained the history of a country, the South is shielding itself behind the plausible screen of defending the honor of its women. This, too, in the face of the fact that only *one-third* of the 728 victims to mobs have been *charged* with rape, to say nothing of those of that one-third who were innocent of the charge. A white correspondent of the Baltimore Sun declares that the Afro-American who was lynched in Chestertown, Md., in May for assault on a white girl was innocent; that the deed was done by a white man who had since disappeared. The girl herself maintained that her assailant was a white man. When that poor Afro-American was murdered, the whites excused their refusal of a trial on the ground that they wished to spare the white girl the mortification of having to testify in court.

This cry has had its effect. It has closed the heart, stifled the conscience, warped the judgment and hushed the voice of press and pulpit on the subject of lynch law throughout this "land of liberty." Men who stand high in the esteem of the public for christian character, for moral and physical courage, for devotion to the principles of equal and exact justice to all, and for great sagacity, stand as cowards who fear to open their mouths before this great outrage. They do not see that by their tacit encouragement, their silent acquiescence, the black shadow of lawlessness in the form of lynch law is spreading its wings over the whole country.

Men who, like Governor Tillman, start the ball of lynch law rolling for a certain crime, are powerless to stop it when drunken or criminal white toughs feel like hanging an Afro-American on any pretext.

Even to the better class of Afro-Americans the crime of rape is so revolting they have too often taken the white man's word and given lynch law neither the investigation nor condemnation it deserved.

They forget that a concession of the right to lynch a man for a certain crime, not only concedes the right to lynch any person for any crime, but (so frequently is the cry of rape now raised) it is in a fair way to stamp us a race of rapists and desperadoes. They have gone on hoping and believing that general education and financial strength would solve the difficulty, and are devoting their energies to the accumulation of both.

The mob spirit has grown with the increasing intelligence of the Afro-American. It has left the out-of-the-way places where ignorance prevails, has thrown off the mask and with this new cry stalks in broad daylight in large cities, the centres of civilization, and is encouraged by the "leading citizens" and the press.

The Malicious and Untruthful White Press

The "Daily Commercial" and "Evening Scimitar" of Memphis, Tenn., are owned by leading business men of that city, and yet, in spite of the fact that there had been no white woman in Memphis outraged by an Afro-American, and that Memphis possessed a thrifty law-abiding, property owning class of Afro-Americans the "Commercial" of May 17th, under the head of "More Rapes, More Lynchings" gave utterance to the following:

"The lynching of three Negro scoundrels reported in our dispatches from Anniston, Ala., for a brutal outrage committed upon a white woman will be a text for much comment on 'Southern barbarism' by Northern newspapers; but we fancy it will hardly prove effective for campaign purposes among intelligent people. The frequency of these lynchings calls attention to the frequency of the crimes which causes lynching. The 'Southern barbarism' which deserves the serious attention of all people North and South, is the barbarism which preys upon weak and defenseless women. Nothing but the most prompt, speedy and extreme punishment can hold in check the horrible and beastial propensities of the Negro race. There is a strange similarity about a number of cases of this character which have lately occurred.

213

In each case the crime was deliberately planned and perpetrated by several Negroes. They watched for an opportunity when the women were left without a protector. It was not a sudden yielding to a fit of passion, but the consummation of a devilish purpose which has been seeking and waiting for the opportunity. This feature of the crime not only makes it the most fiendishly brutal, but it adds to the terror of the situation in the thinly settled country communities. No man can leave his family at night without the dread that some roving Negro ruffian is watching and waiting for this opportunity. The swift punishment which invariably follows these horrible crimes doubtless acts as a deterring effect upon the Negroes in that immediate neighborhood for a short time. But the lesson is not widely learned nor long remembered. Then such crimes, equally atrocious, have happened in quick succession, one in Tennessee, one in Arkansas, and one in Alabama. The facts of the crime appear to appeal more to the Negro's lustful imagination than the facts of the punishment do to his fears. He sets aside all fear of death in any form when opportunity is found for the gratification of his bestial desires.

There is small reason to hope for any change for the better. The commission of this crime grows more frequent every year. The generation of Negroes which have grown up since the war have lost in large measure the traditional and wholesome awe of the white race which kept the Negroes in subjection, even when their masters were in the army, and their families left unprotected except by the slaves themselves. There is no longer a restraint upon the brute passion of the Negro.

What is to be done? The crime of rape is always horrible, but for the Southern man there is nothing which so fills the soul with horror, loathing and fury as the outraging of a white woman by a Negro. It is the race question in the ugliest, vilest, most dangerous aspect. The Negro as a political factor can be controlled. But neither laws nor lynchings can subdue his lusts. Sooner or later it will force a crisis. We do not know in what form it will come."

In its issue of June 4th, the Memphis "Evening Scimitar" gives the following excuse for lynch law:

"Aside from the violation of white women by Negroes, which is the outcropping of a bestial perversion of instinct, the chief cause of trouble between the races in the South is the Negro's lack of manners. In the state of slavery he learned politeness from association with white people, who took pains to teach him. Since the emancipation came and the tie of mutual interest and regard between master and servant was broken, the Negro has drifted away into a state which is neither freedom nor bondage. Lacking the proper inspiration of the one and the restraining force of the other he has taken up the idea that boorish insolence is independence, and the exercise of a decent degree of breeding toward white people is identical with servile submission. In consequence of the prevalence of this notion there are many Negroes who use every opportunity to make themselves offensive, particularly when they think it can be done with impunity.

We have had too many instances right here in Memphis to doubt this, and our experience is not exceptional. *The white people won't stand this sort of thing, and whether they be insulted as individuals or as a race, the response will be prompt and effectual.* The bloody riot of 1866, in which so many Negroes perished, was brought on principally by the outrageous conduct of the blacks toward the whites on the streets. It is also a remarkable and discouraging fact that the majority of such scoundrels are Negroes who have received educational advantages at the hands of the white taxpayers. They have got just enough of learning to make them realize how hopelessly their race is behind the other in everything that makes a great people, and they attempt to 'get even' by insolence, which is ever the resentment of inferiors. There are well-bred Negroes among us, and it is truly unfortunate that they should have to pay, even in part, the penalty of the offenses committed by the baser sort, but this is the way of the world. The innocent must suffer for the guilty. If the Negroes as a people possessed a hundredth part of the self-respect which is evidenced by the courteous bearing of some that the 'Scimitar' could name, the friction between the races would be reduced to a minimum. It will not do to beg the question by pleading that many white men are also stirring up strife. The Caucasian blackguard simply obeys the promptings of a depraved disposition, and he is seldom deliberately rough or offensive toward strangers or unprotected women.

The Negro tough, on the contrary, is given to just that kind of offending, and he almost invariably singles out white people as his victims."

On March 9th, 1892, there were lynched in this same city three of the best specimens of young since-the-war Afro-American manhood. They were peaceful, law-abiding citizens and energetic business men.

They believed the problem was to be solved by eschewing politics and putting money in the purse. They owned a flourishing grocery business in a thickly populated suburb of Memphis, and a white man named Barrett had one on the opposite corner. After a personal difficulty which Barrett sought by going into the "People's Grocery" drawing a pistol and was thrashed by Calvin McDowell, he (Barrett) threatened to "clean them out." These men were a mile beyond the city limits and police protection; hearing that Barrett's crowd was coming to attack them Saturday night, they mustered forces and prepared to defend themselves against the attack.

When Barrett came he led a *posse* of officers, twelve in number, who afterward claimed to be hunting a man for whom they had a warrant. That twelve men in citizen's clothes should think it necessary to go in the night to hunt one man who had never before been arrested, or made any record as a criminal has never been explained. When they entered the back door the young men thought the threatened attack was on, and fired into them. Three of the officers were wounded, and when the *defending* party found it was officers of the law upon whom they had fired, they ceased and got away.

Thirty-one men were arrested and thrown in jail as "conspirators," although they all declared more than once they did not know they were firing on officers. Excitement was at fever heat until the morning papers, two days after, announced that the wounded deputy sheriffs were out of danger. This hindered rather than helped the plans of the whites. There was no law on the statute books which would execute an Afro-American for wounding a white man, but the "unwritten law" did. Three of these men, the president, the manager and clerk of the grocery—"the leaders of the conspiracy"—were secretly taken from jail and lynched in a shockingly brutal manner. "The Negroes are getting too independent," they say, "we must teach them a lesson."

What lesson? The lesson of subordination. "Kill the leaders and it will cow the Negro who dares to shoot a white man, even in self-defense."

Although the race was wild over the outrage, the mockery of law and justice which disarmed men and locked them up in jails where they could be easily and safely reached by the mob—the Afro-American ministers, newspapers and leaders counselled obedience to the law which did not protect them.

Their counsel was heeded and not a hand was uplifted to resent the outrage; following the advice of the "Free Speech," people left the city in great numbers.

The dailies and associated press reports heralded these men to the country as "toughs," and "Negro desperadoes who kept a low dive." This same press service printed that the Negro who was lynched at Indianola, Miss., in May, had outraged the sheriff's eight-year-old daughter. The girl was more than eighteen years old, and was found by her father in this man's room, who was a servant on the place.

Not content with misrepresenting the race, the mob-spirit was not to be satisfied until the paper which was doing all it could to counteract this impression was silenced. The colored people were resenting their bad treatment in a way to make itself felt, yet gave the mob no excuse for further murder, until the appearance of the editorial which is construed as a reflection on the "honor" of the Southern white women. It is not half so libelous as that of the "Commercial" which appeared four days before, and which has been given in this speech. They would have lynched the manager of the "Free Speech" for exercising the right of free speech if they had found him as quickly as they would have hung a rapist, and glad of the excuse to do so. The owners were ordered not to return, "The Free Speech" was suspended with as little compunction as the business of the "People's Grocery" broken up and the proprietors murdered.

The South's Position

Henry W. Grady in his well-remembered speeches in New England and New York pictured the Afro-American as incapable of self-government. Through him and other leading men the cry of the South to the country has been "Hands off! Leave us to solve our problem." To the Afro-American the South says, "the white man must and will rule." There is little difference between the Ante-bellum South and the New South.

Her white citizens are wedded to any method however revolting, any measure however extreme, for the subjugation of the young manhood of the race. They have cheated him out of his ballot, deprived him of civil rights or redress therefor in the civil courts, robbed him of the fruits of his labor, and are still murdering, burning and lynching him.

The result is a growing disregard of human life. Lynch law has spread its insiduous influence till men in New York State, Pennsylvania and on the free Western plains feel they can take the law in their own hands with impunity, especially where an Afro-American is concerned. The South is brutalized to a degree not realized by its own inhabitants, and the very foundation of government, law and order, are imperilled.

Public sentiment has had a slight "reaction" though not sufficient to stop the crusade of lawlessness and lynching. The spirit of christianity of the great M. E. Church was aroused to the frequent and revolting crimes against a weak people, enough to pass strong condemnatory resolutions at its General Conference in Omaha last May. The spirit of justice of the grand old party asserted itself sufficiently to secure a denunciation of the wrongs, and a feeble declaration of the belief in human rights in the Republican platform at Minneapolis, June 7th. Some of the great dailies and weeklies have swung into line declaring that lynch law must go. The President of the United States issued a proclamation that it be not tolerated in the territories over which he has jurisdiction. Governor Northern and Chief Justice Bleckley of Georgia have proclaimed against it. The citizens of Chattanooga, Tenn., have set a worthy example in that they not only condemn lynch law, but her public men demanded a trial for Weems, the accused rapist, and guarded him while the trial was in progress. The trial only lasted ten minutes, and Weems chose to plead guilty and accept twenty-one years sentence, than invite the certain death which awaited him outside that cordon of police if he had told the truth and shown the letters he had from the white woman in the case.

Col. A. S. Colyar, of Nashville, Tenn., is so overcome with the horrible state of affairs that he addressed the following earnest letter to the Nashville "American." "Nothing since I have been a reading man has so impressed me with the decay of manhood among the people of Tennessee as the dastardly submission to the mob reign. We have reached the unprecedented low level; the awful criminal depravity of substituting the mob for the court and jury, of giving up the jail keys to the mob whenever they are demanded. We do it in the largest cities and in the country towns; we do it in midday; we do it after full, not to say formal, notice, and so thoroughly and generally is it acquiesced in that the murderers have discarded the formula of masks. They go into the town where everybody knows them, sometimes under the gaze of the governor, in the presence of the courts, in the presence of the sheriff and his deputies, in the presence of the entire police force, take out the prisoner, take his life, often with fiendish glee, and often with acts of cruelty and barbarism which impress the reader with a degeneracy rapidly approaching savage life. That the State is disgraced but faintly expresses the humiliation which has settled upon the once proud people of Tennessee. The State, in its majesty, through its organized life, for which the people pay liberally, makes but one record, but one note, and that a criminal falsehood, 'was hung by persons to the jury unknown.' The murder at Shelbyville is only a verification of what every intelligent man knew would come, because with a mob a rumor is as good as a proof."

These efforts brought forth apologies and a short halt, but the lynching mania was raged again through the past three months with unabated fury.

The strong arm of the law must be brought to bear upon lynchers in severe punishment, but this cannot and will not be done unless a healthy public sentiment demands and sustains such action.

The men and women in the South who disapprove of lynching and remain silent on the perpetration of such outrages, are particeps criminis, accomplices, accessories before and after the fact, equally guilty with the actual law-breakers who would not persist if they did not know that neither the law nor militia would be employed against them.

Self Help

In the creation of this healthier public sentiment, the Afro-American can do for himself what no one else can do for him, The world looks on with wonder that we have conceded so much and remain law-abiding under such great outrage and provocation.

To Northern capital and Afro-American labor the South owes its rehabilitation. If labor is withdrawn capital will not remain. The Afro-American is thus the backbone of the South. A thorough knowledge and judicious exercise of this power in lynching localities could many times effect a bloodless revolution. The white man's dollar is his god and to stop this will be to stop outrages in many localities.

The Afro Americans of Memphis denounced the lynching of three of their best citizens, and urged and waited for the authorities to act in the matter and bring the lynchers to justice. No attempt was made to do so, and the black men left the city by thousands, bringing about great stagnation in every branch of business. Those who remained so injured the business of the street car company by staying off the cars, that the superintendent, manager and treasurer called personally on the editor of the "Free Speech," asked them to urge our people to give them their patronage again. Other business men became alarmed over the situation and the "Free Speech" was run away that the colored people might be more easily controlled. A meeting of white citizens in June, three months after the lynching, passed resolutions for the first time, condemning it. *But they did not punish the lynchers.* Every one of them was known by name, because they had been selected to do the dirty work, by some of the very citizens who passed these resolutions. Memphis is fast losing her black population, who proclaim as they go that there is no protection for the life and property of any Afro-American citizen in Memphis who is not a slave.

The Afro-American citizens of Kentucky, whose intellectual and financial improvement has been phenomenal, have never had a separate car law until now. Delegations and petitions poured into the Legislature against it, yet the bill passed and the Jim Crow Car of Kentucky is a legalized institution. Will the great mass of Negroes continue to patronize the railroad? A special from Covington, Ky., says:

"Covington, June 13th.—The railroads of the State are beginning to feel very markedly, the effects of the separate coach bill recently passed by the Legislature. No class of people in the State have so many and so largely attended excursions as the blacks. All these have been abandoned, and regular travel is reduced to a minimum. A competent authority says the loss to the various roads will reach $1,000,000 this year."

A call to a State Conference in Lexington, Ky., last June had delegates from every county in the State. Those delegates, the ministers, teachers, heads of secret and other orders, and the head of every family should pass the word around for every member of the race in Kentucky to stay off railroads unless obliged to ride. If they did so, and their advice was followed persistently the convention would not need to petition the Legislature to repeal the law or raise money to file a suit. The railroad corporations would be so effected they would in self-defense lobby to have the separate car law repealed. On the other hand, as long as the railroads can get Afro-American excursions they will always have plenty of money to fight all the suits brought against them. They will be aided in so doing by the same partisan public sentiment which passed the law. White men passed the law, and white judges and juries would pass upon the suits against the law, and render judgment in line with their prejudices and in deference to the greater financial power.

The appeal to the white man's pocket has ever been more effectual than all the appeals ever made to his conscience. Nothing, absolutely nothing, is to be gained by a further sacrifice of manhood and self-respect. By the right exercise of his power as the industrial factor of the South, the Afro-American can demand and secure his rights, the punishment of lynchers, and a fair trial for accused rapists.

Of the many inhuman outrages of this present year, the only case where the proposed lynching did *not* occur, was where the men armed themselves in Jacksonville, Fla., and Paducah, Ky., and prevented it. The only times an Afro-American who was assaulted got away has been when he had a gun and used it in self-defense.

The lesson this teaches and which every Afro-American should ponder well, is that a Winchester rifle should have a place of honor in every black home, and it should be used for that protection which the law refuses to give. When the white man who is always the aggressor knows he runs as great risk of biting the dust every time his Afro-American victim does, he will have greater respect for Afro-American life. The more the Afro-American yields and cringes and begs, the more he has to do so, the more he is insulted, outraged and lynched.

The assertion has been substantiated throughout that the press contains unreliable and doctored reports of lynchings, and one of the most necessary things for the race to do is to get these facts before the public. The people must know before they can act, and there is no educator to compare with the press.

The Afro-American papers are the only ones which will print the truth, and they lack means to employ agents and detectives to get at the facts. The race must rally a mighty host to the support of their journals, and thus enable them to do much in the way of investigation.

A lynching occurred at Port Jarvis, N.Y., the first week in June. A white and colored man were implicated in the assault upon a white girl. It was charged that the white man paid the colored boy to make the assault, which he did on the public highway in broad day time, and was lynched. This, too was done by "parties unknown." The white man in the case still lives. He was imprisoned and promises to fight the case on trial. At the preliminary examination, it developed that he had been a suitor of the girl's. She had repulsed and refused him, yet had given him money, and he had sent threatening letters demanding more.

The day before this examination she was so wrought up, she left home and wandered miles away. When found she said she did so because she was afraid of the man's testimony. Why should she be afraid of the prisoner? Why should she yield to his demands for money if not to prevent him exposing something he knew? It seems explainable only on the hypothesis that a *liason* existed between the colored boy and the girl, and the white man knew it. The press is singularly silent. Has it a motive? We owe it to ourselves to find out.

The story comes from Larned, Kansas, Oct. 1st, that a young white lady held at bay until daylight, without alarming any one in the house, "a burly Negro" who entered her room and bed. The "burly Negro" was promptly lynched without investigation or examination of inconsistent stories.

A house was found burned down near Montgomery, Ala., in Monroe County, Oct. 13th, a few weeks ago; also the burned bodies of the owners and melted piles of gold and silver.

These discoveries led to the conclusion that the awful crime was not prompted by motives of robbery. The suggestion of the whites was that "brutal lust was the incentive, and as there are nearly 200 Negroes living within a radius of five miles of the place the conclusion was inevitable that some of them were the perpetrators."

Upon this "suggestion" probably made by the real criminal, the mob acted upon the "conclusion" and arrested ten Afro-Americans, four of whom, they tell the world, confessed to the deed of murdering Richard L. Johnson and outraging his daughter, Jeanette. These four men, Berrell Jones, Moses Johnson, Jim and John Packer, none of them 25 years of age, upon this conclusion, were taken from jail, hanged, shot, and burned while yet alive the night of Oct. 12th. The same report says Mr. Johnson was on the best of terms with his Negro tenants.

The race thus outraged must find out the facts of this awful hurling of men into eternity on supposition, and give them to the indifferent and apathetic country. We feel this to be a garbled report, but how can we prove it?

Near Vicksburg, Miss., a murder was committed by a gang of burglars. Of course it must have been done by Negroes, and Negroes were arrested for it. It is believed that 2 men, Smith Tooley and John Adams belonged to a gang controlled by white men and, fearing exposure, on the night of July 4th, they were hanged in the Court House yard by those interested in silencing them. Robberies since committed in the same vicinity have been known to be by white men who had their faces blackened. We strongly believe in the innocence of these murdered men, but we have no proof. No other news goes out to the world save that which stamps us as a race of cut-throats, robbers and lustful wild beasts. So great is Southern hate and prejudice, they legally (?) hung poor little thirteen year old Mildrey Brown at Columbia, S.C., Oct. 7th, on the circumstantial evidence that she poisoned a white infant. If her guilt had been proven unmistakably, had she been white, Mildrey Brown would never have been hung.

The country would have been aroused and South Carolina disgraced forever for such a crime. The Afro-American himself did not know as he should have known as his journals should be in a position to have him know and act.

Nothing is more definitely settled than he must act for himself. I have shown how he may employ the boycott, emigration and the press, and I feel that by a combination of all these agencies can be effectually stamped out lynch law, that last relic of barbarism and slavery. "The gods help those who help themselves."

Frances Willard
(1829–1898)

Frances Willard was born on September 28, 1829 in Churchville, New York. The fourth of five children, Frances spent most of her childhood and adolescent years in the wilderness city of Janesville, Wisconsin Territory. With only sporadic attendance at public schools in Wisconsin and one year at the Milwaukee Female College, Frances graduated with a "Laureate in Science" in 1859 from North Western Female College in Evanston, Illinois, after apparently only four years of formal education all together. From 1860 to 1867 she taught at county and local schools in and around the city of Evanston. After a two year tour of Europe, Frances returned to become President of the Evanston College for Ladies from 1870 to 1873. When Northwestern University absorbed the college, she served from 1873 to 1874 as Dean of Women and as Vice President of the Association for Advancement of Women. In 1874 Frances turned her energies to the temperance movement, a reform cause which would deeply involve her for the remainder of her life. From 1874 to 1877 she served as both the secretary of the Illinois Temperance Organization and as corresponding secretary of the National Women's Christian Temperance Union (WCTU). In 1878 she became President of the Illinois WCTU but soon resigned to assume the Presidency of the National WCTU, a position she held until her death. Under Frances' leadership, the National WCTU became more and more political, allying itself with suffrage, with home protection, with prohibition, and numerous other related reform causes. Throughout her reign, Frances achieved prominence as a gifted lecturer and consequently numerous other organizations requested her service. In 1888 she became the first president of the National Council of the National and International Councils of Women; in 1891 she assumed the position of first president of the World's WCTU; in 1893 she became Vice President of the Universal Peace Union; and in the mid-1890's she helped found the General Federation of Women's Clubs. At the relatively young age of 58, Frances fell ill with the grippe and anemia while on a speaking tour in New York, and died shortly thereafter on February 17, 1898.

The following address was delivered at the Third Annual Convention of the Women's Christian Temperance Union in Newark, New Jersey in 1876. It was later printed in Frances Willard, *Woman and Temperance* (Hartford, Ct., 1883), pp. 452–459.

"Temperance and Home Protection"

The rum power looms like a Chimborazo among the mountains of difficulty over which our native land must climb to reach the future of our dreams. The problem of the rum power's overthrow may well engage our thoughts as women and as patriots. To-night I ask you to consider it in the light of a truth which Frederick Douglass has embodied in these words: "We can in the long run trust all the knowledge in the community to take care of all the ignorance of the community, and all of its virtue to take care of all of its vice." The difficulty in the application of this principle lies in the fact that vice is always in the active, virtue often in the passive. Vice is aggressive. It deals swift, sure blows, delights in keen-edged weapons, and prefers a hand-to-hand conflict, while virtue instinctively fights its unsavory antagonist at arm's length; its great guns are unwieldly and slow to swing into range.

Vice is the tiger, with keen eyes, alert ears, and cat-like tread, while virtue is the slow-paced, complacent, easy-going elephant, whose greatest danger lies in its ponderous weight and consciousness of power. So the great question narrows down to one of two (?) methods. It is not, when we look carefully into the conditions of the problem, How shall we develop more virtue in the community to offset the tropical growth of vice by which we find ourselves environed ? but rather, How the tremendous force we have may best be brought to bear, how we may unlimber the huge cannon now pointing into vacancy, and direct their full charge at short range upon our nimble, wily, vigilant foe?

As bearing upon a consideration of that question, I lay down this proposition: All pure and Christian sentiment concerning any line of conduct which vitally affects humanity will, sooner or later, crystallize into law. But the keystone of law can only be firm and secure when it is held in place by the arch of that keystone, which is public sentiment.

I make another statement not so often reiterated, but just as true, viz.: The more thoroughly you can enlist in favor of your law the natural instincts of those who have the power to make that law, and to select the officers who shall enforce it, the more securely stands the law. And still another: First among the powerful and controlling instincts in our nature stands that of self-preservation, and next after this, if it does not claim superior rank, comes that of a mother's love. You can count upon that every time; it is sure and resistless as the tides of the sea, for it is founded in the changeless nature given to her from God.

Now that the stronghold of the rum power lies in the fact that it has upon its side two deeply rooted appetites, namely: in the dealer, the appetite for gain, and in the drinker, the appetite for stimulants. We have dolorously said in times gone by that on the human plane we have nothing adequate to match against this frightful pair. But let us think more carefully, and we shall find that, as in nature, God has given us an antidote to every poison, and in grace a compensation for every loss; so in human society he has prepared against alcohol, that worst foe of the social state, an enemy under whose weapons it is to bite the dust.

Think of it! There is a class in every one of our communities—in many of them far the most numerous class—which (I speak not vauntingly; I but name it as a fact) has not in all the centuries of wine, beer, and brandy-drinking developed, as a class, an appetite for alcohol, but whose instincts, on the contrary, set so strongly against intoxicants that if the liquor traffic were dependent on their patronage alone, it would collapse this night as though all the nitro-glycerine of Hell Gate reef had exploded under it.

There is a class whose instinct of self-preservation must forever be opposed to a stimulant which nerves, with dangerous strength, arms already so much stronger than their own, and so maddens the brain God meant to guide those arms, that they strike down the wives men love, and the little children for whom, when sober, they would die. The wife, largely dependent for the support of herself and little ones upon the brain which strong drink paralyzes, the arm it masters, and the skill it renders futile, will, in the nature of the case, prove herself unfriendly to the actual or potential source of so much misery. But besides this primal instinct of self-preservation, we have, in the same class of which I speak, another far more high and sacred—I mean the instinct of a mother's love, a wife's devotion, a sister's faithfulness, a daughter's loyalty. And now I ask you to consider earnestly the fact that none of these blessed rays of light and power from woman's heart, are as yet brought to bear upon the rum-shop at the focus of power. They are, I know, the sweet and pleasant sunshine of our homes; they are the beams which light the larger home of social life and send their gentle radiance out even into the great and busy world. But I know, and as the knowledge has grown clearer, my heart was thrilled with gratitude and hope too deep for words, that in a republic all these now divergent beams of light can, through that magic lens, that powerful sun-glass which we name the ballot, be made to converge upon the rum-shop in a blaze of light that shall reveal its full abominations, and a white flame of heat which, like a pitiless moxa, shall burn this cancerous excrescence from America's fair form. Yes, for there is nothing in the universe so sure, so strong, as love; and love shall do all this—the love of maid for sweetheart, wife for husband, of a sister for her brother, of a mother for her son. And I call upon you who are here to-day, good men and brave—you who have welcomed us to other fields in the great fight of the angel against the dragon in society—I call upon you thus to match force with force, to set over against the liquor-dealer's avarice our instinct of self-preservation; and to match the drinker's love of liquor with our love of him! When you can centre all this power in that small bit of paper which falls

"As silently as snow-flakes fall upon the sod,
But executes a freeman's will as lightnings do the will of God,"

the rum power will be as much doomed as was the slave power when you gave the ballot to the slaves.

In our argument it has been claimed that by the changeless instincts of her nature and through the most sacred relationships of which that nature has been rendered capable, God has indicated woman, who is the born conservator of home, to be the Nemesis of home's arch enemy, King Alcohol. And further, that in a republic, this power of hers may be most effectively exercised by giving her a voice in the decision by which the rum-shop door shall be opened or closed beside her home.

This position is strongly supported by evidence. About the year 1850 petitions were extensively circulated in Cincinnati (later the fiercest battle ground of the woman's crusade), asking that the liquor traffic be put under the ban of law. Bishop Simpson—one of the noblest and most discerning minds of his century—was deeply interested in this movement. It was decided to ask for the names of women as well as those of men, and it was found that the former signed the petition more readily and in much larger numbers than the latter. Another fact was ascertained which rebuts the hack-neyed assertion that women of the lower class will not be on the temperance side in this great war. For it was found—as might, indeed, have been most reasonably predicted—that the ignorant, the poor (many of them wives, mothers, and daughters of intemperate men), were among the most eager to sign the petition.

Many a hand was taken from the wash-tub to hold the pencil and affix the signature of women of this class, and many another, which could only make the sign of the cross, did that with tears, and a hearty "God bless you." "That was a wonderful lesson to me," said the good Bishop, and he has always believed since then that God will give our enemy into our hands by giving to us an ally still more powerful, woman with the ballot against rum-shops in our land. It has been said so often that the very frequency of reiteration has in some minds induced belief that women of the better class will never consent to declare themselves at the polls. But tens of thousands from the most tenderly-sheltered homes have gone day after day to the saloons, and have spent hour after hour upon their sanded floors, and in their reeking air—places in which not the worst politician would dare to locate the ballot box of freemen—though they but stay a moment at the window, slip in their votes, and go their way.

Nothing worse can ever happen to women at the polls than has been endured by the hour on the part of conservative women of the churches in this land, as they, in scores of towns, have plead with rough, half-drunken men to vote the temperance tickets they have handed them, and which, with vastly more of propriety and fitness they might have dropped into the box themselves. They could have done this in a moment, and returned to their homes, instead of spending the whole day in the often futile endeavor to beg from men like these the votes which should preserve their homes from the whiskey serpent's breath for one uncertain year. I spent last May in Ohio, traveling constantly, and seeking on every side to learn the views of the noble women of the Crusade. They put their opinions in words like these: "We believe that as God led us into this work by way of the saloons,

HE WILL LEAD US OUT BY WAY OF THE BALLOT

We have never prayed more earnestly over the one than we will over the other. One was the Wilderness, the other is the Promised Land."

A Presbyterian lady, rigidly conservative, said: "For my part, I never wanted to vote until our gentlemen passed a prohibition ordinance so as to get us to stop visiting saloons, and a month later repealed it and chose a saloon-keeper for mayor."

Said a grand-daughter of Jonathan Edwards, a woman with no toleration toward the Suffrage Movement, a woman crowned with the glory of gray hairs—a central figure in her native town—

AND AS SHE SPOKE THE COURAGE AND FAITH OF THE PURITANS THRILLED HER VOICE—

"If, with the ballot in our hands, we can, as I firmly believe, put down this awful traffic, I am ready to lead the women of my town to the polls, as I have often led them to the rum shops."

We must not forget that for every woman who joins the Temperance Unions now springing up all through the land, there are at least a score who sympathize but do not join. Home influence and cares prevent them, ignorance of our aims and methods, lack of consecration to Christian work—a thousand reasons, sufficient in their estimation, though not in ours, hold them away from us. And yet they have this Temperance cause warmly at heart; the logic of events has shown them that there is but one side on which a woman may safely stand in this great battle, and on that side they would indubitably range themselves in the quick, decisive battle of election day, nor would they give their voice a second time in favor of the man who had once betrayed his pledge to enforce the most stringent law for the protection of their homes. There are many noble women, too, who, though they do not think as do the Temperance Unions about the deep things of religion, and are not as yet decided in their total abstinence sentiments, nor ready for the blessed work of prayer, are nevertheless decided in their views of Woman Suffrage, and ready to vote a Temperance ticket side by side with us. And there are the drunkard's wife and daughters, who from very shame will not come with us, or who dare not, yet who would freely vote with us upon this question; for the folded ballot tells no tales.

Among other cumulative proofs in this argument from experience, let us consider, briefly, the attitude of the Catholic Church toward the Temperance Reform. It is friendly, at least. Father Matthew's spirit lives to-day in many a faithful parish priest. In our procession on the Centennial Fourth of July, the banners of Catholic Total Abstinence Societies were often the only reminders that the Republic has any temperance people within its borders, as they were the only offset to brewers' wagons and distillers' casks, while among the monuments of our cause, by which this memorable year is signalized, their fountain in Fairmount Park—standing in the midst of eighty

224

drinking places licensed by our Government—is chief. Catholic women would vote with Protestant women upon this issue for the protection of their homes.

Again, among the sixty thousand churches of America, with their eight million members, two-thirds are women. Thus, only one-third of this trustworthy and thoughtful class has any voice in the laws by which, between the church and the public school, the rum shop nestles in this Christian land. Surely all this must change before the Government shall be upon His shoulders "Who shall one day reign King of nations as He now reigns King of saints."

Furthermore, four-fifths of the teachers in this land are women, whose thoughtful judgment, expressed with the authority of which I speak, would greatly help forward the victory of our cause. And, finally, by those who fear the effect of the foreign element in our country, let it be remembered that we have sixty native for every one woman who is foreign born, for it is men who emigrate in largest number to our shores.

When all these facts (and many more that might be added) are marshaled into line, how illogical it seems for good men to harangue us as they do about our "duty to educate public sentiment to the level of better law," and their exhortations to American mothers to "train their sons to vote aright." As said Mrs. Governor Wallace, of Indiana—until the Crusade an opponent of the franchise—"What a bitter sarcasm you utter, gentlemen, to us who have the public sentiment of which you speak, all burning in our hearts, and yet are not permitted to turn it to account."

Let us, then, each one of us, offer our earnest prayer to God, and speak our honest word to man in favor of this added weapon in woman's hands, remembering that every petition in the ear of God, and every utterance in the ears of men, swells the dimensions of that resistless tide of influence which shall yet float within our reach all that we ask or need. Dear Christian women who have crusaded in the rum shops, I urge that you begin crusading in halls of legislation, in primary meetings, and the offices of excise commissioners. Roll in your petitions, burnish your arguments, multiply your prayers. Go to the voters in your town—procure the official list and see them one by one—and get them pledged to a local ordinance requiring the votes of men and women before a license can be issued to open rum-shop doors beside your homes; go to the Legislature with the same; remember this may be just as really Christian work as praying in saloons was in those other glorious days. Let us not limit God, whose modes of operation are so infinitely varied in nature and in grace. I believe in the correlation of spiritual forces, and that the heat which melted hearts to tenderness in the Crusade is soon to be the light which shall reveal our opportunity and duty as the Republic's daughters.

Longer ago than I shall tell, my father returned one night to the far-off Wisconsin home where I was reared; and, sitting by my mother's chair, with a child's attentive ear, I listened to their words. He told us of the news that day had brought about Neal Dow and the great fight for prohibition down in Maine, and then he said: "I wonder if poor, rum-cursed Wisconsin will ever get a law like that?" And mother rocked a while in silence in the dear old chair I love, and then she gently said:

"YES, JOSIAH, THERE'LL BE SUCH A LAW ALL OVER THE
LAND SOME DAY, WHEN WOMEN VOTE."

My father had never heard her say so much before. He was a great conservative; so he looked tremendously astonished, and replied, in his keen, sarcastic voice: "And pray how will you arrange it so that women shall vote?" Mother's chair went to and fro a little faster for a minute, and then, looking not into his face, but into the flickering flames of the grate, she slowly answered: "Well,

I say to you, as the apostle Paul said to his jailor, 'You have put us into prison, we being Romans, and you must come and take us out.' "

That was a seed-thought in a girl's brain and heart. Years passed on, in which nothing more was said upon this dangerous theme. My brother grew to manhood, and soon after he was twenty-one years old he went with his father to vote. Standing by the window, a girl of sixteen years, a girl of simple, homely fancies, not at all strongminded, and altogether ignorant of the world, I looked out as they drove away, my father and my brother, and as I looked I felt a strange ache in my heart, and tears sprang to my eyes. Turning to my sister Mary, who stood beside me, I saw that the dear little innocent seemed wonderfully sober, too. I said: "Don't you wish we could go with them when we are old enough? Don't we love our country just as well as they do?" and her little frightened voice piped out: "Yes, of course we ought. Don't I know that? but you mustn't tell a soul—not mother, even; we should be called strong-minded."

In all the years since then I have kept these things, and many others like them, and pondered them in my heart; but two years of struggle in this temperance reform have shown me, as they have ten thousand other women, so clearly and so impressively, my duty, that

I HAVE PASSED THE RUBICON OF SILENCE

and am ready for any battle that shall be involved in this honest declaration of the faith that is within me. "Fight behind masked batteries a little longer," whisper good friends and true. So I have been fighting hitherto; but it is a style of warfare altogether foreign to my temperament and mode of life. Reared on the prairies, I seemed pre-determined to join the cavalry forces in this great spiritual war, and I must tilt a free lance henceforth on the splendid battlefield of this reform; where the earth shall soon be shaken by the onset of contending hosts; where legions of valiant soldiers are deploying; where to the grand encounter marches to-day a great army, gentle of mein and mild of utterance, but with hearts for any fate; where there are trumpets and bugles calling strong souls onward to a victory which Heaven might envy, and

> "Where, behind the dim Unknown,
> Standeth God within the shadow,
> Keeping watch above His own."

I thought that women ought to have the ballot as I paid the hard-earned taxes upon my mother's cottage home—but I never said as much—somehow the motive did not command my heart. For my own sake, I had not courage, but I have for thy sake, dear native land, for thy necessity is as much greater than mine as thy transcendant hope is greater than the personal interest of thy humble child. For love of you, heart-broken wives, whose tremulous lips have blessed me; for love of you, sweet mothers, who, in the cradle's shadow, kneel this night beside your infant sons, and you, sorrowful little children, who listen at this hour, with faces strangely old, for him whose footsteps frighten you; for love of you have I thus spoken.

Ah, it is women who have given the costliest hostages to fortune. Out into the battle of life they have sent their best beloved, with fearful odds against them, with snares that men have legalized and set for them on every hand. Beyond the arms that held them long, their boys have gone forever. Oh! by the danger they have dared; by the hours of patient watching over beds where helpless children lay; by the incense of ten thousand prayers wafted from their gentle lips to Heaven, I charge you give them power to protect, along life's treacherous highway, those whom they have so loved. Let it no longer be that they must sit back among the shadows, hopelessly mourning over their strong staff broken, and their beautiful rod; but when the sons they love shall go forth to life's battle, still let their mothers walk beside them, sweet and serious, and clad in the garments of power.

Victoria Woodhull
(1838–1927)

Victoria Woodhull was born on September 23, 1838 in the tiny town of Homer, Ohio. The seventh of ten children, her schooling was intermittent while the family wandered from place to place in the midwest. In 1853, at age fifteen, Victoria married Canning Woodhull, a physician, and gave birth to two children over the next several years. Beginning in the late 1850's Victoria travelled throughout the midwest with her sister Tennessee selling a family elixir and offering a variety of psychic remedies for those willing to try them. In 1864 Victoria met Colonel James Harvey Blood and in 1866 she divorced her husband and married Blood. In 1868 Victoria convinced her husband and sister to join her in a move to New York City, supposedly because Demosthenes had spoken to her in a dream and had urged her to go there. After support from Cornelius Vanderbilt, whom Victoria and Tennessee had assisted in psychic ministrations, the two sisters emerged from small successes in real estate ventures to set up shop as a brokerage firm in 1870. Quickly prospering as a businesswoman, Victoria turned her energies to politics and declared herself a candidate for President of the United States. Soon thereafter, the first issue of *Woodhull and Claflin's Weekly* came off the presses to elaborate her program. The *Weekly* expressed a wide range of topics and points of view, including such disparate ones as short skirts, free love, legalized prostitution, tax reform, housing reform, dietary reform, and world government. In 1871, Victoria also assumed leadership of Marx's International Workingmen's Association in New York and her weekly published *The Communist Manifesto* in English for the first time in America. During the same year she also began delivering addresses on woman suffrage and spoke to the House of Representatives urging inclusion under the fourteenth amendment. By election day in 1872, Victoria found herself in jail for publishing her scandalous tales of adultery between Henry Ward Beecher, a prominent minister, and Elizabeth Tilton, wife of a prominent editor. The subsequent court battles resulted in bankruptcy for Victoria and essentially ended her American career. In 1877 she divorced her husband and embarked for England with her sister. Soon after arriving in London Victoria resumed lecturing, and in 1883 she married a wealthy banker who had been an eager listener some six years before. With the help of her daughter, Victoria published the *Humanitarian*, a journal devoted to eugenics, from 1892 to 1901. Surviving her husband, Victoria lived amid affluence for the remainder of her life and died peacefully in her sleep June 10, 1927 at the age of eighty-eight.

The following lecture was delivered in Steinway Hall in New York City on November 20, 1871. It was later printed in *Woodhull and Claffin's Weekly* (August 16, 1873), pp. 2–7.

"The Principles of Social Freedom"

It has been said by a very wise person that there is a *trinity* in all things, the perfect *unity* of the trinity or a tri-unity being necessary to make a complete objective realization. Thus we have the theological Trinity: The Father, the Son and the Holy Ghost; or Cause, Effect and the Process of Evolution. Also the *political* Trinity: Freedom, Equality, Justice or *Individuality, Unity, Ad-*

justment; the first term of which is also resolvable into these parts, thus: Religious freedom, political freedom and social freedom, while Religion, Politics and Socialism are the Tri-unity of Humanity. There are also the beginning, the end and the intermediate space, time and motion, to all experiences of space, time and motion, and the diameter, circumference and area, or length, breadth and depth to all form.

Attention has been called to these scientific facts, for the purpose of showing that for any trinity to lack one of its terms is for it to be incomplete; and that in the order of natural evolution, if two terms exist, the third must also exist.

Religious freedom does, in a measure, exist in this country, but not yet perfectly; that is to say, a person is not entirely independent of public opinion regarding matters of conscience. Though since Political freedom has existed in theory, every person has the *right* to entertain any religious theory he or she may conceive to be true, and government can take no cognizance thereof—he is *only* amenable to *society*-despotism. The necessary corollary to Religious and Political freedom is Social freedom, which is the third term of the trinity; that is to say, if Religious and Political freedom exist, *perfected,* Social freedom is at that very moment guaranteed, since Social freedom is the fruit of that condition.

We find the principle of Individual freedom was quite dormant until it began to speak against the right of religious despots, to determine what views should be advocated regarding the relations of the creature to the Creator. Persons began to find ideas creeping into their souls at variance with the teachings of the clergy; which ideas became so *strongly* fixed that they were compelled to protest against Religious Despotism. Thus, in the sixteenth century, was begun the battle for Individual freedom. The claim that rulers had *no right* to control the consciences of the people was boldly made, and right nobly did the fight continue until the *absolute* right to individual opinion was wrung from the despots, and even the *common* people found themselves entitled to not only entertain but also to promulgate *any* belief or theory of which they could conceive.

With yielding the control over the *consciences* of individuals, the despots had no thought of giving up any right to their *persons.* But Religious freedom naturally led the people to question the right of this control, and in the eighteenth century a new protest found expression in the French Revolution, and it was baptized by a deluge of blood yielded by thousands of lives. But not until an enlightened people freed themselves from English tyranny was the right to self-government acknowledged in theory, and *not yet* even is it fully accorded in practice, as a legitimate result of that theory.

It may seem to be a *strange* proposition to make, that there is no such thing yet existent in the world as self-government, in its political aspects. But such is the fact. If self-government be the rule, every self must be its subject. If a person govern, not only *himself* but others, that is despotic government, and it matters not if that control be over one or over a thousand individuals, or over a nation; in *each* case it would be the *same* principle of power exerted outside of self and over others, and *this* is despotism, whether it is exercised by *one* person over his subjects, or by *twenty* persons over a nation, or by *one-half* the people of a nation over the other half thereof. There is no escaping the fact that the principle by which the *male* citizens of these United States assume to rule the *female* citizens is *not* that of self-government, but that of despotism; and so the fact is that poets have sung songs of freedom, and anthems of liberty have resounded for an empty shadow.

King George III. and his Parliament denied our forefathers the right to make their own laws; they rebelled, and being successful, inaugurated this government. But men do not seem to comprehend that they are now pursuing toward *women* the *same* despotic course that King George pursued toward the American colonies.

But what is freedom? The press and our male governors are *very much* exercised about this question, since a certain set of resolutions were launched upon the public by Paulina Wright Davis at Apollo Hall, May 12, 1871. They are as follows:

Resolved, That the basis of order is freedom from bondage; not, indeed, of such "order" as reigned in Warsaw, which grew out of the bondage; but of such order as reigns in Heaven, which grows out of that undeveloped manhood and womanhood in which each becomes "a law unto himself."

Resolved, That freedom is a principle, and that as such it may be trusted to ultimate in harmonious social results, as in America, it has resulted in harmonious and beneficent political results; that it has not hitherto been adequately trusted in the social domain, and that the woman's movement means no less than the complete social as well as the political enfranchisement of mankind.

Resolved, That the evils, sufferings and disabilities of women, as well as of men, are social still more than they are political, and that a statement of woman's rights which ignores the right of self-ownership as the first of all rights is insufficient to meet the demand, and is ceasing to enlist the enthusiasm and even the common interest of the most intelligent portion of the community.

Resolved, That the principle of freedom is one principle, and not a collection of many different and unrelated principles; that there is not at bottom one principle of freedom of conscience as in Protestantism, and another principle of freedom from slavery as in Abolitionism, another of freedom of locomotion as in our dispensing in America with the passport system of Europe, another of the freedom of the press as in Great Britain and America, and still another of social freedom at large; but that freedom is one and indivisible; and that slavery is so also; that freedom and bondage or restriction is the alternative and the issue, alike, in every case; and that if freedom is good in one case it is good in all; that we in America have builded on freedom, politically, and that we cannot consistently recoil from that expansion of freedom which shall make it the basis of all our institutions; and finally, that so far as we have trusted it, it has proved, in the main, safe and profitable.

Now, is there anything so terrible in the language of these resolutions as to threaten the foundations of society? They assert that every individual has a *better* right to herself or himself than any other person *can have.* No living soul, who does not desire to have control over, or ownership in, another person, can have any *valid* objection to *anything* expressed in these resolutions. Those who are not willing to give up control over others; who desire to *own* somebody beside themselves; who are constitutionally predisposed against self-government and the giving of the same freedom to others that they demand for themselves, will of course object to them, and such are the people with whom we shall have to contend in this new struggle for a greater liberty.

Now, the individual *is* either self-owned and self-possessed or *is not* so self-possessed. If he be self-owned, he is so because he has an *inherent* right to self, which right cannot be delegated to any second person; a right—as the American Declaration of Independence has it—which is "inalienable." The individual must be responsible to self and God for his acts. If he be owned and possessed by some second person, then there is *no such thing* as individuality: and that for which the world has been striving these thousands of years is the merest myth.

But against this irrational, illogical, inconsequent and irreverent theory I boldly oppose the spirit of the age—that spirit which will *not* admit all civilization to be a failure, and all past experience to count for nothing; against that demagogism, I oppose the plain principle of freedom in its *fullest, purest, broadest, deepest* application and significance—the freedom which we see exemplified in the starry firmament, where whirl innumerable worlds, and never one of which is made to lose its individuality, but each performs its part in the grand economy of the universe, giving and receiving its natural repulsions and attractions; we also see its exemplified in every department of nature about us: in the sunbeam and the dewdrop; in the storm-cloud and the spring shower; in the driving snow and the congealing rain—all of which speak more eloquently than can human tongue of the heavenly *beauty, symmetry* and *purity* of the spirit of freedom which in them reigns untrammeled.

Our government is based upon the proposition that: All men and women are born free and equal and entitled to certain inalienable rights, among which are life, liberty and the *pursuit* of happiness. Now what we, who demand social freedom, ask, is simply that the government of this country shall be administered in accordance with the spirit of this proposition. *Nothing* more, *nothing* less. If that proposition mean *anything,* it means *just what* it says, without qualification, limitation or equivocation. It means that *every* person who comes into the world of outward existence is of *equal* right as an individual, and is free as an individual, and that he or she is entitled to pursue *happiness* in whatever direction he or she may choose. Now this is absolutely true of all men and all women. But just here the wise-acres stop and tell us that *everybody* must *not* pursue happiness in his or her own way; since to do so absolutely, would be to have no protection against the action of individuals. These good and well-meaning people only see *one-half* of what is involved in the proposition. They look at a single individual and for the time lose sight of all others. They do not take into their consideration that every other individual beside the one whom they contemplate is *equally* with him entitled to the *same* freedom; and that each is free within the area of his or her individual sphere; and *not* free within the sphere of any other individual whatever. They do not seem to recognize the fact that the moment one person gets out of *his* sphere into the sphere of *another,* that other must protect him or herself against such invasion of rights. They do not seem to be able to comprehend that the moment one person encroaches upon another person's rights he or she ceases to be a *free* man or woman and becomes a *despot.* To all such persons we assert: that it is *freedom* and *not* despotism which we advocate and demand; and we will as rigorously demand that individuals be restricted to *their* freedom as any person dare to demand; and as rigorously demand that people who are predisposed to be *tyrants* instead of free men or women shall, by the government, be so restrained as to make the exercise of their proclivities impossible.

If life, liberty and the pursuit of happiness are *inalienable* rights in the individual, and government is based upon that inalienability, then it *must follow* as a *legitimate* sequence that the *functions* of that government are to *guard* and *protect* the right to life, liberty and the pursuit of happiness, to the end that *every* person may have the most *perfect* exercise of them. And the most perfect exercise of such rights is *only* attained when every individual is not only fully *protected* in his rights, but also *strictly restrained* to the exercise of them within his *own* sphere, and *positively* prevented from proceeding beyond its limits, so as to encroach upon the sphere of another: unless that other first *agree* thereto.

From these generalizations certain specializations are deducible, by which all questions of rights must be determined:

1. Every living person has certain rights of which no law can rightfully deprive him.

2. Aggregates of persons form communities, who erect governments to secure regularity and order.

3. Order and harmony can alone be secured in a community where every individual of whom it is composed is fully protected in the exercise of all individual rights.

4. Any government which enacts laws to deprive individuals of the free exercise of their right to life, liberty and the pursuit of happiness is despotic, and such laws are not binding upon the people who protest against them, whether they be a majority or a minority.

5. When every individual is secure in the possession and exercise of all his rights, then every one is also secure from the interference of all other parties.

6. All inharmony and disorder arise from the attempts of individuals to interfere with the rights of other individuals, or from the protests of individuals against governments for depriving them of their inalienable rights.

These propositions are all self-evident, and must be accepted by every person who subscribes to our theory of government, based upon the sovereignty of the individual; consequently any law in force which conflicts with any of them is not in accord with that theory and is therefore unconstitutional.

A fatal error into which most people fall, is, that rights are conceded to governments, while they are only possessed of the right to perform duties, as a further analysis will show:

In the absence of any arrangement by the members of a community to secure order, *each* individual is a law unto himself, so far as he is capable of maintaining it against all other individuals; but at the mercy of all such who are bent on conquest. Such a condition is anarchy.

But if in individual freedom the *whole* number of individuals unite to secure *equality* and protection to themselves, they thereby surrender *no* individual rights to the community, but they simply *invest* the community with the power to perform certain specified *duties,* which are set forth in the law of their combination. Hence a government erected by the people is invested, *not* with the *rights* of the people, but with the *duty* of *protecting* and maintaining their rights *intact;* and any government is a *failure* or a *success* just so far as it fails or succeeds in this duty; and these are the legitimate functions of government.

I have before said that every person has the right to, and can, determine for himself what he will do, even to taking the life of another. But it is *equally* true that the attacked person has the right to defend his life against such assault. If the person succeed in taking the life, he thereby demonstrates that he is a *tyrant* who is at all times liable to invade the right to life, and that every individual of the community is put in jeopardy by the freedom of this person. Hence it is the *duty* of the government to so restrict the freedom of this person as to make it *impossible* for him to ever again practice such tyranny. Here the duty of the community ceases. It has *no* right to take the life of the individual. That is his own, *inalienably* vested in him, both by *God* and the *Constitution.*

A person may also appropriate the property of another if he so choose, and there is no way to prevent it; but once having thus invaded the rights of another, the whole community is in danger from the propensity of this person. It is therefore the duty of government to so restrain the liberty of the person as to prevent him from invading the spheres of other persons in a manner against which he himself demands, and is entitled to, protection.

The same rule applies to that class of persons who have a propensity to steal or to destroy the character of others. This calls of encroachers upon others' rights, in some senses, are *more* reprehensible than any other, save only those who invade the rights of life; since for persons to be made to appear what they are not may, perhaps, be to place them in such relations with third persons as to destroy their means of pursuing happiness. Those who thus invade the pursuit of happiness by others, should be held to be the *worst* enemies of society; proportionably worse than the common burglar or thief, as what they destroy is more valuable than is that which the burglar or thief can appropriate. For robbery there may be *some* excuse, since what is stolen may be required to contribute to actual needs; but that which the assassin of character appropriates does *neither* good to himself nor to *any one else,* and makes the loser poor indeed. Such persons are the worst enemies of society.

I have been thus explicit in the analysis of the principles of freedom in their application to the common affairs of life, because I desired, before approaching the main subject, to have it *well settled* as to what may justly be considered the rights of individuals; or in other words what individual sovereignty implies.

It would be considered a very unjust and arbitrary, as well as an unwise thing, if the government of the United States were to pass a law compelling persons to adhere during life to everything they should to-day accept as their religion, their politics and their vocations. It would *manifestly* be a departure from the true functions of government. The apology for what I claim to be an invasion of the rights of the individual is found in the law to enforce contracts. While the enforcement of contracts in which *pecuniary* considerations are involved is a matter distinct and different from that of the enforcement of contracts involving the happiness of individuals, *even in them* the government has *no* legitimate right to interfere. The logical deduction of the right of two people to *make* a contract without consulting the government, or any third party, is the right of *either or both* of the parties to *withdraw* without consulting any third party, either in reference to its enforcement or as to damages.

As has been stated, such an arrangement is the result of the exercise of the right of two or more individuals to unite their rights, perfectly independent of every outside party. There is neither right nor duty beyond the uniting—the contracting—individuals. So neither can there be an appeal to a third party to settle any difference which may arise between such parties. All such contracts have their legitimate basis and security in the honor and purposes of the contracting parties. It seems to me that, admitting our theory of government, no proposition can be plainer than is this, notwithstanding the practice is entirely different. But I am now discussing the abstract principles of the rights of freedom, which no practice that may be in vogue must be permitted to deter us from following to legitimate conclusions.

In all general contracts, people have the protection of government in contracting for an hour, a *day*, a *week*, a *year*, a *decade, or* a life, and *neither* the government nor *any other third* party *or* person, or *aggregates* of persons ever *think* of making a scale of respectability, graduated by the length of time for which the contracts are made and maintained. *Least of all* does the government require that any of these contracts shall be entered into for life. Why should the social relations of the sexes be made subject to a different theory? All enacted laws that are for the purpose of perpetuating conditions which are themselves the results of evolution are so many obstructions in the path of progress; since if an effect attained to-day is made the ultimate, progress stops. "Thus far shalt thou go, and no farther," is *not* the adage of a progressive age like the present. Besides, there can be no general law made to determine what individual cases demand, since a variety of conditions cannot be subject to one and the same rule of operation. Here we arrive at the most important of all facts relating to human needs and experiences: That while every human being has a distinct individuality, and is entitled to all the rights of a sovereign over it, it is not taken into the consideration that *no* two of these individualities are made up of the self-same powers and experiences, and therefore cannot be governed by the *same* law to the *same* purposes.

I would recall the attention of all objecting egotists, Pharisees and would-be regulators of society to the true functions of government—to protect the complete exercise of individual rights, and what they are no living soul except the individual has any business to determine or to meddle with, in *any* way whatever, unless his own rights are first infringed.

If a person believe that a certain theory is a truth, and consequently the right thing to advocate and practice, but from its being unpopular or against established public opinion does not have the moral courage to advocate or practice it, *that* person is a *moral coward* and a *traitor* to his own conscience, which God gave for a guide and guard.

What I believe to be the truth I endeavor to practice, and, in advocating it, permit me to say I shall *speak* so *plainly* that *none* may complain that I did not make myself understood.

The world has come up to the present time through the outworking of religious, political, philosophical and scientific principles, and today we stand upon the *threshold* of *greater* discoveries in more *important* things than have ever interested the intellect of man. We have arrived where the very *foundation* of all that *has* been must be analyzed and understood—and this foundation is the relation of the sexes. These are the bases of society—the very last to secure attention, because the most comprehensive of subjects.

All other departments of inquiry which have their fountain in society have been formulated into *special* sciences, and made legitimate and popular subjects for investigation; but the science of *society itself* has been, and still is, held to be too sacred a thing for science to lay its rude hands upon. But of the relations of science to society we may say the same that has been said of the relations of science to religion: "That religion has always wanted to do good, and now science is going to tell it how to do it."

Over the sexual relations, marriages have endeavored to preserve sway to hold the people in subjection to what has been considered a standard of moral purity. Whether this has been successful or not may be determined from the fact that there are *scores of thousands* of *women* who are denominated prostitutes, and who are supported by *hundreds of thousands* of *men* who should, for like reasons, also be denominated prostitutes, since what will change a woman into a prostitute must also necessarily change a man into the same.

This condition, called prostitution, seems to be the *great evil* at which religion and public morality hurl their *special* weapons of condemnation, as the sum total of all diabolism; since for a woman to be a prostitute is to deny her not only all Christian, but also all humanitarian rights.

But let us inquire into this matter, to see just what it is; not in the vulgar or popular, or even legal sense, but in purely *scientific* and *truly moral* sense.

It must be remembered that we are seeking after truth for the *sake* of the truth, and in utter disregard of *everything* except the truth; that is to say, we are seeking for the truth, "let it be what it may and lead where it may." To illustrate, I would say the extremest thing possible. If blank materialism were true, it would be best for the world to know it.

If there by any who are not in harmony with this desire, then such have nothing to do with what I have to say, for it will be said regardless of antiquated forms or fossilized dogmas, but in the *simplest* and *least* offending language that I can choose.

If there is *anything* in the whole universe that should enlist the *earnest* attention of *everybody,* and their support and advocacy to secure it, it is that upon which the true welfare and happiness of everybody depends. Now to what more than to anything else do humanity owe their welfare and happiness? Most clearly to being born into earthly existence with a sound and perfect physical, mental and moral beginning of life, with no taint or disease attaching to them, either mentally, morally or physically. To *be so* born involves the harmony of conditions which will produce such results. *To have* such conditions involves the existence of such relations of the sexes as will in themselves produce them.

Now I will put the question direct. Are not these *eminently* proper subjects for inquiry and discussion, not in that manner of maudlin sentimentality in which it *has been* the habit, but in a *dignified, open, honest* and *fearless* way, in which subjects of so great importance should be inquired into and discussed?

An *exhaustive* treatment of these subjects would involve the inquiry what should be the *chief* end to be gained by entering into sexual relations. This I must simply answer by saying, "Good children, who will not need to be regenerated," and pass to the consideration of the relations themselves.

All the relations between the sexes that are recognized as *legitimate* are denominated marriage. *But of what does marriage consist?* This very pertinent question requires settlement before any real progress can be made as to what Social Freedom and Prostitution mean. It is admitted by everybody that marriage is a union of the opposites in sex, but is it a principle of nature outside of all law, or is it a law outside of all nature? Where is the point before reaching which it is not marriage, but having reached which it is marriage? Is it where two meet and realize that the love elements of their nature are harmonious, and that they blend into and make *one* purpose of life? or is it where a *soulless form* is pronounced over two who know *no* commingling of life's hopes? Or are *both* these processes required—first, the marriage union *without* the law, to be afterward solemnized *by* the law? If *both* terms are required, does the marriage continue after the *first* departs? or if the *restrictions* of the law are removed and the *love* continues, does *marriage* continue? or if the law unite two who *hate* each other, is that marriage? Thus are presented all the possible aspects of the case.

The *courts* hold if the law solemnly pronounce two married, *that they are* married, whether love is present or not. But is this really such a marriage as this enlightened age should demand? No! It is a stupidly arbitrary law, which can find no analogies in nature. Nature proclaims in *broadest terms,* and all her subjects re-echo the same *grand* truth, that sexual unions, which result in reproduction, are marriage. And sex exists wherever there is reproduction.

By analogy, the same law ascends into the sphere of and applies among men and women; for are not they a part and parcel of nature in which this law exists as a principle? This law of nature by which men and women are united by love is God's marriage law, the enactments of men to the contrary notwithstanding. And the precise results of this marriage will be determined by the character of those united; all the experiences evolved from the marriage being the legitimate sequences thereof.

Marriage must consist either of love or of law, since it *may* exist in form with either term absent; that is to say, people may be married by *law* and all love be lacking; and they may also be married by *love* and lack all sanction of law. True marriage must in reality consist entirely either of law or love, since there can be *no* compromise between the law of nature and *statute* law by which the former shall yield to the latter.

Law cannot change what nature has already determined. Neither will love obey if law command. Law cannot compel two to love. It has nothing to do either *with* love or with its absence. Love is superior to all law, and so also is hate, indifference, disgust and all other human sentiments which are evoked in the relations of the sexes. It legitimately and logically follows, if *love* have *anything* to do with marriage, that *law* has *nothing* to do with it. And on the contrary, if *law* have anything to do with marriage, that *love* has nothing to do with it. And there is no escaping the deduction.

If the test of the rights of the individual be applied to determine which of these propositions is the true one, what will be the result?

Two persons, a male and a female, meet, and are drawn together by a *mutual* attraction—a *natural* feeling unconsciously arising within their natures of which *neither* has any control—which is denominated love. This is a matter that concerns *these two,* and *no* other living soul has *any* *human* right to say aye, yes or no, since it is a matter in which none except the two have any right to be involved, and from which it is the duty of these two to exclude every other person, since no one can love for another or determine why another loves.

If true, mutual, natural attraction be sufficiently strong to be the *dominant* power, then it decides marriage; and if it be so decided, no law which may be in force can *any more* prevent the union than a *human* law could prevent the transformation of water into vapor, or the confluence of two streams; and for *percisely* the same reasons: that it is a *natural* law which is obeyed; which law is as *high above human law* as perfection is high above imperfection. They marry and obey this higher law than man can make—a law as old as the universe and as immortal as the elements, and for which there is no substitute.

They are sexually united, to be which is to be married by nature, and to be thus married is to be united by God. This marriage is performed without special mental volition upon the part of either, although the intellect *may* approve what the affections determine; that is to say, they marry because they love, and they love because they can neither *prevent* nor *assist* it. Suppose after this marriage has continued an indefinite time, the *unity* between them departs, could they any more prevent it than they can prevent the love? It *came* without their bidding, may it not also *go* without their bidding? And if it go, does not the marriage cease, and should any third persons or parties, either as *individuals* or as *government,* attempt to compel the *continuance* of a unity wherein *none* of the elements of the union remain?

At no point in the process designated has there been *any* other than an exercise of the right of the two individuals to pursue happiness in their *own* way, *which* way has neither *crossed* nor interfered with *any one else's* right to the *same* pursuit; therefore, there is *no* call for a law to change, modify, protect or punish this exercise. It must be concluded, then, if individuals have the Constitutional right to pursue happiness in their *own* way, that all compelling laws of marriage and divorce are despotic, being *remnants* of the barbaric ages in which they were originated, and *utterly unfitted* for an age so *advanced* upon that, and so *enlightened* in the general principles of freedom and equality, as is this.

It must be remembered that it is the sphere of government to perform the *duties* which are required of it by the people, and that it has, in itself, no rights to exercise. These belong *exclusively* to the people whom it represents. It is *one* of the rights of a citizen to have a voice in determining what the duties of government shall be, and also provide how that right may be exercised; but government should not *prohibit* any right.

To love is a right *higher* than Constitutions or laws. It is a right which Constitutions and laws can *neither give* nor take, and with which they have nothing whatever to do, since in its *very* nature it is forever independent of both Constitutions and laws, and exists—comes and goes—in *spite* of them. Governments might just as well assume to determine how people shall exercise their right to *think* or to say that they shall not think at all, as to assume to determine that they shall not love, or how they may love, or that they shall love.

The proper sphere of government in regard to the relations of the sexes, is to enact such laws as in the present conditions of society are necessary to *protect each* individual in the *free* exercise of his or her *right* to love, and also to protect each individual from the forced interference of *every other* person, that would compel him or her to submit to *any* action which is against their *wish* and *will.* If the law do this it fulfills its duty. If the law do not afford this protection, *and worse still,* if it *sanction* this *interference* with the rights of an individual, then it is *infamous* law and worthy only of the *old-time* despotism; since individual tyranny forms *no* part of the guarantee of, or the right to, individual freedom.

It is therefore a strictly legitimate conclusion that where there is *no* love as a basis of marriage there should be *no* marriage, and if that which was the *basis* of a marriage is taken away that the *marriage* also ceases from that time, statute laws to the contrary notwithstanding.

Such is the character of the law that permeates nature from simplest organic forms—units of nucleated protoplasm to the most complex aggregation thereof—the human form. Having determined that marriage consists of a union resulting from love, without any regard whatever to the sanction of law, and consequently that the sexual relations resulting therefrom are strictly legitimate and natural, it is a very simple matter to determine what part of the sexual relations which are maintained are prostitutions of the relations.

It is certain by this Higher Law, that mariages of convenience, and, still more, marriages characterized by mutual or partial repugnance, are adulterous. And it does not matter whether the repugnance arises before or subsequently to the marriage ceremony. Compulsion, whether of the law or of a false public opinion, is detestable, as an element even, in the regulation of the most tender and important of all human relations.

I do not care where it is that sexual commerce results from the dominant power of *one sex* over *the other,* compelling him or her to submission against the *instincts of love,* and where hate or disgust is present, whether it be in the gilded palaces of Fifth avenue or in the lowest purlieus of Greene street, *there* is prositution, and *all* the law that a *thousand* State Assemblies may pass cannot make it otherwise.

I know whereof I speak; I have seen the most *damning* misery resulting from legalized prostitution. Misery such as the most degraded of those against whom society has shut her doors never know. Thousands of poor, weak, unresisting wives are yearly murdered, who stand in spirit-life looking down upon the sickly, half made-up children left behind, imploring humanity for the sake of honor and virtue to look into this matter, to look into it to the very bottom, and bring out into the fair daylight all the blackened, sickening deformities that have so long been hidden by the screen of public opinion and a sham morality.

It does not matter how much it may still be attempted to *gloss* these things over and to *label* them sound and pure; you, each and every one of you, *know* that what I say is truth, and if you question your own souls you *dare* not reply: it is not so. If these things to which I refer, but of which I shudder to think, are not abuses of the sexual relations, what are?

You may or may not think there is help for them, but I say Heaven help us if *such* barbarism cannot be cured.

I would not be understood to say that there are no good conditions in the present marriage state. By no means do I say this; on the contrary, a very large proportion of present social relations are commendable—are as good as the present status of society makes possible. But what I *do* assert, and that most *positively,* is, that *all* which *is* good and commendable, now existing, would *continue* to exist if all marriage laws were repealed to-morrow. Do you not perceive that law has nothing to do in continuing the relations which are based upon continuous love? These are not results of the law to which, perhaps, their subjects yielded a willing or unwilling obedience. Such relations exist in *spite* of the law; would have existed *had there been* no law, and would continue to exist were the law *annulled*.

It is not of the *good* there is in the present condition of marriage that I complain, but of the *ill,* nearly the *whole* of which is the *direct* result of the law which continues the relations in which it exists. It seems to be the general argument that if the law of marriage were annulled it would follow that *everybody* must necessarily separate, and that all *present family* relations would be sundered, and complete anarchy result therefrom. Now, whoever makes that argument either does so thoughtlessly or else he is dishonest; since if he make it after having given any consideration thereto, he must know it to be false. And if he have given it no consideration then is he no proper judge. I give it as my opinion, founded upon an extensive knowledge of, and intimate acquaintance with, married people, if marriage laws were repealed that less than a *fourth* of those now married would immediately separate, and that *one-half* of these would return to their allegiance *voluntarily* within *one* year; only those who, under every consideration of virtue and good, should be separate, would permanently remain separated. And objectors as well as I know it would be so. I assert that it is *false* to assume that chaos would result from the abrogation of marriage laws, and on the contrary affirm that *from that very hour* the *chaos* now existing would *begin* to turn into order and harmony. What then creates social disorder? Very clearly, the attempt to exercise powers over human rights which are not warrantable upon the hypothesis of the existence of human rights which are inalienable in, and sacred to, the individual.

It is true there is no *enacted* law compelling people to marry, and it is therefore *argued* that if they *do* marry they should always be compelled to abide thereby. But there is a law *higher* than any human enactments which does compel marriage—the law of nature—the law of God. There being this law in the constitution of humanity, which, operating freely, guarantees marriage, why should men enforce arbitrary rules and forms? These, though having no virtue in themselves, if not complied with by men and women, they in the meantime obeying the law of their nature, bring down upon them the condemnations of an interfering community. Should people, then, voluntarily entering legal marriage be held thereby "till death do them part?" Most *emphatically* NO, if the desire to do so do not remain. How can people who enter upon marriage in utter *ignorance* of that which is to render the union happy or miserable be able to say that they will always "love and live together." They may take these vows upon them in perfect good faith and repent of them in sackcloth and ashes within a twelve-month.

I think it will be generally conceded that without love there should be no marriage. In the constitution of things *nothing* can be more certain. This basic fact is fatal to the theory of marriage for life: since if love is what *determines* marriages, so, also, should it determine its continuance. If it be primarily right of men and women to take on the marriage relation of their own free will and accord, *so,* too, does it remain their right to determine *how* long it shall continue and when it shall cease. But to be respectable (?) people must comply with the law, and thousands do comply therewith, while in their hearts they protest against it as an unwarrantable interference and proscription of their rights. Marriage laws that would be consistent with the theory of individual rights would be such as would *regulate* these relations, such as regulate *all other* associations of people. They should only be obliged to file marriage articles, containing whatever provisions may be agreed upon, as to their personal rights, rights of property, of children, or whatever else they may deem proper for them to agree upon. And whatever these articles might be, they should in all cases be equally entitled to public respect and protection. Should separation afterward come, nothing more should be required than the simple filing of counter articles.

There are hundreds of lawyers who subsist by inventing schemes by which people may *obtain* divorces, and the people *desiring* divorces resort to *all sorts* of tricks and crimes to get them. And *all this* exists because there are laws which would *compel* the *oneness* of those to whom *unity* is beyond the realm of possibility. There are another class of persons who, while virtually divorced, endeavor to maintain a respectable position in society, by *agreeing* to *disagree,* each following his and her individual ways, behind the cloak of legal marriage. Thus there are *hundreds* of men and women who to *external* appearances are husband and wife, but in reality are husband or wife to quite different persons.

If the conditions of society were completely analyzed, it would be found that *all* persons whom the law holds married against their wishes find *some* way to *evade* the law and to live the life they desire. Of what use, then, is the law except to make *hypocrites* and *pretenders* of a sham respectability?

But, exclaims a very fastidious person, then you would have all women become prostitutes! By *no means* would I have *any* woman become a prostitute. But if by nature women *are* so, *all* the *virtue* they possess being of the *legal* kind, and not that which should exist with or without law, *then* I say they will not become prostitutes because the law is repealed, since at heart they are already so. If there is no virtue, no honesty, no purity, no trust among women except as created by the *law,* I say heaven help our morality, for nothing human can help it.

It seems to me that no grosser insult could be offered to woman than to insinuate that she is honest and virtuous only because the law compels her to be so; and little do men and women realize the obloquy thus cast upon society, and still less do women realize what they admit of their sex by such assertions. I honor and worship that purity which exists in the soul of every noble man or woman, while I pity the woman who is virtuous simply because a law compels her.

But, says another objector, though the repeal of marriage laws might operate well enough in all those cases where a *mutual* love or hate would determine *continuous* marriage or *immediate* divorce, how can a third class of cases be justified, in which but *one* of the parties desire the separation, while the other clings to the unity?

I assume, in the first place, when there is not mutual love there is no union to continue and nothing to justify, and it has already been determined that, as marriage should have love as a basis, if love depart marriage also departs. But laying this aside, see if there can any real good or happiness possibly result from an enforced continuance of marriage upon the part of one party thereto. Let all persons take this question home to their own souls, and there determine if they could find happiness in holding unwilling hearts in bondage. It is *against* the *nature of things* that *any* satisfaction can result from such a state of things except it be the satisfaction of knowing that you have succeeded in virtually imprisoning the person whom you *profess* to love, and that would be demoniacal.

Again. It must be remembered that the individual affairs of two persons are not the subject of interference by any third party, and if one of them choose to separate, there is no power outside of the two which can rightly interfere to prevent. Beside, who is to determine whether there will be more happiness sacrificed by a *continuation* or a *separation.* If a person is *fully* determined to separate, it is proof positive that another feeling *stronger* than all his or her sentiments of duty determine it. And here, again, *who* but the individual is to determine which course will secure the most good? Suppose that a separation is desired because one of the two loves and is loved elsewhere. In this case, if the union be maintained by force, at least *two* of three, and, probably, *all three* persons will be made unhappy thereby; whereas if separation come and the other union be consummated, there will be but one, unhappy. So even here, if the greatest good of the greatest number is to rule, separation is not only legitimate, *but* desirable. In all other things except marriage it is always held to be the right thing to do to *break* a *bad bargain* or *promise* just as soon as possible, and I hold that of *all things* in which this rule should apply, it should *first* apply to marriages.

Now, let me ask, would it not rather be the *Christian* way, in such cases, to say to the disaffected party: "Since you no longer love me, go your way and be happy, and make those to whom you go happy also." I know of no higher, holier love than that described, and of no more beautiful expression of it than was given in the columns of the *Woman's Journal,* of Boston, whose conductors have felt called upon to endeavor to convince the people that it has no affiliation with those who hold to no more radical doctrine of Free Love than they proclaim as follows:

"The love that I cannot command is not mine; let me not disturb myself about it, nor attempt to filch it from its rightful owner. A heart that I supposed mine has drifted and gone. Shall I go in pursuit? Shall I forcibly capture the truant and transfix it with the barb of my selfish affections, pin it to the wall of my chamber? God forbid! Rather let me leave my doors and windows open, intent only on living so nobly that the best cannot fail to be drawn to me by an irresistible attraction."

To me it is impossible to frame words into sentences *more holy, pure* and true than are these. I would ever carry them in my soul as my guide and guard, feeling that in *living* by them happiness would certainly be mine. To the loving wife who mourns a lost heart, let me recommend them as a panacea. To the loving husband whose soul is desolate, let me offer these as words of healing balm. They will live in history, to make their writer the *loved* and *revered* of unborn generations.

The tenth commandment of the Decalogue says: "Thou shalt not covet thy neighbor's wife." And Jesus, in the beautiful parable of the Samaritan who fell among thieves, asks: "Who is thy neighbor?" and answers his own question in a way to lift the conception wholly out of the category of mere local proximity into a sublime spiritual conception. In other words, he spiritualizes the word and sublimates the morality of the commandment. In the same spirit I ask now, Who is *a wife?* And I answer, not the woman who, ignorant of her own feelings, or with lying lips, has promised, in hollow ceremonial, and before the law, to love, but *she who really loves most,* and *most truly,* the man who commands her affections, and who in turn loves her, with or without the ceremony of marriage; and the man who holds the heart of such a woman in such a relation is "thy *neighbor,*" and *that woman is "thy neighbor's wife" meant in the commandment;* and whosoever, though he should have been a hundred times married to her by the law, shall claim, or *covet* even, the possession of that woman as against her true lover and husband in the spirit, sins against the commandment.

We know positively that Jesus would have answered in that way. He has defined for us "the neighbor," not in the paltry and commonplace sense, but spiritually. He has said: "He that looketh on a woman to lust after her hath committed adultery with her already in his heart." So, therefore, he spiritualized the idea of adultery. In the kingdom of heaven, to be prayed for daily, to come on earth, there is to be no "marrying or giving in marriage;" that is to say, formally and legally; but spiritual marriage must always exist, and had Jesus been called on to define a wife, can anybody doubt that he would, in the same spirit, the spiritualizing tendency and character of all his doctrine, have spiritualized the marriage relation as absolutely as he did the breach of it? that he would, in other words, have said in meaning precisely what I now say? And when Christian ministers are no longer afraid or ashamed *to be Christians* they will embrace this doctrine. Free Love will be an integral part of the religion of the future.

It can now be asked: What is the legitimate sequence of Social Freedom? To which I unhesitatingly reply: Free Love, or freedom of the affections. "And are you a Free Lover?" is the almost incredulous query.

I repeat a frequent reply: "I am; and I can honestly, in the fullness of my soul, raise my voice to my Maker, and thank Him that *I am,* and that I have had the strength and the devotion to truth to stand before this traducing and vilifying community in a manner representative of that which shall come with healing on its wings for the bruised hearts and crushed affections of humanity."

And to those who denounce me for this I reply: "Yes, I am a Free Lover. I have an *inalienable, constitutional* and *natural* right to love whom I may, to love as *long* or as *short* a period as I can; to *change* that love *every day* if I please, and with *that* right neither *you* nor any *law* you can frame have *any* right to interfere. And I have the *further* right to demand a free and unrestricted exercise of that right, and it is *your duty* not only to *accord* it, but, as a community, to see that I am protected in it. I trust that I am fully understood, for I mean *just* that, and nothing less!"

To speak thus plainly and pointedly is a *duty I owe* to myself. The press have stigmatized me to the world as an advocate, theoretically and practically, of the doctrine of Free Love, upon which they have placed their stamp of moral deformity; the vulgar and inconsequent definition which they hold makes the theory an abomination. And though this conclusion is a no more legitimate and reasonable one than that would be which should call the Golden Rule a general license to all sorts of debauch, since Free Love bears the *same* relations to the moral deformities of which it stands accused as does the Golden Rule to the Law of the Despot, yet it obtains among many intelligent people. But they claim, in the language of one of these exponents, that "Words belong to the people; they are the common property of the mob. Now the common use, among the mob, of the term Free Love, is a synonym for promiscuity." Against this absurd proposition I oppose the assertion that words *do not* belong to the mob, but to that which they represent. Words are the exponents and interpretations of ideas. If I use a word which exactly interprets and represents what I would be understood to mean, shall I go to the *mob* and *ask* of *them* what interpretation *they* choose to place upon it? If lexicographers, when they prepare their dictionaries, were to go to the mob for the rendition of words, what kind of language would we have?

I claim that freedom means *to be free,* let the mob claim to the contrary as strenuously as they may. And I claim that love means an exhibition of the affections, let the mob claim what they may. And therefore, in compounding these words into Free Love, I claim that united they mean, and should be used to convey, their united definitions, the mob to the contrary notwithstanding. And when the term Free Love finds a place in dictionaries, it will prove my claim to have been correct, and that the mob have not received the attention of the lexicographers, since it will not be set down to signify sexual debauchery, and that only, or in any governing sense.

It is not only usual but also just, when people adopt a new theory, or promulgate a new doctrine, that they give it a name significant of its character. There are, however, exceptional cases to be found in all ages. The Jews coined the name of Christians, and, with withering contempt, hurled it upon the early followers of Christ. It was the most opprobrious epithet they could invent to express their detestation of those humble but honest and brave people. That name has now come to be considered as a synonym of all that is good, true and beautiful in the highest departments of our natures, and is revered in all civilized nations.

In precisely the same manner the Pharisees of to-day, who hold themselves to be representative of all there is that is good and pure, as did the Pharisees of old, have coined the word Free-Love, and flung it upon all who believe not alone in Religious and Political Freedom, but in that larger Freedom, which includes both these, Social Freedom.

For my part, I am extremely obliged to our thoughtful Pharisaical neighbors for the kindness shown us in the invention of so appropriate a name. If there is a more beautiful word in the English language than *love,* that word is *freedom,* and that *these two* words, which, with us, attach or belong to *everything* that is pure and good, should have been *joined* by our enemies, and *handed* over to us *already* coined, is certainly a high consideration, for which we should never cease to be thankful. And when we shall be accused of all sorts of wickedness and vileness by our enemies, who in this have been so just, may I not hope that, remembering how much they have done for us, we may be able to say, "Father, forgive them, for they know not what they do," and to forgive them ourselves with our whole hearts.

Of the love that says: "Bless *me,* darling;" of the love so called, which is nothing but selfishness, the appropriation of another soul as the means of one's own happiness merely, there is abundance in the world; and the still more animal, the mere desire for temporary gratification, with little worthy the name of love, also abounds. Even these are best left free, since as evils they will thus be best cured; but of that celestial love which says: "Bless *you,* darling," and which strives continually to confer blessings; of that genuine love whose office it is to bless others or another, there cannot be too much in the world, and when it shall be fully understood that this is the love which we mean and commend there will be no objection to the term Free Love, and none to the thing signified.

We not only *accept* our name, but we contend that *none* other could so well signify the *real* character of that which it designates—to be free and to love. But our enemies must be reminded that the fact of the existence and advocacy of such a doctrine cannot immediately elevate to high condition the great number who have been kept in degradation and misery by previous false systems. They must *not expect* at this early day of the new doctrine, that all debauchery has been cleansed out of men and women. In the haunts where it retreats, the benign influence of its magic presence has not yet penetrated. They must *not expect* that brutish men and debased women have as yet been touched by its wand of hope, and that they have already obeyed the bidding to come up higher. They must *not expect* that ignorance and fleshly lust have already been lifted to the region of intellect and moral purity. They must *not expect* that Free Love, before it is more than barely announced to the world, can perform what Christianity in eighteen hundred years has failed to do.

They must *not expect any* of these things have already been accomplished, but I will *tell* you what they *may* expect. They may expect *more* good to result from the perfect freedom which we advocate in *one century* than has resulted in a hundred centuries from all other causes, since the results will be in exact proportion to the extended application of the freedom. We have a legitimate right to predicate such results, since *all* freedom that has been practiced in *all* ages of the world has been beneficial *just* in proportion to the extent of human nature it covered.

Will any of you dare to stand up and assert that Religious Freedom ever produced a *single bad* result? or that Political Freedom *ever* injured a *single* soul who embraced and practiced it? If you can do so, then you may legitimately assert that Social Freedom *may* also produce *equally* bad results, but you cannot do otherwise, and be either conscientious or honest.

It is *too late* in the age for intelligent people to cry out *thief,* unless they have first been robbed, and it is equally late for them to succeed in crying down *anything* as of the devil to which a name attaches that angels love. It may be very proper and legitimate, and withal perfectly consistent, for philosophers of the *Tribune* school to bundle all the murderers, robbers and rascals together, and hand them over to our camp, labeled as Free Lovers. We will only object that they ought to hand the whole of humanity over, good, bad and indifferent, and not assort its worst representatives.

My friends, you see this thing we call Freedom is a large word, implying a deal more than people have ever yet been able to recognize. It reaches out its all-embracing arms, and while encircling our good friends and neighbors, does not neglect to also include their less worthy brothers and sisters, every one of whom is just as much entitled to the use of his freedom as is either one of us.

But objectors tell us that freedom is a dangerous thing to have, and that they must be its conservators, dealing it out to such people, and upon such matters, as they shall appoint. Having coined our name, they straightway proceed to define it, and to give force to their definition, set about citing illustrations to prove not only their definition to be a true one, but also that its application is just.

Among the cases cited as evidences of the evil tendencies of Free Love are those of Richardson and Crittenden. The celebrated McFarland-Richardson case was heralded world-wide as a case of this sort. So far as Richardson and Mrs. McFarland were concerned, I have every reason to believe it was a genuine one, in so far as the preventing obstacles framed by the "conservators" would permit. But when they assert that the murder of Richardson by McFarland was the *legitimate result* of Free Love, then I deny it *in toto.* McFarland murdered Richardson because he believed that the law had sold Abby Sage *soul* and *body* to him, and, consequently, that he *owned* her, and that *no* other person had *any* right to her favor, and that she had *no* right to bestow her love upon any other person, unless *that ownership* was first satisfied. The murder of Richardson, then, is not chargeable to his love or her love, but to the fact of the supposed ownership, which right of possession the law of marriage conferred on McFarland.

If anything further is needed to make the refutation of that charge clear, I will give it by illustration. Suppose that a pagan should be converted to Christianity through the efforts of some Christian minister, and that the remaining pagans should *kill* that minister for what he had done, would the crime be chargeable upon the Christian religion? Will any of you make that assertion? If not, neither can you charge that the death of Richardson should be charged to Free Love. But a more *recent* case is a still *clearer* proof of the correctness of my position. Mrs. Fair killed Crittenden. Why? Because she believed in the spirit of the marriage law; that she had a *better right* to him than had Mrs. Crittenden, to whom the law had granted him; and rather than to give him up to her, to whom he evidently desired to go, and where, following his right to freedom, he *did* go, she killed him. Could a more *perfect* case of the *spirit* of the marriage law be formulated? Most assuredly, no!

Now, from the standpoint of marriage, reverse this case to that of Free Love, and see what would have been the result had all those parties been believers in and practicers of that theory. When Mr. Crittenden evinced a desire to return to Mrs. Crittenden, Mrs. Fair, in practicing the doctrine of Free Love, would have said, "I have no right to you, other than you freely give; you loved me and exercised your right of freedom in so doing. You now desire to return to Mrs. Crittenden, which is equally your right, and which I must respect. Go, and in peace, and my blessing shall follow, and if it can return you to happiness, then will you be happy."

Would not *that* have been the *better,* the *Christian* course, and would not every soul in the broad land capable of a noble impulse, and having knowledge of all the relevant facts, have *honored* Mrs. Fair for it? Instead of a murder, with the probability of another to complement it, would not *all* parties have been *happy* in having done right? Would not Mrs. Crittenden have even *loved* Mrs. Fair for such an example of nobility, and could she not *safely* have received her even into her own heart and home, and have been a *sister* to her, instead of the means of her conviction of murder?

I tell you, my friends and my foes, that you have taken hold of the *wrong* end of this business. You are shouldering upon Free Love the results that flow from precisely its antithesis, which is the spirit, if not the letter, of your marriage theory, which is slavery, and not freedom.

I have a better right to speak, as one having authority in this matter, than most of you have, since it has been my province to study it in all its various lights and shades. When I practiced clairvoyance, *hundreds,* aye thousands, of desolate, heart-broken men, as well as women, came to me for advice. And they were from all walks of life, from the humblest daily laborer to the haughtiest dame of wealth. The tales of horror, of wrongs inflicted and endured, which were poured into my ears, first awakened me to a realization of the hollowness and the rottenness of society, and compelled me to consider whether laws which were prolific of so *much* crime and misery as I found to exist should be continued; and to ask the question whether it were not *better* to let the bond go free. In time I was fully convinced that marriage laws were productive of precisely the *reverse* of that for which they are supposed to have been framed, and I came to recommend the grant of entire freedom to those who were complained of as inconstant; and the frank asking for it by those who desired it. My *invariable* advice was: "Withdraw lovingly, but completely, all claim and all complaint as an injured and deserted husband or wife. You need not perhaps disguise the fact that you suffer keenly from it, but take on yourself all the fault that you have not been able to command a more continuous love; that you have not proved to be *all* that you once seemed to be. Show magnanimity, and in order to *show* it, try to *feel* it. Cultivate that kind of love which loves the happiness and well-being of your partner *most,* his or her person next, and yourself last. Be kind to, and sympathize with, the new attraction rather than waspish and indignant. Know for a certainty that love *cannot* be clutched or gained by being *fought* for; while it is not *impossible* that it may be won back by the nobility of one's own deportment. If it cannot be, then it is gone forever, and you must make the best of it and reconcile yourself to it, and do the next best thing—you may perhaps continue to *hold on* to a slave, but you have *lost* a lover."

Some may indeed think if I can keep the *semblance* of a husband or wife, even if it be not a lover, *better still* that it be so. Such is not my philosophy or my faith, and for such I have no advice to give. I address myself to such as have *souls,* and whose souls are in question; if you belong to the other sort, take advice of a Tombs lawyer and not of me. I have seen a *few* instances of the most magnanimous action among the persons involved in a knot of love, and with the most angelic results. I believe that the love which goes forth to bless, and if it be to *surrender* in order to bless, is love in the *true* sense, and that it tends greatly to beget love, and that the love which is demanding, thinking only of self, is not love.

I have learned that the first *great* error most married people commit is in endeavoring to *hide* from each other the little irregularities into which all are liable to fall. *Nothing* is so conducive to continuous happiness as mutual confidence. In *whom,* if not in the husband or the wife, should one confide? Should they not be each other's *best* friends, *never* failing in time of anxiety, trouble and temptation to give disinterested and unselfish counsel? From such a perfect confidence as I would have men and women cultivate, it is *impossible* that bad or wrong should flow. On the contrary, it is the *only* condition in which love and happiness can go hand in hand. It is the *only* practice that can insure continuous respect, without which love withers and dies out. Can you not see that in mutual confidence and freedom the very *strongest* bonds of love are forged? It is more blessed to grant favors than to demand them, and the blessing is large and prolific of happiness, or small and insignificant in results, just in proportion as the favor granted is large or small. Tried by this rule, the greater the *blessing* or happiness you can confer on your partners, in which your own selfish feelings are not consulted, the greater the satisfaction that will redound to yourself. Think of this mode of adjusting your difficulties, and see what a clear way opens before you. There are none who have once felt the influence of a high order of love, so *callous,* but that they *intuitively* recognize the true grandeur and nobility of such a line of conduct. It must always be remembered that you can never do *right* until you are first free to do *wrong;* since the doing of a thing under *compulsion* is evidence *neither* of good nor bad intent; and if under compulsion, who shall decide what would be the substituted rule of action under full freedom?

In freedom *alone* is there safety and happiness, and when people learn this great fact, they will have just begun to know how to live. Instead then of being the destroying angel of the household, I would become the angel of purification to purge out all insincerity, all deception, all baseness and all vice, and to replace them by honor, confidence and truth.

I know very well that much of the *material* upon which the work must begin is very bad and far gone in decay. But I would have everybody perfectly free to do either right or wrong, according to the highest standard, and if there are those so unfortunate as not to know how to do that which can alone bring happiness, I would treat them as we treat those who are intellectually without culture—who are ignorant and illiterate. There are none so ignorant but they may be taught. So, too, are there none so unfortunate in their understanding of the true and high relation of the sexes as not to be amenable to the right kind of instruction. First of all, however, the would-be teachers of humanity must become truly Christian, meek and lowly in spirit, forgiving and kind in action, and ever ready to do as did Christ to the Magdalen. We are not so greatly different from what the accusing multitude were in that time. But Christians, forgetting the teaching of Christ, condemn and say, "Go on in your sin." Christians must learn to claim *nothing* for themselves that they are unwilling to accord others. They must remember that *all* people endeavor, so far as lies in their power, and so far as it is possible for them to judge, to exercise their human right, or determine what their action shall be, that will bring them most happiness; and instead of being *condemned* and *cast out* of society therefor, they should be *protected* therein, so long as others' rights are not infringed upon. We think they do not do the *best* thing; it is our duty to endeavor to *show* them the better and the higher, and to induce them to walk therein. But because a person chooses to perform an act that *we* think a *bad* one, we have no right to put the brand of excommunication upon him. It is our Christian and brotherly duty to persuade him instead that it is more to his good to do something better next time, at the same time, however, assuring him he only did what he had a right to do.

If our sisters who inhabit Greene street and other filthy localities *choose* to remain in debauch, and if our brothers *choose* to visit them there, they are only exercising the *same* right that we exercise in remaining away, and we have no *more right* to abuse and condemn *them* for exercising their rights that way, than they have to abuse and condemn us for exercising our rights our way. But we have a *duty,* and that is by our love, kindness and sympathy to endeavor to prevail upon them to desert those ways which we feel are so damaging to all that is high and pure and true in the relations of the sexes.

If these are the *stray sheep* from the fold of truth and purity, should we not go out and gather them in, rather than remain within the fold and hold the door shut, lest they should enter in and defile the fold? Nay, my friends, we have only an assumed right to thus sit in judgment over our unfortunate sisters, which is the same right of which men have made use to prevent women from participation in government.

The sin of all time has been the exercise of assumed powers. This is the essence of tyranny. Liberty is a great lesson to learn. It is a great step to vindicate our own freedom. It is more, far more, to learn to leave others free, and free to do just what we perhaps may deem wholly wrong. We must recognize that others have consciences and judgment and rights as well as we, and religiously abstain from the effort to make them better by the use of any means to which we have no right to resort, and to which we cannot resort without abridging the great doctrine, the charter of all our liberties, the doctrine of Human Rights.

But the public press, either in real or affected ignorance of what they speak, denounce Free Love as the justification of, and apologist for, all manner and kind of sexual debauchery, and thus, instead of being the *teachers* of the people, as they *should* be, are the power which inculcates falsehood and wrong. The teachings of Christ, whom so many now profess to imitate, were *direct* and simple upon this point. He was not too good to acknowledge all men as brothers and all women as sisters; it mattered not whether they were highly advanced in knowledge and morals, or if they were of low intellectual and moral culture.

It is seriously to be doubted if any of Christ's disciples, or men equally as good as were they, could gain fellowship in *any* of your Fifth avenue church palaces, since they were nothing more than the *humblest* of fishermen, of no social or mental standing. Nevertheless, they were *quite* good enough for *Christ* to associate with, and *fit* to be appointed by Him to be "fishers of men." The Church seems to have forgotten that good *does* sometimes come out of the Nazareths of the world, and that wisdom *may* fall from the mouths of "babes and sucklings." Quite *too much* of the old pharisaical spirit exists in society to-day to warrant its members' claims, that they are the representatives and followers of Christ. For they are the I-am-holier-than-thou kind of people, who affect to, and to a great extent do, prescribe the standards of public opinion, and who ostracise *everybody* who will not bow to their mandates.

Talk of Freedom, of equality, of justice! I tell you there is scarcely a *thought* put in practice that is *worthy* to be the offspring of those noble words. The *veriest systems of despotism* still reign in *all* matters pertaining to social life. Caste stands as boldly out in this country as it does in political life in the kingdoms of Europe.

It is true that we are obliged to accept the situation *just as it is.* If we accord freedom to all persons we must expect them to make their own best use thereof, and, as I have already said, must protect them in such use until they learn to put it to better uses. But in our predication we must be consistent, and now ask who among you would be *worse* men and women were *all* social laws repealed?

Would you *necessarily* dissolve your present relations, *desert* your dependent husbands—for there are even some of them—and wives and children simply because you have the *right* so to do? You are all trying to deceive yourselves about this matter. Let me ask of husbands if they think there would be fifty thousand women of the town supported by them if their wives were ambitious to have an *equal* number of men of the town to support, and for the same purposes? I tell you, nay! It is because men are held *innocent* of this support, and all the vengeance is visited upon the *victims,* that they have come to have an immunity in their practices.

Until women come to hold men to equal account as they do the women with whom they consort; or until they regard these women as just as respectable as the men who support them, society will remain in its present scale of moral excellence. A man who is well known to have been the constant visitor to these women is accepted into society, and if he be *rich* is eagerly *sought* both by mothers having marriageable daughters and by the daughters themselves. But the women with whom they have consorted are *too vile* to be even acknowledged as worthy of Christian burial, to say nothing of common Christian treatment. I have heard women reply when this difficulty was pressed upon them, "We cannot ostracise *men* as we are compelled to *women,* since we are de-pendent on them for *support.*" Ah! here's the rub. But do you not see that these *other* sisters are *also* dependent upon men for *their* support, and *mainly* so because you render it next to impossible for them to follow any *legitimate* means of livelihood? And are only those who have been fortunate enough to secure *legal* support entitled to live?

When I hear *that* argument advanced, my heart sinks within me at the degraded condition of my sisters. They submit to a degradation simply because they *see no alternative* except self-support, and they see no means for that. To put on the semblance of holiness they cry out against those who, for like reasons, submit to like degradation; the only difference between the two being in a licensed ceremony, and a slip of printed paper costing twenty-five cents and upward.

The good women of one of the interior cities of New York some two years since organized a movement to put down prostitution. They were, by stratagem, to find out who visited houses of prostitution, and then were to ostracise them. They pushed the matter until they found their own husbands, brothers and sons involved, and then suddenly desisted, and nothing has since been heard of the eradication of prostitution in that city. If the same experiment were to be tried in New York the result would be the same. The supporters of prostitution would be found to be those whom women cannot ostracise. The same disability excuses the presence of women in the very home, and I need not tell you that Mormonism is practiced in *other* places beside Utah. But what is the logic of these things? Why, simply this: A woman, be she wife or mistress, who consorts with a man who consorts with *other* women, is equally, with *them and him,* morally responsible, since the receiver is held to be as culpable as the thief.

The false and hollow relations of the sexes are thus resolved into the mere question of the *dependence* of women upon men for support, and women, whether married or single, are supported *by* men because they *are* women and their opposites in sex. I can see no moral difference between a woman who marries and lives with a man because he can provide for her wants, and the woman who is *not* married, but who is provided for at the same price. There is a *legal* difference, to be sure, upon one side of which is set the seal of respectability, but there is no virtue in law. In the *fact* of law, however, is the evidence of the lack of virtue, since if the law be *required* to enforce virtue, its real presence is wanting; and women need to comprehend this truth.

The sexual relation, must be rescued from this *insidious* form of slavery. Women must rise from their position as *ministers* to the passions of men to be their equals. Their entire system of education must be changed. They must be trained to be *like* men, permanent and independent individualities, and not their mere appendages or adjuncts, with them forming but one member of society. They must be the companions of men from *choice, never* from necessity.

It is a libel upon nature and God to say this world is not calculated to make women, equally with men, self-reliant and self-supporting individuals. In present customs, however, this is apparently impossible. There must come a change, and one of the direct steps to it will be found in the newly claimed political equality of women with men. This attained, one degree of subjugation will be removed. Next will come, following equality of right, equality of duty, which includes the duty of self-hood, or independence as an individual. Nature is male and female throughout, and each sex is equally dependent upon nature for sustenance. It is an infamous thing to say a condition of society which requires women to enter into and maintain sexual relations with men is their legitimate method of protecting life. Sexual relations should be the result of entirely different motives than for the purpose of physical support. The *spirit* of the present theory is, that they are entered upon and maintained as a *means* of physical gratification, regardless of the consequences which may result therefrom, and are administered by the dictum of the husband, which is often in direct opposition to the will and wish of the wife. She has *no* control over her own person, having been taught to "submit herself to her husband."

I protest against this form of slavery, I *protest* against the custom which compels women to give the control of their maternal functions over to anybody. It should be *theirs* to determine *when,* and under what circumstances, the greatest of all constructive processes—the formation of an immortal soul—should be begun. It is a *fearful* responsibility with which women are intrusted by nature, and the very *last* thing that they should be compelled to do is to *perform* the office of that responsibility against their will, under improper conditions or by disgusting means.

What can be more terrible than for a delicate, sensitively organized woman to be compelled to endure the presence of a beast in the shape of a man, who knows nothing beyond the blind passion with which he is filled, and to which is often added the delirium of intoxication? You do not need to be informed that here are many persons who, during the acquaintance preceding marriage, preserve a delicacy, tenderness and regard for womanly sensitiveness and modest refinement which are characteristic of true women, thus winning and drawing out their love-nature to the extreme, but who, when the decree has been pronounced which makes them indissolubly theirs, cast all these aside and reveal themselves in their *true* character, as without regard, human or divine, for aught save their own desires. I know I speak the truth, and you too know I speak the truth, when I say that thousands of the most noble, loving-natured women by whom the world was ever blessed, prepared for, and desirous of pouring their whole life into the bond of union, prophesied by marriage, have had all these generous and warm impulses thrust back upon them by the rude monster into which the previous gentleman developed. To these natures thus frosted and stultified in their fresh youth and vigor, life becomes a burden almost too terrible to be borne, and thousands of pallid cheeks, sunken eyes, distorted imaginations and diseased functions testify too directly and truly to leave a shade of doubt as to their real cause. Yet women, in the first instance, and men through them as their mothers, with an ignorant persistence worthy only of the most savage despotism, seem determined that it shall not be investigated; and so upon this voluntary ignorance and willful persistence society builds. It is *high* time, however, that they should be investigated, *high* time that your sisters and daughters should no longer be led to the *altar* like sheep to the shambles, in ignorance of the uncertainties they must inevitably encounter. For it is no slight thing to hazard a life's happiness upon a single act.

I deem it a false and perverse modesty that shuts off discussion, and consequently knowledge, upon *these* subjects. They are *vital,* and I never performed a duty which I felt *more* called upon to perform than I *now* do in denouncing as *barbarous* the ignorance which is allowed to prevail among young women about to enter those relations which, under present customs, as often bring a life-long *misery* as happiness.

Mistakes made in this most important duty of life can never be rectified; a commentary upon the system which of itself is sufficient in the sight of common sense to forever condemn it. In marriage, however, common sense is *dispensed* with, and a *usage* substituted therefor which barbarism has bequeathed us, and which becomes *more* barbarous as the spiritual natures of women gain the ascendancy over the mere material. The former slaves, before realizing that freedom was their God-appointed right, did not feel the *horrors* of their condition. But when, here and there, some among them began to have an *interior* knowledge that they were held in obedience by an *unrighteous power,* they then began to *rebel* in their souls. So, too, is it with women. So long as they knew nothing beyond a blind and servile obedience and perfect self-abnegation to the will and wish of men, they did not rebel; but the time *has* arrived wherein, here and there, a soul is awakened by some terrible ordeal, or some divine inspiration, to the fact that women as much as men are *personalities, responsible* to themselves for the use which they permit to be made of themselves, and they rebel demanding freedom, freedom to hold their own lives and bodies from the demoralizing influence of sexual relations that are not founded in and maintained by love. And this rebellion will continue, too, until love, unshackled, shall be free to go to bless the object that can call it forth, and until, when called forth, it shall be respected as holy, pure and true. Every day *farther* and wider does it spread, and *bolder* does it speak. None *too soon* will the yoke fall by which the unwilling are made to render a hypocritical obedience to the despotism of public opinion, which, distorted and blinded by a sham sentimentality, is a false standard of morals and virtue, and which is utterly destructive to true morality and to real virtue, which can only be fostered and cultivated by freedom of the affections.

Free Love, then, is the law by which men and women of all grades and kinds are attracted to or repelled from each other, and does not describe the results accomplished by either; these results depend upon the condition and development of the individual subjects. It is the *natural* operation of the *affectional* motives of the sexes, unbiased by *any* enacted law or *standard* of public opinion. It is the opportunity which gives the opposites in sex the conditions in which the law of chemical affinities raised into the domain of the affections can have unrestricted sway, as it has in *all* departments of nature *except* in enforced sexual relations among men and women.

It is an impossibility to compel incompatible elements of *matter* to unite. So also is it impossible to compel incompatible elements of *human nature* to unite. The sphere of chemical science is to bring together such elements as will produce harmonious compounds. The sphere of social science is to accomplish the same thing in humanity. Anything that stands in the way of this accomplishment in either department is an *obstruction* to the natural order of the universe. There would be just as much common sense for the chemist to write a law *commanding* that two incompatible elements should unite, or that two, once united, should so remain, even if a third, having a stronger affinity for one of them than they have for each other, should be introduced, as it is for chemists of society to attempt to do the same by individuals; for both are impossible. If in chemistry two properties are united by which the environment is not profited, it is the same law of affinity which operates as where a compound is made that is of the greatest service to society. This law holds in social chemistry; the results obtained from social compounds will be just such as their respective properties determine.

Thus I might go on almost infinitely to illustrate the difference which *must* be recognized between the operations of a law and the *law itself.* Now the whole difficulty in marriage law is that it endeavors to *compel* unity between elements in which it is impossible; consequently there is an attempt made to subvert not only the general order of the universe, but also the special intentions of nature, which are those of God. The results, then, flowing from operations of the law of Free Love will be *high, pure* and *lasting,* or *low, debauched and promiscuous, just in the degree* that those loving, are high or low in the scale of sexual progress; while each and all are strictly natural, and therefore legitimate in their respective spheres.

Promiscuity in sexuality is simply the *anarchical stage of development* wherein the passions rule supreme. When spirituality comes in and rescues the real man or woman from the domain of the purely material, promiscuity is simply impossible. As promiscuity is the analogue to anarchy, so is spirituality to scientific selection and adjustment. Therefore I am fully persuaded that the very highest sexual unions are those that are monogamic, and that these are perfect in proportion as they are lasting. Now if to this be added the fact that the highest kind of love is that which is utterly freed from and devoid of *selfishness,* and whose *highest* gratification comes from rendering its object the *greatest* amount of happiness, let that happiness depend upon whatever it may, then you have my ideal of the highest order of love and the most perfect degree of order to which humanity can attain. An affection that does not desire to bless its object, instead of appropriating it by a selfish possession to its own uses, is not worthy the name of love. Love is that which exists to *do* good, not merely to *get good,* which is constantly giving instead of desiring.

A Cæsar is admired by humanity, but a Christ is revered. Those persons who have lived and sacrificed themselves most for the good of humanity, without thought of recompense, are held in greatest respect. Christians believe that Christ died to save the world, giving His life as a ransom therefor. That was the greatest gift He could make to show His love for mankind.

The general test of love to-day is entirely different from that which Christ gave. That is now deemed the greatest love which has the strongest and most uncontrollable wish to be made happy, by the appropriation, and if need be the sacrifice, of all the preferences of its object. It says: "Be mine. Whatever may be your wish, yield it up to me." How different would the world be were this sort of selfishness supplanted by the Christ love, which says: Let this cup pass from me. Nevertheless, not my will but thine be done. Were the relations of the sexes thus regulated, misery, crime and vice would be banished, and the pale, wan face of female humanity replaced by one glowing with radiant delight and healthful bloom, and the heart of humanity beat with a heightened vigor and renewed strength, and its intellect cleared of all shadows, sorrows and blights. Contemplate this, and then denounce me for advocating Freedom if you can, and I will bear your curse with a better resignation.

Oh! my brothers and sisters, let me entreat you to have more faith in the self-regulating efficacy of freedom. Do you not see how beautifully it works among us in other respects? In America everybody is free to worship God according to the dictates of his own conscience, or even not to worship anything, notwithstanding you or I may think that very wicked or wrong. The respect for freedom we make paramount over our individual opinions, and the result is peace and harmony, when the people of other countries are still throtling and destroying each other to enforce their individual opinions on others. Free Love is only the appreciation of this beautiful principle of freedom. One step further I entreat you to trust it still, and though you may see a thousand dangers, I see peace and happiness and steady improvement as the result.

To more specifically define Free Love I would say that I prefer to use the word *love* with *lust* as its antithesis, *love* representing the spiritual and *lust* the animal; the perfect and harmonious interrelations of the two being the perfected human. This use has its justification in other pairs of words; as good and evil; heat and cold; light and dark; up and down; north and south; which in *principle* are the same, but in *practice* we are obliged to judge of them as *relatively* different. The point from which judgment is made is that which we occupy, or are related to, individually, at any given time. Thus what would be up to one person might be down to another differently situated, along the line which up and down describe. So also is it of good and evil. What is good to one low down the ladder may not only be, but actually is, evil to one further ascended; nevertheless it is the same ladder up which both climb. It is the comprehension of this scientific fact that guarantees the *best* religion. And it is the *non-comprehension* of it that sets us as judges of our brothers and sisters, who are below us in the scale of development, to whom we should reach down the kind and loving hand of assistance, rather than force them to retreat farther away from us by unkindness, denunciation and hate.

In fine, and to resume: We have found that humanity is composed of men and women of all grades of development, from the most hideous human monster up to the highest perfected saint: that all of them, under our theory of government, are entitled to worship God after the dictates of their several consciences; that God is worshiped just as essentially in political and social thought and action as He is in religious thought and action; that no second person or persons have any right to interfere with the action of the individual unless he interfere with others' rights, and then only to protect such rights; that the thoughts and actions of all individuals, whether high and pure, or low and debauched, are equally entitled to the protection of the laws, and, through them, to that of all members of the community. Religious thought and action already receive the equal protection of the laws. Political thought and action are about to secure the equal protection of the laws. What social thought and action demand of the laws and their administrators is the same protection which Religion has, and Politics is about to have.

I know full well how strong is the appeal that can be made in behalf of marriage, and appeal based on the sanctions of usage and inherited respect, and on the sanctions of religion reinforced by the sanctions of law. I know how much can be said, and how forcibly it can be said, on the ground that women, and especially that the children born of the union of the sexes, must be protected, and must, therefore, have the solemn contract of the husband and father to that effect. I know how long and how powerfully the ideality and sentiment of mankind have clustered, as it were in a halo, around this time-honored institution of marriage. And yet I solemnly believe that *all that* belongs to a dispensation of force and contract, and of a low and unworthy sense of mutual ownership, which is passing, and which is destined rapidly to pass, completely away; not to leave us without love, nor without the happiness and beauty of the most tender relation of human souls; nor without security for woman, and ample protection for children; but to lift us to a higher level in the enjoyment of every blessing. I believe in *love with liberty;* in *protection without slavery;* in *the care and culture of offspring by new and better methods, and without the tragedy of self-immolation on the part of parents.* I believe in the family, *spiritually constituted,* expanded, amplified, and scientifically and artistically organized, as a unitary home. I believe in the most wonderful transformation of human society as about to come, as even now at the very door, through general progress, science and the influential intervention of the spirit world. I believe in more than all that the millennium has ever signified to the most religious mind; and I believe that in order to prepare minds to contemplate and desire and enact the new and better life, it is necessary that the old and still prevalent superstitious veneration for the legal marriage tie be relaxed and weakened; not to pander to immorality, but as introductory to a nobler manhood and a more glorified womanhood; as, indeed, the veritable gateway to a paradise regained.

Do not criticise me, therefore, from a commonplace point of view. Question me, first, of the grounds of my faith. Conceive, if you can, the outlook for that humanity which comes trooping through the long, bright vista of futurity, as seen by the eyes of a devout spiritualist and a transcendental socialist. My whole nature is prophetic. I do not and cannot live merely in the present. Credit, first, the burden of my prophecy; and from the new standing-ground so projected forth into the future, look back upon our times, and so judge of my doctrine; and if, still, you cannot concede either the premises or the conclusion, you may, perhaps, think more kindly of me personally, as an amiable enthusiast, than if you deemed me deliberately wicked in seeking to disturb the foundations of our existing social order.

I prize dearly the good opinion of my fellow-beings. I would, *so gladly,* have you think well of me, and not ill. It is because I love you all, and love your well-being still more than I love you, that I tell you my vision of the future, and that I would willingly disturb your confidence, so long cherished, in the old dead or dying-out past. Believe me honest, my dear friends, and so forgive and think of me lovingly in turn, even if you are compelled still to regard me as deceived. I repeat, that I love you all; that I love every human creature, and their well being; and that I believe, with the profoundest conviction, that what I have urged in this discourse is conducive to that end.

Thus have I explained to you what Social Freedom or, as some choose to denominate it, Free Love, is, and what its advocates demand. Society says, to grant it is to precipitate itself into anarchy. I oppose to this arbitrary assumption the logic of general freedom, and aver that order and harmony will be secured where anarchy now reigns. The order of nature will soon determine whether society is or I am right. Let that be as it may, I repeat: "The love that I cannot command is not mine; let me not disturb myself about it, nor attempt to filch it from its rightful owner. A heart that I supposed mine has drifted and gone. Shall I go in pursuit? Shall I forcibly capture the truant and transfix it with the barb of my selfish affection, and pin it to the wall of my chamber? Rather let me leave my doors and windows open, intent only on living so nobly that the best cannot fail to be drawn to me by an irresistible attraction."

Frances Wright
(1795–1852)

Frances Wright was born on September 6, 1795 in Dundee, Scotland. The second of three children, she lost both of her parents when she was two years old and was reared by a succession of relatives in London. After Frances' twenty-first birthday she went to live with a great uncle who taught moral philosophy at Glasgow College. Here she read widely in the college library and became fascinated with the United States. In August, 1818, accompanied by her sister, Frances embarked for a tour of the United States. Back in England in 1820, she published a book of her travels, *Views of Society and Manners in America* (1821), which became one of the most celebrated travel memoirs of the early nineteenth century. Her book reached the Marquis de Lafayette in France, another ardent lover of America, and in 1824 he urged Frances to accompany him on a final visit to his adopted country. Giving in to gossip and dissension within Lafayette's family, she followed him to America in a separate vessel. By the time of Lafayette's return to France in 1825 their relationship had cooled and Frances decided to remain in America. Concerned about the evils of slavery, Frances' first reform efforts were devoted to *A Plan for the Gradual Abolition of Slavery in the United States without Danger of Loss to the Citizens of the South*, which she published as a pamphlet in 1825. In the same year she purchased 640 acres on the Wolf River near Memphis, Tennessee, and set up her plantation "Nashoba" to illustrate how her plan would work. Purchasing several slaves she set them to work on the plantation to earn enough money to acquire their emancipation. However, the project never prospered and, upon returning from a respite in England, she found the place a ruin and arranged to have the slaves transported to Haiti where she freed them and helped them find housing and employment. In 1829 Frances instituted a series of anticlerical lectures and travelled to most of the major cities of the East and Midwest delivering addresses condemning organized religion. In the same year she bought a small church near the Bowery in New York City and transformed in into a "Hall of Science" where she and Robert Dale Owen regularly lectured and edited and published the *Free Enquirer*. In her many lectures and essays Frances condemned capital punishment and demanded improvements in the status of women, including equal education, legal rights for married women, liberal divorce laws, and birth control. By 1830 her interests turned more and more to educational reform, and she delivered numerous lectures trying to convince audiences to set up a national system of free state boarding schools financed by a graduated property tax. In 1830, Frances sailed for France with her sister Camilla in hopes the trip would improve her sister's health. After her sister's death a few months later, she turned to a French physician, D'Asusmont, whom she had met before in America. In 1831 she married the frenchman and soon gave birth to two children, only one of which survived. In 1835, Frances and her husband and daughter returned to America to settle her financial affairs and soon she was back on the lecture platform campaigning for the Democratic ticket in 1836, and offering a new series of lectures on the evils of contemporary society. In the next decade she made five more trips back and forth between Europe and America trying to untangle her financial affairs. On December 13, 1852, Frances died at the age of fifty-seven in Cincinnati, Ohio, having never recovered from a broken hip suffered in a fall the previous winter.

The following address was delivered numerous times as part of a series of lectures presented in Cincinnati, Philadelphia, Baltimore and New York in 1828. It was later printed in Frances Wright, *Course of Popular Lectures*, Lecture II (New York, N.Y., 1829), pp. 41-62.

"Of Free Enquiry"

There is a common error that I feel myself called upon to notice; nor know I the country in which it is more prevalent than in this. Whatever indifference may generally prevail among men, still there are many eager for the acquisition of knowledge; willing to enquire, and anxious to base their opinions upon correct principles. In the curiosity which motives their exertions, however, the vital principle is but too often wanting. They come selfishly, and not generously, to the tree of knowledge. They eat, but care not to impart of the fruit to others. Nay, there are who, having leaped the briar fence of prejudice themselves, will heap new thorns in the way of those who would venture the same. . . .

But will this imputation startle my hearers? Will they say, America is the home of liberty, and Americans brethren in equality. Is it so? and may we not ask here, as elsewhere, how many are there, not anxious to monopolize, but to universalize knowledge? how many, that consider their own improvement in relation always with that of their fellow beings, and who feel the imparting of truth to be not a work of supererogation, but a duty; the withholding it, not a venial omission, but a treachery to the race. Which of us have not seen fathers of families pursuing investigations themselves, which they hide from their sons, and, more especially, from their wives and daughters? As if truth could be of less importance to the young than to the old; or as if the sex which in all ages has ruled the destinies of the world, could be less worth enlightening than that which only follows its lead!

The observation I have hazarded may require some explanation. Those who arrogate power usually think themselves superior *de facto* and *de jure*. Yet justly might it be made a question whether those who ostensibly govern are not always unconsciously led. Should we examine closely into the state of things, we might find that, in all countries, the governed decide the destinies of the governors, more than the governors those of the governed; even as the labouring classes influence more directly the fortunes of a nation than does the civil officer, the aspiring statesman, the rich capitalist, or the speculative philosopher.

However novel it may appear, I shall venture the assertion, that, until women assume the place in society which good sense and good feeling alike assign to them, human improvement must advance but feebly. It is in vain that we would circumscribe the power of one half of our race, and that half by far the most important and influential. If they exert it not for good, they will for evil; if they advance not knowledge, they will perpetuate ignorance. Let women stand where they may in the scale of improvement, their position decides that of the race. Are they cultivated?—so is society polished and enlightened. Are they ignorant?—so is it gross and insipid. Are they wise?—so is the human condition prosperous. Are they foolish?—so is it unstable and unpromising. Are they free?—so is the human character elevated. Are they enslaved?—so is the whole race degraded. . . .

. . . It is my object to show, that, before we can engage successfully in the work of enquiry, we must engage in a body; we must engage collectively; as human beings desirous of attaining the highest excellence of which our nature is capable; as children of one family, anxious to discover the true and the useful for the common advantage of all. It is my farther object to show that no co-operation in this matter can be effective which does not embrace the two sexes on a footing of equality; and, again, that no co-operation in this matter can be effective, which does not embrace human beings on a footing of equality. Is this a republic—a country whose affairs are governed by the public voice—while the public mind is unequally enlightened? Is this a republic, where the interests of the many keep in check those of the few—while the few hold possession of the courts of knowledge, and the many stand as suitors at the door? Is this a republic, where the rights of all are equally respected, the interests of all equally secured, the ambitions of all equally regulated, the services of all equally rendered? Is this such a republic—while we see endowed colleges for the rich, and barely *common schools* for the poor; while but one drop of colored blood shall stamp a fellow creature for a slave, or, at the least, degrade him below sympathy; and while one half of the whole population is left in civil bondage, and, as it were, sentenced to mental imbecility?

Let us pause to enquire if this be consistent with the being of a republic. Without knowledge, could your fathers have conquered liberty? and without knowledge, can you retain it? Equality! where is it, if not in education? Equal rights! they cannot exist without equality of instruction. "All men are born free and equal!" they are indeed so *born,* but do they so *live?* Are they educated as equals? and, if not, can they *be* equal? and, if not equal, can they be free? Do not the rich command instruction? and they who have instruction, must they not possess the power? and when they have the power, will they not exert it in their own favor? I will ask more; I will ask, *do* they not exert it in their own favor? I will ask if two professions do not now rule the land and its inhabitants? I will ask, whether your legislatures are not governed by lawyers and your households by priests? And I will farther ask, whether the deficient instruction of the mass of your population does not give to lawyers their political ascendancy; and whether the ignorance of women be not the cause that your domestic hearths are invaded by priests? . . .

. . . Your political institutions have taken equality for their basis; your declaration of rights, upon which your institutions rest, sets forth this principle as vital and inviolate. Equality is the soul of liberty; there is, in fact, no liberty without it—none that cannot be overthrown by the violence of ignorant anarchy, or sapped by the subtilty of professional craft. That this is the case your reasons will admit; that this is the case your feelings *do* admit—even those which are the least amiable and the least praiseworthy. The jealousy betrayed by the uncultivated against those of more polished address and manners, has its source in the beneficial principle to which we advert, however, (in this, as in many other cases,) misconceived and perverted. Cultivation of mind will ever lighten the countenance and polish the exterior. This external superiority, which is but a faint emanation of the superiority within, vulgar eyes can see and ignorant jealousy will resent. This, in a republic, leads to brutality; and, in aristocracies, where this jealously is restrained by fear, to servility. Here it will lead the wagoner to dispute the road with a carriage; and, in Europe, will make the foot passenger doff his hat to the lordly equipage which spatters him with mud, while there he mutters curses only in his heart. The unreasoning observer will refer the conduct of the first to the *republican institutions*—the reflecting observer, to the *anti-republican education.* The instruction befitting free men is that which gives the sun of knowledge to shine on all; and which at once secures the liberties of each individual, and disposes each individual to make a proper use of them.

Equality, then, we have shown to have its seat in the mind. A proper cultivation of the faculties would ensure a sufficiency of that equality for all the ends of republican government, and for all the modes of social enjoyment. The diversity in the natural powers of different minds, as decided by physical organization, would be then only a source of interest and agreeable variety. All would be capable of appreciating the peculiar powers of each; and each would perceive that his interests, well understood, were in unison with the interests of all. Let us now examine whether liberty, properly interpreted, does not involve, among your unalienable rights as citizens and human beings, the right of equal means of instruction.

Have ye given a pledge, sealed with the blood of your fathers, for the equal rights of all human kind sheltered within your confines? What means the pledge? or what understand ye by human rights? But understand them as ye will, define them as ye will, how are men to be secured in *any* rights without instruction? how to be secured in the *equal exercise* of those rights without *equality of instruction?* By instruction understand me to mean, knowledge—*just knowledge;* not talent, not genius, not inventive mental powers. These will vary in every human being; but knowledge is the same for every mind, and every mind may and *ought to be* trained to receive it. If, then, ye have pledged, at each anniversary of your political independence, your lives, properties, and honor, to the securing your common liberties, ye have pledged your lives, properties, and honor, to the securing of *your common instruction.* Or will you secure the end without securing the means? ye shall do it, when ye reap the harvest without planting the seed. . . .

All men are born free and equal! That is: *our moral feelings acknowledge it to be just and proper, that we respect those liberties in others, which we lay claim to for ourselves; and that we permit the free agency of every individual, to any extent which violates not the free agency of his fellow creatures.*

There is but one honest limit to the rights of a sentient being; it is where they touch the rights of another sentient being. Do we exert our own liberties without injury to others—we exert them justly; do we exert them at the expense of others—unjustly. And, in thus doing, we step from the sure platform of liberty upon the uncertain threshold of tyranny. Small is the step; to the unreflecting so imperceptibly small, that they take it every hour of their lives as thoughtlessly as they do it unfeelingly. . . .

Who among us but has had occasion to remark the ill-judged, however well intentioned government of children by their teachers; and, yet more especially, by their parents? In what does this mismanagement originate? In a misconception of the relative position of the parent or guardian, and of the child; in a departure, by the parent, from the principle of liberty, in his assumption of rights destructive of those of the child; in his exercise of authority, as by right divine, over the judgment, actions, and person of the child; in his forgetfulness of the character of the child, as a human being, born "free and equal" among his compeers; that is, having equal claims to the exercise and development of all his senses, faculties, and powers, with those who brought him into existence, and with all sentient beings who tread the earth. Were a child thus viewed by his parent, we should not see him, by turns, made a plaything and a slave; we should not see him commanded to believe, but encouraged to reason; we should not see him trembling under the rod, nor shrinking from a frown, but reading the wishes of others in the eye, gathering knowledge wherever he threw his glance, rejoicing in the present hour, and treasuring up sources of enjoyment for future years. We should not then see the youth launching into life without compass or quadrant. We should not see him doubting at each emergency how to act, shifting his course with the shifting wind, and, at last, making shipwreck of mind and body on the sunken rocks of hazard and dishonest speculation, nor on the foul quicksands of debasing licentiousness.

What, then, has the parent to do, if he would conscientiously discharge that most sacred of all duties, that weightiest of all responsibilities, which ever did or ever will devolve on a human being? What is he to do, who, having brought a creature into existence, endowed with varied faculties, with tender susceptibilities, capable of untold wretchedness or equally of unconceived enjoyment; what is he to do, that he may secure the happiness of that creature, and make the life he has given blessing and blessed, instead of cursing and cursed? What is he to do?—he is to encourage in his child a spirit of enquiry, and equally to encourage it in himself. He is never to advance an opinion without showing the facts upon which it is grounded; he is never to assert a fact, without proving it to be a fact. He is not to teach a code of morals any more than a creed of doctrines; but he is to direct his young charge to observe the consequences of actions on himself and on others; and to judge of the propriety of those actions by their ascertained consequences. He is not to command his feelings any more than his opinions or his actions; but he is to assist him in the analysis of his feelings, in the examination of their nature, their tendencies, their effects. Let him do this, and have no anxiety for the result. In the free exercise of his senses, in the fair development of his faculties, in a course of simple and unrestrained enquiry, he will discover truth, for he will ascertain facts; he will seize upon virtue, for he will have distinguished beneficial from injurious actions; he will cultivate kind, generous, just, and honourable feelings, for he will have proved them to contribute to his own happiness and to shed happiness around him.

Who, then, shall say, enquiry is good for him and not good for his children? Who shall cast error from himself, and allow it to be grafted on the minds he has called into being? Who shall break the chains of his own ignorance, and fix them, through his descendants, on his race? But, there are some who, as parents, make one step in duty, and halt at the second. We see men who will aid the instruction of their sons, and condemn only their daughters to ignorance. "Our sons," they say, "will have to exercise political rights, may aspire to public offices, may fill some learned profession, may struggle for wealth and acquire it. It is well that we give them a helping hand; that we assist them to such knowledge as is going, and make them as sharp witted as their neighbors. But for our daughters," they say—if indeed respecting them they say any thing— "for our daughters, little trouble or expense is necessary. They can never *be any thing;* in fact, they *are nothing.* We had best give them up to their mothers, who may take them to Sunday's preaching; and, with the aid of a little music, a little dancing, and a few fine gowns, fit them out for the market of marriage."

Am I severe? It is not my intention. I know that I am honest, and I fear that I am correct. Should I offend, however I may regret, I shall not repent it; satisfied to incur displeasure, so that I render service.

But to such parents I would observe, that with regard to their sons, as to their daughters, they are about equally mistaken. If it be their duty, as we have seen, to respect in their children the same natural liberties which they cherish for themselves—if it be their duty to aid as guides, not to dictate as teachers—to lend assistance to the reason, not to command its prostration,—then have they nothing to do with the blanks or the prizes in store for them, in the wheel of worldly fortune. Let possibilities be what they may in favor of their sons, they have no calculations to make on them. It is not for them to ordain their sons magistrates nor statesmen; nor yet even lawyers, physicians, or merchants. They have only to improve the one character which they receive at the birth. They have only to consider them as *human beings,* and to ensure them the fair and thorough development of all the faculties, physical, mental, and moral, which distinguish their nature. In like manner, as respects their daughters, they have nothing to do with the injustice of laws, nor the absurdities of society. Their duty is plain, evident, decided. In a daughter they have in charge a human being; in a son, the same. Let them train up these *human beings,* under the expanded wings of liberty. Let them seek *for* them and *with* them just knowledge; encouraging, from the cradle upwards, that useful curiosity which will lead them unbidden in the paths of free enquiry; and place them, safe and superior to the storms of life, in the security of well regulated, self-possessed minds, well grounded, well reasoned, conscientious opinions, and self-approved, consistent practice.

I have as yet, in this important matter, addressed myself only to the reason and moral feelings of my audience; I could speak also to their interests. Easy were it to show, that in proportion as your children are enlightened, will they prove blessings to society and ornaments to their race. But if this be true of all, it is more especially true of the now more neglected half of the species. Were it only in our power to enlighten part of the rising generation, and should the interests of the whole decide our choice of the portion, it were the females, and not the males, we should select.

When, now a twelvemonth since, the friends of liberty and science pointed out to me, in London, the walls of their rising university, I observed, with a smile, that they were beginning at the wrong end: "Raise such an edifice for your young women, and ye have enlightened the nation." It has already been observed, that women, wherever placed, however high or low in the scale of cultivation, hold the destinies of humankind. Men will ever rise or fall to the level of the other sex; and from some causes in their conformation, we find them, however armed with power or enlightened with knowledge, still held in leading strings even by the least cultivated female. Surely, then, if they knew their interests, they would desire the improvement of those who, if they do not advantage, will injure them; who, if they elevate not their minds and meliorate not their hearts, will debase the one and harden the other; and who, if they endear not existence, most assuredly will dash it with poison. How many, how omnipotent are the interests which engage men to break the mental chains of women! How many, how dear are the interests which engage them to exalt rather than lower their condition, to multiply their solid acquirements, to respect their liberties, to make them their equals, to wish them even their superiors! Let them enquire into these things. Let them examine the relation in which the two sexes stand, and ever must stand, to each other. Let them perceive, that, mutually dependent, they must ever be giving and receiving, or they must be losing;—receiving or losing in knowledge, in virtue, in enjoyment. Let them perceive how immense the loss, or how immense the gain. Let them not imagine that they know aught of the delights which intercourse with the other sex can give, until they have felt the sympathy of mind with mind, and heart with heart; until they bring into that intercourse every affection, every talent, every confidence, every refinement, every respect. Until power is annihilated on one side, fear and obedience on the other, and both restored to their birthright—equality. Let none think that affection can reign without it; or friendship, or esteem. Jealousies, envyings, suspicions, reserves, deceptions—these are the fruits of inequality. Go, then! and remove the evil first from the minds of women, then from their condition, and then from your laws. Think it no longer indifferent whether the mothers of the rising generation are wise or foolish. . . .

There is a vulgar persuasion, that the ignorance of women, by favoring their subordination, ensures their utility. 'Tis the same argument employed by the ruling few against the subject many in aristocracies; by the rich against the poor in democracies; by the learned professions against the people in all countries. And let us observe, that if good in one case, it should be good in all; and that, unless you are prepared to admit that you are yourselves less industrious in proportion to your intelligence, you must abandon the position with respect to others. But, in fact, who is it among men that best struggle with difficulties?—the strong minded or the weak? Who meet with serenity adverse fortune?—the wise or the foolish? Who accommodate themselves to irremediable circumstances? or, when remediable, who control and mould them at will?—the intelligent or the ignorant? Let your answer in your own case, be your answer in that of women. . . .

Let us understand what knowledge is. Let us clearly perceive that accurate knowledge regards all equally; that truth, or fact, is the same thing for all human-kind; that there are not truths for the rich and truths for the poor, truths for men and truths for women; there are simply *truths,* that is, *facts,* which all who open their eyes and their ears and their understandings can perceive.

There is no mystery in these facts. There is no witchcraft in knowledge. Science is not a trick; not a puzzle. The philosopher is not a conjuror. The observer of nature who envelopes his discoveries in mystery, either knows less than he pretends, or feels interested in *withholding* his knowledge. The teacher whose lessons are difficult of comprehension, is either clumsy or he is dishonest.

We observed . . . that it was the evident interest of our appointed teachers to disguise the truth. We discovered this to be a matter of necessity, arising out of their dependence upon the public favor. We may observe yet another cause, now operating far and wide—universally, omnipotently—a cause pervading the whole mass of society, and springing out of the existing motive principle of human action—competition. Let us examine, and we shall discover it to be the object of each individual to obscure the first elements of the knowledge he professes—be that knowledge mechanical and operative, or intellectual and passive. It is thus that we see the simple manufacture of a pair of shoes magnified into an art, demanding a seven years apprenticeship, when all its intricacies might be mastered in as many months. It is thus that cutting out a coat after just proportions is made to involve more science, and to demand more study, than the anatomy of the body it is to cover. And it is thus, in like manner, that all the branches of knowledge, involved in what is called scholastic learning, are wrapped in the fogs of pompous pedantry; and that every truth, instead of being presented in naked innocence, is obscured under a weight of elaborate words, and lost and buried in a medley of irrelevant ideas, useless amplifications, and erroneous arguments. Would we unravel this confusion—would we distinguish the true from the false, the real from the unreal, the useful from the useless—would we break our mental leading strings—would we know the uses of all our faculties—would we be virtuous, happy, and intelligent beings—would we be useful in our generation—would we possess our own minds in peace, be secure in our opinions, be just in our feelings, be consistent in our practice—would we command the respect of others, and—far better—would we secure our own—let us enquire.

Let us enquire! What mighty consequences, are involved in these little words! Whither have they not led? To what are they not yet destined to lead? Before them thrones have given way. Hierarchies have fallen, dungeons have disclosed their secrets. Iron bars, and iron laws, and more iron prejudices, have given way; the prison house of the mind hath burst its fetters; science disclosed her treasures; truth her moral beauties; and civil liberty, sheathing her conquering sword, hath prepared her to sit down in peace at the feet of knowledge. . . .

Did the knowledge of each individual embrace all the discoveries made by science, all the truths extracted by philosophy from the combined experience of ages, still would enquiry be in its infancy, improvement in its dawn. Perfection for man is in no time, in no place. The law of his being, like that of the earth he inhabits, is *to move always, to stop never.* From the earliest annals of tradition, his movement has been in advance. The tide of his progress hath had ebbs and flows, but hath left a thousand marks by which to note its silent but tremendous influx. . . .

If this be so—and who that looks abroad shall gainsay the assertion?—if this be so—and who that looks to your jails, to your penitentiaries, to your houses of refuge, to your hospitals, to your asylums, to your hovels of wretchedness, to your haunts of intemperance, to your victims lost in vice and hardened in profligacy, to childhood without protection, to youth without guidance, to the widow without sustenance, to the female destitute and female outcast, sentenced to shame and sold to degradation—who that looks to these shall say, that enquiry hath not a world to explore, and improvement yet a world to reform!